Body and Soul

The Critical Edition

<u>Film as Literature Series</u>

Force of Evil: The Critical Edition
You Are There teleplays: The Critical Edition
Odds Against Tomorrow: The Critical Edition
Body and Soul: The Critical Edition

The Center for Telecommunication Studies
Film as Literature Series

Body and Soul

The Critical Edition

by
Abraham Polonsky

Edited
—with Annotations and Critical Commentary—
by
John Schultheiss

The Center for Telecommunication Studies
California State University, Northridge

Printed in the USA
First Edition
2002

Published by
The Center for Telecommunication Studies
California State University, Northridge
18111 Nordhoff Street
Northridge, CA 91330
with assistance from
Sadanlaur Publications
Los Angeles, California

ISBN 0-9635823-5-6
Library of Congress Control Number: 2002111119

Contents

Abraham Polonsky
on
John Garfield

Tyger, tyger, burning bright
In the forests of the night
What immortal hand or eye
Could frame thy fearful symmetry?

Introduction

by Abraham Polonsky

I met John Garfield when I went to see him and his partner, Robert Roberts, to tell them the story of *Body and Soul*. A new friend, Arnold Manoff, had just come to work at Paramount Pictures, just a few blocks away from Enterprise Studios. Manoff had been trying to make something of the Barney Ross story, but somehow he wasn't getting anywhere, and since he found me numb with Paramount, he suggested that I go over and see what I could do with some sort of prizefighter story for Garfield. But first, we had lunch at Lucey's. The match game was going on all around us, but Manoff was telling me about John Garfield and Enterprise. He made it sound like an ironic dream. It was.

Arnold Manoff is one of the best short-story writers of the Depression years. That world of want, poor New York Jews, the Enlightenment, and Utopian Socialism, the Life of Reason haunting the glorious future, was the heart of *Body and Soul*. It is Romance with Rebellion. Clifford Odets, of course, was an electric part of this literary movement, and his plays were their enchanting vision, but Garfield was the star for the whole world, the romantic Rebel himself.

In a way, I found the ambiguity of the movies much like the souls of Odets and Garfield when I got there after the war. John McNulty was at Paramount when I turned up. What was I doing there? he asked me. I belonged back in New York. The race track was the only real thing around. The whole place was a fraud. He himself was just hanging in to get enough money to go back to the city, and he cursed Los Angeles, the sunlight, the palm trees, and the movies. He took me onto a set, the first I saw before the Paulette Goddard one, and he showed me Alan Ladd standing on a box for a tight two-shot in a love scene. "This is it," he said. "Go home."

He never went home, but the Blacklist sent Garfield and me back to New York.

The children of rich Jews in those days when they were attracted to the arts had a tendency to become infatuated with the avant garde and the vitality of the irrational, but most poor Jews who didn't join the money system gravitated to socialism, vague or definite; rebellion, moderate or tough; and self-consciousness, harsh or neurotic. Some became gangsters; most joined the establishment of which crime is, after all, as my friend Ira Wolfert says, "the grease that makes things run" (cf. *Force of Evil,* based on Ira Wolfert's novel *Tucker's People*).

As an actor Garfield was the darling of romantic rebels—beautiful, enthusiastic, rich with the know-how of street intelligence. He had passion and a lyrical sadness that was the essence of the role he created as it was created for him. In the hysterical tragedy in which he found himself he became an exile in his own country. That others before him and others after him in every age would play the same role was no satisfaction to him. He was ambitious. The Group trained him, the movies made him, the Blacklist killed him. The popular story, for instance, is (and he may have said so in public himself, for he was obliging in other things besides politics) that he refused the part of Kowalski in Tennessee Williams's play because the woman's part was better than the man's. I read the play when it was submitted to his company, and I know that part was turned down by Roberts because Irene Selznick wouldn't make a proper moving-picture deal on it, so Roberts decided. Garfield was unlikely to turn down anything because a part was smaller or bigger, although he liked to be the star. Everything he did flowed from his magic and frustrating years in the Group. The play was the heart of it. The ensemble was the soul of it. He knew it and acted like that on both occasions when we worked together.

Garfield felt himself inadequate as an intellectual. Most serious actors feel like this. They aren't actually inadequate, any more than intellectuals are, but they feel that way. Being an intellectual and being an artist aren't genetically paired, any more than being an artist and being a good character. Being an intellectual is a full-time occupation, and although it, like everything else, is enriched by other talents, it has its own universe and its own cast of fools. As an actor Garfield was total, and he could play an intellectual with the same vigor and astonishing rapport as a cab driver. Regarding *Force of Evil* he told me before we started that although he really didn't understand some of the meanings, the minute he hung that Phi Beta Kappa key on his watch chain he was in business. And so he was. He had the true actor's genuine wisdom for the human, and he could play his kind of intellectual just as well as he could play his kind of cab driver. You won't meet either in New York, but you wish you could.

He didn't have the range of an Olivier but then Garfield was a star who represented a social phenomenon of enormous importance for his times and, perhaps, ours too. He lived as a star without contradiction in the imagination of those who loved him for something that lay dormant in themselves, and this was tuned to the social vigor of the time that created him. Naturally, when those times became the political target of the estab-lishment in the United State, Garfield, whose roles, whose training, whose past were the environment of the romantic rebellion the Depression gave birth to, became a public target for the great simplifiers. From his dead body and those of many like him, from the hysteria and know-nothing rage of McCarthyism, HUAC, and Nixon, there rose the ominous star of Watergate, which today bewilders us as Nazism bewilders the German people.

Garfield knew on the night he died that Clifford Odets had that day testified before the House Un-American Activities Committee and there, in general, had made the popular derogatory remarks about the left and communism. In addition, Odets said he had been a member of the Com-munist party in the past.

MR. TAVENNER: Were any of the meetings held in your house?
MR. ODETS: No, I don't think I had a home then. I was a very poor man.

And so were the people he named. John Garfield, who wasn't even a fellow traveler, refused to speculate, refused to name names on the grounds he couldn't remember anyone who was a member of the Commu-nist party, not in the Group, not in Hollywood, not anywhere. For years the federal government used their resources to prove he had perjured him-self, and for years they failed, but they did succeed in killing him.

The former Mrs. Garfield says, "I believe in fate, and he might have died anyway. But he wouldn't have died so angry. He was so angry."

He had a right to die angry. He had a right to be angry, for he could find no way to free himself from those who were destroying him.

Now, here, on this terrible night, wandering like Joe Morse around New York, talking to himself with a voice from the grave, really with no place to go, rejected, he saw far off on those screens his own face, which had become the face of a generation of New York street kids. I joined those same New Yorkers and we stood across the street from the funeral parlor watching the tumult and fifty policemen with white gloves. Later, the pa-pers said ten thousand people had come, nothing so big since the death of Valentino.

The strangers I stood with, and they were quiet, unlike those who got into the event, were the same I saw forming a great line around the Globe Theatre in New York after *Body and Soul* opened, the same faces, the same figures, the same bodies, and the same life. They understood in terms of the romantic rebel from the streets that even though he was torn and tempted, he could never give in.

The political vultures who flew about him and descended after his death to croak that had he lived one more minute he, too, would have confessed to the committee, have vanished into the ultimate irrelevance. I hope this book reminds those who love movies of yet another star in a world that charmed the lives of our generation, and in the end Garfield was right to do as he did, right to act as he acted, true not only to his generation but to the country that spawned him. Is it important? I don't know. But it's a fact.

CALIFORNIA
1974

This elegy by Abraham Polonsky was originally written for Howard Gelman's *The Films of John Garfield* (1975).

BODY AND SOUL

The Screenplay

Body and Soul:
The Shooting & Continuity Texts

The following is a synthesis of Abraham Polonsky's authorship of *Body and Soul*. It is a blending of his **shooting** script (written before the film was shot) and the **continuity** script (a transcription of the dialogue and visual/aural elements of the film itself). The shooting script is dated December 1946, with revisions of 13 January 1947. Shooting scripts are helpful artifacts for the critic, since they usually indicate moods and authorial intentions. The dialogue printed is, of course, a verbatim transcription of the words spoken in the film. And, whenever Polonsky's expository language from the shooting script is compatible with the actual material as shot (i.e., when his first intentions were not altered during production), his original descriptive passages are always utilized. Thus, the texture of Polonsky's writing is conveyed through the original wording of the shooting script, such as: "On the wall, moonlight patterns are changing branch shapes, and the sandbag swings slowly in the wind like conscience from a gibbet."

When the content in the film has no counterpart in the shooting script, the editor provides simple descriptions of the action ["Charley takes the cigar out of Quinn's mouth and tosses it aside."], in order to complete a stenographic continuity record. [All instances of these editorial descriptions are enclosed in bold square brackets.] Significant variations from the shooting script are noted at appropriate points, along with additional commentaries, in the "Annotations" section.

This Enterprise Studios production was shot 9 January through late March 1947; distributed by United Artists Corporation; theatrical opening in New York: August 1947.

[Credits on Screen]

THE
ENTERPRISE STUDIOS[1]

Present

JOHN   and   LILLI
GARFIELD[2]   PALMER

in

<u>BODY AND SOUL</u>[3]

And Introducing

HAZEL BROOKS[4]

as

'ALICE'

With

ANNE REVERE[5]

WILLIAM CONRAD   JOSEPH PEVNEY

LLOYD GOFF   CANADA LEE[6]

Original Screenplay
by
ABRAHAM POLONSKY[7]

Music Composed by
HUGO FRIEDHOFER

Conducted by
EMIL NEWMAN

The song "BODY AND SOUL"[8]
Music by . . . JOHNNY GREEN
Lyrics by EDWARD HEYMAN,
ROBERT SOUR and FRANK EYTON

Director of Photography
JAMES WONG HOWE[9]
A.S.C.

Executive Production Manager
JOSEPH C. GILPIN

Assistant Director . . . . ROBERT ALDRICH[10]

Art Direction . . . . NATHAN JURAN

Set Decoration . . . . EDWARD J. BOYLE

Make-up Supervision . . . . GUSTAF M. NORIN

Wardrobe Designed by . . . . MARION HERWOOD KEYES

Supervising Editor . . . . FRANCIS D. LYON

Film Editor . . . . ROBERT PARRISH[11]

Montages Directed by . . . . GUNTHER V. FRITSCH

Musical Director . . . . RUDOLPH POLK

Sound Engineer . . . . FRANK WEBSTER

Sound Recording by . . . . SOUND SERVICES, INC.

Produced
by
BOB ROBERTS

Directed
by
ROBERT ROSSEN[12]

BODY AND SOUL

Screenplay by
Abraham Polonsky

FADE IN:

EXT. TRAINING CAMP - NIGHT - CRANE

Bright moonlight and deep shadow articulate an outdoor ring and a
heavy punching bag slowly, but just barely, swinging in the night wind.
The CAMERA MOVES past a tree up to a wide window facing on the
clearing, to CHARLEY DAVIS asleep, while the [MUSIC and CRICKETS]
sound a note of melancholy hysteria, moonlight nibbling on his face.

He is struggling with a nightmare, fear sweating on his face, and Charley
wakes up screaming.

> CHARLEY
> (calling desperately from the dream)
> Ben. . . ! Ben. . . ! Ben.

Sitting up, eyes open, he stares around the room. The nightmare still
winds within his mind. On the wall, moonlight patterns are changing
branch shapes, and the punching bag swings slowly in the wind like
conscience from a gibbet.[13] Charley watches, his face tense. The CAM-
ERA MOVES BACK as Charley jumps from the bed [taking off a sweater
and grabbing his suit jacket].

EXT. CAMP GROUNDS - NIGHT

CAMERA PANS Charley [putting on his jacket as he goes] across the
grounds to his car. He rips the canvas cover off his big convertible. [He
puts on an overcoat which has been lying on the front seat.] As he starts
the motor [and begins to drive away], lights come on in the cabins, and
men run out, the puguglies and trainers, all wondering what's up.
QUINN, blowzy from sleep and a hangover, rushes out of the big house,
pulling a bathrobe on. He comes up just as the car starts off. The car
seems to drive straight at them, revealing a New York license plate and
the year 1938 [not discernible in the shot]. The car swings sideways
down the road.

> BOXER
> Where's he going? The champ must be crazy. He's
> gotta fight tomorrow night.

> QUINN
> Yeah. I know ...
> (turning away)
> I'll get him.

EXT. HIGHWAY - NIGHT

[Charley intently behind the wheel, staring into CAMERA], the car races
through the moonlit countryside.

EXT. CITY APPROACHES

The city towers loom in the distance, their spires lighted.

[*INT. CAR -*

SHOOTING from behind Charley through the windshield, the MUSIC
intensifying, the car crosses a bridge, its parallel lights streaming ahead.

> DISSOLVE TO:

SAME PERSPECTIVE, as car plunges deeper down city streets.]

EXT. EAST SIDE STREET - NIGHT

Car as it slowly rolls down the street and stops.

[Charley is in f.g. In the b.g., on the wall of a building,] a poster announces the MARLOWE-DAVIS fight, with a picture of *Charlie* [*sic.* the only instance of "Charlie" spelling in the film] [14] Davis in boxing togs. Some men and boys are on the street.

> MAN
>
> Hi ya, champ!

Charley starts to get out of the car.

> BOY
> (whispering, royalty is coming)
> It's Charley Davis!
> (gesturing back toward the poster)

Charley comes by, and the boys step back, admiration and excitement on their faces. Charley starts [toward a store with a large sign marked CANDIES over its front].

Charley pauses on the stoop and looks at the sign on the candy store window, which reads: A. DAVIS, PROP. His grave, disturbed face looks past the sign [through to the darkened interior]. Then he goes up the stairs into the house.

INT. KITCHEN - CLOSE SHOT - ANNA DAVIS

ANNA is seen at the stove with her back to us, pouring herself a glass of tea. [The CAMERA pulls back.] She turns, sees her son. A twist of feeling gathers her features, and the glass shakes in her hand.

> ANNA
> (almost soundlessly)
> Charley. . .

> CHARLEY
> (a small boy again)
> Hello, Ma.

As she watches Charley, Anna walks slowly to the table. Hands shaking, she starts to put the glass down, but it misses the table and crashes to the floor.

Charley hurries over, kneels down, and starts to scoop up the wet pieces.

> ANNA
> (with neutral words)
> Careful, Charley, you'll cut yourself.

She turns away, [and puts some of the broken pieces in a waste basket. She returns to the table.] She is extremely upset, a little cold, extremely careful.

Anna sits down.

> ANNA
> What do you want, Charley?

> CHARLEY
> Ben died.

> ANNA
> (a little shock in her voice)
> When?

> CHARLEY
> Today . . . I hada come down anyway for the fight
> tomorrow . . . I couldn't sleep, Ma . . . I thought
> maybe I . . .

> ANNA
> (holding tight to her feelings)
> Peg is sleeping here, Charley.

> CHARLEY
> (a little stunned)
> Oh . . .

Charley walks [into the bedroom and turns on the light]. In the bedroom are the big double bed and a bureau on which are a girl's hat, gloves, brush and comb, toiletries, etc.

[Charley notices and then reaches over and fingers a nightgown.]
After a backward glance, Charley turns to the dresser and picks up the
sliver-handled brush which is inscribed: "TO PEG FROM CHARLEY."

                    CHARLEY
            (almost to himself)
    I couldn't stand it up there, Ma, after they took
    Ben away. I couldn't sleep, so I came down. I had
    to find a place where I could lie down.
            (turning to Anna)
    Well, you know, Ma, you have to have a place . . .
            (stepping toward her)
    I didn't mean all those things I said to Peg. You
    know that.
            (Anna doesn't answer, but continues
            to watch)
    What'samatter? Don't you want me here?

At this moment the kitchen door opens. Anna looks towards it. Charley
stands within the bedroom as the door closes, and PEG BORN, carrying
an armful of bundles, moves across his line of vision and dumps the
groceries on the table.

                    PEG
    The butcher was closed, but I got everything else
    from the grocer.

Charley takes a step forward, the brush still in his hand. Charley walks
slowly into the kitchen towards Peg.

                    CHARLEY
            (deeply emotional)
    Peg . . .

As he comes up to her, Peg suddenly moves past him into the bedroom,
closes the door, [and turns off the light].

Charley enters the bedroom and comes up behind Peg and takes her in
his arms.

CHARLEY
(in agony, loneliness, desperation)
Peg . . . Peg . . .

[Anna stands in f.g. with her back to the bedroom, where Charley is forcing his kisses on Peg.] She turns her face away and starts to cry. Her body loosens, and she [collapses on the bed].

ANNA
(intensely)
Go away, Charley, go away.

Charley turns blindly from the girl to his mother and walks into the kitchen. [He walks past his mother and exits through the kitchen door.] Anna listens to the footsteps rushing downstairs outside, and turns to Peg, who is sobbing on the bed.

EXT. EAST SIDE STREET - NIGHT

Charley comes rushing down the stoop and runs to his car, where a big crowd of kids and neighbors stands.

MAN
(to another in the crowd admiring
Charley's car)
I remember when he was a kid in the poolroom—
he used to beat everybody! What a fighter!
(seeing Charley near the car)
You leaving, Champ?

Anna stands at the window in the front room and looks down on the street. We see the pantomime of Charley's popularity as he gets into the car. He screeches off, while Anna stands at the window.

INT. THREE CLUBS NIGHT CLUB

Foyer and wide entrance to the long, narrow club. ALICE is singing off screen to a four-piece band. Now the double doors to the street swing open, and Charley walks in, tight.

CHECK GIRL
Oh, hello, Champ. She'll be through in a few
minutes. Can I check your coat?

Charley slowly walks in and goes to the bar.

BARTENDER
Hello, Champ.

CHARLEY
Bourbon.

The bartender puts a glass and the bourbon bottle on the bar.

[BARTENDER
Chaser?

Charley pours himself a shot and drinks it. He walks away from the bar
toward the bandstand and sits down at a front table and watches Alice.]

Alice finishes her number. She walks down off the podium to the table.

She comes up to Charley.

ALICE
Hello, Sweetie . . .
        (upset)
Quinn's been going nuts. You've been every place
in town but here. Why didn't you come here first,
Charley?

He looks steadily at her, his face ravaged by his inner doubts, fears, and
struggle.

ALICE (CON'T)
How does it look, Charley? The night before the
fight, three A.M., and you loaded . . .

CHARLEY
        (taking her arm)
C'mon, Alice. Let's go . . .

Alice looks at him steadily, then a little smile breaks at the corners of her mouth.

                    ALICE
          Okay, Champ . . .

EXTREMELY CLOSE SHOT - SCALE CALIBRATION - DAY

The CAMERA PULLS BACK as an official straightens up and turns towards the CAMERA, as it reveals Charley, nude except for shorts, standing on the scale.

                    OFFICIAL
          Just on the nose, Davis.

                MARLOWE'S VOICE
                (loud, belligerent)
          All fat. Night club fat.

The camera continues to move back to reveal JACK MARLOWE, the contender, speaking. Like Charley, he is wearing shorts.

                MARLOWE (CON'T)
          Whiskey fat. Thirty-five year old fat!

[Marlowe gets on the scale.] We contrast the two men — the younger, much-muscled boy against the older, smoother-bodied man of thirty-five. A flashlight bulb explodes. There is the lightning violence of the glare, and Charley moves past Marlowe as if he were non-existent. The room is jampacked, overflowing into the corridor with reporters, observers, photographers, officials, friends, etc. The crowd makes way for Charley, who is followed by Quinn. Marlowe brings up the rear with his manager, DANE. The scene is continuously punctuated by flashlight bulbs, as Charley stands near the doctor. In the background is ROBERTS.

                    DOCTOR
          Too bad about Ben . . .

                    CHARLEY
          Yeah . . .

                    REPORTER
You in good shape tonight, Marlowe?

                    MARLOWE
Great shape!

                ANOTHER REPORTER
Two pounds under Davis!

                    REPORTER
Think you're going to lick him?

Shooting between Charley's torso and the examining head and hands of
the doctor. Marlowe is in the middle, visible through the narrow space
between Charley's chest [on the right, and Quinn and Dane on the left.]

                    MARLOWE
            (truculent)
I've licked everybody in the division.

                    REPORTER
Are you nervous?

                    MARLOWE
Nervous! He's nervous. It took the Boxing
Commish two years . . . it took every sports writer
two years . . . it took me two years, to pressure
Davis into this fight.

                    DOCTOR
            (to Charley)
Turn around.

The doctor taps Charley on the shoulder. Charley turns around. The
doctor is examining Charley's eyes as he stands side by side with
Marlowe.

                    REPORTER
What round do you think you're going to stop
him?

MARLOWE
I'll stop him in two, if his legs hold out.

Quinn comes close to Marlowe and his manager, Dane.

QUINN
(to Marlowe)
Look, you, lay off with the propaganda.
(to Dane)
Can't you keep this loud-mouth shut?

He gestures towards Marlowe. Dane shrugs his shoulders.

DANE
(with Southern accent)
Ah'm in charge of the muscles, not the brain.

[MARLOWE
(focusing on Charley's eye examination)
What are you using, Champ, the good eye or the
glass one?]

Without any change of expression, without looking at Marlowe, Charley
suddenly snaps a terrific left into his face. Marlowe staggers back, [but
then strikes back at Davis with his right]. There is the hullabaloo of
holding the fighters back, voices up, photographers, etc.

DISSOLVE TO:

INT. ARENA, CORRIDOR AND TUNNEL LEADING TO CHARLEY'S
DRESSING ROOM

There are police, stragglers, etc., and SOUND of the crowd stomping
overhead. Long shot as Roberts and THE DRUMMER come up to the
camera, nodding to the police, etc., on the way to Charley's dressing
room, where the Drummer remains outside. Roberts enters.

INT. DRESSING ROOM

Quinn and Charley, as Charley pulls on socks. But as Roberts enters,
Quinn signals Prince out of the room.

> QUINN
> Prince, go see what bout's on.

> ROBERTS
> That was great publicity, Charley . . . smacking
> Marlowe this afternoon.

> CHARLEY
> I meant to hit him.

> ROBERTS
> The kid was putting on an act to make it look
> good.

> CHARLEY
> I could knock that Marlowe on his ear in two
> rounds.

Roberts [moves closer to Charley and sits down on the rubbing table
next to him], and the probing interchange continues.

> ROBERTS
> What's wrong, Charley? The books are all bal-
> anced; the bets are in. You've bet your purse
> against yourself. You gotta be businesslike,
> Charley. Just because the kid talks a little fresh . . .

His voice trails away.

> CHARLEY
> (raising his voice)
> Gimme the tape, Quinn.

> ROBERTS
> You thinking about Ben, Charley? Everybody
> dies . . . Ben . . . Shorty . . . Even you.

CHARLEY

What's the point?

ROBERTS

(casually)

No point. That's life.

> (Roberts [is talking] close to Charley
> as Charley painstakingly wraps his
> hand.)

You go in there and just box that kid for fifteen rounds, Charley, like we agreed. Nobody get hurt. Nobody get knocked out. You'll lose by a clean decision. You'll get your money, and we're squared away.

> (Charley doesn't reply)

You know the way the betting is, Charley. The numbers are in. Everything is addition and subtraction. The rest is conversation.[15]

CHARLEY

I still think I could knock that Marlowe on his ear in two rounds.

Roberts takes hold of the long end of the bandage and jerks it with a sudden fierceness.

ROBERTS

Maybe you could, Charley. But the smart money is against it, and you're smart.

CHARLEY

(resigned)

It's a deal . . . it's a deal.

ROBERTS

(smiling)

You gotta be businesslike, Charley, and business-men have to keep their agreements.

He starts towards the door. Charley continues to wrap the bandage around his hand.

CHARLEY
Fifteen rounds is along time, Mister Roberts.

Roberts pauses, looks back.

ROBERTS
Make it short then.

He opens the door and walks out.

Conflict, indecision, and memory touch Charley's face. Suddenly he lies back on the table. The bandage [is draped over his body].

CHARLEY
Get out of here!

Quinn exits.

Charley covers his face with his hands.

CHARLEY
(murmuring)
All gone down the drain . . . everything down the drain . . . All these years . . . everything down the drain . . . All these years . . .

BLUR DISSOLVE TO:

[BEGINNING OF FLASHBACK:]

INT. TRIUMPH MEETING HALL - NIGHT - SNARE DRUM

Marked: IROQUOIS DEMOCRATIC CLUB, and the painted head of an Indian. It beats time, drives into a drum roll, and the final clash of a cymbal, as the camera moves to reveal SHELTON, standing in a spot on the dance floor. He has just signaled the end of the drum roll. Now he faces around and booms out.

SHELTON
And now the Iroquois Democratic club of the 14th
A.D. has a big surprise for a very lucky young
man. The boy who won his first amateur bout in
one minute and twelve seconds . . . our own
neighborhood Champ . . . Charley Davis!

The spot picks out Charley. Charley is just glowing with pride. The boys
are looking at him with envy [and are applauding. Charley, exuberantly
standing up, is applauding himself.]

SHELTON'S VOICE
. . . Quiet! Quiet! Quiet! . . . who's got the privilege of dancing a solo with Miss Iroquois Democratic Club, 14th A.D.

There is applause all around as Charley sits stunned and embarrassed.
A corny little band plays a flourish. Pan to Peg, who walks to Shelton.
He takes her robe and walks over to get Charley.

SHELTON'S VOICE
Don't make her anxious, Charley. Hurry . . .

Shelton faces Charley to Peg in the center of the dance floor. She stands
there in the typical bathing beauty outfit. A band across her bosom
reads: "Miss Iroquois Demo Club." Charley hesitates . . .

SHELTON
Take her around, Charley. She won't bite ya.

There is a big laugh from the audience. Charley is beginning to get
angry, feeling his humiliation with a sudden vividness. As he still
hesitates . . . Peg's deadpan breaks a little, and a little human pity comes
into her face. She steps forward and comes close to Charley.

SHELTON
You can dance, can't ya? Can you walk?

There is another big howl, especially from the fighters' table. Charley is
on the point of bolting or fighting.

SHELTON
Come on, she's willing, like I am. Go ahead.

Shelton pushes him into her arms.

Mechanically Charley puts out his arms and takes her around closely.
The drummer bangs the big drum, a bump. There is another laugh.

SHELTON
He's a ringer. A wrestler. . .

Charley darts a murderous glance at him and starts to push the girl away
to go at him, but Peg starts Charley dancing. They dance off, and the
spot moves to Shelton.

SHELTON
(to crowd)
Now why ain't I young and lucky?
(he shrugs)
Okay, friends, before we get lost in fun, don't
forget to vote for the people's choice—Jack
Shelton, the man who never said no to a friend.

And at once the spot breaks out on a big poster of Shelton, who is
running for alderman, as Charley and Peg continue to dance. [The M.C.
stands next to the Shelton poster, with a look on his face identical to that
of the man in the picture, revealing that the M.C. and the candidate are
one and the same.]

[INT. TAXICAB - NIGHT

Charley is sitting between Peg and Shorty in the cab's back seat. Charley
reaches his right hand over and places it on Peg. She ostentatiously
removes it. Shorty notices the rebuff. Charley is planning his next move,
when a sharp swerving of the cab propels both Charley and Shorty
against Peg on her side of the vehicle. Short readjusts his position, but
Charley remains pressed against Peg.

PEG
Ever hear of the law of gravity?

CHARLEY

What's gravity?

PEG

Sit up straight.

Charley reluctantly sits up, causing Shorty to break out in laughter.
Charley elbows him to shut up.

DISSOLVE TO:]

EXT. MOUNT STREET GREENWICH VILLAGE - NIGHT

A taxicab pulls up at the high stoop of a four story converted brownstone. As the taxi door opens, Charley gallantly gets out and extends his
hand within to help Peg. [Peg turns to shake hands with Shorty.

PEG

Well, good night.

SHORTY

'Night.]

Peg shoots past Charley in a flash. A quick tattoo of high heels across the
sidewalk, and she is running up the brownstone steps. He races up after
her, two at a time, passes her, and reaches the apartment house door
before she does. He leans casually, arms folded, with his back to the
door.

CHARLEY
(easily)

I win.

PEG
(panting as she comes up)

Well, you're in better shape.

CHARLEY
(looking her over)

Depends on the point of view.

PEG
[a brief downward glace]
Well, goodnight.

CHARLEY
(affably)
Aw, it's early yet.

Peg is trying to get past him. She has taken the key out of her purse.

PEG
(innocently)
Why don't you go to a movie?

[Charley laughs, but remains in place before the door.]

PEG
Excuse me.

CHARLEY
Certainly.

Charley steps away slightly, and Peg, as if absentmindedly, inserts the key in the lock. Before turning it, she maneuvers herself into a position of advantage so that she can slip inside the door before Charley can follow her. He pretends not to notice what's gong on.

PEG
(suddenly looking past his shoulder)
Is your friend going to wait for you?

Charley turns away to look down the steps to the cab. Shorty has leaned forward and is looking out of the cab up at Charley and Peg, his expression partly incredulous, partly amazed.

[Charley pantomimes to Shorty to leave.] Peg quickly turns the key, pushes the door open, slides in, and tries to slam it shut.

CLOSE SHOT - CHARLEY'S TOE IN DOOR

Peg stamps down on it vigorously. The toe is withdrawn, and [Peg retreats further into the building].

CLOSE SHOT - CAB

Shorty and the driver are leaning out of the cab like firstnighters at the opera. [The cab driver begins to laugh at Charley being out-maneuvered, but Shorty nudges him to stop.]

INNER GLASS DOOR

[Peg makes her way behind an inner glass door which she locks.] From within, Peg draws the curtain of the glass door back and peeps out at Charley, who leans closer to the glass and pantomimes.

> CHARLEY
>
> My friend . . .
> (gesturing to indicate Shorty)
> It don't look good . . .

He holds up his hands in prayer. Peg starts to smile. Charley pronounces soundlessly "five minutes," holding up five fingers for additional clarity. Again he points over his shoulder. Peg hesitates, and then slowly opens the door. She is in full command now and somewhat intrigued by this muscular naiveté.

> PEG
>
> Alright, but as soon as your friend leaves, you leave. Promise?

> CHARLEY
>
> Promise.

[She begins to move back in.]

> CHARLEY
>
> Say, what's your name?

PEG
(smiling)
Peg . . .

She opens the door wider. [Charley adjusts his tie and moves in.]

[*CLOSE SHOT - CAB*

SHORTY
(smiling)
Still the undefeated champ!

CAB DRIVER
(shaking his head)
Amateur!]

INT. LANDING - APARTMENT DOOR

This is the dark and narrow hallway of a brownstone, the head of a flight of stairs in the background. Peg is [in front of her apartment door.]

PEG
(calling)
Irma!

IRMA'S VOICE
Yes!

CHARLEY
Don't you live alone?

Peg shakes her head.

PEG
Are you decent?

                    IRMA'S VOICE
                    (drawling)
Not particularly. . .
                    (a pause)
Bring him in!

Peg turns around and swings the door open.

                        PEG
                  (a lifted brow)
          Are you decent?

[Peg enters.] Charley [laughs], fixes his collar uneasily and walks in.

INT. STUDIO ROOM - FULL SHOT

Charley enters and looks curiously around, closing the door. To
Charley's surprise, and ours, this is a studio apartment, a big, old-
fashioned room with a skylight. Artists' materials are everywhere,
canvasses, sculpture, complete and incomplete. A glass paned door
leads off to a bedroom. IRMA SHAW has been reading. She is a very
sophisticated girl, thoroughly Greenwich Village, long earrings, short
bob, long legs, etc. She looks curiously at Charley.

                        PEG
          This is Irma.

                      CHARLEY
          Hello.

                        PEG
          She sculpts.

Irma turns to Charley who looks blank.

                      CHARLEY
          Huh?

                        IRMA
          I make statues.

                    CHARLEY
              (with understanding)
        Oh!

                      PEG
              (to Irma)
        And this is Charley Davis . . .
              (voice grows orotund)
        . . . amateur boxing champion of the universe . . .
              (in normal voice)
        . . . as of tonight.

                     IRMA
              (with feline, interested smile,
              looking him over from head to toe)
        Re-ally!

                   CHARLEY
              (mumbling)
        Pleased to meet you.

Removing her coat, Peg walks into the bedroom. Irma gives Charley a
long, slow look.

                     IRMA
        Well — sit down, Champ.

                   CHARLEY
        Thanks.

Uneasily, Charley sits down.

                     IRMA
        Take your coat and shirt off.

                   CHARLEY
        What?

                     IRMA
        Like to pose for me?

Around the room there are a few semi-nude statues of women. He is floundering, terribly embarrassed. Peg reenters the room. Charley stands.

                    PEG
          Sit down.

Irma uncovers a statue.

                    IRMA
          I've got a longshoreman posing for me now.

Charley follows her with a hypnotized stare.

                    CHARLEY
          Longshoreman?

Irma reveals a surrealist statue. Charley swallows and lamely smiles. Irma looks at Peg.

                    IRMA
          Very graceful too. . . . Any time you'd like to be
          preserved for posterity, Champ, come up and see
          me. Goodnight, Champ . . .
                    (meaningfully to Peg, as she walks
                    to door of bedroom)
          Peg. . . .

                    PEG
          Irma . . .

Irma gives Charley a long, slow look, smiles, and disappears into the bedroom.

                    CHARLEY
          Is she kidding?

[Peg laughs.] Charley looks at her, deluged by this new experience.

                    CHARLEY
          What do you do here?

PEG
(with little gesture around the room)
Oh, I paint.

CHARLEY
(astounded)
Paint?

PEG
Pictures. . . . I go to art school because I want to be
a painter.

CHARLEY
Well what about this Miss This and Miss That?

PEG
Oh, there's an agency which arranges these little
jobs for me . . . I get twenty-five dollars, and the
crowd gets to whistle.

CHARLEY
Well, what's with that accent?

PEG
What accent?

CHARLEY
Well, the way you say, "crowd" and "whistle".

PEG
(laughing)
Well, I talk that way.

CHARLEY
Why?

PEG
Well, because . . . because I learned it that way.

CHARLEY
Where?

PEG
(quietly)
Oh, in Paris ... Berlin ... London ... Montreal.[16]

CHARLEY
(after a pause)
And you paint, too?

PEG
Yes.

CHARLEY
Paint me!

PEG
Sure.

Peg crosses and sits down at the drawing board.

PEG
Did your friend leave?

CHARLEY
(Charley crosses to window and
looks out)

[The street is empty.]

That character's still there.

PEG
Well, pull the shade up.

CHARLEY
What?

PEG
That'll send him away.

CHARLEY
Okay.

Charley pulls up the shade and turns to Peg.

> CHARLEY
> Should I take my coat off?

> PEG
> Oh, makes no difference.

> CHARLEY
> (striking a pose)
> How's this?

> PEG
> (amused)
> Are you going to be a professional prizefighter, or
> are you going to run for President?

Charley starts walking toward Peg.

> CHARLEY
> I just want to be a success.

> PEG
> You mean you want other people to *think* you're a
> success.

He stands right beside her now, looking down on her arm and shoulder
as she sketches. He looks at the inviting softness of Peg and then puts
his hand out and places it on her shoulder.

> CHARLEY
> Sure. Sure. Every man for himself.

Peg looks up quickly and sees his mood. She suddenly picks up a big,
heavy drawing ruler and smacks his arm. Charley jerks his hand back as
if it were burned. Peg rises, the sketch in hand.

> PEG
> (matter-of-factly, [giving him the
> sketch])
> Time to go home now.

She walks to the apartment door and opens it. Charley slowly follows, not very happy. Charley walks out.

[Peg tries to shut the door quickly behind him, but Charley steps back in.]

                    CHARLEY
          (trying)
     Could I see you again, sometime.

                    PEG
     What for?

                    CHARLEY
          (earnestly)
     Well, just to see you, anything. . . .

                    PEG
          (with a slight smile)
     Try some time.

                    CHARLEY
          (eagerly)
     Will you?

                    PEG
     Try.

She starts to close the door, but he forces it open again.

                    CHARLEY
          (with slow astonishment)
     I don't get it, Peg. Why should you want to see
     me?

                    PEG
          (coyly)
     Why do you want to see me?

As if drawn by a magnet, Charley comes towards her.

CHARLEY
(looking for words)
Because you're beautiful, and you're level, and
you're different . . .

He winds down. He is standing very close to her.

PEG
(estimating him)
Well, Charley, you're sort of innocent . . .
(she leans against the door jamb)
You know, when I went to school, I learned a
poem. Went:
"Tiger! Tiger! Burning bright
In the forests of the night,
What immortal hand or eye
Could frame thy fearful symmetry?"

CHARLEY
(hoarsely)
What's symmetry?

PEG
(with a smile)
Well built.

He suddenly takes her in his arms and kisses her. She gives in, then
frantically pushes him off and closes [in his face]. Charley stands for one
long, hypnotized moment, and then, sketch in hand, runs down the
stairs.

EXT. EAST SIDE STREET - NIGHT - AT POOLROOM

Shorty and a circle of boys are propped [around the stairs leading down
to the poolroom]. The boys listen as Shorty regales them with the whole
evening's adventures.

SHORTY
. . . after I show him how to knock this guy out, we
get this big feed, see, and then they bring this
quail out . . .

[BOYS
(all excited with anticipation)
Yeah! And then what happened? . . . then what
happened?

Shorty looks around, and then theatrically turns to walk away, as if too
bored to continue. All of them grab him at once.

BOYS
Come here! Come on . . . come on! Finish the
story!]

SHORTY
Well . . . she and Charley begin to dance, see. . . .
And before you know it . . .
          (gesturing them closer)
she's inviting him up to her apartment. . . Well . . .
Charley, perfect man of the world. . . gives me the
sign, see . . . and, me, I blow. . . . Fellows . . .
          (snaps his fingers)
just like that . . . Charley, very nonchalant . . .

FIRST BOY
Hello, Charley!

Charley approaches, the rolled up picture in his hand. Shorty [turns
eagerly].

SHORTY
Well . . . well?

Charley walks into silence, the laughing glances. After a felt moment, he
extends the rolled picture to Shorty.

CHARLEY
She draws pictures . . .

SHORTY
(incredulous)
You mean she was drawing your picture?

CHARLEY

Yeah. They got a big room with big paintings and
statues and all that kind of stuff.
(hunches his shoulders)
I'm going to see her again.

FIRST BOY

(coming up)
She give you a diploma?

CHARLEY

Wise guy.

Charley whirls, but Shorty grabs the picture.

SHORTY

Lemme see that. Look, she drew his picture.

FIRST BOY

(looking at it, then to his friend)
Hey, look . . . fur. . . . Doesn't look like you.

CHARLEY

Alright . . . alright . . . alright!

Charley grabs the picture back.

FIRST BOY

What are you gettin' sore about?

CHARLEY

I'm not sore. Who's sore?

Quinn walks down the stairs to the poolroom.

SHORTY

Hiya, Mister Quinn. . . . He was at the fights . . .

CHARLEY

No kiddin'?

SHORTY

Yeah, I saw him.

CHARLEY

You mean when I knocked that guy out?

SHORTY

Sittin' right at the ringside. C'mon . . .

CHARLEY

What for?

SHORTY

C'mon, don't be a dope. Hit him while you're hot!

CHARLEY

Okay . . .

Shorty and Charley run down into the poolroom.

INT. POOLROOM

A crap game or card game is going on desultorily in the very rear. Quinn is playing a pool game. The other tables are more or less deserted. The table lights illuminating the place give it a shadowed poetry. The two boys enter.

Shorty leads Charley close to Quinn's table. Shorty quickly supplies chalk. Quinn chalks his cue. [Shorty attentively takes back the chalk.] Quinn breaks.

SHORTY
(enthusiastically)
Verrrrry strong! You see that, Charley!

Quinn is looking the balls over.

SHORTY

Like the fights tonight, Mister Quinn?

                    QUINN
So-so.

                    SHORTY
How'd ya like that quick knockout Charley made?

                    QUINN
I've seen knockouts before.

He shoots.

                    SHORTY
Everybody said it was sensational. . . . Ever meet
Charley personally, Mister Quinn?

                    QUINN
          (to partner)
You shoot.

Quinn turns around slowly, and Shorty brings Charley forward.

                    SHORTY
This is Charley Davis.

                    QUINN
Hello . . .

                    SHORTY
          (a pause)
How about you taking a hand and setting up a
few money fights now? Charley's on his way up.

                    QUINN
          (bored, lighting cigar)
Uh uh.

                    SHORTY
          ([with greater enthusiasm])
Charley's a great fighter, Mister Quinn. He's got
the natural stuff. . . . He's got the style. A little
training and . . .

                    QUINN
          So what?

Charley is watching with growing resentment.

                    SHORTY
          So what! He won the amateurs . . .

                    QUINN
               (turning on Shorty)
          So what? Kids win this and that every day. . .
          thousands of them. One out of a hundred fights
          professionally. One out of a thousand is worth
          watching. One out of a million is worth coffee and
          doughnuts. . . . Now, tell your boy to get himself
          an honest job.

Charley knocks Quinn's ball away.

                    CHARLEY
               (angrily, turning away)
          Nobody's asking you for coffee and doughnuts . . .

Charley exits. Quinn watches Charley walk towards the entrance and
out. [The anger on Quinn's face slowly dissolves into a smile.]

                    SHORTY
               (with desperate salesmanship)
          You see that, Mister Quinn? He's a natural fighter.
          You got a champion.

Quinn turns to his partner.

                    QUINN
          Throw me the ball.

EXT. STREET

Charley walks over to the candy store. Charley's father, DAVID, is
outside the store, closing down for the night, removing newspapers from
the stand.

                    CHARLEY
          Hi ya, Pop!

Charley grabs a stack of newspapers and takes them inside.

INT. CANDY STORE

His mother, Anna, stands behind the old, short fountain cleaning a glass.

                    CHARLEY
          Good evening, Ma.

                    ANNA
              (ironically)
          Good evening, champion.

She continues to clean.

                    ANNA
          We had a delegation tonight from the poolroom.
          They congratulated your parents.

Charley deflates.

                    CHARLEY
          Well, it's better to win than to lose.

                    ANNA
              (sarcastically)
          Surely. . . and the other boy, you hurt him good,
          champion?

David is putting some cartons on a high shelf.

                    CHARLEY
          Ah, it was only a prizefight. It's a sport.

Charley hands the boxes to him.

ANNA
(milking each word of its irony)
A fine sport! A fine sport, indeed!

Shorty bursts excitedly in, and grabs Charley.

SHORTY
Charley, why'd you run? Quinn'll take you on.
He'll teach you to be a professional fighter. All we
got to do is raise ten or fifteen bucks for equipment . . . we can dig up the dough. . . and. . . good
evening, Mrs. Davis . . . good evening, Mr. Davis.
. . . I'll see you later, Charley.

Shorty exits.

CHARLEY
Yeah.

ANNA
So now you'll be a professional sport and make a
living hitting people . . . knocking their teeth out,
smashing their noses, breaking their heads in.
Sportsman, this is what you want?

DAVID
All right, Anna, if we're closing up, let's close.

Anna turns a bitter face to her husband.

ANNA
Twenty years ago I wanted to move to a nice place
so our Charley'll grow up a nice boy and learn a
profession. But instead we live in a jungle, so he
can only be a wild animal.

DAVID
You think I picked the East Side like Columbus
picked America? It was possible to buy the candy
store with a small cash down payment. . .

ANNA

A fine investment! Next door, a speakeasy. . . .
Across the street a poolroom . . . Loafers on the
corner . . . Children like wolves.

DAVID

Could I help it that J. P. Morgan refused to advance me credit? I would have opened a fancy
store on Fifth Avenue. We could have lived at the
Ritz, Charley would be wearing a monocle.

Charley's face is hard with humiliation and fury.

CHARLEY

You think I want to spend the rest of my life
selling kids two-cent soda? Mister Davis, gimme a
penny candy! Mister Davis gimme a pack of
cigarettes! Mind the baby. . . make mine
raspberry . . .
    (thrusts down fountain soda water
    lever, seltzer spurts)
But not me, ma, understand, not me. I don't want
to end up like Pa.

ANNA

    (turning angrily on him)
Don't talk that way about your father!

DAVID

Let the boy alone. He don't mean what he says.

ANNA

No . . . let him alone . . . like you do, to fight in
poolrooms, to hang around street corners. I want
him to study . . . to be something.

CHARLEY

I want to be a fighter!

ANNA

So fight for *something*, not for money!

Anna angrily departs. David looks at Charley's sullen face, motions him over.

                    DAVID
          Charley!

David slowly turns to the cash register and rings the "no sale." He takes out ten dollars and gives it to Charley.

                    CHARLEY
          That's ten dollars!

                    DAVID
          For your boxing equipment. You don't have to
          discuss this with your mother.

                    CHARLEY
              (softly)
          Thanks, Pop.

Charley leaves the candy store, as David closes the door and goes back to the cash register.

EXT. STREET

Charley crosses over to the poolroom. At this moment a big sedan turns the corner and screams down the street, and a bomb is thrown into the speakeasy.

                    SHORTY
              (screaming)
          They're bombing the speak . . .

He pulls Charley down the steps to the poolroom. There is an enormous explosion. Debris flies, smokes, etc., and then the car screams off.

The street fills with people. A few torn and bloody men stagger out of the speakeasy. Shorty and Charley run to the store. The glass of the candy store is broken. Through the window we see that the adjoining wall to the speakeasy has caved in over the fountain.

Charley steps through the broken glass into the store, followed by Shorty. David lies crushed under the wreckage. Charley reaches down to him.

CHARLEY
(a boy again)
Pa . . . . . . Pa!

[Charley lifts a piece of heavy wood off his father.] Anna rushes in, goes to her husband. [She sees that her husband is dead. She and Charley look at each other with great sadness. Then grief overcomes her and she begins to sob, embracing her husband.] Charley puts his arm on her shoulders.

[CHARLEY
Don't cry, ma. Don't cry.]

Charley's face is rigid, all feeling washed from it. He holds tightly to his mother.

FADE TO BLACK:

EXT. EAST SIDE STREET - NIGHT

The candy store is boarded up, the Davis name half burned off the sign, and there is a "for rent" notice plus neighborhood movie advertisements, etc.

Charley stands in the corner formed by the stoop and candy store, kicking his heels against the winter cold. Across the street the poolroom lights warmly burn, but Charley keeps looking up the street. [A man from the adjacent grocery store sees Charley standing there.

MAN
Charley, it's cold out . . . why don't you come in and get a little warm?

CHARLEY
Uh, thanks. I'm waiting for somebody.

                                MAN
        Okay.]

A girl comes in view, appearing from the alley, and his attention perks,
but as she passes beneath the street light, we see a stranger, and his and
our attention lapses. Charley looks over to the poolroom again and
starts to drift across the street towards it [and goes down the stairs].

INT. POOLROOM - NIGHT

In the front Shorty is playing poker with four other boys. One boy is
reading a newspaper. The atmosphere is of the slump, except that a
heavy set young boxer, MARINO, is flashily dressed.

The door opens, and Charley enters, shaking himself against the cold.

                            SHORTY
        Cold outside. . . huh?

                            CHARLEY
                    (looking out in street)
        Yeah.

                            SHORTY
        She didn't come yet, huh?

                            CHARLEY
                    (looking at Shorty)
        No!

                            SHORTY
        Maybe she won't come.

                            CHARLEY
        She'll come. She'll come. That's what I'm afraid
        of . . . It's gonna be *great*. . . . She and my mother.

                            SHORTY
        Well, if you're goin' with a girl . . .

CHARLEY
Who's goin' with a girl? I won't have a dime in a
hundred years.

Shorty looks at the paper which a boy is reading and takes it from him.
A big splash of type in the sports sections reads: "BEN CHAPLIN GETS
CRACK AT TITLE. SENSATIONAL MIDDLEWEIGHT FINALLY GETS
CHANCE."

SHORTY
No unemployment for him.

Charley [takes the paper and reads] the page and [says] in frustration.

CHARLEY
Alright, alright, don't rub it in. I got troubles of
my own.

SHORTY
You and me both. . .
(to the dealer)
Deal me in next hand.
(to Charley)
Well, look through the want ads . . . Maybe
somebody died, and you can carry the corpse . . .

As Charley [continues to look at the paper], Shorty saunters over to
Quinn.

SHORTY
[(lighting Quinn's cigar)]
How's business, Mister Quinn?

QUINN
Always pitching, huh punk!

SHORTY
Why don't you talk to Charley?

QUINN
What for?

SHORTY
Well, he might listen to you. He ain't got a job,
nothing.

QUINN
It ain't my headache. He don't wanta fight.

SHORTY
His old lady won't let him.

QUINN
That never stopped anybody, kid. You know that
Charley just doesn't have the drive, the fighting
spirit.

SHORTY
(indicates Marino)
How about Marino?

QUINN
He stinks, but he's willing. That's half the racket.
Now, stop dreaming, kid. You'll have to make a
buck some other way.
[(turns to man behind counter)
Let me see that form, will you Sam?

MAN
Yeah, that Four Leaf Clover is running again.]

Shorty returns to the poker game and sits down as Marino deals, while
Charley stands and watches.

SHORTY
Hey, Marino. . . you did great in your last fight . . .
(looks at Charley)
You know Marino, don't you, Charley? He's a real
mutt. Couldn't even lick my kid brother.

MARINO
Aw, lay off of that stuff, Shorty . . .

SHORTY

Even got knocked out last week. But he's still got plenty of dough in his pockets.

MARINO

The guy was a ringer . . .

SHORTY

How much do you get when you lose?

MARINO

Fifty bucks . . .

SHORTY

Fifty bucks! Fifty bucks! You hear that, Charley? He don't have to take his girl walking on the streets . . .

MARINO
(laying down hand)
Jacks.

SHORTY

Queens.

He starts to rake in the money, but Marino grabs his hand.

MARINO

Let me see the cards. . .

SHORTY

Oh, you don't trust me, eh?
(picks up cards, throws them in
Marino's face)
There!

Marino explodes with fury. He reaches over for Shorty, who runs.

MARINO
(frothing)
I'll murder you.

SHORTY
Charley! Charley!

Marino starts around towards Shorty, but Charley steps in between.
Marino hauls off and hits at Charley, who ducks and hits back. They
tangle, Charley suddenly fighting with a wild fury, as if to get rid of all
his troubles. He lashes Marino, while the boys yell: "fight, fight". . .
Shorty stands near Quinn. Charley drops Marino at Quinn's feet.

SHORTY
(smiling, [brushing his hands])
See what I mean. . . ? And your boy don't get fifty
bucks this time. . .

QUINN
You just burned up my cigar money, Charley.
(looks him over with admiration, at
ferocity which is draining off)

SHORTY
I bet he'd be willing to pay expenses now,
wouldn't you?

CHARLEY
[(grabbing Shorty)]
Hey, you know, you're a pretty cute kid. I ought
to take a sock at you.

SHORTY
Charley! Charley!

[CHARLEY
(smiling at Shorty, pushing him
away)
All right.

QUINN
You could make a lot of dough, Charley . . .]

SHORTY
(sees Peg)
Hey, there's Peg!

CHARLEY
Get my hat, will you! . . . Peg! Oh, Peg!

They run out.

EXT. STOOP OF DAVIS HOUSE

Peg is just going up the steps, a package under her arm. As Charley
comes up, followed by Shorty, she sees his bloody lip.

PEG
She left her lipstick on you, Charley.

He touches his mouth, and a smear of blood comes off.

PEG
Did another girl show you her paintings?

CHARLEY
(grinning sheepishly)
Oh, I ran into a door. . . . Let's take a walk around
the block . . .

PEG
What for?

CHARLEY
Well, my mother's been talking like I was bringing
you around for approval or something . . . Well, I
don't want to embarrass you and make you sore.

PEG
(smiling)
Oh, I won't be sore.

SHORTY
(cheerfully)
Look, Charley, you can't call it off. Just tell her
you like long engagements.

[PEG
(to Charley)
Is this a proposal?

SHORTY
From Mama. She'll say, eh . . . "And where do you
come from, Miss Born?" . . .]

Peg and Shorty laugh.

DISSOLVE TO:

INT. DAVIS KITCHEN - NIGHT

Close shot on table, which pulls back to reveal Anna, Peg, Charley, and
Shorty sitting around it. Anna is being very polite and dignified despite
the poverty stricken surroundings. Charley is nervous, watchful. Shorty
is having a good time, and Peg is docile as she tries to cut through
Anna's company behavior.

ANNA
And where do you come from, Miss Born?

Shorty laughs. [Charley hits him to stop.]

CHARLEY
She told you, Ma.

ANNA
(politely reproving)
I heard Miss Born, Charley.

PEG
(with inviting smile)
Call me Peg, Mrs. Davis. My friends call me Peg.

ANNA
Thank you, Peg. . . . I mean where did you come
from in this country?

PEG
Highlandtown. My father was a druggist there.

ANNA
A professional man. . . .Very nice. . . . Charley's
father's brother was a teacher . . . very smart.
Charley's going to night school. . . . He told you?

PEG
Yes. I think it's an excellent idea.

ANNA
And you came to New York to study . . .

PEG
I want to be a painter!

They look towards the bureau where her self-portrait stands.

PEG
Oh, Charley made me bring this.

CHARLEY
Talented, huh?

ANNA
Very talented.

Shorty offers Peg a cigarette, which she declines.

ANNA
(back to main business)
And you live in Greenwich Village . . . ?

PEG
Yes . . .

ANNA
It must be very lonely for a girl all alone. . . . You
live alone?

Peg gives Charley a roguish glance.

PEG

With a friend. . . . *She*. . . . makes statues.

ANNA

Wonderful. . . . Your father's a druggist, a professional man, and you're an artist . . .

CHARLEY
(desperately)
Peg, have another cookie. They're home made.

He holds the plate out to her as if to beg her to save him.

PEG

Thank you.

As she takes one, Charley hands it to Shorty.

CHARLEY

Shorty?

Shorty takes one, as Anna clears her throat to begin again.

CHARLEY
(willing to say anything)
You know, Shorty lives on the same block. He's
got ten brothers and sisters.

SHORTY

Yeah, and seven of them are out of work.

ANNA
(significantly)
The times are very hard. It's not easy for a boy to
get started nowadays . . . but if his friends encour-
age him, if he . . . if he goes to school and gets an
education, if he makes sacrifices . . .

CHARLEY

You end up wearing glasses . . . and still broke.

Charley is very embarrassed. Peg looks around at their embarrassment, leans forward towards Mrs. Davis, and speaks in all honest sincerity.

> PEG
> We're very poor, Mrs. Davis, we've always been poor. My father scraped and scraped, and when prohibition came he sold some of the bonded medicinal whiskey, you know, without prescription.

> ANNA
> And what happened?

> PEG
> Oh they arrested and fined him, and I got fed up anyway, so I came to New York. We're nothing fancy.

> ANNA
> (she pauses)
> Did Charley show you his medal?

> PEG
> No.

> ANNA
> He won it at basketball, the very best in the whole school.

> CHARLEY
> Aw, Ma . . .

> [SHORTY
> (enjoying Charley's discomfort)
> Show it to her. Show it to her.]

> ANNA
> Now don't be bashful, Charley. Peg *wants* to see it.

There is a knock on the door. It is Anna who goes to the door and opens it.

MISS TEDDER
(refined and thin)
Mrs. Davis?

ANNA
Yes . . .

MISS TEDDER
May I come in? I heard your voices in the kitchen.
I'm Miss Tedder.

ANNA
Oh . . . would you come in here, please?

Anna takes Mrs. Tedder into the living room. Charley, Shorty, and Peg
react. Charley gets up and follows Anna and Miss Tedder.

MISS TEDDER
I'm terribly sorry to interrupt your dinner. It's
hurry, hurry, hurry all the time . . .
(she trips past Anna to table, opens
briefcase)
So many cases and so few people . . . and so little
cooperation. I won't be long. I have your letter
here. Mrs. Anna Davis. Is that right?

ANNA
(in low voice)
Yes. I'm Anna Davis . . .

Anna sits.

MISS TEDDER
Now, just a form to make a proper check. . . .
Race: white. Religion: Jewish. Nationality:
American . . .

[Charley walks toward the women.

MISS TEDDER (CON'T)
(looking up, seeing Charley)]
Is this your boy?

CHARLEY

I'm Charley Davis.

MISS TEDDER

Are you unemployed?

CHARLEY

(impertinently)
You got a job for me?

The muscles of his face are frozen, his eyes like slits.

MISS TEDDER

Have you tried?

ANNA

He tried.

MISS TEDDER

All these questions must be answered. I'm sorry.
(turning to Anna)
Have you tried to get a job, Mrs. Davis?

ANNA

Would I be asking for a loan from charity if I could
find work?

MISS TEDDER

It isn't personal. We're supposed to ask. Have
you any resources . . . any jewelry?

CHARLEY

(viciously)
She has her wedding ring.

MISS TEDDER

(embarrassed)
We don't ask our clients to sell their wedding
rings.
(to Charley)
I wish you'd understand. I have to ask these
questions.

ANNA
(desperately)
Charley, please, go in the other room.

Miss Tedder takes a glance at the old, dilapidated furniture in the room.

MISS TEDDER
Is this furniture yours?

CHARLEY
(yelling)
Get out of here!

He is beyond himself. He walks to door and opens it. Anna follows.

ANNA
Charley! I won't have you talking like this.

CHARLEY
Get out! Get out of here!

[Shorty and Peg watch from the kitchen doorway. Miss Tedder goes to the front door, where she pauses.]

MISS TEDDER
We have to ask questions if we're going to help.

CHARLEY
(shouting)
We don't want any help. Tell 'em we're dead. We don't want any help.

Charley slams the door behind Miss Tedder. He turns furiously on his mother.

ANNA
(desperately)
I did it to buy myself fancy clothes? Fool! It's for you . . . to learn, to get an education, to make something of yourself.

CHARLEY
(wheeling to Shorty)
Shorty! Shorty, get me that fight from Quinn. I
want money . . .
(hysterically)
You understand? Money! Money!

ANNA
(with same hysteria as Charley's)
No! I forbid! I forbid! Better buy a gun and shoot
yourself.

CHARLEY
(yelling)
You need *money* to buy a gun!

He runs from the room, swinging the door open. It yawns as Anna
stares after Charley. We hear his steps clatter up to the roof. [Peg exits
from the kitchen door and runs after Charley up the stairs. The camera
pans back to Anna, still frozen in the doorway staring.]

EXT. DAVIS ROOF - NIGHT

Shooting from closed roof door, across graveled roof to parapet against
which Charley stands, his back to the camera, looking out over the city to
the lighted towers, the bright security. The roof door opens, and Peg
anxiously appears. She steps out into the cold wind, and the door slams
shut.

PEG
Charley!

Charley turns, looks, faces out again. Peg moves up along side of
Charley, stands there, trembling in the cold. After a long moment. . .

PEG
(in a small voice)
It's cold.

Charley reaches out with the left side of his open jacket, and she quickly moves close to him. He drops his arm and the coat over her shoulder so that they are both joined by the coat.

> CHARLEY
> I don't want any handouts. You think I like the idea of waiting around for the whole world to make up its mind what to do with me? . . . My mother don't understand . . .

> PEG
> What is it you want to do?

> CHARLEY
> There's only one thing I know how to do—fight!

> PEG
> Well, if you want to fight, fight.

> CHARLEY
> Then, it's all right with you?

> PEG
> Anything you want is all right with me. I love you, Charley.

> CHARLEY
> (with a sudden fierceness, making a
> fist)
> It'll be quick!

> PEG
> Tiger . . . Tiger!

She caresses his fist, then embraces him.

> CHARLEY
> Yeah . . . That's right. I got claws . . . .
> But not for you, Peg . . . not for you.

They kiss, then look down into street.

MONTAGE

[Kaleidoscope of scenes: a series of advertising posters announcing
Charley's fights—"RED SWEENY vs. CHARLEY (first instance of this
spelling) DAVIS" . . . "CHARLEY DAVIS vs. SUNNY FULLER" . . .
"CHARLEY DAVIS vs. K.O. PHIL MARCO" . . . "SLAT McCOY vs.
CHARLEY DAVIS" —intercut with images of Charley training, on the
phone to Peg, Shorty and Quinn at ringside, Charley surrounded by the
bodies of his fallen opponents, as he and Shorty move by train from the
prelims up to the main events. We see Charley's face emerge through the
blood, the cuts, the bruises, the beatings he takes changing him, the
knockouts he gives changing him, the life he leads changing him, a long
rush of fierceness, of the time serving across the continent, causing him
to relive the fights in his nightmares. The final element in the montage is
a segment of a newspaper column, "THE SPORTING CIRCLE," by
Dennis Dare; headline: "How Long Before Ben Chaplin Gives Charley
Davis a Crack at Title?" The initial sentences of the article read: "This
question is being asked around the bars and betting parlors of the town.
I think that Chaplin is sitting on his title waiting for the best contenders
to die off. Followers of the fistic arena are complaining about not seeing
a good title match in years. . . . "]

DISSOLVE TO:

TRAIN STATION - DAY

A train enters 125th Street Station.

[INT. TRAIN CORRIDOR

Quinn, well-dressed, a cigar in his mouth, walks up to a drawing room
door, adjusts his coat, and enters.]

INT. DRAWING ROOM

The double decker beds are still unmade, a table is set up before the seat,
and on the seat next to Shorty is an open valise, etc.

SHORTY
(looking up)
Quinn!

QUINN
Hello, Shorty.

Quinn closes the door and comes forward, camera panning, to shake hands with Shorty. We get the feeling of confinement in the room and see that good times have come: the clothes, the attitudes, the luggage, etc.

SHORTY
What you doing up here, Quinn? Couldn't you wait for Grand Central?

QUINN
(after a pause)
I got big news. . . .

Charley's feet come into scene from upper berth.

CHARLEY
Hey, Quinn!

QUINN
Hello, boy!

CHARLEY
Gee, that cigar stinks.

[Charley takes the cigar out of Quinn's mouth and tosses it aside].

QUINN
Hey, wait a minute! Wait a minute . . .

Charley jumps down and grabs Quinn.

CHARLEY
What do you say, pal? You got that news? You got that fight for me?

QUINN

Well, I don't know . . .

CHARLEY

Come on, tell me about it!
          (maneuvering Quinn to sit down)
Oh . . . the hats!

[Charley and Shorty adjust Quinn's position to avoid sitting on the hats.
They notice his fine apparel.]

SHORTY

How do you like the new coat, huh? And the tie,
Charley!

CHARLEY

Oh, never mind that . . . come on, give us the dope,
will ya.

QUINN

          (sitting down)
Well, we got a few business arrangements to take
care of first, Charley.

Shorty looks at Quinn more soberly.

SHORTY

          (to Quinn)
With who? Roberts?

QUINN

Who else? Nobody fights a championship for
anything unless Roberts gets cut in. You know
that. He's the dough, the real estate, everything.
The business . . .

SHORTY

What does Roberts want, Quinn?

QUINN

Nothing much, only . . . *Charley* . . .

SHORTY
(vehemently)
They'll be cutting you to pieces, Charley.

CHARLEY
Ah, it only means more dough cut more ways. A
bigger pie, more slices . . . more to eat for everybody.

[Charley moves to the basin and begins to lather his face for a shave.]

SHORTY
And Roberts'll be telling us what and when . . .

Charley, his face hard, tuns around and looks at Shorty.

CHARLEY
So what! Everybody's been telling us what and
when . . . the guy who owned the arena, the guy
who owned the fighter, the guy who owned the
books, cheap mobsters, gangsters, guys who
owned nothing. We've been fighting for peanuts
and eatin' them. Right?

SHORTY
Right.

CHARLEY
You know you can't get a fight in New York
without Roberts's say-so. Right?

QUINN
Right.

CHARLEY
Right. Okay, Quinn. Make the deal. I'll be
Champ, then I'll give the orders. I'll say what or
when . . .

Charley turns away and gets razor.

                    SHORTY
          (bitterly)
You can tell us what and when, but you can't tell
Roberts.

                    CHARLEY
But the Champ can!

                    SHORTY
Not if he gives away his right arm.

[Shorty grabs Charley's arm.] Charley cuts himself.

                    CHARLEY
          (furiously)
Aw. . . you made me cut myself!
          [(touching the cut, laughing, relax-
          ing a bit)]
It's my arm, isn't it?

He steps into the washroom.

                                        DISSOLVE TO:

[EXT. CHARLEY'S APARTMENT

A card on the door reads "Charles Davis." A finger pushes the buzzer.]

INT. CHARLEY'S APARTMENT

Medium shot of Peg looking out the window. Victor opens door, admitting Charley, Shorty, and bellboy.

Peg runs towards Charley as he enters. He sweeps her up in his arms.

                    CHARLEY
          (hefting her)
Gee, you're lighter.

PEG
(laughing)
You're stronger . . .

CHARLEY
(squeezing her)
Boy, you feel good.

Shorty comes up close. Charley is looking around him.

CHARLEY
(looking at Victor)
Hey, who's that?

VICTOR
I'm Victor. Mister Quinn employed me.

CHARLEY
Doing what?

SHORTY
The butler . . .
(with real happiness, to Peg)
Hello, Peg. . . .

PEG
Hello, Shorty.
(kissing him)
You look beautiful.

SHORTY
You take the words out of my mouth. How's the
new job?

PEG
Wonderful. . . . I'm the third assistant designer
now . . .

They react to Victor. Charley pokes Shorty. Shorty turns to Victor, who
is enjoying his new job much too soon.

SHORTY
Where do the bags go?

VICTOR
(indicating bedroom)
In there, sir.

Shorty walks into the bedroom, followed by Victor with the bags.

As soon as the door closes, Peg lets herself go and returns as much as she gets from Charley. The fall back on the couch.

PEG
Oh, it's been a long year, Charley . . .

CHARLEY
Yeah . . . twenty-one fights . . . nineteen knockouts, two decisions. . .

PEG
A lonely year . . .

CHARLEY
I missed you, too.

Peg takes his hand, and Charley winces, pulling it away.

CHARLEY
Hey, easy . . .

PEG
What's the matter?

CHARLEY
Guy had a head like rock. . . . It'll be all right.

Peg kisses his hand, and Charley withdraws it, embarrassed. She leans close to kiss him on the mouth, running her fingers over his face.

PEG
And this . . . and this . . . and this . . .

CHARLEY

Chicago . . . Philadelphia . . . Boston. . . . You get
something everytime, but it's worth it as long as
you win . . .
(as he looks around)
Look, lots of money . . . lots of clothes . . . lots of
everything. . . .
(calling)
Hey, Shorty . . . Shorty. . . .

The bedroom door opens, and Shorty appears.

CHARLEY (CON'T)

What about the reservations, the tickets for
tonight?

SHORTY

Well, I . . . want to talk to you about

CHARLEY

How about a drink?

VICTOR

Yes, sir.

PEG

(lightly)
Well, it's early in the morning yet, Charley. . . . We
haven't said hello. . . .

CHARLEY

Hello. . . .
(looking at her)
Morning, noon, or night, what's the difference
how you cut up the twenty-four hours?

His face opens wide with astonishment and pleasure as Victor presses a
button, and the wall revolves, revealing a well-stocked bar. Charley gets
up.

CHARLEY

Well, what do you know?

SHORTY

The only trouble is, Peg's picture's on the other
side.

PEG

Oh, we'll find another wall that stands still.

His whole interest is riveted on the little bar.

CHARLEY

Sure! . . . Look, it's even got a little sink . . .
        (examines bottles)
Bourbon, Scotch . . .
Like milk . . . Like cream . . .
        (slaps bar like bartender)
What'll you have, folks?
        (looks at ranged bottles)
Just like the candy store . . .
        (turns, shoots some seltzer into a
        glass)
Want a two-cent soda, Peg?
        (to Shorty)
Hey, Shorty, I thought I told you . . .

SHORTY

Charley. . . . I'd like to . . .

CHARLEY

Come on, come on . . . we got no secrets here.

SHORTY

I need some money.

CHARLEY

What do you mean, you need money? I thought I
gave you some in Detroit . . .

SHORTY

That was Detroit.

CHARLEY

All the time he needs money. Well, what do you
do with it?

SHORTY

I steal it! I go through your pockets every night
to see if there's any left to send to your old lady.

CHARLEY

Get the reservations.
       (to Victor)
You, bring my bags in.

Charley exits. Shorty crosses to behind the bar. Victor crosses through
and gets the bags.

PEG

What's wrong, Shorty?

SHORTY

Nothing . . . nothing.

Victor exits with the bags. Peg crosses to the bar.

PEG

Come on, Shorty . . . not with me.

SHORTY

He's restless . . . he's had a lot of fights . . . he's
wound up . . . like a guy on a jag. Peg, you got
to . . .

PEG

What have I got to . . . ?

SHORTY

You two still getting married?

PEG

Well, I haven't had time to say no.

SHORTY

Then get married right away.

PEG

Why? Have I got a rival. . . . ?

SHORTY

Yeah . . . money. You know what Charley is . . .
what they're making him . . . a money machine . . .
like gold mines, oil wells, ten percent of the U.S.
mint. . . . They're cutting him up a million
ways. . . . You're the only one left, Peg . . . the only
one. He won't listen to me. If you don't hold onto
him, it's good-bye Charley Davis. Marry him,
Peg . . . but do it now . . . now. . . .

Charley re-enters with a new coat on.

CHARLEY

How do you like this coat? Handmade . . .
Shorty's got one like this, too. Come on, honey . . .
we're gonna burn up the town . . . we'll rob the
stores. Oh, wait a minute, wait a minute, I forgot
. . . Oh yeah, Mom . . . Mom . . . Mom's coming up!
Will you do me a favor, Shorty, the old lady's
coming up. Keep her happy . . . make with the
jokes.

SHORTY

Where'll you be?

CHARLEY

On the town.

The exit. Shorty reacts.

INT. ROBERTS' APARTMENT

Quinn, ARNOLD, and BEN are in the living room in the foreground.
ROBERTS enters.

> ROBERTS
> Quinn, Arnold, Ben . . .
>> (sitting down)
> What did you decide, Arnold?

> ARNOLD
> The Champ and I talked it over. We owe you
> about forty grand . . .

> ROBERTS
> Exactly forty grand.

> ARNOLD
> Yeah . . . but we figure if we could hold the title for
> six months or more, we could pick up some easy
> money . . . you know . . . making appearances,
> and . . .

> ROBERTS
> The Champ hasn't fought a real match in two
> years, Arnold. That costs money, no gates. We
> waited for a real contender. He's here.

> ARNOLD
> I know.

> ROBERTS
> It's a business, Arnold. We get one fight now,
> another in six months. That's money at the gate,
> and the betting. Besides, I've been carrying you
> and your boy. Debts have to be paid, or it
> wouldn't be business.

> QUINN
> I guess you're right, Mr. Roberts. Too bad about
> Ben getting hurt in that last fight. I liked Ben. He
> was a real fighter.

                    ARNOLD
Our luck.

                    QUINN
Accidents happen.

                    ARNOLD
Let them happen to other people. After Ben's
head cracked into that post, I wanted to die. It's
still there—the blood clot. The doctors say no
more fights. . . . What do you want me to do?

                    ROBERTS
I told you . . . get your boy in the ring.

[Arnold gets up and walks over to Ben.]

                    ARNOLD
It's up to you, Ben. If you say no, no.

                    ROBERTS
If it's no, I want the money right away—and I hold
you responsible, Arnold.

Ben slowly gets up and walks over to look harshly at Roberts.

                     BEN
People don't count with you, do they Mister
Roberts?
          (looks at Arnold who awaits his
          fate)
You been square with me, Arnold. I'll fight Davis.

Arnold looks at Roberts.

                    ARNOLD
Okay, Mister Roberts.

                    ROBERTS
In two months.

ARNOLD

In two months. But we agree it's for a decision.
No slugging. I don't want my Champ killed,
Mister Roberts. . . .

ROBERTS

Nobody's gonna get killed.

BEN

Thank you, Mister Roberts. . . . Thank you.

[Arnold and Ben leave.] Quinn blows out his breath with relief after the
tension, [starts to leave]. Roberts holds a box of cigars out to Quinn.

ROBERTS

Have a good cigar, Quinn . . . for the new champ.

QUINN

(taking one)
Thanks, Mr. Roberts. Too bad about Ben's head.
He was a great fighter.

ROBERTS

Yeah, I like fighters, Quinn, better than horses.
But you got to look out for business. So we don't
tell Charley anything about this. Let him go in
fighting and knock Ben out.

QUINN

But Ben's sick, Mr. Roberts. Charley might kill
him.

ROBERTS

The crowd likes a killer, and Charley's a hard
fighter. It'll look fixed if he takes it easy.

QUINN

I know, Mr. Roberts . . .

                    ROBERTS
So, wipe your nose and forget the whole thing.
          [(Quinn lights match for Roberts's
          cigarette)]
Where's your boy? I asked you to bring him
down.

                    QUINN
He said you'd know where to find him . . .

                    ROBERTS
          (with his famous smile)
A fresh kid, huh?

                    QUINN
          [(awkward laughter)]
Yeah . . .

                    ROBERTS
I'll see him. . . .

                                        DISSOLVE TO:

INT. CHARLEY'S APARTMENT - NIGHT

A big head close-up of ALICE, her soft hair flowing goldenly on the
pillow of the couch. The camera angle widens to include Quinn tentatively, tenderly playing with the loose strands of her hair. Alice lies on
the couch, her head pillowed, her hair being caressed by Quinn's hand.
As the camera slowly lifts, Anna is revealed in the background [drinking
tea], as Shorty walks by, watching Quinn with embarrassment. They
have all been waiting a long time for Charley and Peg.

Shorty swallows and slowly drifts over to Quinn.

                    SHORTY
          (a little loud)
Why don't you freshen your drink, Quinn?

                                        Body and Soul 83

QUINN
(oblivious)
It tastes all right.

SHORTY
(leaning over and whispering)
Lay off in front of the old lady, will you!

Quinn draws a hand back as if burned, stands up, and goes to the bar.
Shorty looks down at Alice.

SHORTY
If you're sleepy, why don't you go home?

ALICE
I'm not sleepy. I'm just thinking.

SHORTY
Don't tell me. It's getting kind of late, Mrs. Davis.

ANNA
I've waited, Shorty. I'll wait. I wouldn't want to
disappoint Charley.

ALICE
(slowly sitting up)
I'm waiting for Charley, too. Quinn promised me.
It's lucky to meet lucky people.
(looks around at Anna)
You're a lucky woman, Mrs. Davis.

ANNA
You think so? In what way?

ALICE
(rising, approaching)
Well, your son's going to be champ. And that
means he's going to be rich, and that means you're
going to be rich.

ANNA
(with a twinkle)
I'm beautiful. Why should I want to be rich?

Quinn comes over and hands her a glass.

At this moment the door clicks and opens, while everyone expectantly
looks. Peg, a luxurious mink coat draped about her shoulders, walks
delicately in, watching her steps carefully, a little light-headed. Charley
follows. There is a momentary tableau.

PEG
Well, hello!

CHARLEY
(exuberantly)
Ma!

ANNA
Charley!

Anna stands as Charley rushes to her and exuberantly embraces her.

CHARLEY
You look fine! You look wonderful!

ANNA
(softly)
Let me look. Let me see.

She holds him off, examining him.

CHARLEY
I haven't changed. Neither have you.
(with wide gesture)
How do you like everything, huh?

ANNA
(still looking at him)
It's wonderful.

CHARLEY

I'm sorry we kept you waiting, but Peg and I
we've been on the town.

PEG
(moving in from entrance)
My fault, Mrs. Davis. My fault, everybody. We
danced and danced, and Charley just couldn't get
me home. Look at my dress. We robbed the
stores.
(pirouettes in front of Anna)
And what do you think of my wedding present?

CHARLEY

Yeah, we're going to get married. Right away. We
decided this afternoon.

ANNA
(beaming from her son to Peg)
Now I am rich.

SHORTY

Getting married. . . that's great.
Peg, makes me feel fine.
(kisses Peg on cheek)

CHARLEY
(pushing him away)
Okay, Shorty, that's enough.

PEG

Oh, it's been such a night . . . such a day. Did you
ever drink an ocean full of champagne? Every
place we went there were millions of people, and
everyone an intimate, personal friend of Charley's.
And everyplace we went there was another party
and more champagne. And Charley was the king,
and I was Charley's girl.
(pointing to Anna)
And you're Charley's mother.

(MORE)

                    PEG (CON'T)
                (pointing to Quinn)
            And you're Charley's manager.
                (pointing to Shorty)
            And you're Charley's friend.
                (noticing Alice)
            And . . . who are you?

[Peg props herself on the arm of the sofa.]

                    ALICE
    I'm nobody.

                    PEG
    Oh, now don't sulk. We're all nobody. You know
    who nobody is? Nobody is anybody who belongs
    to somebody. So if you belong to nobody— you're
    somebody. . . . Understand?

[Caught up in the (perhaps inebriated) enthusiasm of her words, Peg
leans backwards and falls off the sofa—right into Charley's arms.
Everybody laughs.]

                    QUINN
    I'm sorry. This is Alice, Charley, she's a friend of
    mine.
                (proudly)
    She sings in a night club.

                    ALICE
    Glad to meet you, Charley.

                    CHARLEY
    Hello.

                    QUINN
    And Miss Born.

                    PEG
    Hello.

ALICE
(indicating coat)
Could I try it on.

PEG

It's all yours.

Alice walks to the mirror with the coat.

SHORTY
Well, when's the wedding?

CHARLEY
Right away.

SHORTY
Good, good.

ANNA
We'll invite the whole neighborhood. You want to
have it uptown or downtown?

Peg and Charley, together:

PEG
Downtown.

CHARLEY
Uptown.

SHORTY
(quickly)
Any place as long as it's legal.

ALICE
(at mirror)
Gee, soft like baby's skin. Bet it cost a lot of
dough.

QUINN
Too rich for your blood.

The door buzzer rings off screen.

> QUINN (CON'T)
> Probably Roberts.

Quinn crosses to the door and admits Roberts [and his hood THE DRUMMER].

> QUINN (CON'T)
> Hello, Mister Roberts. We've been waiting for you.

> ROBERTS
> Who asked you to wait?
> > (crosses to Charley)
> I'm Roberts. You're Charley Davis.

> QUINN
> Come on, Alice . . . let's go.

> CHARLEY
> Pleased to meet you, Mister Roberts. This is my mother . . . this is my girl . . . we're gonna get married. . . . Just bought her a mink coat for a wedding present.

[Quinn and Alice leave.]

> ROBERTS
> > (indicating Shorty)
> And who's this?

> CHARLEY
> That's my friend, Shorty.   How about a drink, Mister Roberts . . . ?

> ROBERTS
> Never touch it.

> CHARLEY
> How do you like the layout, huh? . . .

ROBERTS

Very nice.

CHARLEY

You know, we got a wonderful view. You can see the whole park from here.

SHORTY

What's on your mind, Roberts.

ROBERTS

Oh, social call.

SHORTY

Social call, huh? What kind of a deal did you cook up with Quinn?

CHARLEY

Lay off, Shorty.

ROBERTS

Who'd you say this was?

CHARLEY

That's my friend.

ROBERTS

For how much?

SHORTY

Ten percent.

ROBERTS

Good evening, friend.

SHORTY

Good evening, *partner*. . . . Watch your arm, Charley.

[Shorty places his hand on Charley's arm, and Charley pulls it angrily away.]

CHARLEY
I told you it was my arm, didn't I?

[Shorty goes into the other room. Anna is quite disturbed by what she sees, follows Shorty.]

ROBERTS
Well, can we talk?

CHARLEY
(indicating The Drummer)
Yeah . . . who's this?

ROBERTS
He's with me.

CHARLEY
(indicating Peg)
Well, she's with me.

ROBERTS
We have to get straightened out on this deal, Charley.

CHARLEY
I thought you arranged that with Quinn.

ROBERTS
I don't talk money with Quinns.

CHARLEY
What do you want?

ROBERTS
I only make one kind of deal, Charley. From now until the time when you retire, fifty percent.

CHARLEY
(curtly)
Fifty percent of what? Quinn gets thirty percent, Shorty gets ten percent, and I get sixty.

ROBERTS

You want a crack at the title, don't you, Charley?
We start fresh. You're a fresh young kid, so we
start fresh. There's always one hundred percent.
You take fifty, and I take fifty.

CHARLEY

Well, what about Quinn?

ROBERTS

He's your manager . . . we both need him. You
give him five percent, and I'll give him five
percent.

CHARLEY

What about Shorty?

ROBERTS
(stops, looks at him)
I don't ask you what you give your mother,
Charley . . . or your girl. If you want Shorty for
laughs, give him the ten percent. I pay my expenses. You pay yours.

CHARLEY

Well, Shorty gets ten percent.

ROBERTS

I told you, I only make one kind of deal, Charley.
This way you fight for the championship right
away.

There is a pause in which Charley stares a little guiltily at Roberts.

CHARLEY

Okay, I'll take care of Shorty myself, but . . . don't
say anything about it.

ROBERTS

He's your friend. You're *my* partner.

CHARLEY

It's a deal.

PEG

What about me, Mister Roberts? What percent do
I get? After all, I made him what he is, because I
told him to fight.

ROBERTS
(looking her over carefully)
In my business there is only one hundred percent.
(turning to Charley)
I'd like to say goodnight to your mother, Charley.

CHARLEY

Oh, yeah, sure.
(calling)
Ma! Ma!

The bedroom door opens, and Anna appears, followed by Shorty. Anna
walks slowly into the room, her face grave, her attitude wary, concerned.

CHARLEY
Mister Roberts would like to say goodnight.

ROBERTS
I was awfully glad to meet you, Mrs. Davis.
You're a lucky woman to have a boy like Charley.
He's going to make a lot of money. Enough for
everybody. No more candy store for you, huh!
This is a lot nicer, ain't it?
(reaches into his pocket)
Oh, I almost forgot.

[Roberts gives Charley an envelope of money.]

CHARLEY
What's this?

ROBERTS

Just a little on account, Charley. I know you must
be running short. Goodnight, Mrs. Davis. By the
way, Charley, you want to start training right
away. The fight goes in two months, you know.

CHARLEY

Oh, it can't be too soon for me.

ROBERTS

And take a tip, kid.

CHARLEY

What's that?

ROBERTS

Postpone the wedding bells. Keep your mind on
the fight.
        (looks at Peg)
Goodnight, Charley's girl. Very nice coat. Remember, after mink comes sable. See you, Charley.

CHARLEY

Good night.

Roberts exits. Charley stands in the foreground by the couch. Shorty
crosses to a table by the window, Peg crosses to piano in background.

CHARLEY

Shorty . . . we got a lot of work to do. I want you
to set up that training camp, get ahold of Quinn,
tell him to get me the best sparring partners in
town.

SHORTY

When do you want to start?

CHARLEY

You heard him . . . right away.

ANNA

Then you're not going to get married.

CHARLEY

Why, sure we're going to get married . . . but it will
wait.

ANNA

Why can't the fight wait?

CHARLEY

Ma, you can't do a thing like that. Explain it to
her, will you Shorty.

PEG

Charley's absolutely right, Mrs. Davis. You can't
postpone a *fight*. We can wait.

Charley crosses to her at the piano.

SHORTY

Why don't we drive up to Greenwich tonight?
You can get married right away.

PEG

No, Shorty . . . we'll wait.

CHARLEY

That's my baby.
      (kisses Peg on cheek)
And you know what else, Ma? I think you ought
to get rid of the candy store and come and live
here in a decent place.

ANNA

I live in a decent place, Charley.

SHORTY

Yeah, and it's paid for.

CHARLEY

Sure. By who?

SHORTY

Not by Roberts.

CHARLEY

What's the difference? What are you beefing
about? It's money, ain't it? You get it, Peg, don't
you?

PEG

Yeah . . . I get it.

EXT. TRAINING CAMP - DAY

Punching bag is rhythmically beating against backboard as Charley
hammers it. [In the background, as the obstruction of the bag is removed
with each punch,] Alice is observed sitting on a wagon. Alice crosses her
legs. Charley knocks the bag off.

SHORTY

Whatsamatter, Charley? He oughta keep walkin'
around. I don't want him to cool off.

QUINN

I've been thinking, Charley. You've been working
too hard. Why don't you take a few days off and
go to the city and see Peg, huh?

[Charley looks at Alice.]

CHARLEY

I feel fine.

Charley jumps down off the ring platform.

ALICE

Last few weeks got tough don't they, Charley?

CHARLEY

Yeah.

He trots to the punching bag under the tree. Alice follows.[17]

ALICE

I'm getting to feel the strain myself.

CHARLEY

You're overtrained.

ALICE

So are you.

CHARLEY

Maybe.

ALICE

Awful edgy. . . . You don't want to overdo it.

CHARLEY

Neither do you.

ALICE

What have I got to lose?

CHARLEY

What have you got to win?

ALICE

Everything.

Quinn is listening in the background.

QUINN

Time, Charley.

Charley turns and runs back to the ring, stops. Quinn walks up foreground.

QUINN

(to Alice)
When are you going back to the city?

ALICE

No hurry. The club doesn't open for another week.

QUINN

Maybe you need a week to get ready.

ALICE

I don't think so. I'm beginning to like it up here.
Think I'll stay.

QUINN

Now, listen, Alice . . .

ALICE

No, you listen to me. . . . Don't forget—you made
me come up here.

QUINN

Yeah. . . . I like to see you get ahead, Alice. . . .

ALICE

What did you ever do about it?

QUINN

Nothing. I never done anything about it. You
done everything about it. . . . that job in the night
club?

ALICE

That lousy job.

QUINN

Those clothes you're wearing?

ALICE

You want 'em. I'll give you 'em back in spades.

[There is laughter from the group in the ring.]

QUINN

Take it easy, will you?

ALICE

Can't take that, can you?

QUINN

No, I guess I can't. . . . From me to you, a word of
advice . . . people shouldn't be too ambitious at
first. You drive too fast, you break your neck.

Quinn exits. Alice watches Charley beating up his sparring partner.

ALICE

Kill him, Charley. . . . Kill him . . . !

RINGSIDE - NIGHT

Close shot of Alice. Her face distorted with excitement, Alice is pounding on the canvas.

ALICE
(screaming)
Kill him, Charley, kill him . . . ! Kill him, Charley!

Shooting low from behind to the corner of the ring. Peg, [still sitting in
her chair between Alice and Roberts, who are standing], her face flinch-
ing with horror, is watching the ring as the enormous blood roar of the
crowd exults about her. Now Charley's feet dance in, around, and out.
Now Ben's feet move in, backing towards the ropes.

ALICE
(shrieking)
Kill him. . . . Kill him!

We see the beaten, bloody face of the champion, BEN CHAPLIN, sweaty,
in pain. Charley's gloved fist comes in and smacks him solid, and the
head snaps back.

Charley stands above the crumpling champion as he hits the ropes and
sags. Charley hits him again and again.

It seems to go on endlessly, the crowd screeching madly, and then Ben
starts to weaken. Charley's blows on the head have had their effect.
Like a tree that has been weakened at the root , Ben starts to go down, as
Charley piles on top of him, hitting in fury . . . and then Ben writhes to
the canvas, rolls over, and tries to get up. The crowd is in a maniacal

state of excitement. [At the count of nine, by pulling himself back up by the ropes, Ben gets to his feet. He attempts a final wild swing at Charley, but he collapses unconscious to the floor of the ring.]

[Arnold, Ben's manager, knowing that they have been sold out, looks over despondently at Roberts, who returns the look with a cynical smile.]

[The referee counts Ben out.]

Charley holds his hands above his head, the raging victor.

The crowd starts piling in, filling the ring, blacking out the lights as scene and immense crowd roar.

INT. BEN'S DRESSING ROOM - NIGHT

(Champion's room in major arena.) An utter silence as the DOCTOR, Arnold, and Shorty are grouped around the rubbing table on which Ben lies in a heavy breathing coma.

[In the background are Roberts and The Hammer. Charley and Quinn enter.]

                    DOCTOR
          We'll get him down to the hospital, take some
          x-rays. I'll call an ambulance.

                    ARNOLD
          He's not gonna live.

                    DOCTOR
               (putting Ben's robe more tightly
               over him)
          Well, we'll see . . .

As he goes to the door, the doctor pauses, turns to Charley.

                    DOCTOR
          You must've hit him awful hard.

The doctor leaves. Charley, marked with plaster on the forehead, but strong and triumphant, gazes with a kind of uneasy apprehension at Ben's still form.

CHARLEY
(to everybody)
Anything I can do, anything. Any money, just . . .

ROBERTS
He'll be all right.

ARNOLD
He won't be all right. You know that.

ROBERTS
Take it easy, Arnold. Go ahead, Charley . . . Everybody'll be waiting. I'll clean up here. . . . Go ahead, Quinn. . . . Shorty, keep the champagne cold.

QUINN
C'mon, Charley.

Quinn moves to the door, but Shorty remains near Ben.

CHARLEY
Mr. Arnold, anything I can do . . . just say the word . . . anything.
(Arnold nods slightly)
C'mon, Shorty . . .

SHORTY
I'll stick around and drive down to the hospital with him.

CHARLEY
That's a good idea. I'll see ya later.

ROBERTS
Run along, Shorty. I'll take care of everything here.

Arnold looks up, his stupefied face gathering anger.

> ARNOLD
> (raising his voice to Roberts)
> You promised to have Davis take it easy.
> (pointing at Ben)
> Look at him! Maybe he'll die . . .

Shorty is startled.

> ROBERTS
> You better beat it, Shorty.

> SHORTY
> What for? Who promised to take care of what?

> ROBERTS
> Have it your way.
> (turning to Arnold)
> You got any complaints?

> ARNOLD
> (shrinking back a little)
> No, *I* got no complaints. . .
> (nodding to Ben)
> *He* got complaints. . . . Maybe he'll die . . .

> ROBERTS
> Everybody dies . . .

> ARNOLD
> (angrily to Roberts)
> You knew Ben had the blood clot in the brain . . .
> You promised me . . .

> ROBERTS
> What do you want? A few grand more? You got
> it.

He wheels upon Shorty, on whom understanding has dawned, in whom anger, shock, and horror have joined.

ROBERTS
Anything on your mind, Shorty?

SHORTY
(looking at Ben)
Plenty.

ROBERTS
Spill it.

SHORTY
(venomously)
I don't like being your partner, Roberts. I'm out,
and I think after tonight, Charley'll be out too.

ROBERTS
You're a little behind the times, Shorty. We're not
partners. You were out already. Whatever you get,
you get from Charley. He's giving you a handout.
Didn't he tell you?

SHORTY
(whispering)
No . . .

ROBERTS
Check it.
(turning, slapping Arnold with his
gloves)
Send me the hospital bills.

[Roberts exits. Shorty looks down, then to Ben.] Arnold is watching Ben,
tears in his eyes.

INT. THREE CLUBS NIGHT CLUB - CELEBRATION PARTY

[Composition in depth: in the foreground—prominent in a third of the
frame—is an image of a camera's large flash apparatus. The flash
illuminates the scene, and the silhouette of the photographer exits screen
right. Charley is seen at the far end of a long table.] He is high, nervous,

happy, triumphant, eating lobster and drinking champagne. He gestures with a claw to the circle around him, as the camera reveals Peg at his side and the faces of the choice sporting crowd: Alice, Quinn, Roberts, The Drummer, gamblers, reporters, girls, the top rabble of Broadway.

                    CHARLEY
          I thought he'd never go down. . . . He was like a
          rock.

                    ALICE
          Who's sitting here . . . you or him?

                    CHARLEY
               (gleefully)
          That's right . . . that's right. He sure went down.
          You saw him, Peg . . . you saw him.

                    PEG
               (the brutal shock of the prizefight
               still on her)
          I saw him, Charley . . . I saw him . . .

Suddenly her face lights up as she looks out to the entrance of the night club. She touches Charley's arm.

                    PEG
               (rising)
          Charley, there's Shorty!

Charley and Peg in the foreground to Shorty entering the nightclub. He walks slowly to the bar. Charley looks up, puts down his lobster claw, and yells.

                    CHARLEY
          Shorty . . . hey, Shorty!

Charley picks up a glass of champagne, rises, [and walks toward Shorty. Roberts, knowing what Shorty's appearance forecasts, looks meaningfully at Peg, who then gets up and follows Charley.]

Shorty in the foreground shooting towards the party in the background.

CHARLEY
(happy extravagance)
We're kings of the world, Shorty.

PEG
Aren't you going to join us, Shorty?

SHORTY
No!

PEG
Why not?

CHARLEY
What's the matter?

Roberts and The Drummer come over to the bar.

SHORTY
You didn't win the title, Charley. Ben was double-
crossed. They promised him an easy go . . .

CHARLEY
(bridling)
Where did you get that stuff. Who promised who?

SHORTY
(holding back feeling of hysterical
revolt)
Ben was sick . . . he had a blood clot. And they all
knew.

PEG
A blood clot! . . . You didn't know that, Charley,
did you?

CHARLEY
No . . . I didn't . . .

ROBERTS
It's the old alibi, Champ. You'll get used to it . . .
Come on, let's sit down, everybody, and celebrate.

CHARLEY

Whatsamatter, Shorty? Don't you think I beat him square?

SHORTY

You beat him foul. Ask Quinn — ask Roberts. I don't like partners like Roberts, Charley. It's rotten enough without him. Tell him he's out.

CHARLEY

What are you talking about, Shorty? Are you crazy? You wanna make trouble? You can't believe everything you hear.

SHORTY

Can I believe Roberts? He told me to check with you. He said I was out. Am I out or are you going to keep on giving me the ten percent for old time's sake?

PEG

Yes.

ROBERTS

I had to tell him, Champ. There's only room for one in the driver's seat, and that's you.

CHARLEY

Sure. . . . What's the difference? We won, didn't we? That's what we wanted.

SHORTY

We didn't win . . . he won.

CHARLEY

Oh, come on . . . let's sit down. We'll talk about it some other time.

PEG

We're going to talk about it right now.

SHORTY

That's right . . . now's the time . . . now. It's not
enough to be great, Charley. I tried to tell you in
Philly. I tried to tell you in L.A. We're infested
with rats. He's not just a kid who can fight . . .
he's money. And people want money so bad they
make it stink . . . and they make you stink.

CHARLEY

If you don't like the racket, Shorty, you can always
quit.

SHORTY

I quit before I ever came in here. And if he has any
sense left he'll do the same. I'm through, and you
can keep your pension.

ROBERTS

Come on, Shorty . . . let's all relax.

Roberts puts his hand on Shorty's shoulder. Shorty swings around, but
The Drummer catches his arm. Shorty reacts and exits. Peg looks at
Charley, then follows Shorty. The Drummer follows them both.

EXT. STREET - ENTRANCE TO THREE CLUBS NIGHT CLUB

Shorty comes out in the first rush of trembling disappointment and
anger, starts to walk past the brownstone stoops. Peg rushes after him.

PEG

(calling)
Shorty! Shorty!

He looks back and stops as she runs up to him. [While she talks, The
Drummer walks past them.]

PEG
(swiftly appealing)
Don't run out on me . . . don't leave me alone,
'cause I can't do it all by myself. Now, remember,
long ago, he came to us and asked us, and we said,
it's all right, Charley, go ahead. . . . Now we've got
to help him.

SHORTY
Nobody can help him. He's gotta help himself.

He turns away from her and slowly starts down the street. She sees The
Drummer turn behind Shorty as he passes, sap him, catch him in his
arms, and brutally dump him down the areaway steps below the brownstone stoops. Peg screams in horror. The Drummer runs down the steps
after Shorty. Frantically, Peg runs into the night club.

INT. THREE CLUBS NIGHT CLUB

Quinn, Alice, Charley, and Roberts are at the bar. Peg runs in from the
background.

PEG
Charley!

They all run out after her.

EXT. THREE CLUBS NIGHT CLUB

They all run out. Charley runs downstairs to where The Drummer is
beating Shorty. They all crowd around. Charley runs in, grabs The
Drummer, and starts beating him mercilessly. Peg watches. Roberts
runs in and tries to pull Charley away.

ROBERTS
(losing his calm for the first time)
Charley, your hands!

Charley lets go of The Drummer, who slides limply to the ground. We
see Charley trembling with rage, Peg almost nauseous from the whole
evening's brutality, Shorty [getting up].

                    SHORTY
               (to Charley)
          We all know you can fight. . . .
               (to Roberts)
          Thanks, friend. . . .

He turns to walk to the street. Peg grabs him.

                    PEG
          Shorty, you're hurt!

                    SHORTY
          I'm all right. Take care of Charley.

                    QUINN
               (helping Shorty)
          Come on, Shorty . . .

[Shorty begins to walk across the street.]

                    PEG
          Charley, Shorty's hurt.

Shorty is blindly crossing the street. A taxi swerves, its headlights
blazing, and suddenly squeals to a stop. Peg turns, looks, and screams.
She calls to Charley, then runs to Shorty. The street fills with people as
Charley continues to stand like a man paralyzed. Then slowly he starts
to walk towards the scene of the accident. Shorty is lying in front of the
blazing headlights. Charley looks down on Shorty. A man kneeling at
Shorty's side looks up.

Charley looks [at Peg] lit by the headlights facing him across the chasm
of Shorty's death.

EXT. MOUNT STREET - NIGHT

As Charley and Peg walk slowly towards the entrance to the apartment.
Their steps, their bodies seem to drag with the burden of Shorty's death.
It is very late, hours have passed, and now nothing seems left after all
the triumph Charley felt after winning the fight.

At the stoop to Peg's apartment, Peg stops. They do not look at each
other. Tears have been shed. [Peg begins to look in her purse].

                    CHARLEY
        What's the matter, lose your key?

                    PEG
        No, I'd like to have a cigarette, it you don't mind.
                (her voice frozen)
        If one could only say, Charley, that it started here
        or there . . . but we're in something horrible . . .
        and we've got to get out.

                    CHARLEY
                (almost to himself)
        What can I do? Go back to the candy store?
                (to Peg)
        It was an accident.

                    PEG
        Only the dying. Nothing else. It was all inevi-
        table. You must quit.

                    CHARLEY
        It took a long time, Peg . . . rotten . . . and hard . . .
        and tough. . . . Now I'm a champ. Now it's going
        to be easy. I can't stop now. I can't throw it all
        away. It's what we wanted.

                    PEG
        But, Charley, we can't live with these people. . . . I
        couldn't bear it.

CHARLEY

(eagerly)

You won't have to see them, or meet them again. We'll live fine . . . I'll make the money. I'll look after Ben . . . Believe me, I'll do everything I can . . . But I can't start again . . . from what . . . with what?

PEG

Charley, you'll have to start again with nothing anyway, some day. . . . Only it'll be worse. You'll be like Ben.

CHARLEY

I'm too smart for that.

PEG

It's nothing to argue, Charley . . . I can't live this way. You stop now . . . or I stop.

CHARLEY

But that's not fair.

PEG

Was it fair for Shorty . . . to die?

CHARLEY

It was an accident. . . .

PEG

And for Ben to fight with a blood clot?

CHARLEY

I didn't know.

PEG

Charley . . . one way of the other.

She waits, but he doesn't answer, torn by the past, the lure of the future.

CHARLEY

But I'm the Champ.

PEG
You mean Roberts is. Charley, I can't marry you.
That'd just mean marrying him.

She goes in and closes the door. He sits there, confused, bitter, alone on the street.

MONTAGE

[The spectre of Robert's image is superimposed on shots of Charley fighting. Charley is congratulated for his victories. Charley kisses Alice. Charley and Alice are at the races, and Charley loses. A flurry of betting stubs indicates many losses. Money is spent on jewelry: Charley needs to receive loans from Roberts to cover these excessive expenses. Charley's life consists of a series of night clubs and parties. . . .

Now, he finds himself alone, walking the streets, finally in front of Peg's apartment. He pauses on the stoop, considers going up, but walks away.

Charley is standing in front of Ben Chaplin, who is sitting in a chair in his room.

CHARLEY
(with money in his hand)
Go on, take the money. Take it.

Ben shakes his head.

CHARLEY
Then . . . how about working with me? It's not
charity. I need someone . . . someone I can trust.

BEN
(smiling)
Okay, Charley, okay.

Charley continues to fight more bouts, now with Ben in his corner.

The champagne continues to flow, and Charley is seen in more night clubs, with additional women. Alice is upset. More money is needed. Charley gives Alice a fur coat, and Alice rewards Charley with a kiss.

Newspaper column headlines and story:

THE SPORTING CIRCLE
by Dennis Dare

How Long Before Charley Davis
Gives Jackie Marlowe A Crack at Title?

Nobody seems to know what the plans of Champion Charley Davis are, but many people are asking, is he champion of Broadway or champion of the world in the squared circle?

Roberts is shaking his finger at Charley.

ROBERTS
Huh huh! Not this time, Charley.

CHARLEY
Well, what's the matter? You know I'm good for the money.

ROBERTS
Only if you fight.

CHARLEY
So, I'll fight.

ROBERTS
And it's gotta be Marlowe.

DISSOLVE TO:]

INT. GYM

Usual activity. Quinn and Roberts walk through the assemblage of various fighters in the locker room to reach Charley's dressing room.

INT. CHARLEY'S DRESSING ROOM

Charley is finishing getting dressed as Quinn and Roberts enter. Quinn begins to close the door.

>   ROBERTS
> Leave the door open, you dope.

>   CHARLEY
>   (disturbed)
> You crazy, coming in here in front of everybody!

>   ROBERTS
> It's a gym . . . people come and go here.
> Besides, I'm an admirer of yours. I like to watch
> you train. . . . So you're all set for the Marlowe
> match.

>   CHARLEY
> Yeah . . . we're all set.

>   ROBERTS
> That's great. The odds are two to one for you to
> win. That's a lot of dough if you bet on Marlowe.

>   CHARLEY
>   (doggedly)
> I ain't handing no title over to any kid. I can beat
> him.

>   ROBERTS
>   (ironically)
> Betting on yourself to win, Charley?
>   (a pause)
> I didn't think you were punch drunk yet.

>   CHARLEY
>   (stubbornly)
> Well, I think I can beat him.

ROBERTS

You're not thinking, Charley, you're dreaming. It's only natural after all these years of living good . . . a fight now and then . . . the dough rolling in, the dough rolling out. . . . You begin to dream this can go on forever.

CHARLEY

When I lose the championship, they'll have to carry me out.

ROBERTS

The gym's full of guys who were carried out.

QUINN

Mister Roberts is right, Charley.

CHARLEY
(turning to Quinn)
You'd like to see me take a dive, wouldn't you?

QUINN

No, why should I? You've been money in the bank to me . . . but facts are facts, Charley.

CHARLEY

Yeah? How much of my money you got in the bank, Quinn?

ROBERTS

How much you got, Charley?
(takes envelope out of his pocket
and places it on the table)
There's sixty grand in there. Want to count it? Sixty grand. A clean, fast fight, fifteen rounds to a decision. Sixty grand at two to one. Your end of the purse at two to one. I'm good at figures, Charley. It'll add up to a fortune. Besides, you don't like fighting any more . . . you like living too much. So, why not live the easy life? Maybe you open a cafe with this singer . . . this—what's her name?

QUINN
Alice.

ROBERTS
Yeah—Alice. You punch the cash register instead
of getting punched. You've got a million friends,
Charley . . . you can't miss.
(he grows cold)
All right, Charley, let's stop being nice to each
other. We agreed to make a killing on this fight
months ago. You're into me for a lot of dough.
I've made my arrangements with Marlowe and a
lot of other people. Nobody backs out now . . .
that's the way it is. Besides, a lot of guys think
Marlowe can beat you on the square.

CHARLEY
I don't take no dive for nobody. What do you
think I am . . . a tanker?

ROBERTS
Who's asking you to take a dive? Fifteen rounds
to a decision.

[Charley looks down at the envelope of money.]

CHARLEY
Fifteen round decision?

ROBERTS
That's right.

Charley picks up the money.[18]

ROBERTS
When you get ready to bet that dough, Charley,
see that you give it to me to bet for you. I'll get
you a few extra points.

Roberts and Quinn exit.

INT. HALLWAY LEADING TO DRESSING ROOM

As Roberts and Quinn come out of Charley's dressing room, they meet Ben.

> ROBERTS
> How's the head, Ben?

> BEN
> Still on, Mister Roberts . . . no thanks to you.

> ROBERTS
> You still sore? I should have done something for
> you, Ben.

> BEN
> I like being Charley's trainer.

> ROBERTS
> Here's a little something to sweeten the past.

Charley comes out of his dressing room. [Ben is looking at the money in Roberts's hand.]

> BEN
> I don't take blood money, Mister Roberts . . . mine
> or anybody else's.

[Roberts drops the money on the floor.]

> ROBERTS
> You only have to bend down to pick it up, Ben.

Roberts exits. Ben cracks up.

> CHARLEY
> Hey, take it easy, Ben. You mustn't get excited.

> BEN
> It's just that pressure, Charley. The last couple of
> weeks I've been fighting in my head all the time.

CHARLEY
We got to get you a real examination, Ben.

BEN
Yeah, after the fight.

CHARLEY
You all right now?

BEN
Yeah . . . I'm all right.

Charley pick up the money lying on the floor.

CHARLEY
Here . . . take the money, Ben. It's not like people.
It got no memory . . . it don't think.

BEN
Did you sell the fight, Charley?

[Tight close up of Charley, stunned.

Tight close up of Ben, his eyes fixed intently on Charley.]

CHARLEY
Are you crazy! I'll see you up in camp. Take it
easy.

Ben watches as Charley exits.

INT. CHARLEY'S APARTMENT WITH PARTY - NIGHT

Crap game in foreground, girl dancing on the table. Alice greets some
guests, they turn and watch the crap game. She walks away.

EXT. TERRACE - CHARLEY'S APARTMENT - NIGHT

Charley stands smoking on the terrace. In the background the party is
going on.

INT. CHARLEY'S APARTMENT - BEDROOM

Alice walks into the bedroom. She sits at foreground dressing table.
Quinn follows her in and closes the bedroom doors.

> ALICE
>
> Leave the doors open, Quinn. What'll people
> think?

> QUINN
>
> (walking to her)
> Do you care?
> (stands next to her)
> You sure you're not worried?

> ALICE
>
> I got nothing to be worried about.

> QUINN
>
> Not as long as you keep your mind on the dough.
> (holding up his drink)
> To the money. . . . You gonna bet?

> ALICE
>
> If I have to beg, borrow and steal, I'm gonna bet
> this fight.

> QUINN
>
> Just remember, baby . . . I told you about it.
> You get in on a big fix once in a lifetime.
> (sits down on bed)
> And after it's over?

> ALICE
>
> No problem. The boy's going to make a snootful
> of dough.

> QUINN
>
> He'll go through it in a year with your help.

> ALICE
>
> That gives me a year, Quinn. What about you?

QUINN

I'll find myself another mug. They come and they
go . . . but I stay. That's the reason you should
listen to me, baby.

ALICE

Don't you ever get tired?

[Quinn stands up.]

QUINN

No. I got no time for pride. He could have had
the whole world. So he leaned over sideways and
grabbed you.

[Quinn angrily grabs Alice's arm.]

ALICE

Nobody grabbed me. I grabbed him.

QUINN

Sure, baby . . . all love and a yard wide. But every
time he's low down, he's gone to Peg. And he's
not going to feel so high after this fight.

ALICE

I don't care where his heart is . . . only the money.

QUINN

What about me . . . how I feel?

ALICE

Don't romance me, Quinn. You're getting old.

QUINN

You could use a new paint job yourself.

ALICE
(stands and looks at him)
And I know were to get it.

[Alice walks through the French doors to the terrace, leaving Quinn in the foreground where he finishes his drink. He moves back to the doors, and in the background on the terrace are Alice and Charley talking. They walk off, while Quinn watches.

Quinn walks back into the party and takes a position by the crap game. In the background, a drunk pushes the button for the revolving bar and it rotates back into the wall.

The wall with Peg's picture on it has now replaced the bar.

Charley, angered by the drunk's actions, moves quickly to the man and shoves him down. Charley pushes the button to return the bar to its former position, and then he makes a move to hit the drunk again. Alice intervenes, maneuvers him to the bar, and hands him a drink. He violently jerks it from her, spilling most of it, and drinks the rest.

DISSOLVE

Same location, morning: the aftermath of the party. A man is snoring on the sofa. The camera pans left; debris from the party, overturned furniture reflect the shambles of Charley's apartment. Another man is passed out in a chair, with Peg's picture in his lap. Charley emerges from his bedroom rubbing his head, trying to shake off his hangover. He turns off a light.

Charley is trying to make an accounting of what happened the night before—he feels his pockets. He takes out a wad of money and fingers it. He puts it back into his pocket.

Charley sees Peg's picture resting on the drunk's lap, and he angrily grabs it away. He looks at the picture, contemplates his situation, and walks out.]

EXT. LANDING - PEG'S APARTMENT - MORNING

Charley walks to Peg's door, picks up the milk and paper and knocks.

[Inside Peg sleepily puts on her robe and opens the door.]

                    CHARLEY
              (with embarrassed grin)
          Early delivery today.

                       PEG
              (surprised, opens door wide)
          Charley . . . Come in.

He enters, still carrying the painting.

INT. ROOM

Peg closes door, puts milk in kitchen, walks to window and pulls down
shade. She turns and observes him.

                       PEG
               (lightly)
          Trouble?

                    CHARLEY
               (with difficulty)
          No . . . no . . .

She begins moving toward the kitchen.

                       PEG
          Well, I better make some coffee. You look as if
          you need some.

She walks to the alcove, and starts to prepare coffee, running water into
the pot, etc.

                       PEG
          Isn't this a trifle early for you?

                    CHARLEY
          I got up a little early this morning.
               (a pause)
          That is . . . I didn't get to sleep.

PEG
(measuring coffee)
Celebrating the Marlowe match?

CHARLEY
I tried to . . .
(a pause)
I thought you skipped all the places in the paper
that mentioned my name.

PEG
(continuing preparing the coffee)
On the contrary . . . I read about you religiously.
. . . Orange juice?

CHARLEY
Sure.

Peg enters with the juice. [Charley is looking through Peg's sketches.]

PEG
Yes, I've been promoted since you were last here.
I'm a fully fledged designer now.

CHARLEY
That's great.

PEG
(ceremonial gesture)
Well, good health . . .
(she lowers her glass)
What's it this time, Charley?

Charley wondering how to begin.

PEG
(without hostility)
Last time you came it was because you were
bored. And the year before you were lonely. . . .
Once it was your birthday, twice it was mine . . .
What's the occasion now?
(MORE)

PEG (CON'T)
(a wry smile, a little weary)
I don't understand. I worked very late last night,
so I'm not very bright this morning . . . But I'll try
now . . . What do you want? Advice . . . comfort
. . . recriminations . . . ?

CHARLEY
(indicating the painting)
I brought this, too.

PEG
(looking at the painting)
Doesn't looks like me, it's bad technique.
Is this your problem? Don't you want it any
more?

CHARLEY
No.

PEG
(half turning away)
I just don't understand. I'm still half asleep. If
you don't want it any more, why return it after all
these years?

CHARLEY
I want you.

It strikes her full at the heart, makes her tremble, but she turns to look at
him. He looks full in her face, then lowers his eyes. She sits down and
holds her tears back, the catch of feeling that runs like water through her
flesh.

PEG
(finally, in one quick breath)
Well, here I am, Charley. . . .

He puts his hands on hers.

CHARLEY
(a tight whisper)
Peg, I'm scared . . . so low down . . . I had to see
you . . . I wondered . . . I had to find out once and
for all . . . I had to know. And we won't be broke.
. . . It's my last fight. . . . Look!
(reaches into his pocket)
I got sixty grand, and more to come . . . and I'll
buy you . . .

PEG
(placing her hand on his mouth,
speaking rapidly)
Don't tell me what you'll get me. . . . Don't tell me
what you can buy. You've got nothing to buy.

CHARLEY
I said all that once before, didn't I?

PEG
Don't talk, Charley. Just sit. 'Cause you'll only
start saying those things you've learned to say . . .
not what you once were . . . what you are . . .
(on stove the coffee pot runs over,
hisses)
Oh . . .
(jumping to her feet, running to it)
Ever since Irma left, it runs over.

CHARLEY
(a safe question)
Irma! Where is she?

PEG
Texas.

CHARLEY
Texas? Doing what?

Peg can't stop talking now, the emotion bubbling in her voice, almost
hysterical happiness.

PEG
(bringing in a cup of coffee)
She's married. . . . She married the first guy that
ever bought a statue from her.

CHARLEY
(a brief laugh)
Is she happy?

PEG
Deliriously. It all happened on a rainy afternoon.

Charley watches her, drinking her in, and Peg, aware, rattles on.

PEG (CON'T)
Things happen that way. . . . Sometimes you wait
very long for happiness. And sometimes you fall
all over it before you learn to walk. She just
walked in all . . . jumpy . . . jumping. . . . Well, I
must be jumping . . . I can't think why . . . I think
I'm ill . . .
(holding her pulse)
. . . running a high . . . What am I talking about?
Do you know?

They are facing each other. She kneels beside him.

PEG
Do you know what it's like to love and be alone?

[They kiss.]

DISSOLVE

INT. PEG'S APARTMENT

A note is balanced between an ash tray and a lamp. Charley is on studio
couch. He is fast asleep, and the afternoon light is drifting on dust mites
through the big window. He stirs and wakes, opening his eyes. He
looks around, lost, surprised. He sits up, and he sees that the room is

empty. He looks at his watch. [He sees the note and picks it up to read it.]

INSERT - NOTE

> Charley,
> I talked you to sleep. Meet me at your Mother's.
> > Peg.
> P.S. I took the money.

DISSOLVE TO:

INT. DAVIS KITCHEN - NIGHT

Peg is making a potato pancake. [She is moving it with a spatula.]

ANNA
Ah, ah . . . don't poke it . . . pat it, gently.

PEG
Is it spoiled?

ANNA
(taking the spatula)
No, no.

PEG
I'm trying to be useful.

ANNA
Then get me a saucer.

As Peg gets a saucer, Anna scoops up the pancake and puts it into a saucer.

ANNA
Let the expert have a taste.

A strand of hair hangs across Anna's cheek. Peg gently strokes it into place. [Peg smiles tenderly at Anna.]

ANNA

One pretty woman in the family is enough . . .

Anna shifts her attention to Peg's face, and with a sudden access to love kisses her cheek briefly. Saucer in hand, Peg starts to the bedroom.

INT. BEDROOM

Charley has just finished shaving. Peg walks in and kisses him.

CHARLEY
(closing eyes)
More . . .

Peg takes a piece of the pancake and puts it in his mouth.

PEG
You approve?

He kisses her.

CHARLEY
You know, that's a taste that never leaves your mouth.

PEG
(shouting to Anna)
The expert approves.

CHARLEY
Say, I meant to ask you, what did the old lady say when you told her this is my last fight?

PEG
(whispering)
She cried. And then she said the most beautiful thing I've ever heard in my life.

CHARLEY
What?

PEG

Well, she said she didn't think at her age she could still fall in love again.

CHARLEY

With who?

PEG

Us.

[He moves to kiss her again, but pauses.]

CHARLEY

Oh, by the way, what did you do with all my money?

PEG

I put it in my bank.

CHARLEY

Well, in the morning I'll go down with you and pick it up.

PEG

What for?

CHARLEY

Well, I need it.

PEG

Why?

CHARLEY

Well, to bet on the fight.

PEG

Charley, if you lose the fight *and* the money, then you'll want to fight again. . . . No, no, I'm not going to give you the money to bet. We're rich enough!

The kitchen door opens, interrupting them, and a GROCER enters, carrying a box. Charley and Peg look towards the kitchen. Charley is disturbed, his mind on the money. But Peg is brisk, having decided to run things properly now.

INT. KITCHEN

The grocer [SHIMIN] enters with his box of fruit, bread, etc., and he sees Charley.

> SHIMIN
> Here I am, Mrs. Davis . . . Charley, Charley. . . .
> You're a sight for sore eyes.

> CHARLEY
> Hello, Shimin!

> SHIMIN
> (pumping Charley's hand, [losing
> control of the box, which Charley
> catches])
> It's good to see you. You look wonderful.
> (turns to Anna)
> He looks fine.

> ANNA
> You know Miss Born? Charley's fiancee.

> GROCER
> This I suspected. Here you are, Mrs. Davis.
> (handing Anna a large bunch of
> grapes)
> Charley, something special for you. Straight from
> the Garden of Eden.

> CHARLEY
> Thanks.

> ANNA
> Have some wine, Shimin.

GROCER

What's the occasion?

ANNA
            (as if suggesting toast)
Charley's last fight.

GROCER

You don't say?

CHARLEY
            (hastily)
Don't spread it around, Shimin.

GROCER

I'm like a grave. Does that mean you won't fight
anymore? .

CHARLEY

That's right.

GROCER
            (smiling)
Well, so you'll retire a champeen. . . . That's bad?
It's good.
            (holding up glass)
To the future retired champeen of the world . . .
good luck. And to my five dollars that I bet on the
fight, good luck, too.
            (drinks, picks up his box)
Good. Excuse me. Charley, everybody's betting
on you, the whole neighborhood. Like you was
the Irish sweepstakes.

ANNA

People shouldn't bet.

GROCER

No, no, Mrs. Davis, it isn't the money. It's a way
of showing. . . . Over in Europe the Nazis are
killing people like us—just because of their
religion. But here Charley Davis is champeen. So
you win . . . and you retire champeen . . . and we
are proud. Period.[19]

(to Peg)

I'm glad I met you.

(going out the door, turns back)

Charley, when you leave, stop in and say
toodledoo.

He leaves. The women are emotionally stirred. Anna is even proud. But
Charley's face is clouded.

CHARLEY

What's the matter with people, anyway? Why do
they have to bet? It's a racket. Don't they know?
. . . they know it's a racket.

ANNA

People gamble.

CHARLEY

They're suckers. Tell 'em not to bet on me.

ANNA

I'm too old to walk up and down New York telling
people not to bet . . .

(smiling)

. . . especially when they win.

CHARLEY

You don't win all the time. You can lose too.
Suckers like Shimin shouldn't bet.

ANNA

Suckers like Shimin! You didn't hear what he said,
Charley? It isn't the five dollars that's important,
it's . . . (the principle)

CHARLEY

I heard . . . I heard. I can still lose.

PEG

That's right, Charley. Then why bet? Why take a
chance?

CHARLEY

Well, you don't understand. It's a different thing.
I don't want to quit without money . . . I don't
want to end up broke. . . .

PEG

Broke? You've got sixty thousand dollars. You
could stop now.

CHARLEY

Stop now? Are you kidding? There's a million
bucks riding on my back. If I don't fight I don't
get a dime. I'm all mobbed up, tied hand and foot,
down to my last buck. Do you think I want to end
up like Ben . . . punchy . . . with a blood clot on the
brain . . . waiting to die any day? Or with a bullet
in my back in an alley?

[Tight close up of Anna.]

ANNA

What do you mean, bullet?

CHARLEY

Don't you understand? The fight's fixed.

ANNA

Fixed? What does it mean fixed?

Charley darts a glance to Peg, who now understands everything.

CHARLEY
(in the trap now)
It means I'm throwing the fight.

ANNA

Throwing the fight?

CHARLEY

It means I'm - I'm - I'm gonna lose. It's all arranged. It's a racket anyway. That's why I want to
bet the sixty grand. You get it, Peg, don't you?

PEG

Yeah! I get it.

CHARLEY

It's an investment. A sure thing . . .

After a silence as the women [stare sadly at Charley], he explodes.

CHARLEY

Well, what do you want? What are you looking
at?

ANNA

Then you didn't understand what Shimin said . . .

CHARLEY

It's none of my business what they think or what
they do. Nobody looks out for me.

PEG

Poor Charley. Nobody's looking out for you.

CHARLEY
(a big fury)
You're all so high and mighty!
(to Anna)
You wouldn't even have that dirty candy store if it
wasn't for me. . . . You wouldn't have a dime . . .
the clothes on your back . . . It's my money, isn't it?
You were in such a big hurry to take it and slap it
in the bank. Sure, you said, we're rich enough . . .
(MORE)

CHARLEY (CON'T)
(wheeling to Peg)
. . . like all the rest of them, from what comes out
of my hide. I take the beatings, and you take the
dough, like all the rest of them. Well, this time *I'm*
taking care of the dough. Give me back that sixty
grand.

As he rages on, the blank shock which is Peg's first reaction, moves
through revulsion into a fury greater than his.

PEG
(furiously)
Yeah, that's right . . . I'm like the rest of them! So
you want your money back? Well, take it back.
And everything else you've given me. Here . . .
(strikes him on face; they face each
other like ferocious animals)
what everyone gives you!
[strikes him twice more]
The long years of happiness . . .
[strikes him again, then again]
the promises broken . . . the lonely nights!

[Peg turns away and walks from the room crying.]

FADE TO BLACK.

FADE IN:

EXT. TRAINING CAMP - RING - DAY

[Roberts and The Drummer are at ringside watching.]

In training gear, Ben in the ring refereeing, Charley and a sparring
partner mix it. After a short flurry, Charley hits the man, who takes a
hard fall on the canvas.

BEN
(without enthusiasm)
That's enough, Charley.

Charley is helping his partner up as photographs are taken.
[Quinn is smiling with pleasure at what he sees.]

QUINN
Take it easy for the rest of the day, Charley.

Quinn walks over to Roberts and a few reporters near the ring.

QUINN (CON'T)
(enthusiastically to reporters)
He's been that way for two months, boys. There's
no stopping him. It's gonna be a Marlowe massa-
cre.

Ben has draped a bathrobe over Charley, and they now step through the
ropes and come down the wooden steps.

REPORTER
You're looking great, Champ.

CHARLEY
Thanks, Pete . . . I feel fine. I can even name the
round.

REPORTER
Good.

DISSOLVE TO:

EXT. TRAINING CAMP - NIGHT

[Ben opens the sliding door of a storage shed and begins to put away
some boxing gear.]

Moonlight floods the ring, which has been partly dismantled. Charley
slowly walks through the grass and approaches the ring, goes slowly up
the stairs, punches the sandbag, and then stands there alone, brooding.
From the cottage the lights are lit, but Charley is isolated. The shadow of
the sandbag breaks and beats across the whiteness of the canvas. Now
Ben slowly strolls over towards Charley. He stands at the foot of the
steps, looking up.

BEN
(looking up at Charley)
Last night, eh Charley . . .

CHARLEY
Yeah . . .

BEN
You know, I always get a sorta sad feeling when I
see them breaking camp, tearing down the ring,
collecting the gear. . . . It always felt so good after a
win. . . . Walk down Lennox Avenue, kids all crazy
for you . . . and proud . . . a champion of the world
for the whole world to know. . . .

[Charley sits down next to Ben.]

BEN (CON'T)
You fixed the fight, didn't you?

CHARLEY
I been worried about you, Ben . . . the three or four
times the last month you fainted. But I got it all
arranged. It's not like a hospital . . . they got
doctors, and they give you tests — it's kinda like a
checkup. You know your head's been getting
worse. . . . A fellow's got to take care of himself.

BEN
Yeah . . . head's been pretty bad lately. That's why
I shouldn't have fought you. But look, Charley,
you can lick Marlowe. He's fast, but he ain't got
what it takes . . . If you keep on top of him, he'll go
down, I know.

CHARLEY
I got you covered, Ben. You don't got a thing to
worry about. The bet's in there for you, too . . .

BEN

That's what I figured. . . . I knew it that day at the
gymnasium . . . all this monkey business with the
training to run the odds up against Marlowe
. . . and you not really training at all. . . . What are
you ducking out on, Charley? You can be on top
for years yet.

CHARLEY

That's the way things are, Ben. That's the way
they are. There'll be a big chunk of dough, and
I'm through. . . . It's enough.

BEN

Why? There's nobody in your class. . . .

[Roberts walks out of the cottage and listens to what Ben is saying.]

BEN (CON'T)

Look, I've watched this Marlowe, studied him. . . .
He backs away and shoots a left and backs away.
You keep on top of him . . . he'll go down. I know
he'll go down. Look, I'll show you . . .

[Ben gets into the ring and starts punching the sandbag.]

BEN (CON'T)

Look, Charley. . . . You keep on top of him like this,
see . . . and then one good punch!

CHARLEY

I know, I know . . .

BEN

Maybe you let Roberts talk to you a little too
fast . . .

A shadow falls across the ring.

ROBERTS' VOICE

I'd like a word with you, Ben.

Ben and Charley turn, and there is Roberts walking towards the ring,

                    BEN
Say it, Mister Roberts.

                    ROBERTS
When are you leaving?

                    BEN
Tomorrow when Charley leaves.

                    ROBERTS
I think you better go tonight.

                    BEN
Where to, Mister Roberts?

                    ROBERTS
Where we don't have to see you . . .

                    CHARLEY
Now, take it easy.

                    ROBERTS
I'm taking it easy. We'll get someone else for your
corner, Charley.

                    BEN
Let Charley take care of that.

                    ROBERTS
It's taken care of. Get out tonight, and keep your
mouth shut.

                    CHARLEY
Now, wait a minute, Roberts. . . . Maybe Ben's
right. . . . What's our hurry? Maybe we figured
this Marlowe wrong. Maybe we could
cover . . .

ROBERTS

Don't second guess me, Charley. It's all set.
You've bet your pile on yourself to lose. So what
are we talking about?
          (turning to Ben)
I told Quinn to dump you months ago. He said
Charley wanted you. Well, Charley doesn't want
you any more.

BEN

          (angrily)
Let Charley tell me . . .

[Roberts and Charley look briefly at each other. Charley looks down.
Roberts looks intently at Ben.]

ROBERTS

I'm telling you. Start running.

BEN

          (yelling in sudden fury)
You double-crossed me before. Now I'm through
. . . done . . . washed up. I don't scare easy anymore.

His voice sounds in the quiet air. [The Drummer comes up behind
Roberts, and Charley goes into the ring to restrain Ben.]

ROBERTS

You're punchy, Ben. Your head's soft.

CHARLEY

Leave him alone! He's sick.

ROBERTS

I let you stay on Charley's pension list.

BEN

          (screaming)
You don't tell me how to live!

ROBERTS
(coldly)
No, but I'll tell you how to die.[20]

Ben lunges at Roberts.

ROBERTS (CON'T)
(exploding to Drummer)
Get this crazy punch drunk wreck out of here.

Ben is backing toward the ropes of the ring.

BEN
I don't scare anymore. . . . I don't scare
anymore . . .

Ben falls backwards over the ropes, hitting his head.

The Drummer had started up the steps to the ring, but Charley has
intercepted him at the top of the steps. Charley turns and bends over
Ben.

CHARLEY
Ben . . . Ben . . .

[From Ben's point of view, the image of Charley is blurred.]

CHARLEY (CON'T)
Ben, get up, will you. Come on, Ben . . . Ben . . .
Ben, come on, get up. Ben . . . you're going to be
all right. Get up.

Charley starts to help Ben up. [Ben is mumbling to himself.]

CHARLEY
Get a doctor, will ya.

BEN
(breaking away)
No! No! I don't want a doctor . . . I don't want
anybody.

Ben starts boxing imaginary foe. [Charley is being restrained by Roberts and Quinn.]

                    QUINN
          Let him wear himself out.

Ben is still boxing.

                    BEN
          Got to take it . . . always sold out. . . .

[Ben falls backward to the edge of the ring. He pulls himself back up by the ropes, still shouting deliriously.]

                    BEN (CON'T)
          I can take it! I can take it! I can take it! I gotta
          take it!

[Extreme close up of Ben.]

                    BEN (CON'T)
          I'm the champ!

He falls over and lies still. Charley walks over and stands beside him. Quinn kneels beside him.

                    QUINN
          I think he's dead.

[Camera cranes upward to reveal most of the ring, with Charley, Quinn, Roberts, The Drummer, and the others looking down on Ben.

                              DISSOLVE TO:

The identical angle of the ring, now empty and at night, a camera perspective which is designed to present a repetition of the opening sequence of the film . . .]

REPEAT OPENING SHOTS OF PICTURE:

EXT. TRAINING CAMP - NIGHT - CRANE

Bright moonlight and deep shadow articulate an outdoor ring and a heavy sandbag slowly, but just barely, swinging in the night wind. The CAMERA MOVES past a tree up to a wide window facing on the clearing, to CHARLEY DAVIS asleep, while the [MUSIC and CRICKETS] sound a note of melancholy hysteria, moonlight nibbling on his face.

He is struggling with a nightmare, fear sweating on his face, and Charley wakes up screaming.

                    CHARLEY
          (calling desperately from the dream)
          Ben . . . Ben . . . Ben . . . !

[END OF FLASHBACK SEQUENCE: On Charley's final utterance of Ben's name, which propels him out of his nightmare, the formal design and movement of Charley's body on his bed in the training camp coordinate elegantly in a MATCH CUT which continues, with an additional silent pronunciation of Ben's name, the exact movement of his body on the rubbing table in his dressing room (where he was lying when the flashback sequence began, on page 29)—as he comes out of what appears to be a repetition of his nightmare of Ben's death; or, more precisely, the nightmare of his prolonged descent into corruption, which has culminated in Ben's death.][21]

INT. CHARLEY'S DRESSING ROOM

[The sound of Charley screaming out Ben's name causes PRINCE, Ben's replacement as trainer, to enter the dressing room.

                    PRINCE
          You call, Champ?

                    CHARLEY
          No.

Prince enters the room and closes the door.

PRINCE

It's time to get ready. You only got a few minutes.
Did you have a good sleep?

CHARLEY

Yeah.

PRINCE

I hear Marlowe is so nervous he can hardly sit still.
He ain't taking it easy . . . lying back, so relaxed.
He's got plenty to be nervous about too.

Charley daubs the perspiration on his brow—the residue of his nightmare—with the back of his bandaged hand.

PRINCE (CON'T)

'Cause they're certainly going to carry him out of
that ring. . . . Guess you feel kind of funny not
having Ben with you. He was a great champ!

There is a knock on the door, which opens partially.

MAN

Main event! Get ready.

Door closes.

PRINCE

I was talking to a few of the reporters out in the
hall . . . they asked me how you felt. I says, "How
do you think the Champ feels? He's *sleeping*
inside."

CHARLEY

Yeah, dreamin'.

Charley strikes his left palm with his right fist. Quinn enters with
another trainer or handler, who holds up his right hand for Charley's
practice punches. These last moments before the fight occur without any
talking.]

INT. CORRIDOR CORNER

Charley, accompanied by Quinn, Prince, and the other trainer, guarded by policemen, walks rapidly to the corridor corner, the ever present noise of the crowd filling the air. The camera moves with Charley as he reaches the stairs. Roberts is standing there with The Drummer, and a few cronies. He looks soberly at Charley as the Champ goes by. Now a roar starts in the crowd as Charley enters the arena offscreen.

DISSOLVE TO:

[INT. RING

The boxers and their entourages are in the ring. An ANNOUNCER is speaking into a microphone suspended from a wire above.

> ANNOUNCER
> Introducing the worthy contender, that fast and rugged boy from the Lone Star state, Jackie Marlowe . . .

Marlowe rises to accept the applause from the audience.

> ANNOUNCER
> And, now, introducing a great champion, who has met and defeated all the leading contenders, the champion of the world, Charley Davis . . .

Charley nods in recognition of the cheers and whistles of the crowd. Alice, Arnold (Ben's former manager), Roberts, and The Drummer are in their seats observing.

MONTAGE

Charley and Marlowe receive their fight instructions from the referee. . . . The bell sounds for Round One, and the two fighters begin the bout. . . . Round Five is illuminated on the board, superimposed on the fighters in the ring. . . . Round Seven: the fighters clinching, the referee telling them to break and to fight . . . Round Nine: the crowd increasingly restless, clapping in annoyance over the torpid nature of the fight; Marlowe and

Charley continuing their lethargic movements and clinching . . . Round Eleven: the crowd is now booing in disgust ; Alice is detachedly looking in a mirror and combing her hair; the referee is evaluating the fight— INSERT OF HIS SCORECARD: through eleven rounds, he has scored seven rounds to Marlowe, two to Davis, two a draw. . . . Round Twelve: the fighters are clinching on the ropes; the audience is clapping and booing; a RADIO COMMENTATOR is describing the event: "There is still no action in this fight, ladies and gentlemen. The champion looks badly out of condition."

The bell rings and both fighters go to their respective corners. The referee confers with a fight official at ringside. Charley is being attended to by his trainers.] He is extremely tired, wind and legs and arms, from the long boxing. Quinn stands behind the ropes, looking rather objectively at the champion.

CHARLEY
What round is it?

PRINCE
It's the end of the twelfth.

CHARLEY
(puffing with exhaustion)
I'll fall down by the fifteenth.

The bell rings to start Round Thirteen.

Quinn climbs down to his ringside position and slowly turns to face Roberts.

Quinn nods in some understanding with Roberts, who then gets up and leaves.

Quinn nods a go-ahead signal to DANE, Marlowe's manager.

Dane most intently looks in at the fighters. He pounds the canvas to get Marlowe's attention.

Dane catches Marlowe's inquiring glance and makes a gesture of encouragement with his fist, nodding at the same time.

Marlowe's face suddenly hardens. He pushes Charley with his left, as if to move away, and suddenly drives two quick punches to Charley's head, enormous blows for which Charley is utterly unprepared. Charley goes down. At the count of six, Charley rises.

Marlowe opens up a terrific barrage of blows against Charley, beating him with a wild fury.[22] An enormous roar comes up from the crowd. Suddenly there is the wildest excitement everywhere. Charley hangs onto the ropes helplessly as Marlowe beats him down, and at the same time keeps pushing him back against the ropes so that Charley can't collapse to the canvas. Now Charley hangs onto Marlowe, instinctively trying to tie him up, but Marlowe bangs him in the mouth and nose, starting blood. Marlowe is a dynamo of blows.

The spectators are screaming murder.   Charley is down on his hands and knees. The crowd is howling. Charley attempts to get up as the referee starts to count. He reels into Marlowe and tries to punch back , but the young contender is all strength. Bloody and dazed, Charley hangs on and takes the beating.

Marlowe nails him on the side of the head, and Charley goes down.

Close shot of Charley. Blood instead of sweat on Charley's dazed face. He is kneeling, trying to get up. The referee leans in.

REFEREE
. . . four . . . five . . .

The bell crashes as the round ends. The crowd roars with continuous excitement.

Prince and the handler rush in and pick Charley up from the floor, where he has been saved by the bell.

Prince and the handler are working furiously over Charley, whose face is well smashed at the mouth, the nose, and over the eyes. As Charley starts to come to, he confronts Quinn.

CHARLEY
(panting)
You sold me out, you rat. Sold out . . . like Ben.

[In Marlowe's corner, there is great optimism that Marlowe will be the new champion.]

QUINN
Don't worry about it. He just lost his head, that's all.

[There is a large, tight close up of Charley's eyes.

Dane puts the plug back into Marlowe's mouth.

DANE
Go back in there and finish him, son.

Again, the close up of Charley's eyes.]

CHARLEY
(relaxing, mumbling)
I'm gonna kill him. I'm going to kill him.

The bell rings, and the lights are dimmed. Charley walks forward, as Marlowe rushes in for the kill. The crowd underroar begins, swelling at the surface of the howl of triumph.

Charley hangs on for dear life, tying up the younger fighter so Marlowe can't punch. The referee breaks them forcibly. But Charley gets in again and again, holding on. Charley is fighting on instinct, all his years guiding him as he keeps Marlowe from hitting.

Marlowe sees an opening, and gives Charley a hard blow to the head. Charley goes down on one knee, leaning on the ropes.

At the count of nine, Charley gets back up.

Marlowe aggressively attacks Charley, but unexpectedly Charley counterattacks with two powerful punches that hurt Marlowe and put him on the defensive.

There is a look of anxiety on Dane's face.

An upsurge of emotion from Arnold who yells, "Get him, Charley, get him!"

An expression of alarm from the previously insouciant Alice.

Great excitement and jubilation from Peg, who cries out: "Charley!"

Dismay and fear from Quinn.

Charley has turned the fight around: he is now clearly the stalker, Marlowe the prey.

The bell rings.

Charley is back in his corner, limp on the stool as Prince and the other handler work on him. Quinn is outside the ropes behind Charley.

In Marlowe's corner, there is now apprehension and trepidation.

>   MARLOWE
>   (fearfully)
>   The guy is crazy! He's crazy!

Quinn reaches in through the ropes and is stroking Charley' head. Charley is muttering to himself.

>   CHARLEY
>   I'm going to kill him.

>   QUINN
>   (in Charley's ear)
>   Take a dive and finish it.

Charley, while still looking straight ahead, flips his gloved fist backwards and strikes Quinn on the side of his face.

>   CHARLEY
>   (exhausted; fiercely)
>   I'm gonna kill him. I'm gonna kill him.

In Marlowe's corner, Dane is trying to salvage the fight.

>   DANE
>   Keep running—and you'll be champ.

Quinn is now in the ring next to Charley.

> QUINN
> You're behind in points . . . you got to knock him
> out to win.

Close up of Quinn, staring at Charley.

> QUINN (CON'T)
> Do you know what you're doing, Charley?

The buzzer sounds. Business of clearing the ring.

Last admonition to Marlowe.

> DANE
> Last round coming up. Stay away from him.

The bell: Round Fifteen.

The lights are out. Charley comes out, still tired, but going in.

The crowd, anticipating the dramatic climax, edges forward silently in
their seats.

Marlowe runs away from Charley. He knows the fight is his if he can
stay away. He doesn't even try to box. He just stays away.

[The radio commentator tries to capture the eerie atmosphere in the
arena.

> RADIO COMMENTATOR
> I've never seen anything like it before in my life. A
> great silence has descended over this crowd. They
> seem to sense the cue. There's fear in Marlowe's
> eyes, as Davis looks for an opening.

A slight spasm of reaction from the crowd as Marlowe, in his
backpeddling to stay away from Charley, slips, his gloves going to the
canvas to upright himself.

RADIO COMMENTATOR
Davis is following Marlowe around the ring now
like a tiger stalking his prey.]

Large close up of Charley, poised for the attack.

Large close up of Marlowe, fearful of what is to come.

Charley smashes Marlowe with four powerful blows, and Marlowe goes down.

The crowd is on its feet.

Roberts watches from the rear of the arena.

Peg reacts joyfully.

Marlowe gets back up.

Quinn registers gloom and depression.

Charley's right cross sends Marlow to the deck again.

The crowd is all frenzied excitement.

Marlowe is up again around the count of six.

Charley wallops at him. Marlowe starts to sag again. Charley batters him half through. Charley's blows are unrelenting. Marlowe slowly collapses. The referee is counting. Marlowe is out cold. As the last number is counted in and the referee raises Charley's arm in victory, the crowd erupts in frenzy, and the ring starts to fill with people, police, etc.

Charley is surrounded in the ring by Quinn, Prince, and others. The ring announcer enters to speak into the lowered microphone.

[ANNOUNCER
(holding Charley's arm in the air)
By a knockout, the winner and still champion of
the world, Charley Davis . . .]

Peg, blissfully happy at the announcement, begins to move down the aisle with the rest of the ecstatic crowd.

Close shot of Charley in the ring. His face is dazed, sweaty, bloody.

Full shot of the ring as the pandemonium moves from the crowd into the ring, the disappointed gamblers, the squad of cops surrounding the winner.

Charley comes through the ropes and down and is congratulated by the joyous Arnold. Alice approaches Charley, but, pausing briefly and staring coldly in her eyes, he brushes by her. Stopped in her tracks, she stands there looking at him depart.

Peg fights her way through the crowd.

Corridor and ramp in arena as policeman form a line to keep the excited crowd from pouring through the corridor, which leads to the dressing rooms. Charley files through the mob offering congratulations.

Quinn is next to Alice; he turns to her, holding on to her coat.

                    QUINN
        Back in my league now, aren't you, baby?

Alice contemptuously pulls her coat out of Quinn's grasp and walks quickly away.

Peg is making her way to Charley, passing through a similar gauntlet of wild onlookers.

Charley and his entourage come through the police line and down the steps into the corridor. Roberts is waiting. As Charley comes by, Roberts turns to him.

                    ROBERTS
                   (ironically)
              Congratulations, Champ!

Charley pauses briefly to look at Roberts, and then, without taking his eyes off Roberts, he makes a move to walk on. Roberts stops him.

Charley continues to look intently at Roberts. A tight shot of Roberts and Charley. To the bystanders, an ordinary conversation.

                        CHARLEY
        Get yourself a new boy. I retire.

                        ROBERTS
        What makes you think you can get away with
        this?

                        CHARLEY
                (smiling)
        Whatta you going to do, kill me? Everybody dies.

Peg arrives at the top of the stairs calling Charley's name. She is momentarily stopped by the police.

                        CHARLEY
        Hey, let her through!

Peg rushes down the stairs to Charley.

                        PEG
                (exuding happiness and solicitude)
        Are you all right, Charley? . . . Are you all right?
        . . . Are you all right?

                        CHARLEY
                (looking up at Roberts)
        I never felt better in my life![23]

He and Peg break away from Roberts, toward the camera, and into the depth of the corridor.

                                        DISSOLVE TO:

"THE END" TITLE superimposed over Charley and Peg, walking away from the camera, in his old neighborhood, toward his parents' candy store.

"An ENTERPRISE PICTURE"

FADE OUT:

Cast of Characters

John Garfield (Charley Davis)
Lilli Palmer (Peg Born)
Hazel Brooks (Alice)
Anne Revere (Anna Davis)
William Conrad (Quinn)
Joseph Pevney (Shorty Polaski)
Lloyd Goff [Gough] (Roberts)
Canada Lee (Ben Chaplin)
Art Smith (David Davis)
James Burke (Arnold)
Virginia Gregg (Irma)
Peter Virgo (Drummer)
Joe Devlin (Prince)
Shimen Ruskin (Grocer)
Mary Currier (Miss Tedder)
Milton Kibbee (Dane)
Tim Ryan (Shelton)
Artie Dorrell (Jackie Marlowe)
Cy Ring (Victor)
Glen Lee (Marine)
John Indrisano (Referee)
Dan Tobey (Announcer)
Wheaton Chambers (Doctor)

Abraham Polonsky: "When you tell a story about boxing, corruption is always the main theme . . . the corruption of power . . . the corruption of what money buys . . . or what you will do to get it. If it's about the relationship between characters in terms of who shall be your friend or enemy, it is not only their personal corruption but the influence of society upon that desire and that need. If you're going to make money out of what other people do, you're going to hurt them. Even if you're helping them. In that sense, corruption is the basic theme of every picture I made. But the real theme is *the inability to corrupt*."

Annotations to the Screenplay

by John Schultheiss

[Names or descriptive phrases in **bold** are of especial artistic or historical significance, and will receive extended scrutiny in these annotations and in the various critical essays. Whenever the *Body and Soul* screenplay or the Ernest Hemingway short story, "Fifty Grand," are quoted, the accompanying *bracketed numbers* refer to the pages of the printed texts in this volume.]

[1]**Enterprise Studios**—set up by David L. Loew, with his partners Charles Einfeld, A. Pam Blumenthal, **John Garfield**, and Garfield's business manager, Bob Roberts—represents one of the more interesting challenges to the dominance of the major studios in the 1940s, a reflection of the desire of various producers, directors, and stars to determine their own projects, even if they had to partly finance the films themselves or defer their salaries. Enterprise leased studio lots and financed its own pictures, largely through David Lowe's connections. The films were then distributed by such larger companies as United Artists and MGM. Stars such as Garfield, Ingrid Bergman, Barbara Stanwyck, and Joel McCrea were attracted by a chance to participate in their films' profits. And directors such as Abraham Polonsky, Robert Rossen, André De Toth, Lewis Milestone, and Max Ophuls were given the freedom to develop their own film concepts. Accordingly, Enterprise's assemblage of a distinctive group of independent and creatively experimental artists during the post-WWII period provides a fertile basis of enquiry for those seeking to identify a social-political subtext in art.

"Enterprise was an idealistic attempt at independent filmmaking, and many of the creative people who gathered at the studio shared a liberal philosophy: for them a film could and should do more than entertain. A belief in the essential decency of the 'common man' and a basic distrust of wealth and power were at the heart of many of their pictures. In general, morale was high, interest and excitement were evident at all levels of production, and, most importantly, independent filmmakers could get the money they needed to make their pictures. Fringe benefits for employees ranged from small percs such as free coffee and donuts to big ones like life insurance policies, guaranteed vacations, and exceptionally high salaries."

[Edwin T. Arnold and Eugene L. Miller, *The Films and Career of Robert Aldrich* (Knoxville: The University of Tennessee Press, 1986), pp. 9-14.]

"When the Hollywood witch-hunt started, many of the people who had worked at Enterprise were blacklisted. Director **Robert Aldrich** [assistant director on both *Body and Soul* and *Force of Evil*; see separate Aldrich annotation] remembered the studio as an "unequalled organization" experimenting with a "really brilliant idea of a communal way to make films." He elaborates further: "While Enterprise did have an orientation towards stories with <u>social significance</u>, I think it would be unfair to say that that was its *aim*. The talented people in that period—there were always exceptions, of course—tended to be more liberal than the untalented people, and because they were more liberal, they got caught up in social processes that had political manifestations which later proved to be economically difficult to live with. In its search for talented and interesting people, Enterprise hired a great many followers of that persuasion and its pictures consequently began to acquire more and more social content." In the words of Alan Eyles: "It would seem clear enough that Enterprise had no deliberate policy for the content of its pictures—it wanted to make all kinds of films—and while it is certainly true that Enterprise's collapse predated the blacklist era, it is food for thought as to whether *the company as a whole might have been brought down for some of the associations it had formed*, had it survived [financially] to face HUAC's gaze."

(Allen Eyles, "Films of Enterprise: A Studio History," *Focus on Film* 35, April, 1980, p. 25.)

Pursuing this speculation concerning how the "associations" of Enterprise would have been interpreted by conservative observers during the era of actual blacklisting, the following redbaiting analysis (probably late 1947) by columnist Westbrook Pegler reinforces the ominous suspicion that, indeed, the studio would have been "politically" vulnerable:

Enterprise Studios Foots Travelers' Bill

Enterprise Studios of Hollywood recently released a film on an old theme, the dry splash of the vat-man in pugilism. A champion accepts the gamblers' bribe to take a dive.

The name of this picture is *Body and Soul*. The star is known as John Garfield.

Canada Lee is his opponent in the fight. He is a Negro actor who used to fight in the ring around New York. Not bad. Since he took to speaking recitations with expression and gestures he has developed something called social consciousness, a common malady of actors these days. His name bobs up again and again in the company of other names often cited by the committee on un-American activities.

The Daily Worker [Communist newspaper] of New York rapturously endorsed the movie and this naturally aroused my curiosity, because the *Worker*'s raptures are reserved strictly for works which it deems wholly consistent with its policies. It praises only persons whom it has inspected and approved.

"Canada Lee's superb portrayal is one of the best things about Enterprise Studios *Body and Soul*," the *Daily Worker*'s review says.

ENTERPRISE STUDIOS!

Wasn't that the address to which the 19 defiant and dashing Hollywood glamorites referred all unpaid bills and mislaid personal property the time they came down to Washington to protest against the committee's identification of Communists in Hollywood? There were Humphrey Bogart and Glamorous Baby Bacall, his wife, and so-and-so and you-know-who.

After they had signed tabs for several days, back they swooped to the enchanting land of make-believe, but, as I say, notice was given to the hotel people to send all unpaid bills and forgotten diamonds to Enterprise Studios, Hollywood, Calif. It seemed to be headquarters.

[Westbrook Pegler, no newspaper identified, n.d.—a clipping from the files of Frances Pearson, widow of Canada Lee.]

Note the choice of the word "Travelers" in the article's headline— a Cold War innuendo that describes not only the trip to Washington by the Hollywood stars, but which also, as in "Fellow Traveler," conveys a pejorative implication about persons who sympathize with the Communist party.

While it existed (1946-1949), Enterprise Studios produced nine motion pictures: *Ramrod* (1947), *The Other Love* (1947), *Body and Soul* (1947), *Arch of Triumph* (1948), *Four Faces West* (1948), *So This Is New York* (1948), *No Minor Vices* (1948), *Force of Evil* (1948), and *Caught* (1949).

But a lack of strong leadership produced an unfortunate tendency for the studio to waste enormous sums of money, energy, and talent on weak material. In Robert Aldrich's opinion, "The studio had everything in the world in its favor except one thing: there was no head of that studio. There were a lot of very talented, experienced, intelligent people among its various branches, but there was no knowledgeable guy to run the shop." As a result, few of the films made at Enterprise were commercially profitable. (*Body and Soul* was the only unqualified financial success; *Arch of Triumph* was the unmitigated disaster.)

On 9 October 1953, *Daily Variety* reported: "Bank of America yesterday foreclosed on two old John Garfield starrers, *Body and Soul* and *Force of Evil*, produced by Roberts Productions. Superior Court Judge Frank G. Swain ordered sale of the pix. Bank had loaned Roberts $1,610,000 for *Force* and $1,000,000 for *Body*, and reported there was still outstanding against both pix $187,588 principal, $27,442 interest and $2,470 attorney's fees."

[2]**John Garfield**, veteran actor of New York's **Group Theatre** and socially conscious motion pictures, especially for Warner Bros., was nominated for the 1947 Academy Award as Best Actor in *Body and Soul*.

"The first axiom of *film gris* is John Garfield. Garfield was the first 'method actor' to become a Hollywood star, and he remains the greatest, in my opinion. . . . Garfield starred in the films that defined and inaugurated the *film gris* genre, and it was his power as a movie star that allowed them to be made." (*Film Gris* is a conception of Thom Andersen in his "Red Hollywood." See Annotation #7.)

Note Abraham Polonsky's paean to John Garfield as the Introduction to this book; see Mark Rappaport's "The Candy Store That Dare Not Speak Its Name," Peter Valenti's "Forest of the Night," and John Schultheiss's "The Bitch Goddess and the Blacklist," also in this volume, for discussions of John Garfield's varied presences as acting icon, cultural symbol, and ethical metaphor in American cinema and theatre in the 1930s and 1940s.

[3]*Body and Soul*: **Historical, Social, Political, and Cultural Contexts for Analysis.** It is assumed that the publication of a notable popular culture text like *Body and Soul* would stimulate an interest in interconnected issues worthy of further inquiry. Here are a few initial notes on some of these topics:

A. **Boxing and Society.** In *Boxing and Society: An International Analysis*, John Sugden examines the place occupied by boxing in a "civilized" society. The positions taken in this debate are discussed within a variety of lived cultural settings. As a critical exercise, it might be enlightening for the reader and students of film to locate some points of connection between these categories and the ambiance of *Body and Soul*.

(1) *Boxing and Civilization*. Boxing is often accused of being "uncivilized," that is, the sport encourages manifestations of brutality which have no place in a morally advanced or civilized society. The basic assumption here is that because of a "civilizing process" that has supposedly taken place over the centuries, our appetite for violence has decreased, and therefore people no longer feel impelled to take part in or watch bloodthirsty and violent sports.

The durability of boxing and the facts of modern history cast doubt on this assumption. Events such as the Holocaust, the Dresden fire storms and atomic bombs dropped on Nagasaki and Hiroshima, the ethnic cleansing in the former Yugoslavia and genocide in Rwanda and Burundi, the terrorist attacks in New York suggest "that we remain part of a species which, under certain circumstances, is capable of manifold acts of social degradation."

The persistence of violent sports such cockfighting and the so-called Ultimate Fighting Championship (relatively unlimited use of the violent techniques of Thai and Western boxing and pro-wrestling's painful submission holds) suggests a continuity in the appetite of humans to appreciate and share in the celebration of life and death—a parody of the human condition—which is at the core of a boxing match. For some people "the contest is not mere self-destructive play but life itself . . . and the world is new, fresh, vital, terrifying by turns, a place of wonder. It is the lost ancestral self that is sought, however futilely. . . . When the boxing fan shouts, 'Kill him! Kill him! he [or *she*: observe Alice's violent blood lust in *Body and Soul*, p. 99.] is betraying no individual pathology or quirk but asserting his common humanity and his kinship, however distant, with the thousands upon thousands of spectators who crowded into the Roman amphitheatres to see gladiators fight to the death. That such contests for mass amusement endured not for a few years or even decades but for centuries should arrest our attention." [Joyce Carol Oates, *On Boxing* (Garden City: Doubleday, 1987.)]

Sport is a relatively autonomous theatre within which the conventions of the socio-cultural mainstream can be temporarily suspended, permitting modes of behavior which as a rule, in terms of physical and emotional expression, lag behind the conventions of conduct which govern everyday life. The underlying thesis here is that through both participation and spectatorship, sport provides opportunities for people to express repressed potentials and feel basic human urges in settings which do not pose a threat to a given social order.

(2) *Boxing and Social Class.* While the overwhelming majority of those who box professionally are from marginal working-class environments, the same cannot be said for those whose commercial interests in and vicarious appreciation of the sport ensure that it continues to exist as an important component of the sport entertainment industry. There is little new in this. In Greece and Rome all gladiators, including boxers, were supported by the elite. In Regency England [the period (1811-1820) during which George, Prince of Wales, later George IV, was regent], without the patronage of the gentry, boxing would not have developed at all. Likewise, throughout the twentieth century the economic viability of boxing has been predicated on its appeal to people from the full cross-section of society.

In the United States boxing can be viewed as a symbolic event within which the tensions among rugged individualism, masculinity, bureaucratic rationality and liberalism are worked out. Business people, politicians, theatrical and movie personalities, "classy dames," and stars from other sporting arenas regularly rub shoulders at the "big fight." In this regard, professional boxing differs little from many other professional sports where the performers are drawn mainly from the lower classes, and their performances, particularly those viewed live, are consumed by middle-class audiences.

As Luis Bunuel's savage social satire *The Discreet Charm of the Bourgeoisie* (1972) illustrates so well, the outward sophistication of the middle classes often conceals dark secrets, not the least of which are a liking for violence and related behavior. While participation in and/or being victimized by violence may primarily be the preserve of the "rough" working class, it would appear that violence as spectacle has a much wider appeal—and it is this, not the generic push of the ghetto, which has enabled boxing to survive so long.

(3) *Boxing as Labor.* Boxing was one of the earliest developments of a sports entertainment industry which now has an extremely lucrative worldwide market. As a commercial endeavor, boxing has always been "owned" and controlled by wealthy groups of people for whom the ghetto provides a reservoir of willing labor.

For every one who fights for a purse of a million dollars or more, there are thousands who fight for a pittance on the under-card of some small-town show. "The top of the pyramid is small, the base broad, shading out the anonymous subsoil of humanity at any level of boxing." (Oates, *On Boxing.*) Furthermore, the winner's (and loser's) purse is divided up among a retinue of trainers, managers, cut-men, match makers, and agents. In this regard the boxer's body and the capital it generates cease to be owned and controlled by the fighters themselves.

> SHORTY: "You know what Charley is . . . what they're making him . . . a money machine . . . like gold mines, oil wells, ten percent of the U.S. mint. They're cutting him up a million ways."
> [*Body and Soul*, 79]

With the possible exception of prostitution there can be no other profession within which alienation is so directly experienced. Joyce Carol Oates believes that boxing and prostitution are connected through deprivation: "Impoverished people prostitute themselves in ways available to them, and boxing on its lowest levels offers an opportunity for men to make a living of a kind." (*On Boxing.*)

> BEN: "Did you sell the fight, Charley?"
> [*Body and Soul*, 118]

Selling your own body for the abuse and pleasure of others has been the last refuge of the poor as long as history has been recorded. In the modern world the inner city (where the rich can visit and where the poor must live) is the territory of both boxers and prostitutes.

[The above language and the various contexts for the purpose of analyzing boxing's place in society are derived from John Sugden, *Boxing and Society: An International Analysis* (Manchester UK: Manchester University Press, 1996), pp. 172-196.]

B. Sport, Art, and Aesthetics. The following discussion may provide some insights into an aesthetic and metaphoric relationship of sport and art.

> *This Sporting Life* does in fact have something in common with *Body and Soul*. They are not films about football and boxing.
> —Lindsay Anderson,
> Director of *This Sporting Life* (1963).

Sports have served a long apprenticeship in the movies, from the 1920s to the present, and have generally followed the formulas of inspirational biographies, athlete-meets-girl narratives, and sentimental interpretations of American Dream stories. But, as with all genres in literature and cinema, there is a more mature, ironic, deconstructive potential that would allow for the integration, in a meaningful and significant way, of the drama of sport into the larger drama of human relationships. In the hands of the artist, the sports narrative transcends conventional dramatics (us vs. them, winners vs. losers, fair vs. foul play) to reflect the metaphorical, psychological, or mythical qualities that sport may recursively contribute to theme, character, and structure.

Contemporary example: *Raging Bull* (1980) employs the dramatic possibilities of sport (boxing) to express life situations. The brutality of the fight scenes are woven into the fabric of the film to convey the film's thematic idea—what Joyce Carol Oates calls an attempt "to invite injury as a means of assuaging guilt, in a Dostoyevskian exchange of physical well being for peace of mind." (*On Boxing*.) This exchange clearly manifests itself when, after violently abusing his wife and brother, Jake La Motta (Robert De Niro) takes a beating in defense of his middleweight crown— that is, until the last round when, after "playing possum" (as the radio announcer calls it), he quickly dispatches his opponent.

[Ronald K. Giles, "The Reflexive Vision of Sport in Recent Drama and Film," in *The Achievement of American Sport Literature: A Critical Appraisal*, edited by Wiley Lee Umphlett (Rutherford: Fairleigh Dickinson University Press, 1991), p. 100.]

Body and Soul example:

> It's not about prizefighting. It's about the difficulties ex-
> perienced in an economic system that's not concerned for
> the personality and character of any individual person.
> Only for the value that can be generated by private enter-
> prise. This is a private enterprise.
> —Abraham Polonsky

Boxing is being used by Polonsky as a trope to express a moral and political conception of life.

QUINN

Too bad about Ben's head. He was a great fighter.

ROBERTS

Yeah, I like fighters, Quinn, better than horses.
But we have to look out for business. So we don't
tell Charley. Let him go in fighting and knock Ben
out.

QUINN

But Ben's sick. Charley might kill him.

ROBERTS

The crowd likes a killer. Charley's a hard fighter.
It'll look fixed if he takes it easy.

QUINN

I know, Mr. Roberts . . .

ROBERTS

Wipe your nose and forget the whole thing.
[*Body and Soul*, 82-83]

Abraham Polonsky: "Now when you tell a story about boxing,
corruption is always the main theme. It it's successful, it's the corruption
of power. If it's the use of money, it's the corruption of what money buys.
Or what you will do to get it. If it's the relationship between characters in
terms of who shall be your friend or enemy, it is not only their personal
corruption but the influence of society upon that desire and that need. If
you're going to make money out of what other people do, you're going to
hurt them. Even if you're helping them. In that sense, corruption is the
basic theme of every picture I made. But the real theme is the inability to
corrupt." (Interview with Author, 9 November 1987.)

"The inability to corrupt." Whether Polonsky's statement is interpreted to suggest the redemptive idea of sport, as in Charley Davis's rejec-
tion of his corrupt bargain with Roberts "to regain his soul" (analogously,
Joe Morse's repudiation of Tucker, in *Force of Evil*); or whether the statement signifies Charley's revenge against Roberts for the latter's abroga-
tion of the agreement—the thematic point is the same: one's real "personal
best" (pace Robert Towne and the world of track) depends on moral rather
than athletic stature.

[See also: Daniel J. Herman, "Sport, Art, and Aesthetics: A Decade of Controversy (1978-88)," in *Achievement of American Sport Literature*, pp. 158-164.]

C. The Boxing Movie. *Ali* (2001), a film biography about Muhammad Ali, directed by Michael Mann, is one of the most recent movies set in the world of boxing, but the sport has long been a Hollywood staple. Filmmakers have employed this genre from the beginning of cinema. The dominating influence of the pugilistic Ernest Hemingway on the pre-World War II generation of Hollywood screenwriters ensured that there was a steady diet of tough dramas set within the boxing universe during the early sound era.

> The most popular sport in film noir is also the most violent, existentially intense, ritualistic, and money-driven athletic exhibition that the city has to offer, and invariably it is controlled by organized crime.
>
> The boxer, alone in the ring with his opponent, bathed in harsh white light in a sea of blackness from which voices shout, jeer, hoot, and whistle, is a prototypical, existential noir hero, deep in his labyrinth: that is, the labyrinth of his mind, where the chess match of the fight unfolds milliseconds before the action of the physical fight, which lies within the labyrinth of the ring; the ring's lethal, phantom corridors and chambers—negotiated with jabs, hooks, and feints—invisible to all but the boxers, in turn center the carefully evoked mini-labyrinth of the city itself. The tight rectangular ring both entraps the two fighters and gives them license to do what they would be arrested for doing just twenty feet away, among the spectators.
>
> —Nicholas Christopher,
> *Somewhere in the Night: Film Noir and the American City*
> (New York: The Free Press, 1997), pp. 173, 175.

The fight movies of the late 1940s and 1950s are pessimistic, brooding affairs. If a fighter wakes up screaming in the night with a man's name on his lips, as John Garfield does at the beginning of *Body and Soul* (1947), it is not that of his opponent, but of a fighter whose health he once destroyed. The post-war era, with its rampant inflation, unemployment, labor strife, shifting social patterns and the anxieties of the Cold War, had after all spawned *film noir* and laid bare more complex existential predicaments. According to Deborah Thomas ["How Hollywood Deals with the Deviant Male," in *The Movie Book of Film Noir*]: 'What was normal during the war—close male companionship, sanctioned killing, and more casual sexual behavior—became deviant in the context of post-war calm.' The passive heroes of *film noir* were beset by vampiric women, parasitic criminals and aggressive government agencies, and the boxing movie proved the perfect arena for projecting this crisis of masculine powerlessness. In such socially-conscious films as *Body and Soul*, *The Set-Up* (1948), *Champion* (1949), *The Harder They Fall* (1956) and *Somebody Up There Likes Me* (1956), the climactic bout becomes a moral arena where nothing and no one is 'innocent.' There has to be a motive greater than the simple desire to crush an opponent: John Garfield in *Body and Soul*, Robert Ryan in *The Set-Up* and Paul Newman in *Somebody Up There Likes Me* all have a burden of responsibility towards the women they exclude from their working lives. They refuse to lose rather than need to win. Each of them is fighting to redeem himself from his own violent career, and arguably from its implicit sexuality.

The next wave of boxing movies was the self-conscious product of the 'movie brat' generation. Films such as Walter Hill's debut *Hard Times* (1975), John Avildsen's *Rocky* (1976) and Scorsese's *Raging Bull* (1980) deliberately refer back to the post-war classics that the filmmakers grew up with and which they felt resonated with the 1970s mood of pessimism. The crucial figure for these directors was Marlon Brando's Terry Molloy from *On the Waterfront* (1954). Molloy's significance in the 1970s is partly a matter of due reverence. As Scorsese has suggested, *On the Waterfront* is the iconographic equivalent of Shakespeare for his generation.
[Nick James, "Raging Bulls: Sexuality and the Boxing Movie," in *Boxer: An Anthology of Writings on Boxing and Visual Culture* (London: First MIT Press edition, 1996), n.p.]

There have been crime films dealing with baseball, horse racing, soccer, and American football, but no sport has been as associated with illegality in the cinema as often as boxing.
—Kim Newman,
The BFI Companion to Crime (1997).

A remarkably cogent listing of the best fight pictures—a compilation as well-considered as any to be found in an academic journal—is assembled by Susan King in the *Los Angeles Times*. She divides them into biographies and dramas:

Biographies
> *Gentleman Jim* (1942): Errol Flynn as 19th century boxer Jim Corbett.
> *Somebody Up There Likes Me* (1956): Paul Newman as prizefighter Rocky Graziano; Oscar-winning cinematography by Joseph Ruttenberg, screenplay by Ernest Lehmann, directed by Robert Wise.
> *The Great White Hope* (1970): James Earl Jones as Jack Johnson (named Jack Jefferson in the film); Jones and Jane Alexander had won Tony Awards for their roles in the Broadway play written (screenplay as well) by Howard Sackler, directed by Martin Ritt.
> *The Greatest* (1977): Muhammad Ali plays himself.
> *Raging Bull* (1980): director Martin Scorsese and writer Paul Schrader's character study of prizefighter Jake La Motta (Robert De Niro, Best Actor Oscar).
> *The Hurricane* (1999): Denzel Washington (Golden Globe winner) as Rubin "the Hurricane" Carter.

Dramas
> *The Champ* (1931): Wallace Beery won an Oscar as a washed-up boxer who returns to the ring.
> *The Life of Jimmy Dolan* (1933): Douglas Fairbanks Jr. hides out at a school for disabled children, because he thinks he has killed a man; remade as *They Made Me A Criminal* (1939) with **John Garfield** as the boxer on the lam.
> *Kid Galahad* (1937): Wayne Norris as a naïve young man who is turned into a top fighter by promoter Edward G. Robinson; remade in 1962 as a drama with music starring Elvis Presley.
> *Golden Boy* (1939): adaptation of the **Clifford Odets** play, introducing William Holden to the screen; see "Film as Literature: The Bitch Goddess and The Blacklist," in this volume.
> *City for Conquest* (1940): James Cagney as truck driver-turned-boxer who is blinded in the ring; cinematography by **James Wong Howe**; see Annotations #s 9, 13 and 22.
> *The Killers* (1946): Burt Lancaster as the Swede [named Ole Andreson in the original short story by **Ernest Hemingway**, who "did something wrong . . . once" (probably as Jack Brennan in the previous Hemingway story, **"Fifty Grand,"** and now is paying for his actions at the hands of the killers.] (See "The Bitch Goddess and The Blacklist," Note #39, p. 288, in this volume.)

Body and Soul (1947). Susan King writes: "This boxing classic still packs a wallop because of **James Wong Howe**'s amazing black-and-white cinematography, **Abraham Polonsky**'s literate script, **Robert Rossen**'s taut direction, and **John Garfield**'s gangbuster of a performance as Charley Davis."

Champion (1949): Kirk Douglas received his first Oscar nomination as a boxer, totally without morals or scruples, who punches his way to the top, leaving friends and family in his wake.

The Set-Up (1949): Robert Ryan as a pugilist on the skids who refuses to throw a fight; directed by Robert Wise.

The Harder They Fall (1956): Humphrey Bogart as a world-weary sportswriter-turned-press agent; written by Budd Schulberg, also the writer of *On the Waterfront*.

Requiem for a Heavyweight (1962): Anthony Quinn as a washed-up boxer on a downward spiral of degeneration; written by Rod Serling.

Rocky (1976): Sylvester Stallone as a loser who gets his chance to shine in the ring; won the best film Oscar, beating out *Network* and *All the President's Men*, with John G. Avildsen winning for best director. [Joyce Carol Oates has dismissed the *Rocky* films as being "scarcely about boxing as we know it," noting that Stallone and his opponents are "ludicrously encumbered with bodybuilders' physiques." (*On Boxing*.)]

[*Fat City* (1972): John Huston's adaptation of Leonard Gardner's novel about tanktown prizefighters (Stacy Keach and Jeff Bridges) is not on Susan King's list, but should be included in any respectable citation of key boxing texts.]

(Susan King, "Going Glove to Glove with Some Greats," *Los Angeles Times Calendar*, 27 December 2001, pp. 22-26.)

D. Critical Commentaries and Methodologies. The following are adumbrations of the major critical approaches to *Body and Soul* expressed in the various critical essays in this volume—inevitably dominated (because of Polonsky's general world view) by those that attempt to make comprehensible "the effects of a tight, restrictive capitalistic system" and the need for an individual to create a personal identity in the face of moral and environmental chaos:

- **Marxism**:

"Those wishing to ban boxing should redirect their efforts towards the eradication of poverty, for without the latter, there is little appetite for the former."
[John Sugden, *Boxing and Society: An International Analysis* (Manchester: Manchester University Press, 1996), p. 7.]

- **Existentialism (Individualism):**

"Modern prize-fighting is a remarkable metaphor for the philosophical and social condition of men (and, sometimes, women) in modern mass society. Launched in eighteenth-century England, largely as a way of upper-class betting men to amuse themselves at the expense of lower-class ruffians, prize-fighting was created in anticipation of mass industrialized society, where it has flourished as a sport and, even more startlingly, as an aesthetic: namely, to watch without seeing. The prize-fighter enacts a drama of poor taste that is in truth nothing more than an expression of resentment or a pantomime of rebellion totally devoid of any political content except ritualized male anger turned into a voyeuristic fetish. Boxing is a form of kitsch, which explains why so many intellectuals have been attracted to it: the intellectualization of kitsch is a growth industry. But the boxer symbolizes even more than resentment and human-struggle-as-kitsch; he symbolizes, in some respects, the individual in mass society: marginalized, alone, and consumed by the very demands and acts of his consumption."
[Gerald Early, *The Culture of Bruising: Essays on Prizefighting, Literature, and Modern American Culture* (New York: The Ecco Press, 1994), p. xiv.]

[**Note:** The opposition between Marxist and Existential interpretations is crystallized in the debate over *Body and Soul*'s ending; see Annotation #23. Also, see analogous discussion concerning Jack Brennan's motivation and behavior in Ernest Hemingway's "Fifty Grand," Notes: 5-7, 9-11.]

- **Social Consciousness**:

  "Here are the gin and tinsel, squalor and sables of the Depression era, less daring than when first revealed in *Dead End* or **Golden Boy** but more valid and mature because shown without sentiment or blur. The old tenement films with 'social significance' had general reform in mind. They represented a native protest of our social fabric. But *Body and Soul* gets deeper into its milieu, makes specific the blame, and tightens up the conflicts of its cast with logic."
  (Stephen Belcher, *New Movies*, Vol. 22, No. 6, November 1947, pp. 9-10.)

- **The Bitch Goddess "Success"**:

  See "Film as Literature: The Bitch Goddess and the Blacklist," in this volume, where an individual's ambition for success is discussed as an ambiguous cultural and moral process. The achievement of success is often purchased at the price of the corruption of one's own artistic talent, or obtained by the betrayal of others. Concerning the former, as a prototypical critical commentary that reflects the "selling out" of one's artistic integrity for commercial success, consider this brief profile of James O'Neill (father of dramatist Eugene O'Neill), who is often employed by literary scholars as an axiom of this phenomenon:

  Actor James O'Neill—as celebrated in his day as the son was later, if differently. The son of famine-driven Irish peasants, he had risen by a combination of talent, need, and the looks of a matinee idol into the first tier of the stage, a possible successor to the great Booth, with whom he once played Othello and Iago on alternative nights. He had trained himself into the wide Shakespearean range, but, again like Booth, was fit for a variety of other roles. Then, on a star-crossed February night in 1883 (appropriately, in Booth's theater), he took the part of Edmond Dantès in *The Count of Monte Cristo*. For the next thirty years he was to play the part continually. It made him a rich man and destroyed him as an actor. Photographs show him in his prime, handsome and dashing, then gradually thickening.
  (Thomas Flanagan, "Master of the Misbegotten," *The New York Review of Books*, 5 October 2000, p. 14.)

The emigration from (the modest salaries of) Broadway to (the lucrative contracts of) Hollywood is often characterized as a species of "selling out." Accordingly, here is another historical perspective involving **Clifford Odets**, an oft-cited player in the sellout controversy, considered to be particularly relevant because his politics and socially conscious writing parallel Abraham Polonsky's, and because the themes and moral conflicts in his boxing play, *Golden Boy* (1937), anticipate and foreshadow *Body and Soul* (1947):

> Consider three contemporary playwrights. Sam Shepard becomes a movie star, a heartthrob; Harold Pinter turns out clever screenplays; David Hare directs films—and they do so without looking over their shoulders. Who today would criticize them for diminishing themselves as playwrights, squandering their talents, or just plain selling out? Selling Out—in capitals—the very notion is an anachronism. But in the 30s, for the theatre, the term still meant something. The stage was where 'real' dramatic artists made their stand. Eugene O'Neill never, ever went to Hollywood, Clifford Odets was reminded over and over again. And if Odets wished to be the next O'Neill—or maybe better than O'Neill—he must stay in New York and pump out plays. . . . [But] one of America's major playwrights became only an intriguing footnote among filmmakers. He sold out. Having gone merely to look round, he ended by becoming Hollywood. He was cremated, appropriately enough, at Forest Lawn cemetery.
> (Gerald Peary, "Odets of Hollywood," *Sight and Sound*, Volume 56, Issue 1, 1986, pp. 59, 63.)

Marxism and The Bitch Goddess. During the studio era, then, Communists sneered at Hollywood writers as sellouts. As Paul Buhle and Dave Wagner contend, "Even Hollywood left-wingers often wondered among themselves why they were not out organizing the working class or at least producing documentaries, as a small and demonstrably unsuccessful group of left-wing artists attempted to do from New York." And Abraham Polonsky insisted that the role of radicals in Hollywood was simply beyond the understanding of contemporary Marxists:

> You can't possibly explain it by saying, "They came to Hollywood for the money," although indeed they did. You can't possibly say that they came for the glamour, although some did in fact. But if they had come only for money and glamour they would all have become stool pigeons, to hold their jobs, to continue making money

and doing pictures. According to Marxist theory, no decent pictures could be made in Hollywood.

Polonsky, indeed, denies the very premise held by many of his contemporaries that any Communist working at a Hollywood studio is, by the very nature of the inherent ideological contradictions, selling out:

The dilemma was not solved and it couldn't be solved because it was artificial and didn't exist. Film making in the major studios is the prime way that the film art exists. That doesn't mean that film, as an art form, does not exist apart from the studios. But when you want to get into making movies, then there's only one thing to do: you try to make feature films for studios. It may not be the best solution to an artistic problem. It may end in the total defeat of every impulse that the writer has, the director has, and the actor has. But the fact of the matter is, that's the only choice, and that is why so many people who became Communists in Hollywood didn't rush to go elsewhere.
[Paul Buhle and Dave Wagner, *A Very Dangerous Citizen: Abraham Lincoln Polonsky and the Hollywood Left* (Berkeley: University of California Press, 2001), p. 50.]

While money was the most obvious attraction of movie writing, a profound impetus was the chance to leave one's mark on a new mode of creative writing and communicating. No matter that movie writing was downgraded by the eastern literati; the challenge of celluloid captured many writers' imaginations. Indeed, the sneers of the highbrows were a measure of the attraction of a medium which reached so many more millions of people, and moved them so much more directly, than books or plays could do.
[Larry Ceplair and Steven Englund, *The Inquisition in Hollywood: Politics in the Film Community, 1930-1960* (Berkeley: University of California Press, 1983), p. 4.]

It is interesting to recognize *Body and Soul* within this dynamic. The following perception of the film, which refreshingly does not invoke the sellout cliché, is an overall positive affirmation of the artistic migration from New York to Hollywood and seems compatible with the contentions of Polonsky, Ceplair, and Englund above.

Body and Soul is more than a fight film. As latest example of the influence of Broadway's more serious talents on Hollywood it provides an excuse to reconsider that migration of the mid-thirties. Remember Odets and Irwin Shaw taking their rough talk to Hollywood, Orson Welles turning from experiments on stage and radio to the screen? Remember the excitement of seeing emigrants from the Mercury, Federal and Group theatres in films—Agnes Moorehead, Joseph Cotten, Ruth Warrick, Franchot Tone, John Garfield? They were New Yorkers who went to Hollywood with something to say."

(Stephen Belcher, *New Movies*, November 1947, p. 9.)

- **The Political Blacklist:**
     In the climate of the 1950s Cold War, influential columnist Ed Sullivan, also one of the biggest powerbrokers in the new medium of television, wrote these remarkable paragraphs:

Body and Soul, as a case history, is of tremendous importance to Americans fighting Communism because it illustrates the manner in which Commies and pinks, in the field of communications and ideas, gave employment to one another.

The picture was directed by Robert Rossen, written by Abe Polonsky, included in its cast Garfield, Canada Lee and Ann Revere. All of them later were probed by the House Committee on Un-American Activities. Rossen, Polonsky and Miss Revere defied the committee on the grounds of the Fifth Amendment, and were shelved by moving picture companies.

—Ed Sullivan,
"Little Old New York," *New York Daily News*,
21 May 1952.
(See reprint of Sullivan's entire column, in this volume,
pp. 376-377.)

     Ed Sullivan's involvement in the anti-communism movement is a fascinating one. (See Kevin Lewis's "Shadowboxing," in this volume, for its ramifications in the career of actor **Canada Lee**.) During the odious Cold War period when media artists had to have their personal political beliefs "cleared" by acceptable authorities in order to be employed, Sullivan turned consistently to Theodore Kirkpatrick—of *Counterattack* and *Red Channels: The Report of Communist Influence in Radio and Television*—for guidance. Sullivan told his column readers on 21 June 1950: "Kirpatrick has sat in my living room on several occasions and listened attentively to performers eager to secure a certification of loyalty. On some occasions, after interviewing them, he has given them the green light; on other occasions, he has told them Veterans' organizations will insist on further proof." Sullivan wrote that *Counterattack* was doing "a magnificent American job."

Cultural historian Jerry Bowles offers a possible explanation for Sullivan's behavior:

> Like many men who have not served in the military during war periods, Sullivan was sensitive about it and insecure about his 'patriotism.' He did not want to be accused of not having done his part. Despite the fact that he was to become the first man to present many great Soviet acts to the American public, Sullivan remained a fervent anti-communist.
>
> [Jerry Bowles, *A Thousand Sundays: The Story of The Ed Sullivan Show* (New York: G.P. Putnam's Sons, 1980), pp. 46-47.]

Body and Soul, structurally and thematically, is much like most Robert Rossen's other films, dealing with a young man struggling for self-realization while in the pursuit of money, power or glory. None of Rossen's other films, though, portray this struggle in terms as political as those of *Body and Soul*—surprising, inasmuch as *All the King's Men* is a political biography.

But then again, it is not all that surprising, considering the talent at work here. The credits of *Body and Soul* read like a virtual Who's Who of the Hollywood blacklist. Rossen, scenarist Abraham Polonsky, actors John Garfield, Anne Revere, Canada Lee, [Lloyd Gough, Art Smith] were all put out of work in the Fifties because of old leftist ties.

(Scott Bowles, *CinemaTexas Program Notes*,
Vol. 20, No. 1, 18 February 1981.)

While the House Un-American Activities Committee is recessing, I'd suggest they read the plays put on by the Group Theatre. I think they'll find that despite John Garfield's testimony that the Group Theatre was run 'on an artistic, theatrical basis' and never mixed up in politics, there was considerable communistic party line propaganda in the plays of Clifford Odets, John Howard Lawson and others.

(Irving Hoffman, "Tales of Hoffman,"
The Hollywood Reporter, 1 May 1951, p. 3.)

[4]**Hazel Brooks.** Making her film debut in *Body and Soul*, Hazel Brooks was given elaborate attention by the studio publicity department, which produced this sort of marvelously perfervid flackery: "The 22-year old is causing more furore in the film citadel than any aspiring star since Carole Lombard made her first appearance on the Hollywood scene. For Hazel not only has one of the town's most arresting faces and its indisputably most eye-stopping figure, she is a smart lass who can talk as fluently on Thomas Wolfe, the conflicting philosophies of Aristotle and Berkeley and Hume, and the Brooklyn Dodgers as she can on movie-making."

Ultimately, it was Brooks's physical, rather than intellectual, attributes that were emphasized in the film. See Annotation #17, "Sexuality and the Boxing Movie," where a provocative scene between her and John Garfield, rich in sexual ambiguity, is analyzed.

Brooke's star aspirations were never realized.

[5] **Anne Revere.** An excellent character player of the American stage and screen, Anne Revere made her Broadway debut in 1931, and in 1940 moved to Hollywood to begin a decade-long career in films that culminated in 1945 in an Academy Award as best supporting actress for her performance as Elizabeth Taylor's mother in *National Velvet*. She was also nominated for Oscars for *The Song of Bernadette* (1943) and *Gentleman's Agreement* (1947). She was at the peak of her career in 1951 when she was blacklisted by the industry for taking the Fifth Amendment before the House Committee on Un-American Activities.

Rex Reed wrote: "Anne Revere brought strength and dignity to the screen, and the whole world treated her like the next best thing to apple pie. Then, suddenly, like horsemen from a nightmarish apocalypse, the horror began. The world had gone mad. People were looking for Reds under their beds. It was the sickest era in American history since the Civil War, and Anne Revere, with one Oscar and nominations for two others, was destroyed." ("Anne Revere Looks Ahead!" *Los Angeles Times*, 2 May 1975.)

Unable to obtain any roles in films or on television, she was out of work for several years. In 1958 she returned to Broadway, and two years later won a Tony Award for her performance in *Toys in the Attic*. However, it was not until 1976 that she could be seen again in a substantial film role, in *Birch Interval*. It would be her last film. Near its conclusion, a defeated idealist (Rip Torn) reflects that "man finds true peace in the triumph of principle." Anne Revere had found peace.

(See Clarke Taylor, "Blacklist—Horror Role for Anne Revere," *Los Angeles Times Calendar*, 20 June 1976, p. 39.)

⁶**Canada Lee.** The career of distinguished African American actor Canada Lee—rich on so many social and creative levels—can serve as the springboard for a variety of cultural, artistic, and political annotations.

For the most comprehensive and critically astute portrait of Canada Lee, see Kevin Lewis's "Shadowboxing," in this volume.

• Canada Lee in *Body and Soul*:

In the history of the American film industry, there are a few pictures, possibly half a dozen, which present Negro personality as a normal part of the action. . . . Ben in *Body and Soul* is responsible for the decision that brings the film to a climax. . . . The young prizefighter's attempt to free himself from the corruption that traps him is given depth and meaning by his identification of *his* fate with the fate of the Negro fighter who has been similarly trapped and beaten.
[John Howard Lawson, *Theory and Technique of Screenwriting* (New York: G.P. Putnam's Sons, 1949), pp. 436, 360.]

"There is considerable authenticity given to the pic by the appearance of *Canada Lee*, as the middle-weight champ belted out for the crown by Garfield. (Lee, now a name legit actor, will be recalled as a pretty fair middleweight title contender a dozen years back.)"
—*Variety*, 13 August 1947.

"It is Canada Lee who brings to focus the horrible pathos of the cruelly exploited prize-fighter. As a Negro ex-champion who is meanly shoved aside, until one night he finally dies slugging in a deserted [*sic*.] ring, he shows through great dignity and reticence the full measure of his inarticulate scorn for the greed of shrewder men who have enslaved him, sapped his strength, and then tossed him out to die. The inclusion of this portrait is one of the finer things in the film." (*New York Times*.)

To read the script alone, it would be hard to tell which role Canada Lee would play. Actually, he's one of the prizefighters. But according to the screenplay he's simply a figure illustrating the vicious and corrupt nature of some phases of boxing. The aim was to show a victim of other people's greed. It just happened that he was a Negro. It could easily have been any other fighter.
—John Garfield, *Negro Digest*, November 1947

Censorship. A letter contained in the Production Code Administration's (PCA) file, dated 4 January 1947, indicates that the Breen Office demanded an entire sequence in which a white boxer fights an African American boxer be cut from the script. The stated reason for the deletion was that the Production Code did "not permit any scenes showing the social intermingling of white and colored people or of a boxing contest between two people of these opposite colors." Obviously, this demand was disregarded. To the contrary:

> "Canada Lee gets at his character's insides slowly but steadily, gradually drawing the viewer in, so subtly weaving his spell that you're surprised by the effect his character's death ultimately has on you. It's a classic example of a black performer taking a supporting part and beefing it up with his talent and also his mad conviction and desire to make a statement, to create. This is also a prime example of the gradual change in the depiction of Negro characters in Hollywood films of the post-World War II era. No longer simply comic characters, the black figures are treated more sensitively, used occasionally as statements on the effects of a tight, restrictive capitalistic system."
>
> [Donald Bogle, *Blacks in American Films and Television*
> (New York: Garland Publishing, 1988), p. 33.]

In *Blackface, White Noise: Jewish Immigrants in the Hollywood Melting Pot* (University of California Press, 1998), Michael Rogin writes that *Body and Soul* was the first Hollywood film to place at its center the relationship between an African American and a Jew. The film created one of the first "substantial, ungrotesque" African American film roles—but it "fails to free the African American actor from inheriting the sacrificial role."

Ben Chaplin (Canada Lee) is a black boxer, for whose death Charley Davis feels responsible. Desperate for money and with a blood clot in his brain, Ben plans to throw his match to Charley, receiving the promise that his head would be spared. Charley is not told any of this, and aggressively knocks Ben out. Shocked when he hears the truth, Charley takes on the damaged ex-champ as his trainer.

Once Charley is champ, his agreement to throw his title defense and bet against himself is an "investment." There is thus interracial solidarity between black man and Jew: not only is Charley following Ben in selling out; he has also risen on Ben's back, as the graphic shots of the Jewish fighter knocking down the African American make all too literal. "*Body and Soul* insists that the black face represents the sacrificed immigrant Jewish community. In finishing off Ben and elevating Charley, the film tells the truth about the contrasting prospects in the United States for African Americans and Jews. When the white fighter became Jewish, he inherited the culture's wish for a victory of white over black. *Body and Soul* wanted to repudiate that wish, but it could not film black victory."

Although the word *Negro* is never uttered in *Body and Soul*, Canada Lee plays the black Christ. Eventually, the Jewish boxer follows the African American as mob-sponsored champion paid to throw away his crown. Charley was warned that he would end up like Ben, but he does not. "Ben dies for Charley's sins." (pp. 214-219.)

[7]**Abraham Polonsky in Hollywood.** As with the profile of Enterprise Studios, it might be enlightening to locate Polonsky's career as screenwriter and filmmaker in a specific historical context. Among the *classic* screenwriters (those in Hollywood from the beginning of the silent era through the 1940s), it is possible to detect shifting relationships among studios, directors, the nature of screenwriting, artistic seriousness, and American film style. It is useful to distinguish several different screenwriter waves, each with distinct attitudes about the work, and each effecting various changes in American film.

The First Wave
This early period contains authors who grew up with the industry from its infancy. There is little self-importance about their role in shaping a work. Films are merely vehicles for a star, a project to be done, a job. Hollywood is basically an industry supplying fantasies and entertainment to a giant public; artistic aspirations are minimal. The real excitement for seminal writers like Anita Loos, Frances Marion, and Jeanie Macpherson, for example, is the pleasure of being on the scene in a young industry, where the action is, with life and film taking on the quality of legend, with stars being born and life being lifted out of the ordinary by the success of a fledgling industry. During the 1920s, their scripts were written directly for stars like Mary Pickford, Marion Davies, the Talmadge sisters, and director Cecil B. De Mille.

The Second Wave
The second wave came with sound. Writers like Ben Hecht, Robert Riskin, Nunally Johnson, Dudley Nichols, Jules Furthman, Samson Raphaelson had all been shaped by the freedom of the 1920s, and carried both its style and subject matter into film. The most famous of them aspired to drama and high art, but all had connections with popular art which they were able to draw on for the films of the 1930s. Again, many of the most reliable writers were women: Bess Meredith, Sonja Levien, Vicki

Baum, Jane Murfin. Most of the screenwriters made the adjustment to the new medium unreflectively, drawing on their literary talent in theatre and journalism. Basically apolitical, shaped by the carefree 1920s, they were strong individualists, fulfilled in the release of their wit and intelligence in the scripts of the highly popular genre comedies and melodramas they wrote.

The Third Wave

This was more of a group or movement, though not in a unified sense. Many were from the leftist theatre of the 1930s; most were shaped by the decade's political hopes; almost all were steeped in the 1930s combativeness, ethnic origins, and the sense of the tough city. It is within this third wave that we find **Abraham Polonsky**. Others include: Dalton Trumbo, Ring Lardner, Jr., Robert Rossen, Clifford Odets, John Howard Lawson, Hugo Butler, Albert Maltz, Ben Barzman, Michael Wilson, Ian Hunter, Paul Jarrico, Daniel Fuchs, A.I. Bezzarides, Daniel Mainwaring, James M. Cain, Nathanael West.

The attitude of these writers towards their screenwriting work is more personal than that of the first wave; they want film to be a carrier of their personal and political vision, and they want to put the America they see, not a fantasy, on film. Most of them were unsuccessful with this political agenda. Abraham Polonsky (and a few others, to a certain extent) succeeded.

Film Gris. Critic Thom Andersen has intelligently addressed the important question of whether the most famous victims of the blacklist were talented filmmakers who were responsible for a distinctive kind of cinema. He proposes that **Abraham Polonsky** initiated with *Body and Soul*—and intensified with *Force of Evil*—a new genre of Hollywood films, which was created between the first House Committee on Un-American Activities hearings of October 1947 and the second hearings of May 1951. "Because this genre grew out of the body of films that have come retrospectively to be called *film noir* and because it may be distinguished from the earlier *film noir* by its greater psychological and social realism, I will call the genre *film gris*." Andersen associates this genre with six men who were blacklisted—Polonsky, Robert Rossen, Joseph Losey, Jules Dassin, John Berry, and Cyril Endfield—and their "artistic fellow travelers." He identifies 13 films as composing this genre: Polonsky's *Body and Soul* (1947) and *Force of Evil* (1948) [both starring **John Garfield**], Jules Dassin's *Thieves' Highway* (1949) and *Night and the City* (1950), Nicholas Ray's *They Live by Night* (1949) and *Knock on Any Door* (1949), John Huston's *We Were Strangers* [starring **John Garfield**] (1949) and *The Asphalt Jungle* (1950), Michael

Curtiz's *The Breaking Point* [**John Garfield**] (1950), Joseph Losey's *The Law-less* (1950) and *The Prowler* (1951), Cyril Endfield's *Try and Get Me* (1951), and John Berry's *He Ran All the Way* [**John Garfield**] (1951).

Andersen considers *Body and Soul* the first *film gris*. *Force of Evil* is its more ambitious successor, with dialogue "even more stylized than it had been in *Body and Soul*. It becomes a kind of vernacular blank verse, and it is spoken with an uncanny feeling for its rhythms by Garfield, Thomas Gomez, and Beatrice Pearson. Both these films have received eloquent praise, but their thematic originality has not been appreciated."

[Thom Andersen, "Red Hollywood," in *Literature and the Visual Arts in Contemporary Society*. Edited by Suzanne Ferguson and Barbara Groseclose. (Columbus: Ohio State University Press, 1985), pp. 184-187. The discussion concerning the three waves of screenwriters is adapted from Albert LaValley, "The Emerging Screenwriter," *Quarterly Review of Film Studies*, Volume 1, Number 1, February 1976, pp. 22-27.]

The fascinating tale of how Polonsky came to write the screenplay for *Body and Soul* has been related in academic and anecdotal texts—often entertainingly by Polonsky himself in various interviews and film seminar appearances. A representative rendition can be found in David Talbot and Barbara Zheutlin, *Creative Differences: Profiles of Hollywood Dissidents* (Boston: South End Press, 1978), pp. 73-74. In this volume, Joseph Janeti's "That Affable Familiar Ghost" provides the narrative.

Polonsky's script was nominated for a 1947 Academy Award for "Writing—Original Screenplay" in a very strong field:

> *Body and Soul*, Enterprise, UA.,
> Abraham Polonsky.
> *A Double Life*, Kanin Prod. U-I,
> Ruth Gordon and Garson Kanin.
> *Monsieur Verdoux*, Chaplin, UA.,
> Charles Chaplin.
> *Shoeshine*, Lopert Films (Italian),
> Sergio Amidei, Adolfo Franci,
> C.G. Viola, and Cesare Zavattini.

(Polonsky would often make comments like, "History is the change from one convention of social living to another which seems more liberating or more useful or more satisfying or more enriching.") But that year of the 1947 Academy Awards, with an especially quirky nod to historical whimsy, the Original Screenplay Oscar went to . . .

The Bachelor and the Bobby-Soxer, RKO,
Sidney Sheldon.

Polonsky: "That's what history is. And people must expect to be
disappointed very often. Because your idea of what may happen
in history is not what happens usually in history."
(Interview with Author, 21 October 1997.)

[8]**The Song "Body and Soul,"** originally composed in 1930 by
Johnny Green, with lyric by Edward Heyman, Robert Sour, and Frank Eyton,
is selected by Will Friedwald as one of twelve great standards of twentieth
century popular music—in *Stardust Melodies: A Biography of Twelve of
America's Most Popular Songs* (New York: Pantheon Books, 2002).

Political scientist Michael Rogin perceives provocative cultural
implications in the employment of music in *Body and Soul*, an interpretation reflective of his thesis regarding the theme of **African American sacri-
fice** in Hollywood movies. (This contention is explored more fully in a
thematic analysis in Annotation #6.) Rogin finds it problematic that the
film (he blames Robert Rossen)—instead of selecting some African American jazz versions of the song, such as those by Coleman Hawkins, Teddy
Wilson, or Billie Holiday—chose to incorporate Johnny Green's tune "into
a brooding, melodramatic, orchestral background noise credited to composer Hugo Friedhofer and conductor Emil Newman. That European high-
culture choice, repeated in making Charley's girl friend an artist, came at
black expense." (*Blackface, White Noise*, p. 220.)

"Abraham Polonsky does not remember the music as an important issue in the film" (Rogin, p. 307); however, see Annotation #13 for
another analysis by Michael Rogin which links racial and musical themes.

[9]**James Wong Howe**, born in China, in the United States from age
five, was raised in the northwest, and for a while pursued a career as a
professional boxer. He is one of the few Hollywood cinematographers
known by name to the general public.

Howe won the Academy Award for the cinematography of *The
Rose Tattoo* (1955) and *Hud* (1963); he has Academy Award Nominations
for the following films: *Algiers* (1938), *Abe Lincoln in Illinois* (1939), *Kings
Row* (1941), *The North Star* (1943), *The Old Man and the Sea* (1957), *Seconds*
(1966).

See Annotations #s 13 and 22 for notes on Howe's cinematography.

[10]**Robert Aldrich**—director of such commercial hits as *The Dirty Dozen* (1967) and *What Ever Happened to Baby Jane?* (1962)—did his apprenticeship work from 1946 to 1948 while under contract to Enterprise Productions, where he advanced from assistant director to unit production manager to, finally, studio manager. The first film Aldrich worked on at Enterprise was *Body and Soul*, which, according to Arnold and Miller (*Robert Aldrich*, p. 10), "must be seen as the pivotal artistic experience of his apprenticeship. Over and over again, even in his last film thirty-four years later, he would return to *Body and Soul* for inspiration."

The theme that would become central to Aldrich's work is distilled in *Body and Soul*: a protagonist [in this case, the prizefighter Charley Davis] who is corrupted by his own success tries to atone for his actions, to regain his self-respect, by challenging hostile forces [gangsters who betray him], and will face almost certain death as a consequence. For example, Aldrich's *The Big Knife* (1955, based on the play by Clifford Odets) tells of the last two days in the life of Charlie Castle, a film star who has tired of making "lousy, lousy films." Charlie has come to recognize the artificiality of his life, the disgrace of his betrayed talents, and his urgent need for spiritual and artistic redemption. In a tellingly symbolic moment (notably a *homage* to Abraham Polonsky), there is a jarring cut to a shot of Charlie being knocked bleeding to the mat in a boxing match. We gradually realize that we are seeing on old film—a "good" film (like *Body and Soul?*)—made before Charlie sold out, but which accurately reflects Charlie's present desperate situation.

Aldrich worked once more with Polonsky in 1948 on *Force of Evil*, in which Garfield again plays a character (this time a lawyer for the mob) compromised by money, who attempts in the end (having indirectly caused the death of his brother) to restore some order to the chaotic, hostile environment that he helped create. As Aldrich said about the recurring thread in his own films: "Struggle. You may still win a blessing. Why not struggle and maximize the victories? They may not come, probably *won't* come, but they might come, and if they come you're one victory ahead of total defeat." (*Robert Aldrich*, p. 50.)

Robert Aldrich's friendship with Abraham Polonsky would prove to be one of the most important in his life. Although they never worked together after *Force of Evil*, they remained close and often got together to discuss the madness and corruption of the world they saw around them. In Polonsky's words, "It was an innate, intellectual friendship, based on great affection for each other." As Lukas Heller aptly put it, "I think it's fair to say that Abe Polonsky would be about the one person of whom Aldrich would think he was an intellectual inferior." Polonsky would deliver the warm and moving eulogy for Aldrich at the memorial service held by the Directors Guild of America shortly after his death [1983].

(Arnold & Miller, *Robert Aldrich*, p. 11.)

See Annotation #23 on the debate concerning the ending of *Body and Soul*, which contains further discussion of the cinema of Robert Aldrich.

[11]**Robert Parrish** and Francis Lyon won Academy Awards for Film Editing of *Body and Soul*.

Editor Parrish, who also edited such films as the Academy Award winning *All the King's Men*—and who went on to direct some notable pictures like *Cry Danger*, *The Purple Plain*, *Saddle the Wind*, and *In the French Style*—wrote a delightful memoir, *Growing Up in Hollywood*, in which he tells his memory (probably the most colorfully constructed version) of the genesis of *Body and Soul*:

FADE IN:

"It will be the true story of Barney Ross, the three-time champion of the world, war hero, and model for young people. We'll get John Garfield to star in it and Robert Rossen, the writer-turned-director, to direct. We'll call it *Tiger, Tiger, Burning Bright* [titled *Burning Journey*, in a 20 June 1946 *Hollywood Reporter* story] to give it a classy sound, but it will actually be a straightforward, gutsy melodrama, right off the streets. The kind of stuff Zanuck did at Warner Brothers, only better, and we'll end it with Ross making a comeback at Madison Square Garden, recapturing the title for the fourth time."

FADE OUT:

"FADE IN:

Headline:
BARNEY ROSS CONFESSES
DRUG ADDICTION
Former Welterweight Champion "Hooked" in
Army Hospital after War Injury

Barney Ross, the former three-time welterweight champion, has confessed to an addiction to heroin. "It started as a painkiller during the war," the short, dark, still well-built boxer told a press conference today.

FADE OUT:

FADE IN:

[Charlie Einfeld, one of the owners of Enterprise Studios:] "The picture's off, we can't make a movie where the hero's a junkie. Declare *force majeure* or deception or something, cancel all contracts, and we'll swallow our losses. I think we're probably lucky anyway. Prize-fight pictures are box-office poison. Women don't go to see them."

Robert Rossen said, "I think you're wrong. I say we go ahead. It doesn't *have* to be about Barney Ross. Polonsky's script can be about any bum who comes up the hard way. We'll just change the title and change the ending. We'll use the ending from **Hemingway's 'Fifty Grand.' "**

"We don't own the motion-picture rights to 'Fifty Grand.' "

"OK, so in our picture the payoff will be sixty grand. The thing is, we have a good story, a good cast, and crew, and we're ready to go."

"You haven't got a good story. You *had* a good story until Ross's press conference yesterday. You know the code won't permit movies where drugs are even mentioned, so the Barney Ross story is out. Period. Forget it. And to invent a new ending, then try to patch up the rest of the script by borrowing from other prize-fighting stories, and still meet our contractual dates sound like disaster to me, like putting Band-Aids on a leper." He [Charlie Einfeld] turned to the company lawyer. "What do you think, Al?"

Al said, "We're a new studio. We've got most of our money tied up in *Arch of Triumph*. We know that's a winner. With a best seller, Bergman and Boyer, two of the biggest stars in the business, and a great director, we can't miss. If that were finished and in release it would be different, but it will be a year before we see any money from that one. [It would turn out to be a major financial disaster.]

Our whole publicity campaign on *Tiger, Tiger, Burning Bright* is based on Barney Ross. If we go ahead now, we'll be murdered by the code and the women's clubs and we'll be sued by Ross. I think we should cancel, Charlie, and quick."

"I've always been nervous about boxing pictures anyway," Charlie said. "If it weren't for John Garfield's box-office attraction I wouldn't have gone into this project in the first place. Look, Bob, why don't you give me and Al a couple of hours to go into the legal and contractual aspects, and we'll see you after lunch. I promise we'll consider everything with an open mind and we won't make a decision until this afternoon."

Rossen was now pacing the room, his shoulders hunched, his chubby face a cloud of bitter frustration. He was sweating profusely, cornered, fighting for his life as a movie director. He had directed one picture, a successful melodrama with Dick Powell at Columbia called *Johnny O'Clock* [1947]. *Tiger, Tiger, Burning Bright* was to be his breakthrough into the big time, and he wasn't going to see it go down the drain just because Barney Ross was hooked on heroin.

He turned on his tormentor, i.e., his employer, the head of the studio. "OK, maybe this'll help you make up your open minds. It's going to cost you as much to cancel as it would to shoot. You gotta pay me and Polonsky and Garfield whether you make the picture or not. The sets are built. We've made deals with Lilli Palmer, Bill Conrad, and the New York actors. You're probably even going to have to pay Barney Ross."

"No we won't," Al said. "There's a morals clause in his contract. We'll save some money there."

"There's one in my contract too," Rossen said, "but it won't save you any money. Mine says 'play or pay.'"

He left the room like a wounded, dangerous bear who was going to call his lawyer.

FADE OUT:

FADE IN:

The picture started shooting three weeks later. The title was changed to *Body and Soul*, and announcements were made saying that the picture had nothing to do with Barney Ross.
> [Robert Parrish, *Growing Up in Hollywood* (New York: Harcourt Brace Jovanovich, 1976), pp. 168-170.]

[12] **Robert Rossen.** As a young man, Rossen was a screenwriter at Warner Bros., and was formed by the socially conscious thriller—*Marked Woman* (1937), *They Won't Forget* (1937), *Dust Be My Destiny* (1939), *Out of the Fog* (1941), etc. At a 1943 Writers' Congress at UCLA, many were looking forward to Hollywood's postwar role. Like John Huston, Rossen would develop as a director in the years after WWII, and in his presentation to the Congress, "An Approach to Character, 1943," he indicated his continued interest in intelligent psychological stories in realistic settings. But the people who have been through the war will have realized that you do not "have to be a special kind of guy to be a hero. They will have seen too many ordinary people become heroes, and by ordinary, I mean everybody from a banker's son to a ditch digger, and very few of them will be handsome, tall and cool. They'll be all sizes and shapes and they won't be cool at all. They'll be mad and sweaty and dirty and the gals they meet and know, they'll be different too."
The ordinary man will have discovered a new sense of his own dignity:

> He knows much more about what's going on and he's more and more convinced that he can handle whatever comes his way. This country needs him. There's a place for him, and he has a sense of his own importance. He has pride now and courage and belief that he and a lot of other people like him can work it out. People have found dignity, they've appraised its worth, and they'll live for it, or die for it.
> [Rossen's "An Approach to Character," quoted in Ian Hamilton, *Writers in Hollywood* (New York: Carroll & Graf Publishers, 1990), pp. 276-277.]

Viewed selectively, *Body and Soul* would seem to be an eloquent fulfillment of the redemption-of-dignity principle as expressed in Rossen's "An Approach to Character" essay. But an examination of the extreme difference of opinion between Rossen and Polonsky on the ending of the film [see Annotation #23] may cause the observer to conclude that the "re-assertion-of-self" statement is more the result of Polonsky's vision than any application of character theory by Rossen.

More distressing, Rossen's personal life could not duplicate his fiction—his sellout of principle is detailed in "The Bitch Goddess and the Blacklist," in this volume. In summary: he had appeared before HUAC in 1951, and he had refused to name names. He was consequently blacklisted, but he swore, like Charley Davis, that those "bastards aren't going to get me." However, Rossen testified again in May 1953, cooperated with the committee and, in un-Charley Davis-like fashion, named 50 people as party members. To Carl Foreman, Rossen was a "street fighter" who had destroyed "his image of himself as a tough guy." Cy Endfield remembered meeting Rossen (before he had informed): "a very assured guy with the iron jaw and great personal determination, and [now] he was a shadow of that guy. He had lost his feeling for himself. He had said, 'They won't get me,' and they got him." Rossen seemed diminished in his own eyes by his decision, along with Clifford Odets and others who became informers. Rossen's "Approach to Character, 1943" remained limited to Hollywood fiction only.

Remarkably, as with Robert Aldrich, *Body and Soul* seems to have made a profound impact on Robert Rossen, and in his later films (e.g., *The Hustler*, 1961) he would return to the earlier work for inspiration.

> Rossen, who still saw himself as a radical in the early 1960s, despite the trauma of his committee testimony, was probably thinking less of the American mythology of success, in commenting on the theme of the films, than of the categories of *Body and Soul* and the social drama of the 1930s.

> In this tradition the sensitivity of the "artist" or sportsman is corrupted by the "system," and Rossen linked *The Hustler* to this work by seeing the film as "about the artist in society" and about "what he had to do to be a success." Rossen saw the film in terms of an individual's efforts to preserve his dignity against the "competitive objectives" created by modern industrial society. Yet *The Hustler* is not a "fable of the streets" [as Polonsky has described *Body and Soul*], and while Gordon [George C. Scott] identifies himself as a "businessman," Eddie's [Paul Newman] victory is essentially a moral one. Eddie walks out of the pool hall alone at the end, while in Polonsky's ending for *Body and Soul* the neighborhood swallows Charley up. The emphasis is on personal [existential] growth

and change, but Eddie, in his final attack on Gordon, extends his moral [Marxist] criticism to Gordon's materialist values.
[Brian Neve, *Film and Politics in America: A Social Tradition* (London: Routledge, 1992), pp. 174-175, 218-219.]

[13]**Conscience from a Gibbet.** The cinematography of **James Wong Howe** (see separate Annotation #8) for *Body and Soul* reflects may of the characteristics of his work at Warner Bros. (over 24 films, from 1938 to 1947), and is very much a Warners' kind of production (see Peter Valenti's "*Body and Soul* in the Forest of the Night: Warner Bros. Meets HUAC," in this volume). The setting is gritty lowlife, dealing with common people in a realistic fashion. Typical of Warners, the film had a relatively low budget (around $1,000,000) and was shot entirely on sound stages. Howe was brought in on the production only three days before shooting began.

From the opening scene, the images are typically high contrast with blacks dominating the screen. Though most scenes include a few highlights, there is a dirty, dark gray quality to most of the film which gives it a somber, depressing atmosphere. With a few notable exceptions, the camera maintains a normal point of view with moderate use of foreground and some deep focus. The only obviously artificial lights used in the film are occasional soft hair lights on Lilli Palmer.

The initial scene is representative of the melodramatic, emotive photography of *Body and Soul*. In a studio night sequence, the camera opens with a high-angle, high-contrast shot of a punching bag swinging slowly over the white mat. A bare, silhouetted tree limb looms ominously in the foreground. The bag casts a heavy black shadow on the ring floor. Howe said that the opening shot was intended to be symbolic of the hanged man: Garfield. From this viewpoint, the camera dollies and booms past the dead tree to a high-angle, close shot of Garfield uneasily asleep on the porch. He sits up rapidly, toward the lens, and cries, "Ben!" It is later discovered that Garfield is indirectly responsible for Ben's death. Hard crosslight casts lurid shadows across his face and glistens off his sweat. In one shot, Howe captures the mood of the film and the confused, fearful state of the protagonist.
[Todd Rainsberger, *James Wong Howe: Cinematographer* (New York: A.S. Barnes & Company, 1981), pp. 215-216.]

We will come to learn that punching the bag set off Ben's fatal attack just a few hours before, and as the camera pans from the swaying object to Charley's nightmare, the exercise bag evokes the body of a lynched man. "Black body swinging in the southern breeze,/ Strange fruit hanging from the poplar trees"—the shot pays homage to Billie Holiday's signature song, "Strange Fruit," written for her by the Jewish Communist songwriter Lewis Allen.
(Michael Rogin, *Blackface, White Noise*, p. 218.)

[14]**"Charlie" v. "Charley" Davis.** Polonsky's shooting script is consistent in its spelling of "Charley" Davis. The poster in the background of this shot, with its misspelling of "Charlie," is thus a mistake of the art director or the prop man. Instances of this kind, while certainly not momentous, can be distracting. In François Truffaut's *Shoot the Piano Player* (1960), there is a poster that reads "CHARLIE KOLLER [*sic*.] DANCING NIGHTLY." The name of the character (played by Charles Aznavour) should have been correctly spelled as "Kohler."

[15]**Everybody Dies . . . Everything is Addition and Subtraction . . . The Rest is Conversation.** The influence of Polonsky's screenplays on other filmmakers—such as Quentin Tarentino (*Pulp Fiction*; see Annotation #21), Francis Ford Coppola (*The Godfather*—"It's only business"), and Oliver Stone (*Wall Street*—"It's all bucks, kid. The rest is conversation")—is detectable in the film noir social consciousness, the Marxist critique of economic corruption, the existential tone, and, of course, specific dialogue.

The influence is evident in the British film *Saturday Night and Sunday Morning* (1961, written by Alan Sillitoe, directed by Karel Reisz): "Don't let the bastards grind you down. That's one thing you learn. I'd like to see anybody try to grind me down. That'll be the day. What I am out for is a good time. All the rest is propaganda."

It is evident in *In the Line of Fire* (1993, written by Jeff Maguire, directed by Wolfgang Petersen): "Everyone dies. Some people die because they've done wrong, others simply because they come from Minneapolis."

And when an essay in an academic journal (*Post Script: Essays in Film and the Humanities*, Winter/Spring 2000) is titled, "'It's all about bucks, kid. The rest is conversation.' Framing the Economic Narrative from *Wall Street* to *Reality Bites*," it is a striking recognition that with his original dia-

logue—"Everything is addition and subtraction. The rest is conversation"—
Abraham Polonsky *began* the framing of the economic narrative with *Body and Soul*.

[16]**Lilli Palmer's Accent.** Elegant, worldly, gentle, intelligent star of international films, Lilli Palmer was the daughter of a surgeon and an Austrian actress who made her stage debut in Berlin in 1932. After the Nazi takeover she went to Paris, then to London in 1935, and for the next decade appeared in many British films and plays. *Body and Soul* was her second Hollywood film, and in her autobiography, *Change Lobsters and Dance* (1975), she briefly notes the occasion:

> The script was finished for an excellent story called *Body and Soul*. They finally thought of me and made the necessary changes in the script, turning a girl from Brooklyn into a young French painter, which immediately made the part more interesting. John Garfield, the male lead, the prototype of American working-class youth, falls in love with the "classy old-world dame." Our contrasting personalities added something quite interesting to the relationship. When *Body and Soul* was released in New York, it was an immediate success, became one of the all-time standbys, and is still being shown on television. It was my first winner.

[17]**Sexuality and the Boxing Movie.** There is a familiar pattern in Hollywood's treatment of boxing: framing the brutality and excitement of the spectacle within a context of eroticism and heterosexual validation. But a fight between two trained boxers involves a set of aesthetic and moral relationships which are often antithetical to commercial movie purposes. The movie business likes its male icons to have primarily a heterosexual appeal, and a homosexual appeal only as a by-product. Yet the erotic content of boxing is exclusively homoerotic. As Joyce Carol Oates has stated: "The confrontation in the ring—the disrobing, the sweaty heated combat that is part dance, courtship, coupling; the frequent urgent pursuit by one boxer of the other—surely boxing derives much of its appeal from this mimicry of a species of erotic love." (*On Boxing*.)

Nick James discusses boxing and sexuality by focusing on *Body and Soul*, especially on the obstructing influence of Alice (Hazel Brooks), who is a Delilah to Charley's Sampson:

> It is the absolute necessity of animosity to the sport which accounts for wariness about sexuality within it. Real boxers are supposed to refrain from sex as part of their training ritual, as if the intensity

of their desire to punish the opponent can be weakened only by sexual satisfaction. "Every athlete [is] up against the old question—could the refinement of your best reflexes which sex offer[s] be worth the absence of rapacity it might also leave?" writes Norman Mailer. [*The Fight* (1991).] This "in training" taboo implies that the two states of anticipatory desire—for sex and for combat—are interchangeable. "Instead of focusing his energies and fantasies upon a woman," says Oates, "the boxer focuses them upon an opponent. Where Woman has been, Opponent must be." [*On Boxing*.] Thus for a male fighter to retain his mythic power over his opponent, his "maleness" must be intensified by being cloistered in a hermetic all-male environment.

Nevertheless, boxing movies continually try to invert this process. In *Body and Soul*, Hazel Brooks's gold-digging nightclub floozy sits below the training ring, obscured from the camera by a punching bag. As the troubled boxer, played by John Garfield, starts pounding the bag, each blow reveals her, so that the two images blur together. Later she wraps herself around the bag in front of Garfield, obviating the mixture of dislike and desire that he feels for her. The movie is overlaying her image onto that of the opponent-substitute and she invokes the same mixed emotions in Garfield as a fighter would.

> (Nick James, "Raging Bulls: Sexuality and the
> Boxing Movie," in *Boxer*, n.p.)

Women and Boxing. John Sugden writes that in the 1990s women have begun moving into the previously male-dominated world of boxing from three related directions. First, as a response to increased male violence and harassment, more women have taken up one of the variety of forms of martial arts for self-defense. For many years women were banned from boxing in many countries, but recent advances in women's rights have rendered such legislation obsolete in the United States. Accordingly, boxing has been added as an activity for women to protect themselves.

Related to this, women have discovered that boxing training is an excellent medium for keeping fit and staying in shape. Thus, the female demand for access to boxing has increased dramatically.

Finally, perhaps most importantly, increasing numbers of women have gone beyond training to discover that they actually enjoy and are good at the real thing and are therefore chipping away at the popular perception of boxing as a sport for men only. "Whether or not this movement in the direction of sexual equality represents a progressive movement in

civilization or merely offers women an opportunity to share in the uncivilized barbarity of men is an issue which requires future debate."
(John Sugden, *Boxing and Society*, pp. 193-194.)

[18] **"Fifty Grand" to Sixty Grand.** The continuity from Ernest Hemingway's "Fifty Grand" [and "My Old Man," in terms of a fixed race] and *Body and Soul* extends to *Pulp Fiction* (1994). The latter's Butch Coolidge is a descendent of Jack Brennan and Charley Davis. In common with his predecessors, prizefighter Coolidge enters into an illicit business agreement with gangster Marsellus Wallace to throw his fight, although, unlike his fictional colleagues who insist on losing by decision, he seems to agree to a fake knockout: "In the fifth, my ass goes down." [Quentin Tarantino, *Pulp Fiction* (New York: Hyperion, 1994), p. 27.]

The twist in this pattern of fictional betrayals is that, in *Pulp Fiction*, it is the fighter who betrays the gangster, by not complying with the illegal agreement to throw the fight. (Butch not only does not lose the fight, he beats his opponent to death.) This, then, becomes the contemporary *noir*'s counterpart to the previous characters' ignoble behavior—the existential "falling out of grace" which needs to be redeemed. Butch gets his chance when he makes his choice to rescue Marsellus: "Butch decides for the life of him, he can't leave anybody in a situation like that." (Tarantino, p. 105.) As in the marvelous universe of second chances, from Joseph Conrad to Howard Hawks, Butch squares himself with Marsellus, and drives away on a Big Chrome Chopper named "GRACE." (Tarantino, p. 109.)

See the discussion of "Fifty Grand" and *Body and Soul*, in "Film as Literature: The Bitch Goddess and the Blacklist," in this volume.

[19]**It Isn't the Money. It's a Way of Showing.** The original line of dialogue in Polonsky's shooting script (FINAL: Revised 1-13-47) reads: "In Europe today they're killing people like us . . . just because they're Jewish." The actual dialogue in the film changes this to: ". . . just because of their religion." (The VHS videotape of *Body and Soul*, commercially distributed by Republic Pictures, and the version of the film broadcast by American Movie Classics do not contain *any* of this wording at all, with this result: "It isn't the money. It's a way of showing . . . We are proud. Period." There is no immediate explanation for the elimination of the "Jewish" or "religion" references.)

Lester D. Friedman, in *Hollywood's Image of the Jew*, feels that *Body and Soul* "downplayed its hero's Jewishness" or that its "use of the characters' Jewishness is somewhat ambivalent." The grocer's lines of dialogue convey the idea that "Charley clearly embodies the frustrated hopes of his people. He never, however, acknowledges this or even mentions his own Jewishness. ["Religion: Jewish" is mentioned, however, during the social worker's (Mrs. Tedder) interview of Anna Davis, p. 64.] We assume he wins the last fight, at least partially, so as not to betray those who put their faith in him—including the Jewish community that supports him."

[Lester D. Friedman, *Hollywood's Image of the Jew* (New York: Frederick Ungar Publishing Co., 1982), pp. 115-116.]

Charley Davis: The Other-Directed Character Type. A landmark book describing the formation of an American social identity by examining how media reflects and subtly influences that identity is Harvard sociologist David Riesman's *The Lonely Crowd* (1950). Riesman labels three distinctive American character types: "tradition-directed," "inner-directed," and "other-directed." His main concern is with the other-directed type, which he finds dominant in twentieth-century American urban society. The common trait of an other-directed individual, as described by Riesman, is the psychological need to trust and depend on contemporaries as the main source of self-identity and motivation. These contemporaries include friends, acquaintances, and the mass media. Riesman postulates that through signals from these outside sources, other-directed personalities choose their models of behavior. As a result, the individual becomes extremely sensitive to the actions and wishes of others.

Riesman discusses *Body and Soul*, which he sees—from a sociologist's point of view—as a paradigm of other-directed behavior:

> The hero (John Garfield) is a Jewish boy from the East Side who gets to be boxing champion and proceeds to alienate all surrounding groups: his family circle and faithful girl; his unambitious, devoted retinue; the East Side Jews who see him as a hero. He agrees for a large sum to throw his last fight and bets against himself, which would have brought him wealth—and utter alienation from these groups. En route to the fight he is told that the Jews see him as a hero, a champion in the fight against Hitler. Recalled to "himself" he double-crosses his gangster backers by winning the fight; and, poor again, he is restored to the primary group of family, girl, and Jews.

Here, the other-directed nature of society determines the resolution of the film's narrative. This filmed view of an urban society reflects the other-directed character of the hero and the peer social group.

[Tim Bywater and Thomas Sobchack, *Introduction to Film Criticism* (New York: Longman, 1989), pp. 124-125.]

Riesman's interpretation can certainly be challenged. See Annotation #23.

> Working in *Body and Soul* I was very proud. Proud, because I was an actor in, and co-producer of a well-integrated, entertaining drama. All its characters are people, whether they're Christian or Jewish, Caucasians or Negroes. There are victims in the film who aren't Negroes. In fact, my role, that of Charley Davis, a Jewish boxer, is part of the same pattern of corruption.
> —John Garfield, *Negro Digest*, November 1947.

(See Mark Rappaport's "The Candy Store That Dare Not Speak Its Name," in this volume, for an extended discussion of Jewish themes and iconography in Hollywood cinema.)

Shimin the grocer's comments raise the issue of the ideology of racial superiority and the Holocaust. Within this context, the African American boxer Joe Louis becomes pertinent. Joe Louis was the first black boxer to attain world-wide popularity after the 25-year-long "color bar" that was enforced in the wake of black boxer Jack Johnson's perceived war of transgression. Louis would find himself the symbolic champion of the white establishment's most progressive elements as well as the darling and standard bearer of black communities across the country. The Italian fighter, Primo Carnera, came to be closely associated, at least in the eyes of the American press, with Italian Fascist leader Benito Mussolini, who enthused about boxing as an "exquisitely fascist means of self-expression." Mussolini's invasion of Abyssinia in 1934 led to the Carnera-Louis confrontation of the following year being seen as a symbolic re-enactment of the war between Italy and the small African nation.

The rise to visibility of Max Schmeling, a German fighter closely associated with the Nazi regime, was to generate an even more fevered war of symbols. In fact the Jewish fighter Max Baer, who met and defeated Schmeling in 1933, declared that: "Every punch in the eye I give Schmeling is one for Adolf Hitler." When, against the odds, Louis was defeated in the twelfth round by Schmeling on 22 June 1936, it was read by white supremacists, not only as a victory for Germany or Nazism over America, but as positive proof of the black race's inferiority. George Spandau was to declare, "Through the German Schmeling the white race, Europe and White

America, defeated the black race."

Therefore, the second Louis-Schmeling confrontation on 22 June 1938 took on the symbolic connotations of an epic international conflict. Awareness of the Nazi menace had begun to permeate popular consciousness in the United States and Louis suddenly found himself recast as the standard bearer for the nation in a fight being billed as "democracy versus fascism, pacifism versus militarism, and ultimately good versus evil." In the event Louis destroyed Schmeling in 124 historic seconds and provided prizefighting with one of its most powerful and enduring symbolic moments.

[Keith Piper, "Four Corners, A Contest of Opposites," in *Boxer: An Anthology of Writings on Boxing and Visual Culture* (London: First MIT Press edition, 1996), pp. 76-77.]

The great African American novelist and intellectual Richard Wright (*Native Son*) communicates, from his earliest writing, a contempt for the dehumanizing aspects of boxing. In *Black Boy* (1945), in a section titled "Four Rounds for Five Dollars," Wright's autobiographical protagonist expresses a self-loathing for having been manipulated to engage in a boxing match for white men: "The shame and anger we felt for having allowed ourselves to be duped crept into our blows and blood ran into our eyes, half blinding us. . . . I felt that I had done something unclean, something for which I could never properly atone."

Wright thought that boxing was a manifestation of the inanity of American popular culture.

In a July 1938 piece in *New Masses*, "High Tide in Harlem," Wright calls both Joe Louis and Max Schmeling puppets, which implies that not only are they manipulated but their contrived gyrations are manipulating the public that watches them. He calls the second fight between Schmeling and Louis, probably one of the most famous sporting events in the history of sports on this planet, "a colorful puppet show, one of the greatest dramas of make-believe ever witnessed in America," and "a configuration of social images whose intensity and clarity had been heightened through weeks of skillful and constant agitation."

[Quoted in Gerald Early, *The Culture of Bruising: Essays on Prizefighting, Literature, and Modern American Culture*, p. 23; passages from Richard Wright's *Black Boy* anthologized in Henry B. Chapin, editor, *Sports in Literature* (New York: David McKay Company, 1976), pp. 132-133.]

20You Don't Tell Me How to Live . . . No, But I'll Tell You How to Die. The following is a **Marxist-Existential** analysis of "Abraham Polonsky's Metaphoric Use of Ben Chaplin" by Sam Mithani.

This essay is predicated on the knowledge that at the time he wrote *Body and Soul*, Polonsky was a member of the Communist Party of the United States, and an activist for a socialist state. A major concern was the enfranchisement of the "Negro" (the positive designation "African American" having not yet been coined). In offering the Negro actor, Canada Lee, the role of Ben Chaplin, the creative team of *Body and Soul* consciously attempted to make a potent social statement.

Polonsky's sordid boxing world, mixing black, white, immigrant Americans—for "equality in exploitation"—is a consciously chosen microcosm to illustrate one of his great themes: that oppression causes moral, psychological, and physical degradation not only of the victimized, but also of the society in which the "hunter" and the "prey" co-exist.

In giving Ben Chaplin a Voice, Polonsky sought to violate the conventions of 1940s Hollywood cinema, which had shaped audience subjectivity by its earlier films that made up the field of racial discourse. He uses Ben Chaplin as a metaphor of abject alienation; an alienation not only from the promises of the "just society" of America, but from the spiritual heart of one's own essential humanity. Ben Chaplin's ultimate defeat and humiliation is ultimately significant not because it takes place at the hands of (white) bosses, but because it is the fate of humanity in a world forever corrupt, irredeemably ugly, bent on self-destruction, consumed with self-hate, in love with its own corruption.

Polonsky echoes the nihilism of the Negro plight through Chaplin's final confrontation with Roberts. Ben tries to talk Charley into fighting Marlowe fair and square. He feels confident that Charley will retain his championship if he employs the right tactics. It is Ben's desperate attempt to obtain revenge on Roberts, his degraded life, the whole damn universe. In helping Charley win he seeks to rejuvenate his own dead "center."

Observing the bleakness of the post-WWII American scene, alienated as a Marxist amidst the political currents of Cold War and Red Scare, Polonsky sympathized with the extreme marginalization of the African American. They all lived on the "outside" of "The Great Society," even though they lived in it. Polonsky created a complex social consciousness for Ben Chaplin, and left him hovering unwanted between two worlds— between powerful America and his own stunted place in life. Instead of having a socio-economic psychosis absorb the portrait of Ben, Polonsky provided an *existential metaphor* for Ben: the modern American individualist, cast out from the American Dream, alienated from his deepest moral convictions, desperately and hopelessly struggling against an unrepentant, dehumanizing System (the very symbol of an indifferent Universe), who only finds ultimate justification in his own angry, sacrificial death, a complete self-obliteration—*Nil.*

Within this milieu, Charley Davis and Ben Chaplin struggle to maintain a sincere friendship based on simple humane values of devotion, tenderness, and loyalty. It is Polonsky's urgent Marxist message of ideological unity—based on the humanist principle of equality that transcends racial, ethnic, and class boundaries. In 1947, it was a message much needed, and appreciated, by the Left Wing.

The rest of America sought refuge in its ignorance.

[This essay has been adapted from a previously unpublished manuscript by Sam Mithani, "Giving Voice to Ben Chaplin: Afro-American Representation in Abraham Polonsky's *Body and Soul*," 12 July 1999.]

[21]**MATCH CUT.** Among *Pulp Fiction*'s several cross-references to *Body and Soul*, perhaps the most explicit involves Tarantino's appropriation of *Body and Soul*'s flashback structure for a dramatic transition. There is a parallelism by which the fighters are linked in terms of their dressing room locations, the dream/reality contrast, their orientation on the dressing tables, and their physical gestures of wiping perspiration from their brows.

- Charley Davis is in a troubled sleep on his training table the night of the fight struggling with a nightmare, fear sweating on his face. Sitting up, eyes open, he stares around the room. The nightmare still winds within his mind as he wipes the cold sweat off. In the language of the shooting script: "Charley daubs the perspiration on his brow—the residue of his nightmare—with the back of his bandaged hand." [144]

- In parallel fashion, in *Pulp Fiction* (as the 1972 "watch flashback" scene ends) there is an abrupt transition to Butch Coolidge lying "on a table catching a few zzzzzz's before his big fight. Almost as soon as WE CUT to him, he wakes up with a start. Shaken by the bizarre memory, he wipes his sweaty face with his boxing glove." (Tarantino, p. 69.)

[22]**The Final Fight.** "For pure film realism, no scenes in all of **James Wong Howe**'s cinematography are more effective than the closing fight sequence of *Body and Soul*. In what is perhaps the most visually dynamic

fight ever filmed, Howe employed the subjective camera in a way never before attempted." (Rainsberger, *Howe*, p. 217.)

(Lowell E. Redelings, in his contemporary review of the film, in the *Hollywood Citizen News*, 22 November 1947, supports this from personal experience: "The championship fight scenes are among the most authentic and exciting ever seen on the screen, and I speak from years of observing countless fights as a former sports writer.")

Rainsberger continues on Howe:

> From the beginning, the fight sequences had been a source of concern for the producers. They had intended to rent a local stadium and hire a few thousand extras in an effort to duplicate Madison Square Garden. When Howe was hired he told them not to bother; he promised to create the sense of atmosphere and the crowds with lighting. He knew the attention would be on the ring, so with a couple of hundred extras, carefully chosen camera positions, and the proper lighting, he could re-create the location on a sound stage. The results proved him right.

Since his 1940 *City for Conquest*, Howe had wanted to use a hand-held camera to film a boxing match. Having been a boxer himself, he found that conventional coverage did not convey the violence and reality of a match. He wanted to communicate the essence of the fight to the audience and, in fact, put them in the fighter's place. In an interview, Howe described his approach to the scene:

> I realized the fights I'd seen were not true because I've been around fighters and I know. Usually they put a big bulky dolly in the ring which can't move around and can only go up and down and sideways. But I said, I want something so that when Johnny [Garfield] gets hit and falls I can follow him and turn the camera and suddenly leave his face and see nothing but hot light flashing down on his face—just as the fighter would—and then you cut to the face and the eyes are closed . . . you can see the excitement in that.

> [ABRAHAM POLONSKY: James Wong Howe felt that to get the proper movement in the boxing scene, he wanted to think of it as a war. He felt that combat photographers had a sense of motion that people living other kind of lives knew nothing about. (Interview with Author.)]

Rainsberger:

Howe rented two lightweight Eyemo cameras and experimented with hand-holding techniques. Simply holding the camera and walking around did not permit enough freedom of movement. He decided to strap on roller skates and become a human dolly. He had a grip push him around the ring and warned, "You watch the fighter, it doesn't make any difference if you miss the distance; that's good because I want sometimes to be out of focus." As Win Sharples points out, "This is the way the [groggy] fighter would actually perceive it . . . moving in and out of clear focus."

Howe had the scene shot without sound so that he could give his grip and the fighters directions during the take. The camera moved as a fighter would move, stalking the opponent, moving in and out, from side to side, never steady. Howe did not overdo the technique by having a fighter's glove hit at the lens, for this would draw too much attention to the camera, and Howe wanted to make the audience believe they were in the fight, not watching a film of it. Critic Archer Winston feels that Howe succeeded: "You will find yourself participating in the fight to an extent never before realized on the screen. It is even possible to question a greater sense of participation in anyone who sits beyond the second row at a real fight."

The atmosphere of a fight is meticulously maintained. The lighting is filtered through heavy smoke, and only the people sitting around the ring are visible; the rest is dark. Point-of-view shots from the audience help move the camera into a participatory mode. At the end of the fight, spectators jump up in front of the camera as if it were just another fan.

The fight is the climax of the film and thus warrants such dramatic treatment. It gains greater impact and meaning because of the clarity and unparalleled credibility of the scene. The viewer can feel the punishment Garfield receives and realize the kind of man he truly is.

(Rainsberger, *James Wong Howe*, pp. 217-218.)

[23] **I Never Felt Better In My Life.** Abraham Polonsky has long maintained that this moment for Charley Davis "is a moment of victory, even if he gets shot in the very next scene."

But Bob Rossen, whose temperament is more anarchistic than mine, and more driven to a kind of tragic melodrama than I am, thought that a very good end for the picture would be that Charley Davis, having challenged the forces of evil and walked off triumphantly, should now be shot down and roll over in the street and bang into a garbage can and the garbage can would fall over on him and there he would lie in the garbage of history.

I said the trouble with you, Rossen, is that you want to show the next scene to defeat the whole point of the picture. This is a story about the rediscovery of something in a person. Having rediscovered it he has his moment of triumph. That's where the story ends.

Well, there was a big row. Rossen went to talk to the head of the studio, and the head of the studio said shoot both versions. And so we did.

And this is my compliment to Bob Rossen. After looking at both versions, Rossen said, use the one Polonsky wrote, it's better. And that was for Bob Rossen an act of graciousness for which there is no precedent and no subsequent action to match.

(Interview with Author.)

A debate could develop on whether the ending of *Body and Soul* signifies a "moral redemption or regeneration" on Charley's part, or whether it functions as an amoral, pragmatic act of revenge.

The first year you are in boxing you are in it for the money. After that you are in it for revenge.

—Eddie Walker,
Noted 1940s Manager of Fighters

"Fifty grand is a lot of money," I said.
It's business," said Jack [Brennan].
"I can't win. You know I can't win anyway."
"As long as you're in there you got a chance."
"No," Jack says. "I'm all through.
It's just business."

—Ernest Hemingway,
"Fifty Grand" [223]

See "Fifty Grand," Notes 5-7, 9-11, for a discussion of whether Brennan planned to throw the fight or not.

[The Eddie Walker quotation and an overall candid discussion of the ruthless pragmatics of boxing are to be found in Teddy Brenner's (as told to Barney Nagler) *Only the Ring Was Square* (Englewood Cliffs NJ: Prentice-Hall, 1981).]

QUESTION: *From the existentialist perspective, where does moral authority reside in the film?*

POLONSKY: In self-esteem—in the undestroyed element left in human nature which wants to look at itself and say, "This is myself, I'm not terrible, I believe in myself, I have a good opinion of myself. I have a self that I can recognize, that's mine."

A kind of liberation and freedom comes from failure. What I tried to do there [in the ending] was to get the feeling of that, having reached the absolute moral bottom of commitment, there's nothing left to do but commit yourself. There's no longer a problem of identity when you have no identity left at all. So, in you very next step, you must become something.

———————

Walcott covered up and Jack was swinging wild at Walcott's head. Then he swung the left and it hit Walcott in the groin and the right hit Walcott right bang where he'd hit Jack. Way low below the belt. Walcott went down and grabbed himself there and rolled and twisted around. . . . [230]

"They certainly tried a nice double-cross," John said. "Your friends Morgan and Steinfelt," Jack said. "You got nice friends." He lies there, his eyes open now. His face has still got that awful drawn look. "It's funny how fast you can think when it means that much money," Jack says. "You're some boy, Jack," John says. "No," Jack says. "It's nothing." [231]

—Ernest Hemingway,
"Fifty Grand"

A possible approach to elucidating Polonsky's existential vision may be to place the ending of *Body and Soul* in a literary and philosophical pattern which includes the ending of Hemingway's short story, **"Fifty Grand."** (By extension the links can be made to a world view characteristic of "tough-guy literature," a "hard-boiled style," and the American *film noir*—with motifs which continue even up through the stylized, existential world of *Pulp Fiction*, 1994. See further discussion of these motifs in "The Bitch Goddess and the Blacklist" and in Annotation #18.) A configuration such as this may make more comprehensible a personal code of action observed in these works which depends less on conventional or *official* guidelines for determining "good" and "evil" behavior, and depends more on the creation of *individual* values, such as courage, discipline, integrity, and an image of self-worth—values which are inextricably linked to the specialized worlds that these characters inhabit. These characters live in environments where retribution, revenge, getting even, paying one's debts, honoring agreements (legal or illegal), and settling old scores have more to do with defining the values of self than the more abstract ideals of societal harmony, public good, and adherence to codified law.

Ernest Hemingway influenced generations of writers and filmmakers by his existential portraits of characters who are severely buffeted by an indifferent, hostile universe—who endure extraordinary physical and psychological pain—but who are able to work out some sort of personal accommodation or "separate peace" with their surroundings and learn how "to live in it." The titles of collections of Hemingway's short stories—*In Our Time* (1925) and *Winner Take Nothing* (1933)—suggest something of the unequal fight individuals face in the contemporary world.

> **POLONSKY:** *Charley Davis makes this difficult judgment not out of moral reasons, but simply because he's betrayed. He's not doing it for the good of boxing; he's doing it because they double-crossed him, and he answered back by taking his revenge.*
> (Interview with Author, 9 November 1987.)

Danny Peary [in *Cult Movies* (New York: Dell Publishing, 1981), p. 100] claims that in *Body and Soul* Charley has "learned the difference between right and wrong" and that this is his motivation for refusing to throw the fight. Other critics share this viewpoint, but this interpretation would severely limit richer character dimensions and thematic possibilities for the film. (This "moral redemption" theory also restricts more fertile meanings for the ending of *Force of Evil*.) Charley Davis, Jack Brennan, and others within the tough-guy tradition, transcend the moral platitudes of mainstream culture. It boils down to reverberating Dashiell Hammett's laconic dictum for Sam Spade: "I won't play the sap for you."

QUESTION: *You once said that your films express "a soldier's attitude." Is there an application of an existential idea to the ending of* Body and Soul?

> POLONSKY: The most important thing to understand is that I do not write stories which attempt to sell a certain morality to the audience. I accept the world and our place in it and I know we have to deal with it. I also know that if we have certain concerns about our nature in it, we're going to pay a price for that. If you're not willing to pay the price, then you can't live in that world. That's the soldier's attitude: that's how you survive a battle.

QUESTION: *It has been often asserted that the ending of* Body and Soul *represents a "redemptive" action on Charley's part.*

> POLONSKY: I do not believe in redemption through accident, contrition, confession. I don't believe that you can escape the consequences of your actions by being good natured about it: as in, I've spent all my life killing people, but from now on I'll spend the rest of my life helping people. Like the guys involved in Watergate who became preachers in a church once they were caught. People do that because it makes them more acceptable in society. But my vision of society is to be more realistic. I wanted a real life exit.
>
> ***Charley Davis does not commit to morality. He commits to the destruction of those who betrayed him. That's existential.*** Committing to law and order is liberal, is a Capra ending. Which is okay, but I didn't write a Capra picture. If you say redemption, you imply that a person redeems his sins of the past, you mean that he's taken another kind of attitude. Charley Davis is a product of the streets. This is part of the street action. It is revenge. He revenges himself the best way he can in this particular set up: by winning the fight, even if he loses the money (and possibly his life). The difference between becoming a better person and fulfilling your existence as you've lived it are two different things. Charley is choosing revenge.
>
> (Interviews with Author, 28 July 1990 and 27 May 1995.)

This is an individual, existential, tough-guy resolution: Hemingway and Jack Brennan, out of Dashiell Hammett and Sam Spade, out of Abraham Lincoln Polonsky.

Interestingly, the tough-guy aspect was acknowledged at the time of the film's release. Virginia Wright, in her review of the film for the Los Angeles *Daily News* (22 November 1947), was particularly appreciative of this tone: "One of the most satisfying aspects of this satisfying film is *the avoidance of any hint of nobility at the last. The champion fights from animal instinct, from a fury at being double crossed himself,* and not until it is all over is he quite aware of what he has done."

NEVERTHELESS, there are advocates for more edifying interpretations of the film's ending. Here's an example: "Moved at the last minute not to betray those who have faith in him (he is a Jew, and the Jewish community regards him as their champion), he wins the fight, saving his soul." [Martha Wolfenstein and Nathan Leites, *Movies: A Psychological Study* (New York: Atheneum, 1970), p. 273. See Annotation #18.]

As will be seen below, some of these didactic explanations emanate from those with a "social conception of morality," especially those who tend to infer socially conscious meanings in Polonsky's own description of his screenplay as "a fable of the streets."

> Throughout, Polonsky's script for *Body and Soul* places the fable of the streets in the context of a system of business, of a capitalist system, that is more powerful and all-pervading than any individual character in the film—except, ultimately, Charley Davis.
> (Brian Neve, *Film and Politics in America*, p. 132.)

> Marxism declares without equivocation that the exploitation of man by man is the major causative factor underlying social immorality.

> Counterposed to the social conception of morality is the conception of individual morality: the assumption that the major moral problem facing man is the regeneration of the individual rather than the change of society.
> (James T. Farrell, *Literature and Morality*, p. 4.)

Accordingly, among the cogent analyses that contend that the ending of the film makes a social (political, "Marxist") point is the following by Paul Buhle and Dave Wagner:

> Polonsky's insistence on using the closing scene of *Body and Soul* as he had written it, despite its superficially happy ending, was

emphatically political. Charley's recognition of the need for a sense of decency in human affairs begins with the unmistakable suggestion that the boxing business had lynched Ben. Narratively and politically, Polonsky's need for a defiant ending with a shout of hope derives in part from the social context of Charley's awakening at the moment of Ben's "lynching" as expressed metaphorically in the swinging body bag.

With Rossen's ending, the only meaning in Charley's awakening is personal: Charley glimpses his likely future as a discarded fighter who dies penniless in the ring. His awakening is the American individualist's realization that it is time, in the lingo of another genre, to strap on his guns and clean up the gang that has taken over the boxing business. For Charley to die in a hail of bullets is entirely logical from that view. But that would be mere naturalism, little more than an inverted happy ending suited to the weary wisdom of the postwar audience, a knowing noir grimace.

For Polonsky, the scene evidently had another meaning. In Ben's death, Charley for the first time glimpses beyond himself and comes to terms with the pain of another human being. From that moment, he begins to repair his relations with his family and his community, and his decision not to throw the fight is rooted in his dawning comprehension that he is fighting not only for himself but for Ben and for his neighborhood and for everyone else the system has ground down. That is the meaning of the final "Everybody dies." It is not the defiance of the genre hero who has just killed his enemies but the serene utterance of a soul at peace with itself. Now that he has done the right thing, he is prepared to die—even, in a sense, for Rossen's ending, should that become necessary.

What matters most is the clarity of understanding that Charley attains at that moment. For Polonsky this was nothing less than the hope that all of the world's Charleys one day would make the same declaration. Hence Polonsky's frequently expressed frustration with Rossen's ending: this is not a fable about Charley Davis, it is a fable of the working class; it would be "crazy," as Polonsky once said of Rossen's ending, for a group of left-wing storytellers to conclude their finest work by killing off the proletariat!

(*A Very Dangerous Citizen*, pp. 115-116.)

Robert Aldrich. The influence of Abraham Polonsky on director Robert Aldrich is cited in Annotation #10. Accordingly, "the possibility of the kind of moral regeneration" found in the ending of *Body and Soul* signified the essential story of every Aldrich film. As Lukas Heller, who worked with Aldrich as writer throughout the 1960s and 1970s remembered, "When we would have story problems, Aldrich would revert to the film *Body and Soul* and say, 'That ending was always right. Why don't we use that ending here?' And he tried to work the structure of that story into every other movie."

Aldrich's *The Longest Yard* (1974) is a salient example. Paul Crewe (Burt Reynolds), who as a professional football player had "sold out" his teammates by shaving points, is now in prison for stealing a car. Under physical duress, he finally acquiesces to despotic Warden Hazen's (Eddie Albert) request to put together a team of convicts to give the guards a tune-up game. A good friend called Caretaker is killed in a trap set for Crewe, and, thus, partly inspired by Caretaker's death, Crewe's team plays tough and holds the guards to a 15-13 halftime lead. Hazen orders Crewe to lose the game by a 21-point margin or face life imprisonment (due to false testimony) as an accessory to Caretaker's murder. Crewe submits to the blackmail on the condition that the guards ease up on the inmates after achieving their 21-point-lead. Hazen gives his word to Crewe, but then turns around and orders the guards to inflict as much physical damage as possible on the inmates after the point spread is assured. Unaware of Hazen's intended treachery, Crewe fulfills his part of the bargain and throws the game in the second half, once again (as he had done in the pro's) selling out his teammates. With the score 35-13 in favor of the guards, Crewe sees his team suddenly brutalized and realizes that he has been deceived. Angered and determined to get even, Crewe decides to play, rallies his squad around him, and leads them to a come-from-behind victory in the game's closing seconds.

The two events which solidify Crewe's resolve and lead to his "redemption" are the death of Caretaker and his betrayal at the hands of the warden. In *Body and Soul* the parallels are the death of Ben Chaplin and the mob's betrayal of Charley during the fight by trying to knock him out.

The Longest Yard ends with a freeze frame of Crewe and another friend [Charley and Peg] walking side by side down a darkened, deserted corridor. They face an uncertain future—it is unclear whether Warden Hazen will carry out his threat to frame Crewe for murder.

[Hemingway brought closure to the story of his ex-fighter (Jack Brennan?)—if "The Killers" is read as the next chapter to **"Fifty Grand"** and Ole Andreson is projected as the personification of Brennan (see "The Bitch Goddess and the Blacklist," Note #39). Robert Rossen *would have* *made* the destiny of Charley Davis quite clear in his *proposed* ending to *Body and Soul*. And Robert Wise *does* continue the narrative to show the brutal fate of Robert Ryan at the hands of the mob, as the result of his refusal to throw a fight in *The Set Up* (1949).]

But in *Body and Soul* and *The Longest Yard*, in spite of the open endings, it is the victory itself, no matter how fleeting or ephemeral, that ultimately counts.

Aldrich admits lifting this ending from *Body and Soul* for his film: "There the Garfield character had thrown everything away and had to redeem his self-esteem more than anything else. Without the switch, without the main character having to regain his self-esteem after having sold everybody out, there's no pull, you don't care. So I just stole from Polonsky, stuck it on, wrote in the story of Caretaker's burning to death, and the funeral." Aldrich acknowledges that this theme embodies his most cherished convictions about the possibilities for individual human redemption. And, in these words, one can locate the theme that is philosophically and poetically harmonious with the cinema of Abraham Polonsky:

> I like to believe that my indelible trademark is my affection for the struggle to regain self-esteem. Now, the likelihood of doing that is remote. Still, it's the costs that make it into a gallant struggle. In *The Longest Yard*, perhaps Burt Reynolds is not going to have a happy prison life; perhaps he's not going to go on living at all. And in *Emperor of the North*, perhaps Lee Marvin hasn't really prevailed over anything. But in each case a man has fallen from grace, done something he's ashamed of, and then struggled to recapture his opinion of himself. Now, I think the odds against succeeding in doing that are overwhelming. It's not in the cards that that's probably going to happen. But I think you admire the people beside you who say, "The hell with it. I'm not going to quit. I don't give a shit what other people think about me. I'm going to try and hold myself in esteem." That's what all these pictures are really about.
>
> [Arnold & Miller, *The Films and Career of Robert Aldrich*, pp. 10, 182-185; Alain Silver and James Ursini, *What Ever Happend to Robert Aldrich: His Life and His Films* (New York: Limelight Editions, 1995), pp. 141-142.]

Left, Jackie Marlowe (Artie Dorrell); right, Charley Davis (John Garfield)

Film as Literature. The literary text and its cinematic double: Charley Davis and Jackie Marlowe, in Abraham Polonsky's *Body and Soul*, echo their literary counterparts, Jack Brennan and Walcott, in Ernest Hemingway's "Fifty Grand." While the illicit wagering set-up and the device of the double-cross are specific plot parallels, both narratives exude—in a more textured, formalistic, and philosophical sense—the existential ethos of spiritual and artistic corruption, betrayal, and redemption.

Fifty Grand

by Ernest Hemingway

[*Editor's Note*: Ernest Hemingway's "Fifty Grand," originally published in 1927 in the *Atlantic Monthly* (May) and in his volume of short stories, *Men Without Women* (October), is one of his best known short pieces. It is the tale of an aging athlete who knows he is fighting his last bout against an opponent he cannot beat, and who wants to make sure that he makes money out of it for his family. As in many *noir* narratives, the action taken is in itself dishonest, but we are made (by the brilliance of storytelling form) to sympathize with or to understand, if not morally condone, the motivation. Jack Brennan (like other Hemingway protagonists—for example, Manuel in "The Undefeated," Harry Morgan in *To Have and Have Not*) is a so-called **code-hero** who, in facing the perilous conditions of life, makes a personal accommodation with them (a "separate peace," which in Brennan's situation involves betting on his opponent) and then, impelled by the code, sticks to the bargain if it kills him. The "code" asks of a man that he try to impose meaning where none seems possible, that he try in every gesture to impress his will on the raw material of life. Brennan's real enemy is time. When the gamblers attempt to betray him, Brennan must undergo a severe test of courage, and (reflecting the subversive nature of the *noir* idiom) this ordeal transcends the immoral quality of the wager. He achieves an ironic triumph-in-loss. For many critics the story represents an approximation of tragedy.

The thematic connections of this story (and other works by Hemingway) to Abraham Polonsky's *Body and Soul* are discussed in "Film as Literature: The Bitch Goddess and the Blacklist," in this volume.]

FIFTY GRAND

by Ernest Hemingway

"How are you going yourself, Jack?" I asked him.

"You seen this, Walcott?" he says.

"Just in the gym."

"Well," Jack says, "I'm going to need a lot of luck with that boy."

"He can't hit you, Jack," Soldier said.

"I wish to hell he couldn't."

"He couldn't hit you with a handful of bird-shot."

"Bird-shot'd be all right," Jack says. "I wouldn't mind bird-shot any."

"He looks easy to hit," I said.

"Sure," Jack says, "he ain't going to last long. He ain't going to last like you and me, Jerry. But right now he's got everything."

"You'll left-hand him to death."

"Maybe," Jack says. "Sure. I got a chance to."

"Handle him like you handled Kid Lewis."

"Kid Lewis," Jack said. "That kike!"[1]

The three of us, Jack Brennan, Soldier Bartlett, and I were in Hanley's. There were a couple of broads sitting at the next table to us. They had been drinking.

"What do you mean, kike?" one of the broads says. "What do you mean, kike, you big Irish bum?"

"Sure," Jack says. "That's it."

"Kikes," this broad goes on. "They're always talking about kikes, these big Irishmen. What do you mean, kikes?"

"Come on. Let's get out of here."

"Kikes," this broad goes on. "Whoever saw you ever buy a drink? Your wife sews your pockets up every morning. These Irishmen and their kikes! Ted Lewis could lick you too."

"Sure," Jack says. "And you give away a lot of things free too, don't you?"

We went out. That was Jack. He could say what he wanted to when he wanted to say it.

Jack started training out at Danny Hogan's health farm over in Jersey. It was nice out there but Jack didn't like it much. He didn't like being away from his wife and the kids, and he was sore and grouchy most of the time. He liked me and we got along fine together; and he liked Hogan, but after a while Soldier Bartlett commenced to get on his nerves. A kidder gets to be an awful thing around a camp if his stuff goes sort of sour. Soldier was always kidding Jack, just sort of kidding him all the time. It wasn't very funny and it wasn't very good, and it began to get to Jack. It was sort of stuff like this. Jack would finish up with the weights and the bag and pull on the gloves.

"You want to work?" he'd say to Soldier.

"Sure. How you want me to work?" Soldier would ask. "Want me to treat you rough like Walcott? Want me to knock you down a few times?"

"That's it," Jack would say. He didn't like it any, though.

One morning we were all out on the road. We'd been out quite a way and now we were coming back. We'd go along fast for three minutes and then walk a minute, and then go fast for three minutes again. Jack wasn't ever what you would call a sprinter. He'd move around fast enough in the ring if he had to, but he wasn't any too fast on the road. All the time we were walking Soldier was kidding him. We came up the hill to the farmhouse.

"Well," says Jack, "you better go back to town, Soldier."

"What do you mean?"

"You better go back to town and stay there."

"What's the matter?"

"I'm sick of hearing you talk."

"Yes?" says Soldier.

"Yes," says Jack.

"You'll be a damn sight sicker when Walcott gets through with you."

"Sure," says Jack, "maybe I will. But I know I'm sick of you." So Soldier went off on the train to town that same morning. I went down with him to the train. He was good and sore.

"I was just kidding him," he said. We were waiting on the platform. "He can't pull that stuff with me, Jerry."

"He's nervous and crabby," I said. "He's a good fellow, Soldier."

"The hell he is. The hell he's ever been a good fellow."

"Well," I said, "so long, Soldier."

The train had come in. He climbed up with his bag.

"So long, Jerry," he says. "You be in town before the fight?"

"I don't think so."

"See you then."

He went in and the conductor swung up and the train went out. I rode back to the farm in the cart. Jack was on the porch writing a letter to his wife. The mail had come and I got the papers and went over on the other side of the porch and sat down to read. Hogan came out the door and walked over to me.

"Did he have a jam with Soldier?"

"Not a jam," I said. "He just told him to go back to town."

"I could see it coming," Hogan said. "He never liked Soldier much."

"No. He don't like many people."

"He's a pretty cold one," Hogan said.

"Well, he's always been fine to me."

"Me too," Hogan said. "I got no kick on him. He's a cold one, though."

Hogan went in through the screen door and I sat there on the porch and read the papers. It was just starting to get fall weather and it's nice country there in Jersey, up in the hills, and after I read the paper through I sat there and looked out at the country and the road down below against the woods with cars going along it, lifting the dust up. It was fine weather and pretty nice-looking country. Hogan came to the door and I said, "Say, Hogan, haven't you got anything to shoot out here?"

"No," Hogan said. "Only sparrows."

"Seen the paper?" I said to Hogan.

"What's in it?"

"Sande² booted three of them in yesterday."

"I got that on the telephone last night."

"You follow them pretty close, Hogan?" I asked.

"Oh, I keep in touch with them," Hogan said.

"How about Jack?" I says. "Does he still play them?"

"Him?" said Hogan. "Can you see him doing it?"

Just then Jack came around the corner with the letter in his hand. He's wearing a sweater and an old pair of pants and boxing shoes.

"Got a stamp, Hogan?" he asks.

"Give me the letter," Hogan said. "I'll mail it for you."

"Say, Jack," I said, "didn't you used to play the ponies?"

"Sure."

"I knew you did. I knew I used to see you out at Sheepshead."

"What did you lay off them for?" Hogan asked.

"Lost money."

Jack sat down on the porch by me. He leaned back against a post. He shut his eyes in the sun.

"Want a chair?" Hogan asked.

"No," said Jack. "This is fine."

"It's a nice day," I said. "It's pretty nice out in the country."

"I'd a damn sight rather be in town with the wife."

"Well, you only got another week."

"Yes," Jack says. "That's so."

We sat there on the porch. Hogan was inside at the office.

"What do you think about the shape I'm in?" Jack asked me.

"Well, you can't tell," I said. "You got a week to get around into form."

"Don't stall me."

"Well," I said, "you're not right."

"I'm not sleeping," Jack said.

"You'll be all right in a couple of days."

"No," says Jack, "I got the insomnia."

"What's on your mind?"

"I miss the wife."

"Have her come out."

"No. I'm too old for that."

"We'll take a long walk before you turn in and get you good and tired."

"Tired!" Jack says. "I'm tired all the time."

He was that way all week. He wouldn't sleep at night and he'd get up in the morning feeling that way, you know, when you can't shut your hands.

"He's stale as poorhouse cake," Hogan said. "He's nothing."

"I never seen Walcott," I said.

"He'll kill him," said Hogan. "He'll tear him in two."

"Well," I said, "everybody's got to get it sometime."[3]

"Not like this, though," Hogan said. "They'll think he never trained. It gives the farm a black eye."

"You hear what the reporters said about him?"

"Didn't I! They said he was awful. They said they oughtn't to let him fight."

"Well," I said, "they're always wrong, ain't they?"

"Yes," said Hogan. "But this time they're right."

"What the hell do they know about whether a man's right or not?"

"Well," said Hogan, "they're not such fools."

"All they did was pick Willard at Toledo. This Lardner, he's so wise now, ask him about when he picked Willard at Toledo."[4]

"Aw, he wasn't out," Hogan said. "He only writes the big fights."

"I don't care who they are," I said. "What the hell do they know? They can write maybe, but what the hell do they know?"

"You don't think Jack's in any shape, do you?" Hogan asked.

"No. He's through. All he needs is to have Corbett pick him to win for it to be all over."

"Well, Corbett'll pick him," Hogan says.

"Sure. He'll pick him."

That night Jack didn't sleep any either. The next morning was the last day before the fight. After breakfast we were out on the porch again.

"What do you think about, Jack, when you can't sleep?" I said.

"Oh, I worry," Jack says. "I worry about property I got up in the Bronx, I worry about property I got in Florida. I worry about the kids. I worry about the wife. Sometimes I think about fights. I think about that kike Ted Lewis and I get sore. I got some stocks and I worry about them. What the hell don't I think about?"

"Well," I said, "tomorrow night it'll all be over."

"Sure," said Jack. "That always helps a lot, don't it? That just fixes everything all up, I suppose. Sure."

He was sore all day. We didn't do any work. Jack just moved around a little to loosen up. He shadow-boxed a few rounds. He didn't even look good doing that. He skipped the rope a little while. He couldn't sweat.

"He'd be better not to do any work at all," Hogan said. We were standing watching him skip rope. "Don't he ever sweat at all any more?"

"He can't sweat."

"Do you suppose he's got the con? He never had any trouble making weight, did he?"

"No, he hasn't got any con. He just hasn't got anything inside any more."

"He ought to sweat," said Hogan.

Jack came over, skipping the rope. He was skipping up and down in front of us, forward and back, crossing his arms every third time.

"Well," he says. "What are you buzzards talking about?"

"I don't think you ought to work any more," Hogan says. "You'll be stale."

"Wouldn't that be awful?" Jack says and skips away down the floor, slapping the rope hard.

That afternoon John Collins showed up out at the farm. Jack was up in his room. John came out in a car from town.

He had a couple of friends with him. The car stopped and they all got out. "Where's Jack?" John asked me.

"Up in his room, lying down."

"Lying down?"

"Yes," I said.

"How is he?"

I looked at the two fellows that were with John.

"They're friends of his," John said.

"He's pretty bad," I said.

"What's the matter with him?"

"He don't sleep."

"Hell," said John. "That Irishman could never sleep."

"He isn't right," I said.

"Hell," John said. "He's never right. I've had him for ten years and he's never been right yet."

The fellows who were with him laughed.

"I want you to shake hands with Mr. Morgan and Mr. Steinfelt," John said. "This is Mr. Doyle. He's been training Jack."

"Glad to meet you," I said.

"Let's go up and see the boy," the fellow called Morgan said.

"Let's have a look at him," Steinfelt said.

We all went upstairs.

"Where's Hogan?" John asked.

"He's out in the barn with a couple of his customers," I said.

"He got many people out here now?" John asked.

"Just two."

"Pretty quiet, ain't it?" Morgan said.

"Yes," I said. "It's pretty quiet."

We were outside Jack's room. John knocked on the door.

There wasn't any answer.

"Maybe he's asleep," I said.

"What the hell's he sleeping in the daytime for?"

John turned the handle and we all went in. Jack was lying asleep on the bed. He was face down and his face was in the pillow. Both his arms were around the pillow.

"Hey, Jack!" John said to him.

Jack's head moved a little on the pillow. "Jack!" John says, leaning over him. Jack just dug a little deeper in the pillow. John touched him on the shoulder. Jack sat up and looked at us. He hadn't shaved and he was wearing an old sweater.

"Christ! Why can't you let me sleep?" he says to John.

"Don't be sore," John says. "I didn't mean to wake you up."

"Oh no," Jack says. "Of course not."

"You know Morgan and Steinfelt," John said.

"Glad to see you," Jack says.

"How do you feel, Jack," Morgan asks him.

"Fine," Jack says. "How the hell would I feel?"

"You look fine," Steinfelt says.

"Yes, don't I," says Jack. "Say," he says to John. "You're my manager. You get a big enough cut. Why the hell don't you come out here when the reporters was out! You want Jerry and me to talk to them?"

"I had Lew fighting in Philadelphia," John said.

"What the hell's that to me?" Jack says. "You're my manager. You get a big enough cut, don't you? You aren't making me any money in Philadelphia, are you? Why the hell aren't you out here when I ought to have you?"

"Hogan was here."

"Hogan," Jack says. "Hogan's as dumb as I am."

"Soldier Bahtlett was out here wukking with you for a while, wasn't he?" Steinfelt said to change the subject.

"Yes, he was out here," Jack says. "He was out here all right."

"Say, Jerry," John said to me. "Would you go and find Hogan and tell him we want to see him in about half an hour?"

"Sure," I said.

"Why the hell can't he stick around?" Jack says. "Stick around, Jerry."

Morgan and Steinfelt looked at each other.

"Quiet down, Jack," John said to him.

"I better go find Hogan," I said.

"All right, if you want to go," Jack says. "None of these guys are going to send you away, though."

"I'll go find Hogan," I said.

Hogan was out in the gym in the barn. He had a couple of his health-farm patients with the gloves on. They neither one wanted to hit the other, for fear the other would come back and hit him.

"That'll do," Hogan said when he saw me come in. "You can stop the slaughter. You gentlemen take a shower and Bruce will rub you down."

They climbed out through the ropes and Hogan came over to me.

"John Collins is out with a couple of friends to see Jack," I said.

"I saw them come up in the car."

"Who are the two fellows with John?"

"They're what you call wise boys," Hogan said. "Don't you know them two?"

"No," I said.

"That's Happy Steinfelt and Lew Morgan. They got a poolroom."

"I been away a long time," I said.

"Sure," said Hogan. "That Happy Steinfelt's a big operator."

"I've heard his name," I said.

"He's a pretty smooth boy," Hogan said. "They're a couple of sharpshooters."

"Well," I said. "They want to see us in half an hour."

"You mean they don't want to see us until a half an hour?"

"That's it."

"Come on in the office," Hogan said. "To hell with those sharpshooters."

After about thirty minutes or so Hogan and I went upstairs. We knocked on Jack's door. They were talking inside the room.

"Wait a minute," somebody said.

"To hell with that stuff," Hogan said. "When you want to see me I'm down in the office."

We heard the door unlock. Steinfelt opened it.

"Come on in, Hogan," he says. "We're all going to have a drink."

"Well," says Hogan. "That's something."

We went in. Jack was sitting on the bed. John and Morgan were sitting on a couple of chairs. Steinfelt was standing up.

"You're a pretty mysterious lot of boys," Hogan said.

"Hello, Danny," John says.

"Hello, Danny," Morgan says and shakes hands.

Jack doesn't say anything. He just sits there on the bed. He ain't with the others. He's all by himself. He was wearing an old blue jersey and pants and had on boxing shoes. He needed a shave. Steinfelt and Morgan were dressers. John was quite a dresser too. Jack sat there looking Irish and tough.

Steinfelt brought out a bottle and Hogan brought in some glasses and everybody had a drink. Jack and I took one and the rest of them went on and had two or three each.

"Better save some for your ride back," Hogan said.

"Don't you worry. We got plenty," Morgan said.

Jack hadn't drunk anything since the one drink. He was standing up and looking at them. Morgan was sitting on the bed where Jack had sat.

"Have a drink, Jack," John said and handed him the glass and the bottle.

"No," Jack said, "I never liked to go to these wakes."

They all laughed. Jack didn't laugh.

They were all feeling pretty good when they left. Jack stood on the porch when they got into the car. They waved to him.

"So long," Jack said.

We had supper. Jack didn't say anything all during the meal except, "Will you pass me this?" or "Will you pass me that?" The two health-farm patients ate at the same table with us. They were pretty nice fellows. After we finished eating we went out on the porch. It was dark early.

"Like to take a walk, Jerry?" Jack asked.

"Sure," I said.

We put on our coats and started out. It was quite a way down to the main road and then we walked along the main road about a mile and a half. Cars kept going by and we would pull out to the side until they were past. Jack didn't say anything. After we had stepped out into the bushes to let a big car go by Jack said, "To hell with this walking. Come on back to Hogan's."

We went along a side road that cut up over the hill and cut across the fields back to Hogan's. We could see the lights of the house up on the hill. We came around to the front of the house and there standing in the doorway was Hogan.

"Have a good walk?" Hogan asked.

"Oh, fine," Jack said. "Listen, Hogan. Have you got any liquor?"

"Sure," says Hogan. "What's the idea?"

"Send it up to the room," Jack says. "I'm going to sleep tonight."

"You're the doctor," Hogan says.

"Come on up to the room, Jerry," Jack says.

Upstairs Jack sat on the bed with his head in his hands.

"Ain't it a life?" Jack says.

Hogan brought in a quart of liquor and two glasses.

"Want some ginger ale?"

"What do you think I want to do, get sick?"

"I just asked you," said Hogan.

"Have a drink?" said Jack.

"No, thanks," said Hogan. He went out.

"How about you, Jerry?"

"I'll have one with you," I said.

Jack poured out a couple of drinks. "Now," he said, "I want to take it slow and easy."

"Put some water in it," I said.

"Yes," Jack said. "I guess that's better."

We had a couple of drinks without saying anything. Jack started to pour me another.

"No," I said, "that's all I want."

"All right," Jack said. He poured himself out another big shot and put water in it. He was lighting up a little.

"That was a fine bunch out here this afternoon," he said. "They don't take any chances, those two."

Then a little later, "Well," he says, "they're right. What the hell's the good in taking chances?"

"Don't you want another, Jerry?" he said. "Come on, drink along with me."

"I don't need it, Jack," I said. "I feel all right."

"Just have one more," Jack said. It was softening him up.

"All right," I said.

Jack poured one for me and another big one for himself.

"You know," he said, "I like liquor pretty well. If I hadn't been boxing I would have drunk quite a lot."

"Sure," I said.

"You know," he said, "I missed a lot, boxing."

"You made plenty of money."

"Sure, that's what I'm after. You know I miss a lot, Jerry."

"How do you mean?"

"Well," he says, "like about the wife. And being away from home so much. It don't do my girls any good. 'Who's your old man?' some of those society kids'll say to them. 'My old man's Jack Brennan.' That don't do them any good."

"Hell," I said, "all that makes a difference is if they got dough."

"Well," says Jack, "I got the dough for them all right."[5]

He poured out another drink. The bottle was about empty.

"Put some water in it," I said. Jack poured in some water.

"You know," he says, "you ain't got any idea how I miss the wife."

"Sure."

"You ain't got any idea. You can't have an idea what it's like."

"It ought to be better out in the country than in town."

"With me now," Jack said, "it don't make any difference where I am. You can't have an idea what it's like."

"Have another drink."

"Am I getting soused? Do I talk funny?"

"You're coming on all right."

"You can't have an idea what it's like. They ain't anybody can have an idea what it's like."

"Except the wife," I said.

"She knows," Jack said. "She knows all right. She knows. You bet she knows."

"Put some water in that," I said.

"Jerry," says Jack, "you can't have an idea what it gets to be like.',

He was good and drunk. He was looking at me steady. His eyes were sort of too steady.

"You'll sleep all right," I said.

"Listen, Jerry," Jack says. "You want to make some money? Get some money down on Walcott."

"Yes?"

"Listen, Jerry," Jack put down the glass. "I'm not drunk now, see? You know what I'm betting on him? Fifty grand."

"That's a lot of dough."

"Fifty grand," Jack says, "at two to one. I'll get twenty-five thousand bucks. Get some money on him, Jerry."

"It sounds good," I said.

"How can I beat him?" Jack says. "It ain't crooked. How can I beat him? Why not make money on it?"

"Put some water in that," I said.

"I'm through after this fight," Jack says. "I'm through with it. I got to take a beating. Why shouldn't I make money on it?"[6]

"Sure."

"I ain't slept for a week," Jack says. "All night I lay awake and worry my can off. I can't sleep, Jerry. You ain't got an idea what it's like when you can't sleep."

"Sure."

"I can't sleep. That's all. I just can't sleep. What's the use of taking care of yourself all these years when you can't sleep?"

"It's bad."

"You ain't got an idea what it's like, Jerry, when you can't sleep."

"Put some water in that," I said.

Well, about eleven o'clock Jack passes out and I put him to bed. Finally he's so he can't keep from sleeping. I helped him get his clothes off and got him into bed.

"You'll sleep all right, Jack," I said.

"Sure," Jack says, "I'll sleep now."

"Good night, Jack," I said.

"Good night, Jerry," Jack says. "You're the only friend I got."

"Oh, hell," I said.

"You're the only friend I got," Jack says, "the only friend I got."

"Go to sleep," I said.

"I'll sleep," Jack says.

Downstairs Hogan was sitting at the desk in the office reading the papers. He looked up. "Well, you get your boy friend to sleep?" he asks.

"He's off."

"It's better for him than not sleeping," Hogan said.

"Sure."

"You'd have a hell of a time explaining that to these sport writers though," Hogan said.

"Well, I'm going to bed myself," I said.

"Good night," said Hogan.

In the morning I came downstairs about eight o'clock and got some breakfast. Hogan had his two customers out in the barn doing exercises. I went out and watched them.

"One! Two! Three! Four!" Hogan was counting for them. "Hello, Jerry," he said. "Is Jack up yet?"

"No. He's still sleeping."

I went back to my room and packed up to go in to town. About nine-thirty I heard Jack getting up in the next room. When I heard him go downstairs I went down after him. Jack was sitting at the breakfast table. Hogan had come in and was standing beside the table.

"How do you feel, Jack?" I asked him.

"Not so bad."

"Sleep well?" Hogan asked.

"I slept all right," Jack said. "I got a thick tongue but I ain't got a head."

"Good," said Hogan. "That was good liquor."

"Put it on the bill," Jack says.

"What time you want to go into town?" Hogan asked.

"Before lunch," Jack says. "The eleven o'clock train."

"Sit down, Jerry," Jack said. Hogan went out.

I sat down at the table. Jack was eating a grapefruit. When he'd find a seed he'd spit it out in the spoon and dump it on the plate.

"I guess I was pretty stewed last night," he started.

"You drank some liquor."

"I guess I said a lot of fool things."

"You weren't bad."

"Where's Hogan?" he asked. He was through with the grapefruit.

"He's out in front in the office."

"What did I say about betting on the fight?" Jack asked. He was holding the spoon and sort of poking at the grapefruit with it.

The girl came in with some ham and eggs and took away the grapefruit.

"Bring me another glass of milk," Jack said to her. She went out.

"You said you had fifty grand on Walcott," I said.

"That's right," Jack said.

"That's a lot of money."

"I don't feel too good about it," Jack said.

"Something might happen."

"No," Jack said. "He wants the title bad. They'll be shooting with him all right."

"You can't ever tell."

"No. He wants the title. It's worth a lot of money to him."

"Fifty grand is a lot of money," I said.

"It's business," said Jack. "I can't win. You know I can't win any-way."

"As long as you're in there you got a chance."

"No," Jack says. "I'm all through. It's just business."

"How do you feel?"

"Pretty good," Jack said. "The sleep was what I needed."

"You might go good."

"I'll give them a good show," Jack said.

After breakfast Jack called up his wife on the long-distance. He was inside the booth telephoning.

"That's the first time he's called her up since he's out here," Hogan said.

"He writes her every day."

"Sure," Hogan says, "a letter only costs two cents."

Hogan said good-by to us and Bruce, the nigger rubber, drove us down to the train in the cart.

"Good-by, Mr. Brennan," Bruce said at the train, "I sure hope you knock his can off."

"So long," Jack said. He gave Bruce two dollars. Bruce had worked on him a lot. He looked kind of disappointed. Jack saw me looking at Bruce holding the two dollars.

"It's all in the bill," he said. "Hogan charged me for the rubbing."

On the train going into town Jack didn't talk. He sat in the corner of the seat with his ticket in his hat-band and looked out of the window. Once he turned and spoke to me.

"I told the wife I'd take a room at the Shelby tonight," he said. "It's just around the corner from the Garden. I can go up to the house tomorrow morning."

"That's a good idea," I said. "Your wife ever see you fight, Jack?"

"No," Jack says. "She never seen me fight."

I thought he must be figuring on taking an awful beating if he doesn't want to go home afterward. In town we took a taxi up to the Shelby. A boy came out and took our bags and we went in to the desk.

"How much are the rooms?" Jack asked.

"We only have double rooms," the clerk says. "I can give you a nice double room for ten dollars."

"That's too steep."

"I can give you a double room for seven dollars."

"With a bath?"

"Certainly."

"You might as well bunk with me, Jerry," Jack says.

"Oh," I said, "I'll sleep down at my brother-in-law's."

"I don't mean for you to pay it," Jack says. "I just want to get my money's worth."

"Will you register, please?" the clerk says. He looked at the names. "Number 238, Mister Brennan."

We went up in the elevator. It was a nice big room with two beds and a door opening into a bath-room.

"This is pretty good," Jack says.

The boy who brought us up pulled up the curtains and brought in our bags. Jack didn't make any move, so I gave the boy a quarter. We washed up and Jack said we better go out and get something to eat.

We ate a lunch at Jimmy Hanley's place. Quite a lot of the boys were there. When we were about half through eating, John came in and sat down with us. Jack didn't talk much.

"How are you on the weight, Jack?" John asked him. Jack was putting away a pretty good lunch.

"I could make it with my clothes on," Jack said. He never had to worry about taking off weight. He was a natural welterweight and he'd never gotten fat. He'd lost weight out at Hogan's.

"Well, that's one thing you never had to worry about," John said.

"That's one thing," Jack says.

We went around to the Garden to weigh in after lunch. The match was made at a hundred forty-seven pounds at three o'clock. Jack stepped on the scales with a towel around him. The bar didn't move. Walcott had just weighed and was standing with a lot of people around him.

"Let's see what you weigh, Jack," Freedman, Walcott's manager said.

"All right, weigh *him* then," Jack jerked his head toward Walcott.

"Drop the towel," Freedman said.

"What do you make it?" Jack asked the fellows who were weighing.

"One hundred and forty-three pounds," the fat man who was weighing said.

"You're down fine, Jack," Freedman says.

"Weigh him," Jack says.

Walcott came over. He was a blond with wide shoulders and arms like a heavyweight. He didn't have much legs. Jack stood about half a head taller than he did.

"Hello, Jack," he said. His face was plenty marked up.

"Hello," said Jack. "How you feel?"

"Good," Walcott says. He dropped the towel from around his waist and stood on the scales. He had the widest shoulders and back you ever saw.

"One hundred and forty-six pounds and twelve ounces."

Walcott stepped off and grinned at Jack.

"Well," John says to him, "Jack's spotting you about four pounds."

"More than that when I come in, kid," Walcott says. "I'm going to go and eat now."

We went back and Jack got dressed. "He's a pretty tough-looking boy," Jack says to me.

"He looks as though he'd been hit plenty of times."

"Oh, yes," Jack says. "He ain't hard to hit."

"Where are you going?" John asked when Jack was dressed.

"Back to the hotel," Jack says. "You looked after everything?"

"Yes," John says. "It's all looked after."

"I'm going to lie down a while," Jack says.

"I'll come around for you about a quarter to seven and we'll go and eat."

"All right."

Up at the hotel Jack took off his shoes and his coat and lay down for a while. I wrote a letter. I looked over a couple of times and Jack wasn't sleeping. He was lying perfectly still but every once in a while his eyes would open. Finally he sits up.

"Want to play some cribbage, Jerry ?" he says.

"Sure," I said.

He went over to his suitcase and got out the cards and the cribbage board. We played cribbage and he won three dollars off me. John knocked at the door and came in.

"Want to play some cribbage, John?" Jack asked him.

John put his hat down on the table. It was all wet. His coat was wet too.

"Is it raining?" Jack asks.

"It's pouring," John says. "The taxi I had got tied up in the traffic and I got out and walked."

"Come on, play some cribbage," Jack says.

"You ought to go and eat."

"No," says Jack. "I don't want to eat yet."

So they played cribbage for about half an hour and Jack won a dollar and a half off him.

"Well, I suppose we got to go eat," Jack says. He went to the window and looked out.

"Is it still raining?"

"Yes."

"Let's eat in the hotel," John says.

"All right," Jack says, "I'll play you once more to see who pays for the meal."

After a little while Jack gets up and says, "You buy the meal, John," and we went downstairs and ate in the big dining room.

After we ate we went upstairs and Jack played cribbage with John again and won two dollars and a half off him. Jack was feeling pretty good. John had a bag with him with all his stuff in it. Jack took off his shirt and collar and put on a jersey and a sweater, so he wouldn't catch cold when he came out, and put his ring clothes and his bathrobe in a bag.

"You all ready?" John asks him. "I'll call up and have them get a taxi."

Pretty soon the telephone rang and they said the taxi was waiting.

We rode down in the elevator and went out through the lobby, and got in a taxi and rode around to the Garden. It was raining hard but there was a lot of people outside on the streets. The Garden was sold out. As we came in on our way to the dressing-room I saw how full it was. It looked like half a mile down to the ring. It was all dark. Just the lights over the ring.

"It's a good thing, with this rain, they didn't try and pull this fight in the ball park," John said.

"They got a good crowd," Jack says.

"This is a fight that would draw a lot more than the Garden could hold."

"You can't tell about the weather," Jack says.

John came to the door of the dressing-room and poked his head in. Jack was sitting there with his bathrobe on, he had his arms folded and was looking at the floor. John had a couple of handlers with him. They looked over his shoulder. Jack looked up.

"Is he in?" he asked.

"He's just gone down," John said.

We started down. Walcott was just getting into the ring. The crowd gave him a big hand. He climbed through between the ropes and put his two fists together and smiled, and shook them at the crowd, first at one side of the ring, then at the other, and then sat down. Jack got a good hand coming down through the crowd. Jack is Irish and the Irish always get a pretty good hand. An Irishman don't draw in New York like a Jew or an Italian but they always get a good hand. Jack climbed up and bent down to go through the ropes and Walcott came over from his corner and pushed the rope down for Jack to go through. The crowd thought that was wonderful. Walcott put his hand on Jack's shoulder and they stood there just for a second.

"So you're going to be one of these popular champions," Jack says to him. "Take your goddam hand off my shoulder."

"Be yourself," Walcott says.

This is all great for the crowd. How gentlemanly the boys are before the fight. How they wish each other luck.

Solly Freedman came over to our corner while Jack is bandaging his hands and John is over in Walcott's corner. Jack puts his thumb through the slit in the bandage and then wrapped his hand nice and smooth. I taped it around the wrist and twice across the knuckles.

"Hey," Freedman says. "Where do you get all that tape?"

"Feel of it," Jack says. "It's soft, ain't it? Don't be a hick."

Freedman stands there all the time while Jack bandages the other hand, and one of the boys that's going to handle him brings the gloves and I pull them on and work them around.

"Say, Freedman," Jack asks, "what nationality is this Walcott?"

"I don't know," Solly says. "He's some sort of a Dane."

"He's a Bohemian," the lad who brought the gloves said.

The referee called them out to the center of the ring and Jack walks out. Walcott comes out smiling. They met and the referee put his arm on each of their shoulders.

"Hello, popularity," Jack says to Walcott.

"Be yourself."

"What do you call yourself 'Walcott' for?" Jack says. "Didn't you know he was a nigger?"

"Listen—" says the referee, and he gives them the same old line. Once Walcott interrupts him. He grabs Jack's arm and says, "Can I hit when he's got me like this?"

"Keep your hands off me," Jack says. "There ain't no moving-pictures of this."

They went back to their corners. I lifted the bathrobe off Jack and he leaned on the ropes and flexed his knees a couple of times and scuffed his shoes in the rosin. The gong rang and Jack turned quick and went out. Walcott came toward him and they touched gloves and as soon as Walcott dropped his hands Jack jumped his left into his face twice. There wasn't anybody ever boxed better than Jack. Walcott was after him, going forward all the time with his chin on his chest. He's a hooker and he carries his hands pretty low. All he knows is to get in there and sock. But every time he gets in there close, Jack has the left hand in his face. It's just as though it's automatic. Jack just raises the left hand up and it's in Walcott's face. Three or four times Jack brings the right over but Walcott gets it on the shoulder or high up on the head. He's just like all these hookers. The only thing he's afraid of is another one of the same kind. He's covered everywhere you can hurt him. He don't care about a left-hand in his face.

After about four rounds Jack has him bleeding bad and his face all cut up, but every time Walcott's got in close he's socked so hard he's got two big red patches on both sides just below Jack's ribs. Every time he gets in close, Jack ties him up, then gets one hand loose and uppercuts him, but when Walcott gets his hands loose he socks Jack in the body so they can hear it outside in the street. He's a socker.

It goes along like that for three rounds more. They don't talk any. They're working all the time. We worked over Jack plenty too, in between the rounds. He don't look good at all but he never does much work in the ring. He don't move around much and that left-hand is just automatic. It's just like it was connected with Walcott's face and Jack just had to wish it in every time.[7] Jack is always calm in close and he doesn't waste any juice. He knows everything about working in close too and he's getting away with a lot of stuff. While they were in our corner I watched him tie Walcott up, get his right hand loose, turn it and come up with an uppercut that got Walcott's nose with the heel of the glove. Walcott was bleeding bad and leaned his nose on Jack's shoulder so as to give Jack some of it too, and Jack sort of lifted his shoulder sharp and caught him against the nose, and then brought down the right hand and did the same thing again.

Walcott was sore as hell. By the time they'd gone five rounds he hated Jack's guts. Jack wasn't sore; that is, he wasn't any sorer than he always was. He certainly did used to make the fellows he fought hate boxing. That was why he hated Kid Lewis so. He never got the Kid's goat. Kid Lewis always had about three new dirty things Jack couldn't do. Jack was as safe as a church all the time he was in there, as long as he was strong. He certainly was treating Walcott rough. The funny thing was it looked as though Jack was an open classic boxer. That was because he had all that stuff too.

After the seventh round Jack says, "My left's getting heavy."

From then he started to take a beating. It didn't show at first. But instead of him running the fight it was Walcott was running it, instead of being safe all the time now he was in trouble. He couldn't keep him out with the left hand now. It looked as though it was the same as ever, only now instead of Walcott's punches just missing him they were just hitting him. He took an awful beating in the body.

"What's the round?" Jack asked.

"The eleventh."

"I can't stay," Jack says. "My legs are going bad."

Walcott had been just hitting him for a long time. It was like a baseball catcher pulls the ball and takes some of the shock off. From now on Walcott commenced to land solid. He certainly was a socking-machine. Jack was just trying to block everything now. It didn't show what an awful beating he was taking. In between the rounds I worked on his legs. The muscles would flutter under my hands all the time I was rubbing them. He was sick as hell.

"How's it go?" he asked John, turning around, his face all swollen.

"It's his fight."

"I think I can last," Jack says. "I don't want this bohunk[8] to stop me."

It was going just the way he thought it would. He knew he couldn't beat Walcott. He wasn't strong any more. He was all right though. His money was all right and now he wanted to finish it off right to please himself. He didn't want to be knocked out.[9]

The gong rang and we pushed him out. He went out slow. Walcott came right out after him. Jack put the left in his face and Walcott took it, came in under it and started working on Jack's body. Jack tried to tie him up and it was just like trying to hold on to a buzz-saw. Jack broke away from it and missed with the right. Walcott clipped him with a left-hook and Jack went down. He went down on his hands and knees and looked at us. The referee started counting. Jack was watching us and shaking his head. At eight John motioned to him. You couldn't hear on account of the crowd. Jack got up. The referee had been holding Walcott back with one arm while he counted.

When Jack was on his feet Walcott started toward him.

"Watch yourself, Jimmy," I heard Solly Freedman yell to him.

Walcott came up to Jack looking at him. Jack stuck the left hand at him. Walcott just shook his head. He backed Jack up against the ropes, measured him and then hooked the left very light to the side of Jack's head and socked the right into the body as hard as he could sock, just as low as he could get it. He must have hit him five inches below the belt. I thought the eyes would come out of Jack's head. They stuck way out. His mouth come open.

The referee grabbed Walcott. Jack stepped forward. If he went down there went fifty thousand bucks.[10] He walked as though all his insides were going to fall out.

"It wasn't low," he said. "It was a accident."

The crowd were yelling so you couldn't hear anything.

"I'm all right," Jack says. They were right in front of us. The referee looks at John and then he shakes his head.

"Come on, you polak son-of-a-bitch," Jack says to Walcott.

John was hanging onto the ropes. He had the towel ready to chuck in. Jack was standing just a little way out from the ropes. He took a step forward. I saw the sweat come out on his face like somebody had squeezed it and a big drop went down his nose.

"Come on and fight," Jack says to Walcott.

The referee looked at John and waved Walcott on.

"Go in there, you slob," he says.

Walcott went in. He didn't know what to do either. He never thought Jack could have stood it. Jack put the left in his face. There was such a hell of a lot of yelling going on. They were right in front of us. Walcott hit him twice. Jack's face was the worst thing I ever saw—the look on it! He was holding himself and all his body together and it all showed on his face. All the time he was thinking and holding his body in where it was busted.

Then he started to sock. His face looked awful all the time. He started to sock with his hands low down by his side, swinging at Walcott. Walcott covered up and Jack was swinging wild at Walcott's head. Then he swung the left and it hit Walcott in the groin and the right hit Walcott right bang where he'd hit Jack. Way low below the belt. Walcott went down and grabbed himself there and rolled and twisted around.

The referee grabbed Jack and pushed him toward his corner. John jumps into the ring. There was all this yelling going on. The referee was talking with the judges and then the announcer got into the ring with the megaphone and says, "Walcott on a foul."[11]

The referee is talking to John and he says, "What could I do? Jack wouldn't take the foul. Then when he's groggy he fouls him."

"He'd lost it anyway," John says.

Jack's sitting on the chair. I've got his gloves off and he's holding himself in down there with both hands. When he's got something supporting it his face doesn't look so bad.

"Go over and say you're sorry," John says into his ear. "It'll look good."

Jack stands up and the sweat comes out all over his face. I put the bathrobe around him and he holds himself in with one hand under the bathrobe and goes across the ring. They've picked Walcott up and they're working on him. There're a lot of people in Walcott's corner. Nobody speaks to Jack. He leans over Walcott.

"I'm sorry," Jack says. "I didn't mean to foul you."

Walcott doesn't say anything. He looks too damned sick.

"Well, you're the champion now," Jack says to him. "I hope you get a hell of a lot of fun out of it."

"Leave the kid alone," Solly Freedman says.

"Hello, Solly," Jack says. "I'm sorry I fouled your boy."

Freedman just looks at him.

Jack went to his corner walking that funny jerky way and we got him down through the ropes and through the reporters' tables and out down the aisle. A lot of people want to slap Jack on the back. He goes out through all that mob in his bathrobe to the dressing-room. It's a popular win for Walcott. That's the way the money was bet in the Garden.

Once we got inside the dressing-room Jack lay down and shut his eyes.

"We want to get to the hotel and get a doctor," John says.

"I'm all busted inside," Jack says.

"I'm sorry as hell, Jack," John says.

"It's all right," Jack says.

He lies there with his eyes shut.

"They certainly tried a nice double-cross," John said.

"Your friends Morgan and Steinfelt," Jack said. "You got nice friends."

He lies there, his eyes are open now. His face has still got that awful drawn look.

"It's funny how fast you can think when it means that much money," Jack says.

"You're some boy, Jack," John says.

"No," Jack says. "It was nothing."

NOTES
by John Schultheiss

[1] Jack Brennan has just called Ted Lewis a "kike," a term which for Jack has nothing to do with ethnicity, but points instead to Lewis's propensity to fight dirty in the ring. Susan F. Beegel explains, in her analysis of the original typescript of the story, Jack's "unique attitudes toward ethnicity":

> The deleted opening elaborates on Jack's original use of ethnic slurs. Kid Lewis, a dirty fighter Jack detests, is a "kike," although Lewis is a gentile name. Benny Leonard, a Jewish boxer Jack admires, is "no kike," but "a Jewish boy" and "a damn fine fighter." The omitted lines about Leonard, Lewis, and "kikes" explain why later in the published version Jack taunts the blond, blue-eyed, and possibly Danish Walcott by calling him a "nigger" and a "polak." In the deleted opening, Hemingway has established Jack Brennan as a man who uses racist language without bigotry.
> [Susan F. Beegel, *Hemingway's Craft of Omission: Four Manuscript Examples* (Ann Arbor: UMI Research, 1988).]

[2] Earl Sande, a famous jockey of the era.

[3] Everybody's got to get it sometime. Everyone loses. It is *how* that matters. "If life must beat you, there is nothing 'unethical' about getting some small consideration for participating in the game which can only go against you." Jack Brennan ultimately exhibits the same resignation as the World War I soldier, and it is this feeling that pushes him to fix the fight—as long as he is going to be badly beaten, he says, he ought to be well paid. [James J. Martine, "Hemingway's 'Fifty Grand': The Other Fight(s)," in *The Short Stories of Ernest Hemingway: Critical Essays*. Edited by Jackson J. Benson. (Durham: Duke University Press, 1975), pp. 198-203.]

[4] Jess Willard, world heavyweight champion, was defeated by Jack Dempsey in Toledo, Ohio in 1919. Lardner is Ring Lardner, a famous sportswriter of the day, a writer of short stories (including "Champion," one of the most famous boxing tales in American literature), a columnist, and a father of two writer sons (including Ring Lardner, Jr., one of the so-called "Hollywood Ten.")

[5] It is during Jack's drunken conversation with Jerry that we see his hopes for his daughters. He knows that the next day will be his last as a boxer, and we see him assessing the cost of the profession he has pursued. Jack's glum resignation makes clear that the money alone is no longer enough. He realizes that the "dough" is a poor substitute for something, but he cannot quite imagine what that something might be. He knows that his daughters will not fit in with the society girls, no matter how much money he makes, and he has been absent from much of their lives. As in the conversation revolving around moral distinctions, Jerry is too ob-

tuse to understand what Jack is driving at. The only yardstick Jerry understands is money.

(David Thoreen, "Poor Ernest's Almanac: The Petty Economies of 'Fifty Grand's' Jack Brennan," in *The Hemingway Review*, Vol. 13, No. 2, Spring 1994, pp. 31-32.)

[6]Many critics have maintained that Jack Brennan sold the fight—that, prior to the bout, he arranged with the gamblers Morgan and Steinfelt to lose intentionally so that he might win his bet. This notion derives from the secret meeting between the boxer and the gamblers who visit the champ's training camp the day before his title bout with Walcott. Jerry Doyle brings the gamblers to Jack's room and then is asked to leave; consequently, neither Doyle nor we witness whatever deal transpired between Jack and the gamblers. Many readers assume that, during this meeting, Jack agrees to lose to Walcott on purpose.

However, neither Brennan's comments after that meeting (referenced here) nor his actions in the boxing ring suggest that he fixes the title fight. Indeed, the discussion between Brennan and Doyle after the gamblers have left suggests otherwise. Brennan does advise Doyle to bet on Walcott, and Brennan does inform Doyle that he has bet fifty grand on the challenger, at two-to-one odds. But Brennan denies fixing the fight. "'How can I beat him?' Jack asks Jerry. 'It ain't crooked. How can I beat him? Why not make some money on it?'"

Brennan is out of shape, over the hill; this fight will be his last. He has not trained well and has slept poorly. He knows that Walcott will defeat him soundly. Jack has assessed his chances for victory honestly and has decided that he cannot win. So, he bets against himself, but he does not agree to lose the fight on purpose.

(See subsequent notes.)

[7]During his bout with Walcott, Brennan certainly does not fight like a boxer who intends to lose on purpose. After four rounds, "Jack has him bleeding bad and his face all cut up." Any of those hard left jabs to the face is a potential knockout punch. A man of great integrity, Brennan is trying very hard to win this fight, even though he will lose $50,000 if he beats Walcott.

[8]An opprobrious term for a person of Slavic descent.

[9]Brennan, as expected, begins to tire in the late rounds. The younger Walcott begins to pommel him badly. By the twelfth and final round, Brennan can barely walk, but he refuses to quit; he intends to avoid a knockout, finish the fight, and win his bet.

[10]The fix becomes apparent in the final round, but it is Walcott's fix, not Brennan's. Walcott intentionally fouls Brennan with a low blow. If Brennan falls and is unable to continue, Walcott is disqualified, and Brennan wins the fight but loses his bet.

When Hemingway wrote this story, the rules of boxing stated that, in the case of a low blow—below the belt—the attacker is to be penalized or disqualified, even if it might be accidental. Later, fighters were required to wear protective devices, and the rules were changed to minimize the penalty for fouls. While a low blow can still cost a fighter the loss of a round, the foul is no longer the basis of a decision.

[11]Quickly sensing the fix, and seeing his fifty grand slipping away, Brennan courageously remains standing, despite incredible pain, and waves away the referee. In the next exchange, Brennan belts Walcott twice in the groin, and Walcott falls to the canvas. Brennan is disqualified for the low blows, and Walcott is declared the winner.

In the end, Brennan did throw the fight, but he made that decision in the middle of the final round, not during the pre-fight meeting with Steinfelt and Morgan. During the fight, Brennan maintains his integrity; he fights to win, even though winning would cost him fifty grand.

(See James Tackach, "Whose Fix Is It, Anyway?: A Closer Look at Hemingway's 'Fifty Grand,'" *The Hemingway Review*, Spring 2000, Vol. 19, No. 2, pp. 113-117.)

Analogously, it could be asserted that Charley Davis in *Body and Soul* had *not* planned to defeat his opponent in an effort to achieve moral redemption; or because he wants to assert (pace Shimin the grocer) Jewish pride in the face of Nazi genocide; or because of feelings of guilt over the fate of Ben Chaplin—interpretations which are all circumscribed by the generalized assumption that Charley experienced some sort of afflatus of moral conscience or social responsibility. On the contrary, like Jack Brennan, it is only after he is betrayed in the ring, in the final stages of the bout, that Charley defeats Marlowe as an act of **existential revenge**. (See Abraham Polonsky's comments in Screenplay Annotation #23: "Charley Davis makes this difficult judgment not out of moral reasons, but simply because he's betrayed. He's not doing it for the good of boxing; he's doing it because they double-crossed him, and he answered back by taking his revenge.")

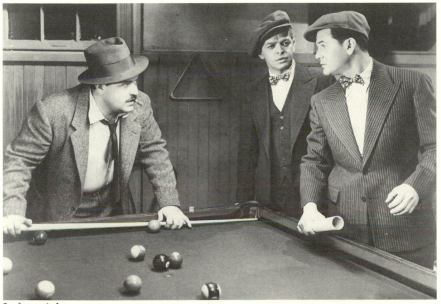

Left to right:
Quinn (William Conrad), Shorty (Joseph Pevney), Charley Davis (John Garfield)

The Great Depression Years. "That world of want, poor New York Jews, the Enlightenment, and Utopian Socialism, the Life of Reason haunting the glorious future, was the heart of *Body and Soul*. It is Romance with Rebellion. Clifford Odets, of course, was an electric part of this literary movement, and his plays were their enchanting vision, but Garfield was the star for the whole world, the romantic Rebel himself."

—Abraham Polonsky

Left to right:
Anna Davis (Anne Revere), Shorty (Joseph Pevney), Charley Davis (John Garfield)

The Sell-Out. "The exclusive worship of the bitch-goddess SUCCESS is our national disease" (William James)—our culture teaches us to shape our lives in accordance with the hunger for worldly things; on the other hand, a contempt for success is the consensus of the national literature for the past hundred years or more.

> SHORTY: "You know what Charley is, what they're making him: a money machine—like gold mines, oil wells, ten percent of the U.S. mint. They're cutting him up a million ways."

Film as Literature:
The Bitch Goddess and the Blacklist

by John Schultheiss

The habit of creation, that intellectual maternity which is so difficult to acquire, is remarkably easy to lose. Inspiration gives genius its opportunity. It runs, not on a razor's edge, but on the very air and takes wing with the quick alarm of a crow. It wears no scarf that the poet can grasp; its hair is a flame; it flies away like those beautiful pink and white flamingoes that are the despair of huntsmen. So work is a wearing struggle that is both feared and loved by the fine and powerful constitutions that are often shattered by it. A great poet of our own day said, speaking of this appalling toil, "I begin it with despair and leave it with sorrow."

—Honoré de Balzac,
Cousin Bette (1846)

"He had two hits running on Broadway at the same time. Even Nathan liked 'em. Popular 'n satirical. Like Barry, only better. The critics kept waiting for him to write that great American play."
"What happened to him?"
"Hollywood."

—Budd Schulberg,
The Disenchanted (1950)

Half-idealism is the peritonitis of the soul.

—Clifford Odets,
The Big Knife (1949)

"I didn't have enough strength to resist corruption but I was strong enough to fight for a piece of it."

—Abraham Polonsky,
Force of Evil (1948)

CHARLEY

Here. . . take the money, Ben. It's not like people.
It got no memory. . . it don't think.

BEN

Did you sell the fight, Charley?

—Abraham Polonsky,
Body and Soul (1947)

The Sell-Out. A major theme of art and politics--of literature, of film, of life itself: bartering away moral principle for money, job security, power , and status. "Selling out"—a conceit or process which always seems to connote deep ethical ambiguity and psychological complexity—could be *personal* by the corruption of one's own literary or artistic talent, or it could be *political* by the betrayal of others.

Here is a straightforward expression of this phenomenon from the world of fiction, in the persona of the dying writer Harry, in Ernest Hemingway's "The Snows of Kilimanjaro": "He had destroyed his talent by not using it, by betayals of himself and what he believed in, by drinking so much that he blunted the edge of his perceptions, by laziness, by sloth and by snobbery, by pride and by prejudice, by hook and by crook. . . . It was a talent all right but instead of using it he had traded on it."[1]

Here is an example from real life, from the life of Robert Rossen, director of *Body and Soul*, whose appearance before the House Committee on Un-American Activities was a personal dramatization of the central conflict and moral dilemma of the film itself. During an earlier round of the HUAC hearings (25 June 1951), Rossen refused to testify about his own ostensible past membership in the Communist Party or about anybody else. Rossen said, "I didn't want to give any names, and that is what I conceived to be a moral position." He was consequently blacklisted for two years. On 7 May 1953, he testified again, and this time (unlike Charley Davis's resolution of *his* professional and moral crisis in *Body and Soul*) Rossen retailored his conception of what constituted a moral position, became a "friendly witness," and informed on 50 people. Now that he had thought the matter over for those two years, Rossen said, "I didn't think that any one individual can indulge himself in the luxury of individual morality or pit it against what I feel today very strongly is the security and safety of this nation." There was, of course, a professional dividend: the naming of names allowed his filmmaking career to resume.[2]

Betrayals of oneself, betrayals of others; betrayals portrayed in fiction, betrayals occurring in real life—the American dream, the American nightmare—this is the universe circumscribed by the "bitch goddess of success " and the blacklist.

A Brief Review of Some Pertinent Sell-Out Texts. On the artistic side of the debate there exists the potential crisis which has plagued writers and intellectuals from the first instant that creative ideas began to have monetary value. This is the enduring axiom that financial and material success tend to corrupt the talent of intellectuals and ineffably erode their will and spirit to continue the productive and inventive work which earned them success in the first place. Richard Hofstadter summarizes the problem in *Anti-Intellectualism in American Life*:

> One hears more and more that the intellectual who has won a measure of freedom and opportunity, and a new access to influence, is thereby subtly corrupted; that, having won recognition, he has lost his independence, even his identity as an intellectual. Success of a kind is sold to him at what is held to be an unbearable price. He becomes comfortable, perhaps even moderately prosperous, as he takes a position in a university or in government or working for the mass media, but he then tailors himself to the requirements of these institutions. He loses that precious tincture of rage so necessary to first-rate creativity in a writer, that capacity for negation and rebellion that is necessary to the candid social critic, that initiative and independence of aim required for distinguished work in science. It appears, then, to be the fate of intellectuals either to berate their exclusion from wealth, success, and reputation, or to be seized by guilt when they overcome this exclusion.[3]

Norman Podhoretz has written an autobiographical study of his own career, *Making It* (1967), in which he closely echoes Hofstadter's comments about the ambivalence toward success in American culture:

> My second purpose in telling the story of my own career is to provide a concrete setting for a diagnosis of the curiously contradictory feelings our culture instills in us toward the ambition for success, and toward each of its various goals: money, power, fame, and social position. On the one hand, "the exclusive worship of the bitch-goddess SUCCESS," as William James put it in a famous remark, "is our national disease;" on the other hand, a contempt for success is the consensus of the national literature for the past hundred years or more. On the one hand, our culture teaches us to shape our lives in accordance with the hunger for worldly things;

on the other hand, it spitefully contrives to make us ashamed of the presence of those hungers in ourselves and to deprive us as far as possible of any pleasure in their satisfaction.[4]

American literature, theatre, and cinema have all carried on an extended engagement with bitch-goddess SUCCESS. From **literature**, *Arrowsmith* (1925) by Sinclair Lewis is an example of a novel which deals with the temptation of the artist or the intellectual. In this work, bacteriology is a symbol for art and Dr. Martin Arrowsmith is the embattled artist. As Arrowsmith moves from obscurity to international fame, he learns that his continued success is assured if he will renounce the principle of pure research (the search for the truth of science in the world around him) and capitalize on his name. Society tends to contribute to the "corruption" process by showering acclaim on the successful artist. But Arrowsmith, significantly, decides to resist the temptations which initially triggered his entry into science (fame, money, and the love of women), to return to isolation and the search for truth.

Another literary example is useful to set the stage for a discussion below of how fact and fiction intersect in the parallel lives of Clifford Odets and Abraham Polonsky. The narrative category for these works might be called the "literature of seduction,"[5] and the novel is F. Scott Fitzgerald's *Tender Is the Night* (1934), whose protagonist could symbolize Fitzgerald himself. Together with Fitzgerald's *The Crack-Up* (1931-1945), this novel creates his version of the popular legend: the American artist, supposedly ruined by success, worn out at 30, a life with "no second act," unable to duplicate his early triumphs or to attain maturity for more profound undertakings. *Tender Is the Night*, in effect, could be read as a fictionalized account of Fitzgerald's own decline: his sudden rise to the top, the wasting of his talent, his steady alcoholic atrophy, the final years in Hollywood.[6]

In *Tender Is the Night*, as in *Arrowsmith*, science again serves as a guise for the dilemma confronting the artist, the American writer unable to endure success. Dick Diver begins his career as an idealist, but he meets Nicole Warren and by marrying her inherits both her wealth and the problem of her schizophrenia. The energy and intelligence which once had made him a promising research psychoanalyst are slowly drained away; Nicole, in recovering from her disease, has somehow infected Dick. He will die in obscurity searching for his vanished youth. Early in the novel, Nicole asks why it is that only Americans dissipate. Fitzgerald's answer in *The Crack-Up* was no different from Dick Diver's: "Material success means the end of idealism and the death of art."[7]

In *The Disenchanted* (1950), working with the fictionalized biography of Fitzgerald, Budd Schulberg is quite emphatic that a problem for the writer is *Hollywood*, but the overriding dilemma remains linked to that "problem" of SUCCESS:

> "Why must Hollywood always take the rap? Why didn't Bane have enough guts to stay with his plays?"

> "Temptation," Manley said. "That's writers in America. Your high mortality on writers, that goes on all the time in America. Y' know why? ... American idea of success. *Nothing fails like success.* Write one bestseller, one hit play, Big Success. Do one thing, get rich 'n famous. Writers get caught up in American system. Ballyhoo. Cocktail parties. Bestseller list. Worship of Success."[8]

For most of a century American authors have regularly accepted work in the movie industry, and for most of a century there have been warnings that there is no territory more dangerous for a talented writer than Hollywood. The industry's need for experienced writers mushroomed when the studios converted from silent to sound production (1927-1930), and the desire for serious writers intensified a few years later when the Depression crippled the publishing industry and the commercial theatre.

> "Once in Hollywood, within a two-mile radius you could find two-thirds of the great talent of the world. Poets and painters and philosophers. Lured here by the gold."
>
> —Ben Hecht[9]

"Selling out in Hollywood" is a phrase often used to describe the popular view that writing for Hollywood constitutes a deep betrayal (there's that word again) of a writer's talents. The inevitable result of movie employment is a diminishment of creative energy and a loss of artistic inspiration.[10]

> What shining phantom folds its wings before us?
> What apparition, smiling yet remote?
> Is this—so portly yet so highly porous—
> The old friend who went west and never wrote?[11]

As the poem implies, this sell-out issue really concerns "Eastern" writers, those whose literary origins and reputations are in *non-movie* fields, authors who had achieved or were in the early stages of achieving careers as novelists, dramatists, short story writers, poets, or critics. (The use of the term "Eastern" recognizes that the eastern seaboard, particularly New York and Boston, has traditionally symbolized America's literary establishment.)[12]

"Playwrights who go to Hollywood for any length of time seldom come back without a fatal *streptococcus septicus*."
—George Jean Nathan[13]

"The failure of writers of conscience and with natural gifts rare enough in America or anywhere to get the best out of their best years may certainly be laid partly to Hollywood, *with its already appalling record of talent depraved and wasted*."
—Edmund Wilson[14]

"There was enough brilliance and even genius in those lists of writers in Hollywood to have produced a golden age and one is inclined to ask whatever happened to it? What mattered was the fearful devouring of talent by the insatiable studios. Young writers of exceptional promise were whisked away to Hollywood and never heard from again."
—Robert E. Sherwood[15]

So was born the Hollywood-as-destroyer legend, nurtured through the years by both writers and their partisans. Novelists and playwrights of acute sensibility and talent, so the legend goes, were lured to Hollywood by offers of huge amounts of money and the promise of challenging assignments; once in the studios they were required to work on mundane, hackneyed scripts; they were treated without respect by the mandarins who ruled the studios; and they were subjected to petty interferences by their intellectual inferiors. In the process, they were destroyed as artists.[16]

This is a theorem so entrenched that it has become, in Tom Dardis's words, "a myth that won't go away."[17] It is so embedded as a cliché that it flows effortlessly, almost as an aside, from a John Updike novel, *Bech: A Book* (1970), which is not even about Hollywood: "His favorite Jewish writer was the one who turned his back on his three beautiful Brooklyn novels and went into the desert to write scripts for Doris Day."[18] (There is nothing further on this point in the novel; it is just a parenthetical comment, made with the easy assumption that the reader would automatically grasp the context.)

A more pointedly sardonic riff is provided by newspaperman Gene Fowler, who worked off and on as a screenwriter for almost 20 years. He did not let his independent writing suffer as a result, but he must have nevertheless felt sufficient guilt about his lucrative movie employment to write this:

"Hollywood Horst Wessel"[19]

The boys are not speaking to Fowler
Since he's taken the wine of the rich.
The boys are not speaking to Fowler—
That plutocrat son of a bitch.

For decades he stood with the bourgeois,
And starved as he fumbled his pen.
He lived on the cheapest of liquor,
And, aye, was the humblest of men.

Then Midas sneaked up to the gutter
Where old Peasant Fowler lay flat.
And the King of Gilt ticked the victim,
Who rose with a solid gold pratt.

Gone, gone was the fervor for justice,
And fled was the soul of this man,
This once fearless child of the shanty
Was cursed with an 18-K can.

O, where was this once valiant spokesman,
Who gave not a care nor a damn?
Alas, when they scaled his gray matter
It weighed hardly one epigram.

The boys are not nodding to Fowler
Since he rose from the alms-asking ditch.
The boys will not cotton to Fowler,
That sybarite son of a bitch![20]

Another relevant aspect of the selling out process is picked up by Fowler in the fourth quatrain—"gone was the fervor for justice, / and fled was the soul of this man." Again foreshadowing a cross-reference to Clifford Odets in the analysis below, this raises the issue of the socially engaged writer who is diverted from serious (though less lucrative) themes by the production of lighter (more commercially successful) work. George S. Kaufman and Moss Hart devote *Merrily We Roll Along* (1934) to the problem of a playwright with great literary potential selling out to easy materialistic gain. This play indicts the writer who popularizes, who aims his work at the mass audience to insure its financial success. The protagonist, Richard Niles, had a viable, "artistic" beginning with a play about a coal mine disaster (which was evidently a literary triumph, but which played only two weeks at the Provincetown Playhouse). He is accused of abandoning this critically promising start.

Johathan Crale, Niles's "conscience," is always jibing him: "I used to come into the studio and find you bubbling over with ideas—good, juicy ones. And in the past year all I've heard you talk about is how much the play grossed, and what you got for the movie rights, and that you met Noel Coward." A key point here seems to be that serious art must have some socially significant theme (racial injustice, political activism, the betterment of humanity), be of somber intention, and resist easy public comprehension. Comedies, melodramas, or any work with accessible content, by contrast, are looked on as frivolous, decadent, and meretricious.

Prominent critic George Jean Nathan, the epitome of the sophisticated, urbane New Yorker of the 1930s-1940s, was a self-appointed guardian of the ideals of the "serious" **theatre**. In an essay called "The Business of Laughter," he scornfully rebukes those playwrights who resort to lightweight material to make money:

> Clare Boothe started out with an Ibsen frown in *Abide with Me*, failed to make a cent, and then turned to laugh shows and became rich.

> Philip Barry hasn't made a dime on such sober attempts as *John*, *Hotel Universe* and *Bright Star* but has gone big when he has peddled comic stuff to the crowd.

> George Abbot lived in a dingy two-by-four hole in the West Fifties when he put on such exhibits as *Those We Love*, *Four Walls*, *Heat Lightning*, and *Lilly Turner*, and was able to move to the St. Regis only when he put on *Three Men on a Horse*, *Boy Meets Girl*, *Room Service*, *Brother Rat* and *What a Life*.[21]

To Nathan, money is incompatible with artistic integrity. Writers who manage to win approval from the mass audience are selling their talent down the river for a fast buck. He prefers the struggling, impecunious playwright who still possesses his conscience and his soul, but little else: "I am on the side of any writer, good or bad, who values his independence and integrity above the beckoning finger of potential mauve motor-cars, marble dunking pools, English butlers, and seven-dollar neckties."[22]

Novelist James T. Farrell (the Studs Lonigan trilogy) decided he wanted no part of Hollywood after his brief exposure to it. He was not successful as a screenwriter, but he claims this was because he refused to compromise his personal integrity. He rejected the lucrative movie work for the freedom of literature, and seems secure in his decision: "I am proud not to be rich because I gave myself and my time to creative struggle."[23] In the appropriately titled *The League of Frightened Philistines* (1945), Farrell provides a succinct recapitulation of the usual rhetorical buzz words, a coda of sorts for this "selling out" dossier:

> A large proportion of the literary talent of America is now diverted to Hollywood. Such talent, instead of returning honest work for the social labor that made its development possible, is used up, burned out, in scenario writing. This is a positive and incalculable social loss. And there can be little doubt of the fact that a correlation exists between the success of this commercial culture and the loss of esthetic and moral vigor in so much contemporary writing. This must be the result when talent is fettered and sold as a commodity, when audiences are doped, and when tastes are confused, and even depraved.[24]

But not all writers felt betrayed by the studios. Hollywood's defenders—including many writers, industry executives, and film historians—have maintained that the film industry during these earlier decades merely offered much needed employment at a time when authors could not hope to support themselves and their families by the sale of their serious writing; that work in the film industry was not inherently more damaging than selling commercial fiction to middle-brow magazines like the *Saturday Evening Post*; and that their talents were anything but wasted in Hollywood.[25] Indeed, it was in large part due to their efforts in producing literate and entertaining scripts, many argue, that films reached maturity in the 1930s. "Hollywood destroyed them," wrote Pauline Kael (while arguing that *Citizen Kane* in a complex way was the result of their influence), "but they did wonders for the movies."[26] Robert Kirsch, book critic for the *Los Angeles Times*, contends that many of the writers hired by the studios "found in Hollywood and in movies material and techniques which enhanced their [serious] work."[27]

A careful study of scores of writers' careers reveals the following:

- writers of real talent were unaffected by their years in Hollywood;
- writers whose careers were sidetracked from other forms of writing most likely would have derailed in any case;
- many writers discovered that their talent was more amenable to the screen than to drama or fiction [D.W. Griffith (for starters), Robert Riskin, Dudley Nichols, Preston Sturges, Nunnally Johnson, Herman Mankiewicz, among others].[28]

"There is no [stereotype] of a screen or television writer which," in the view of Michael Blankfort, "has any truth in it. There are only writers, each of whom makes his own wars or his own peace; some despise themselves for winning, some despise themselves for losing; some take their work seriously, some say they are overpaid and live in fear of the day when they will be found out. No one of us can speak for the other."[29]

In *The Green Hills of Africa* (1935), Ernest Hemingway tells how America destroys its writers.

> We destroy them in many ways. First, economically. They make money. It is only by hazard that a writer makes money although good books always make money eventually. Then our writers when they have made some money increase their standard of living and they are caught. They have to write to keep up their establishments, their wives, and so on, and they write slop. It is slop not on purpose but because it is hurried. Because they write when there is nothing to say or no water in the well. Because they are ambitious.[30]

In other words, writers live in the world and have to confront the world's temptations. Can affluence, publicity, or power corrupt the artist? In "Writers and the World," Gore Vidal answers:

> In themselves, no. Or as Ernest Hemingway nicely put it: "Every whore finds his vocation." Certainly it is romantic melodrama to believe that publicity in itself destroys the artists. Too many writers of the first rank have been devoted self-publicists (Frost, Pound, Yeats), perfectly able to do their work quite unaffected by a machine they have learned how to run. Toughness is all. Neither Hollywood nor the World destroyed Scott Fitzgerald. He would

have made the same hash of things had he taught at a university, published unnoticed novels and lived in decorous obscurity. *The spoiling of a man* occurs long before his first encounter with the World.[31]

"The spoiling of a man." This is Gore Vidal's phrase for a universal theme. But, having established the general "sell out/corruption" motif, we need to move now from the random to the particular.

Three Writers: Biographical and Artistic Comparisons

The Sell-Out theme is one idiom by which to make comprehensible the artistic works and the parallel lives of Ernest Hemingway (1899-1961), Clifford Odets (1906-1963) and Abraham Polonsky (1910-1999). All three writers deal with ethical dilemmas, moral compromise, and betrayals in their artistic work, and two of them engaged those crises in their own lives in front of HUAC. In that arena, one failed and one passed the moral challenges. This essay attempts to perceive *Body and Soul* within this tapestry.

Ernest Hemingway   Clifford Odets   Abraham Polonsky

Ernest Hemingway	Clifford Odets	Abraham Polonsky
Themes. The disillusionments of contemporary men in their struggle to come to terms with a world they cannot truly understand; individuation or the quest for self-illumination; early conflicts are initiatory in nature, subsequently generating the tensions of the long and arduous journey towards understanding. All protagonists experience the same needs in meeting the struggle and frustration of twentieth-century man. Some become involved in war, suffer wounds, and are forced to reconcile the psychological disturbances created by these hurts. Others are forced to come to terms with the reality of the traumas created by the pressures of a hostile environment. Themes are connoted by the carefully calculated titles of his volumes of short stories: *In Our Time* (1925), *Men Without Women* (1927), *Winner Take Nothing* (1933). No Hollywood involvement other than providing literary source material.[32]	**Themes.** The sweet smell of success[33] and what it does to people; selling oneself and others for money; compromise in art. Plays—*Waiting for Lefty, Awake and Sing, Till the Day I Die* (all 1935), *Golden Boy* (1937), *The Big Knife* (1948). Films—*Humoresque* (1946), *Sweet Smell of Success* (1957), *The Story on Page One* (1959).	**Themes.** Man's malignant, manipulative drive for material success, and the need to overcome it; informer, betrayer, blacklisting motifs; self-esteem—courage, discipline, integrity—in the face of physical hostility and moral chaos. Films—*Body and Soul* (1947), *Force of Evil* (1948), *I Can Get It for You Wholesale* (1951), *Odds Against Tomorrow* (1959), *Madigan* (1968), *Tell Them Willie Boy Is Here* (1969), "Season of Fear" (1987, rewritten and produced as *Guilty by Suspicion* by Irwin Winkler, 1991). Television—"fronted" teleplays for CBS series *You Are There*, specifically "The Fate of Nathan Hale" (Air Date: 30 Aug 53), "The Recognition of Michelangelo" (15 Nov 53), "The Vindication of Savonarola" (13 Dec 53), "The Tragedy of John Milton" (30 Jan 55). Novels—*The World Above* (1951), *Season of Fear* (1956).[34]

Ernest Hemingway	Clifford Odets	Abraham Polonsky
Boxing Allegory. Short Story: "Fifty Grand."	**Boxing Allegory.** Play: *Golden Boy.*	**Boxing Allegory.** Film: *Body and Soul.*
Character as Metaphor. Jack Brennan, "Fifty Grand" (boxing); Butler, "My Old Man" (horse racing); Ad Francis, "The Battler" (boxing); Ole Andreson, "The Killers" (boxing); Jesus Christ, "Today Is Friday" (boxing), Manuel Garcia, "The Undefeated" (bullfighting); Harry, "The Snows of Kilimanjaro" (hunting); Francis Macomber, "The Short Happy Life of Francis Macomber" (hunting).	**Character as Metaphor.** Joe Bonaparte, *Golden Boy* (boxing); Charlie Castle, *The Big Knife* (Hollywood).	**Character as Metaphor.** Charley Davis, *Body and Soul* (boxing); Joe Morse, *Force of Evil* (gambling—numbers racket).
Actor Persona. John Garfield. Films: *Under My Skin*, as Dan Butler (1950, from "My Old Man"); *The Breaking Point*, as Harry Morgan (1950, from *To Have And Have Not*).	**Actor Persona.** John Garfield. Plays: *The Big Knife*, as Charlie Castle (National Theatre, 1949); *Golden Boy*, as Joe Bonaparte (ANTA Playhouse, 1952).	**Actor Persona.** John Garfield. Films: *Body and Soul*, as Charley Davis, and *Force of Evil*, as Joe Morse.
	Real Life Personage as Metaphor. Clifford Odets. Play: *Names* (1995) by Mark Kemble.[35]	**Real Life Personage as Metaphor.** John Garfield. Play: *Names* (1995) by Mark Kemble.
FBI. Not intimidated by investigations.[36] Career unaffected.	**HUAC.** Informer. Named at least six names.[37] Career continued.	**HUAC.** Refused to name names.[38] Blacklisted for seventeen years.

Film as Literature

Body and Soul was not *Golden Boy* or "Fifty Grand." Boxing clichés have been a part of the screen since 'way back and in the mythology of the movies the cliché is practically a bible. We based our story on boxing clichés but we felt we got an original story which developed the realities behind the standard yarn about a prize fighter, a girl and the crooked manipulator.

—Abraham Polonsky,
New York Times, 16 Nov 1947

Ernest Hemingway. Generations of writers and filmmakers have been influenced by Hemingway's existential portraits of characters who are severely buffeted by an indifferent, hostile environment—but who are able to work out some sort of personal accommodation or "separate peace" with their surroundings and learn how "to live in it." The titles of collections of his short stories—*In Our Time* and *Winner Take Nothing*—suggest something of the unequal fight individuals face in the contemporary world.

There are certain Hemingway short stories—(1) those that impinge on the milieu of gambling sports and the specific metaphor of boxing, and (2) those that engage the sell-out motif, the themes of spiritual & artistic corruption, and redemption—that would seem to be immediately relevant to *Body and Soul*. Two will receive the most attention here: "Fifty Grand" (1927), because of its intimate boxing parallels, and "My Old Man" (1922), because of the John Garfield persona in the film adaptation. But these stories should be read in the context of six other stories from 1924 to 1927: "The Undefeated" (1924), "The Battler" (1925), "Today Is Friday" (1926), "The Killers" (1927), "The Short Happy Life of Francis Macomber" (1936), and "The Snows of Kilimanjaro" (1936). (See note[39].)

In "My Old Man" Hemingway introduces the plot in which a fixed game is spoiled and the cheaters cheated. What makes Hemingway's "My Old Man" such an important cross-reference to *Body and Soul* and the character of Charley Davis is the jockey Butler's ambiguous morality. Butler is both good and evil, and the ways in which the reader responds to his morality are shaped by the first-person narration of his son Joe. One of the most important incidents in the story occurs when Butler wins a race called the Premio Commercio. The son hears a gambler named Holbrook contemptuously call his father a son of a bitch, because Butler apparently reneged on an agreement to throw the race by holding his horse back. It is precisely because he has dishonored his agreement with Holbrook that Butler is forced to accept the abuse of being called a son of a bitch in front of his only son who loves him dearly. Butler also bets on fixed races; but while Joe knows that fixed races are wrong, he feels that they are not as wrong as disloyalty to his father. Eventually, Butler decides to "stay straight" by refusing to fix races, and, in so doing, incurs the wrath of crooked gamblers who can no longer count on him.

In the movie based on this story, *Under My Skin* (1950, screenplay by Casey Robinson), a redemptive action is reserved for the climax—in a decision by Dan Butler (played by our abiding icon, John Garfield) to win the race which he had committed himself to lose. Butler had been told by his girl "that it will kill Joe if you throw that race," and Butler agrees that he owes his son "an honest race."

In Hemingway's story, Butler is killed *during* the race, provoking an exchange between two insiders, who apparently lost money because of Butler's accident. This is Hemingway's ending:

> "Well, Butler got his all right."
> The other guy said, "I don't give a goddam if he did, the crook. He had it coming to him on the stuff he's pulled."
> "I'll say he had," said the other guy, and tore the bunch of tickets in two.
> And George looked at me to see if I'd heard and I had all right and he said, "Don't you listen to what those bums said, Joe. Your old man was one swell guy."
> But I don't know. Seems like when they get started they don't leave a guy nothing.[40]

So as to avoid this ending, which was considered too harsh, *Under My Skin* has Butler first winning the race—and *then* being thrown from his horse. He is taken to the track emergency room where Joe is with him when he dies. The son will thus always be able to remember that his father won the race (not as in the story), and he will always know that his father died riding an honest race. Compare Casey Robinson's movie dialogue to Hemingway's:

GEORGE
Joe, your dad was a great jockey. He rode the
greatest race I ever saw. He died winning honest.
They can't take that away from him ever.

JOE
(seeing the statue that memorializes
great jockeys who have been killed)
Will they put his name on the roll of honor?

GEORGE
They couldn't keep it off. He was a great jockey
and a great guy.[41]

"Fifty Grand" (reprinted in this volume) is not only philosophically allied to Abraham Polonsky's vision of experience, but its boxing milieu is replicated visually in *Body and Soul*. The surface of "Fifty Grand" is gray, bleak, and forbidding. In the dirty, gritty world of big-time boxing, with crooked fighters, crooked managers, and crooked gamblers, Jack Brennan, the aging welterweight champion, has managed to survive only by being as dirty as the next man. Brennan is approached by gamblers (Morgan and Steinfelt), and it has often been assumed that during a specific part of this meeting [pp 216-218]—which Hemingway does *not* allow us to witness—Brennan agrees to lose to Walcott on purpose, that he bets fifty thousand of his own money on his opponent, planning to retire for good. But it could also be argued that, while he *does* bet against himself, he does *not* agree to lose the fight on purpose. He has realistically assessed his chances for victory and has decided that he cannot win. (See "Fifty Grand," Note #6.)

In any event, in the thirteenth round Brennan is suddenly and deliberately fouled by the challenger. He realizes that he has been double-crossed. The gamblers have secretly bet on him to win. If he falls to the canvas, the referee will award the fight to him on a foul, and he will lose his money. Though in extreme pain he manages to continue the bout. He fouls Walcott with equal viciousness. He fouls him twice: the first to set things even for the double-cross, the second to win the money—the way the gamblers tried to. Walcott is awarded the match, and Brennan, temporarily at least, has managed something of an escape. But at heavy cost: "I'm all busted inside," Jack says after the fight [231].

The last line of the story, "It was nothing," is the epitome of the character's stoicism. Brennan's pride will not allow him to be knocked out. The defeat must be on his own terms. Though not in "good shape" physically, Brennan is in peak condition spiritually—as interpreted within the peculiar ethic that imbues the worlds of "Fifty Grand," *Body and Soul*, and *Force of Evil*.[42]

The existential ethos of these works is quite similar, but *Body and Soul*'s closest plot parallels to "Fifty Grand" involve the set-up and the double cross. In this instance, Charley Davis *has* agreed with the gangster Roberts to lose his fight with Marlowe—but on a fifteen-round *decision*! Charley does not want to take a dive.

• *Body and Soul*:

> CHARLEY
> I don't dive for nobody. What do you think I am
> . . . a tanker?

> ROBERTS
> Nobody's asking you to dive. You fight fifteen
> rounds to a decision. [116]

This preference for a "decision" over a "knockout" denotes a traditional code of the ring.

• "Fifty Grand":

> "It was going just the way he thought it would. He knew he couldn't beat Walcott. He wasn't strong any more. He was all right though. His money was all right and now he wanted to finish it off right to please himself. He didn't want to be knocked out."[43] [229]

Charley bets sixty thousand dollars on himself to lose. He plans to lose on his own terms. But late in the fight, the gangsters violate the agreement and order Marlowe to knock Charley out. Charley is outraged at the betrayal and, in spite of great physical pain, retaliates furiously ("fighting on instinct, all his years guiding him," [148] as Polonsky writes in the screenplay), and wins the fight. He is willing to renounce the money (and probably his life), rather than obtain it on somebody else's terms.

> ABRAHAM POLONSKY: Charley Davis makes this difficult judgment not out of moral reasons, but simply because he's betrayed. He's not doing it for the good of boxing; he's doing it because they double-crossed him, and he answered back by taking his revenge.[44]

Charley Davis's existentially memorable line in *Body and Soul* — "What are you going to do, kill me? Everybody dies."—is paralleled by Jack Brennan's equally stoic closing comment, "It was nothing."

POLICING AMERICA'S WRITERS: Ernest Hemingway.

In *Dangerous Dossiers: Exposing the Secret War Against America's Greatest Authors*, Herbert Mitgang writes: "For a great part of the twentieth century, the federal government policed many of the most revered American authors and playwrights and also watched well-known writers from other countries who are read and admired here. Furthermore, the practice of maintaining dossiers that cast a shadow of criminality over certain prominent literary personalities continues up to our own time."[45]

Why should the government be suspicious of writers? *Because,* bristles the govenment, of the themes of their books (both fiction and nonfiction) . . . the professional writers' guilds they belonged to and the writers' meetings they attended . . . the petitions they signed and the publications they subscribed to . . . the places where they traveled in their own country and abroad.

The FBI, the State Department, and other agencies began tracking Hemingway's activities as a correspondent and Loyalist supporter during the Spanish Civil War. Here are extracts from internal FBI memoranda on Hemingway, obtained under the Freedom of Information Act:

> Hemingway engaged actively on the side of the Spanish Republic during the Spanish Civil War, and it is reported that he is very well acquainted with a large number of Spanish refugees in Cuba and elsewhere. Hemingway, it will be recalled, joined in attacking the bureau early in 1940 [he had called the FBI "anti-liberal, pro-Fascist, and dangerous of developing into an American Gestapo"], at the time of the "general smear campaign" following the arrests of certain individuals in Detroit charged with violation of federal statutes in connection with their participation in Spanish Civil War activities. Hemingway signed a declaration, along with a number of other individuals, severely criticizing the bureau in connection with the Detroit arrests. Hemingway has been accused of being of Communist sympathy, although we are advised that he has denied and does vigorously deny any Communist affiliation or sympathy. . . . His actions have indicated that his views are "liberal" and that he may be inclined favorably to Communist political philosophies.[46]

Hemingway's FBI dossier mentions the names of every organization he belonged to, comments about his personal life and marriages, details about his trips, the titles of his books, the magazines he wrote for.

He has contributed to *Scribner's*, *Atlantic Monthly*, *New Republic*, *Esquire*, *Cosmopolitan*, and other magazines. In addition, he has had articles published in the *New Masses*, his "Fascism is a Lie" having appeared therein on June 22, 1937. In 1937 and 1938, he covered the Spanish Civil War for the North American Newspaper Alliance. . . . In the fall of 1940 Hemingway's name was included in a group of names of individuals who were said to be engaged in Communist activities. These individuals were reported to occupy positions of the "intellectual front" and were said to render valuable service as propagandists. They loaned their efforts politically as writers, artists and speakers and traveled throughout the country supporting and taking part in Communist-front meetings and in the program of the party generally. . . . Hemingway, according to a confidential source who furnished information on October 4, 1941, was one of the "heads" of the Committee for Medical Aid to the Soviet Union. This informant alleged that the above-mentioned committee was backed by the Communist party. . . . In January 1942, it was reported that the American Russian Cultural Association of New York City put out a small pamphlet soliciting support. The name of Ernest Hemingway appeared therein as a member of the Board of Honorary Advisors. This group was purportedly organized to foster better relations between the United States and Russia. . . . Hemingway was a member of the board of directors of the League of American Writers, Inc., which is reportedly a Communist-front organization.[47]

During the last twenty years of his life, Hemingway suspected that he was a target of the FBI. His longtime lawyer, Alfred Rice, tells the story: "Whenever Ernest and I were at the Floridita in Cuba, he would sit at the end of the bar, protecting his back. Once he said to me, 'You see those three guys over there? They're agents, keeping an eye on me.' It sounded a little strange at the time, but you know something? He may have been right."[48]

Clifford Odets. One reads the following statement from a basic study of the subject, *Hollywood and the Profession of Authorship*, to discern some figures who are deemed prototypical of the whole corruption pattern—and one name, for our purposes, stands out:

Herman Mankiewicz, Edward Justice Mayer, Preston Sturges, Vincent Lawrence, **Clifford Odets**, John Monk Saunders, Lawrence Stallings and Robert Riskin. With scores of other playwrights and novelists, both apprentice and established, their experiences in

Hollywood provided the *foundation* upon which the Hollywood-as-destroyer legend was built.[49]

Clifford Odets, in 1931, joined the Group Theatre, co-founded by Harold Clurman, Lee Strasberg, and Cheryl Crawford to apply the methods developed by Stanislavski and the Moscow Art Theatre: an emphasis on the ideal of theatricalized (psychological) realism and a presiding belief in acting as the artistic illumination of human behavior—plays set in a real world, with characters who are complex, ambivalent, layered, recognizable, and every bit as neurotic as the people in the audience.[50]

Almost without exception, analyses of Odets's career are divided into initial words of praise:

"In one extraordinary year, 1935, the Theatre presented four Odets plays—*Waiting for Lefty*, *Till the Day I Die*, *Awake and Sing*, and *Paradise Lost*—that unleashed four years' worth of the Group's psychic and artistic energy. . . ."

and sighs of remorse over what was perceived to be his subsequent diminished artistry:

"1935 was the year of Odets. Photographed, interviewed, written about as the wunderkind of the American theatre, he was sought after by society matrons and Hollywood moguls. Sadly, for him and his theatre, nothing he wrote after that banner year was ever to be as good."[51]

His obituary in *Newsweek* (26 August 1963) is the quintessential model of this praise/remorse dichotomy:

Died: CLIFFORD ODETS, 57, playwright and film writer, author of social-protest dramas (*Waiting for Lefty*, *Awake and Sing*) in the 1930s, when he was hailed as an emerging titan of the American theater only to have his stature stunted in Hollywood, Aug. 14. Son of a well-to-do Bronx printer, Odets drifted in his youth into acting and Communism—owning up later to brief membership in the party—before winning acclaim as a dramatist. After *Golden Boy* in 1937 he turned to Hollywood, marrying twice (first wife: Luise Rainer), commanding huge fees for writing and doctoring scripts, and turning out occasional plays. But the plays all flopped except for *The Country Girl* in 1950, and a critic roasted the whole faltering career in one pan: "Odets, where is thy sting?"[52]

In the 1930s, plays and novels—like everything else—were scrutinized, then applauded or denounced, on the basis of their politics. What a writer had to say about what was wrong with America and how to fix it was often more to the point than how it was said. "Money figured importantly in all of the major Group Theatre productions. Whether the characters had it or didn't have it, money remained a fixed central part of the American experience that the plays chronicled. Money was temptation, corruption, dream, and necessity. Without it, you couldn't survive; with too much of it, you were driven crazy. A recurrent theme was: What does it profit a man to gain the whole world if he loses his soul?

"[Consistently] the plays supported the common man against the capitalist machine. Repeatedly bamboozled and confounded by the system, the average man, the lone individual rises up to challenge the way things are by his strength of character, his will, his integrity, his ability to conceive of a fairer system, and his capacity to have dreams."[53]

The crises in Odets's later works reveal more about his strictly personal conflicts between art and money, between holding on and selling out. It is difficult to disentangle the work and the man in Odets's career, and the critical consensus seems to be that his major plays on the subject of selling out, *Golden Boy* and *The Big Knife*, are rooted in his personal experience. In these plays, "Odets's own disappointment, his lingering sense of having been corrupted by American commerce, his sorrow at his inability to continue the power and the purity of the work of 1935 [and the guilt over the political betrayal of his friends (after May 1952)] can be read."[54]

All of this *inexorably* (because of its important cross-reference to *Body and Soul*) takes us to *Golden Boy* (1937), Odets and the Group Theatre's greatest commercial success. In this play Odets depicts the degeneracy of a young Italian-American (Joe Bonaparte) who should have become a violinist but who thinks it will be easier to win fame and fortune in the boxing ring. He has an affair with his manager's mistress (Lorna), becomes arrogant and conceited, and kills an opponent in the ring. In a wild flight, he and the girl take a furious ride in his new automobile and are killed in a crash.

The polarities in the play are "self-realization" or "success." The moral appears to be that man must live, not for his false self (the ring), but for his real self (the violin). But Joe and Lorna cannot be happy, because Joe has lost his real self, and because society is corrupted by false values. The only power that is respected in our society, Odets suggests, is economic power; and this power is generated by fists, bullets, and machines. An individual's frustration can easily find an outlet in socially approved power drives. "People have hurt my feelings for years. I never forget," Joe informs Lorna. "You can't get even with people by playing the fiddle. If music shot bullets I'd like it better."[55]

Should Joe Bonaparte be a prizefighter or a violinist? Is he to live by the fist or the fiddle? This is the play's central question, and, to one critic, its nagging spurious metaphor. "Joe's moral crisis, as he struggles with a choice between a life dedicated to great music or to brute strength, has always seemed ludicrous to me," writes Foster Hirsch. "He's clearly a special case, a man too talented and too lucky to be believable, and I don't see how his story has any of the social significance that Odets seems to think it does. Who in the Depression, or at any other time, had such luscious options as between a steller career on the concert stage or heroism in the boxing arena?"[56]

Abraham Polonsky's dialectics in *Body and Soul* are more basic than violins and violence. In Richard Corliss's words, "Charley Davis has no musical genius to suppress for the sake of pugilistic renown. He's out of work; his only conservatory is a pool hall. And his only choice is between Money and No money." What it takes to make him decide is a look at his mother answering embarrassing family questions to get a loan for her son's education. Over his mother's adamant objections, he tells Shorty to set up a bout. "Mother and son explode at each other like cheap fireworks in a slum hallway."[57]

CHARLIE
(wheeling to Shorty)
Shorty! Shorty, get me that fight from Quinn.
I want money. . .
(hysterically)
You understand? Money! Money!

ANNA
(with same hysteria as Charlie's)
No! I forbid! I forbid! Better buy a gun and shoot yourself.

CHARLIE

(yelling)

You need *money* to buy a gun! [67]

In *Golden Boy*, as well, Joe Bonaparte's major motivation for selling out is money. What Joe wants is what society esteems: success, fame, and the status that comes with owning a Deusenberg. As his brother-in-law Siggie (played by *John Garfield* in the 1937 production[58]) puts it, "Joe went into the boxing game 'cause he's ashamed to be poor. That's his way to enter a little enterprise. All other remarks are so much alfalfa!" (I, 5).

Intriguingly, the complexities of the sell-out scenario now envelop John Garfield. Note the following imbroglio: Odets had promised the title role of Joe Bonaparte to Garfield, who on the surface seemed perfect. At twenty-four he was close to the character's age (twenty-one), he had Joe's tough streak and animal magnetism, and by virtue of his starring role in a hit play he would be a box-office draw as well. But director Harold Clurman felt Garfield lacked the pathos and variety the part demanded, and Luther Adler was cast. Garfield swallowed his anger and pride—it had been widely reported in the papers that he would play the lead—and left a $300-a-week star's salary to take the supporting role of Siggie and a $100 paycheck. His belief in the Group Theatre was still strong.

But a few months later Garfield announced that he had signed a two-picture deal with Warner Bros. Garfield had never really forgiven Clurman for casting Luther Adler instead of him as Joe Bonaparte, and he had been pursued avidly by movie studios ever since his good impression in *Awake and Sing!* (1935). Three years of turning down lucrative offers was enough. The Group's promise of artistic fulfillment rang slightly hollow to somebody who had lost out on the part of a lifetime. His fellow Group members were stunned and angry.

Most upset was Morris Carnovsky, who had poured his own passionate idealism into his performance as Papa Bonaparte. He saw Garfield's departure as just the kind of tragic mistake that the fictional Joe had made in *Golden Boy*! Life was imitating art. "Many of our most genuinely talented young people prefer to make their marks as successes in the conventional and material sense of the word to retaining their integrity," Carnovsky told an interviewer, describing *Golden Boy*'s theme as an indictment of selling out. "They prefer the meretricious, immediate rewards, the popular recognition of success to the best uses of their own peculiar genius." It was painful, from his perspective, to see his words verified by an actor he had loved and regarded as a protégé.[59]

It was an undeniable fact that Hollywood offered an alternative to the Group players (or to any stage actors for that matter) that Broadway even in its best days never had. Work in the New York theatre was irregular. A career on the New York stage was a chancy thing for all but the biggest stars. The movie studios, by contrast, offered long-term contracts and large salaries even to lower-ranked actors; it was the only way they could guarantee the steady supply of talent they needed for the hundreds of films they cranked out each year. "The theatre—why, it's just an art," Harold Clurman had remarked to Walter Wanger during his first visit to Hollywood. "But this—this is an industry!"[60]

Odets's *The Big Knife*, a wonderful title reflecting a multifaceted metaphor, deals with this dilemma for actors. It is "about the struggle of a gifted actor, Charlie Castle, to retain his integrity against the combination of inner and outer corruptions which assail him." (Odets, *New York Times*, 20 February 1949.) When the play opens, Castle—played by John Garfield in the original production at the National Theatre in 1949—is already corrupted, a famous movie star worth "millions a year in ice-cold profits" to employer Marcus Hoff, who wants Charlie to renew his contract. But the protagonist is reluctant to do so because part of him loathes film work,[61] and also because his wife, Marion, threatens to divorce if he commits himself to Hoff. If Charlie does not sign, however, Hoff will reveal that the star was responsible for an automobile accident in which a child was killed, and that the drunken actor had permitted his friend and publicity man to go to jail for him. Even without the threat of blackmail, Charlie would face uncertain employment as a stage actor if he failed to sign the contract. He is described by his agent as "a special, idealistic type" (Act I.); the venomous Smiley Coy characterizes him as "the warrior minstrel of the forlorn hope" (II.); and his wife Marion recalls "the critic who called you the Van Gogh of the American theatre" (II.). Charlie Castle's conflict, then, is between integrity and corruption , or between idealism and materialism.

Hank Teagle, his author-friend, exposes the deepest source of the actor's suffering:

> You've *sold* out! You'll be here for another fourteen years! Stop torturing yourself, Charlie—don't resist! Your wild, native idealism is a fatal flaw in the context of your life out here. Half-idealism is the peritonitis of the soul—America is full of it! Give up and really march to Hoff's bugle call! Forget what you used to be!
> (III, 1.)

Odets's enemies insisted that he sold himself again and again to Hollywood, and even his friends found it difficult to defend the paradox of a revolutionary playwright in the Depression era "who maintained a penthouse at One University Place and an apartment at Beekman Place, and in later years decorated the walls of his Beverly Hills mansion with Klees and the French impressionists. The accounts of his associations with the great and famous, his peregrinations to the Mecca of Materialism he alternately praised and despised, were exploited in the press at the expense of Odets the artist, the writer of passionate plays about serious dilemmas in American life."[62]

POLICING AMERICA'S WRITERS: Clifford Odets.

Artistic dilemmas were compounded by the ugly postwar political climate. Socially conscious artists, some who had been Communists in the 1930s, considered themselves patriotic Americans who had taken actions during the war years that seemed logical at the time to support a political party they believed was dedicated to the best, most progressive aspects of the American way of life: justice for working people, equal rights for black Americans, a militant struggle against European fascism. Those who seemed so commendably patriotic during the war years were viewed as suspiciously subversive by 1945, when the *Hollywood Reporter* called them "as red as a burlesque queen's garters."[63] One's own acts of betrayal were no longer to be restricted to personal creative sensibilities, but were about to become extended, through political pressure, to include others.

What were the choices before the House Committee on Un-American Activities? The artists could do what the committee wanted—beat their breasts, repent of their communist associations (implicitly admitting that membership in the party was the hideous offense HUAC claimed it was), and inform on friends and co-workers who had made the same commitment—or they could take the Fifth Amendment (which also implied that being a Communist was a crime) and rest assured that they would not work in film, television, or the New York theatre for a very long time.

Thus, in the rottenness of postwar America—where McCarthyism, race prejudice, affluence, and militarism rub shoulders—the person who sold out became a national protagonist. The stakes for Clifford Odets were high: he was a well-paid, successful Hollywood screenwriter who would lose his principal means of support if he refused to testify. A couple of months before he faced the Committee, Odets had postured that he was "going to show them the face of a radical man," that he was going to be "a resister, not a namer."[64] But Elia Kazan writes of how he and Odets worked out a plan for cooperating with HUAC, and telling what they knew about the Communist Party in the Group Theatre. Kazan: "I'd name the others in the cell with us, all seven of them, and name [Odets] too. Then I told him that if he did not agree to my naming him, I'd do as others had done, refuse to cooperate with the Committee." To Kazan's surprise, "I found that what he needed from me was what I needed from him, permission to name the other. We were, it turned out, in agreement, and when his time came he did the same thing I did, he named names."[65]

Odets was going to lose the moral fight, but, like Jack Brennan and Charley Davis, he did not want to take a dive. He was going to give the Committee names, but he was going to do it in his fashion. Perhaps implicitly signifying Odets's ambivalence about his actions to save his career, note a linguistic tension present in the various descriptions of his (reluctant) testimony before HUAC (19-20 May 1952):

- Odets was a "combative informer" . . .[66]
- "He put on a show of independence and some defiance of the Committee's questions" . . .[67]
- "Clifford Odets lectured the Committee even while he acceded to it" . . .[68]
- "Odets was considerably less friendly toward the Committee— he had to be persistently prompted" . . .[69]

but he *did* name names and *did* give a detailed account of Communist Party meetings and procedures. Clifford Odets's Hollywood sell-out was no longer a strictly personal matter, and he would pay a psychic price. In Elia Kazan's words: "The sad fact is that what was possible for me hurt Clifford mortally. He was never the same after he testified. He gave away his identity when he did that; he was no longer the hero-rebel, the fearless prophet of a new world. It choked off the voice he'd had. The ringing tone, the burst of passion, were no longer there. What in the end gave me strength drained him of his. I realize now that my action in the matter had influenced him strongly. I wish it had not. I believe he should have remained defiant, maintained his treasured identity, and survived as his best self. He was to die before he died."[70]

> I am not like those in the land, who, having shared the life of the republic, would now find safety by being first to cry down their own companions. I am not eager, sir, that my tombstone should read: "Here lies a man who survived despite all." He who dies after his principles have died, sir, has died too late.
> —Abraham Polonsky,
> "The Tragedy of John Milton,"*You Are There* (1955).

Abraham Polonsky. Human regeneration is the essence of Polonsky's work. His main characters are always caught between the suppressing force of social conventions and the need to express their humanity. Victory in this struggle comes through commitment of individuals to creating and fulfilling their human identity. Polonsky offers no general solutions to human or social problems. He depicts moments of existential choice: any single person can say no to evil at any time.[71]

The following are meant to be provocative juxtapositions:

- "Neither a nation nor a woman can be forgiven for the unguarded hour in which a chance comer has seized the opportunity for an act of rape," wrote Karl Marx.

- "No more can the gifted writer be forgiven for the unguarded hour when he has allowed a chance literary agent, a chance Hollywood producer, a chance publisher to violate his artistic honor with a fat contract, [or chance political opportunism]— and thereby turn him into a wretched hack [or informer]," writes James T. Farrell, in another of his portentously titled books, *Literature and Morality* ("A Crucial Question of Our Times").

- Karl Marx again: "A writer must certainly earn money in order to exist and write, but he should not exist and write in order to earn money. A man's writing must always be an end in itself."[72]

As we have seen, these existential assertions are relevant both to the world of fiction and to life. Abraham Lincoln Polonsky's fictional works may very well exemplify a literature and cinema of seduction—but in real life he never sold out.

Polonsky's subject remains the bitch goddess *success*, and he explores it within the framework of Hollywood genre films. As Stephen Farber maintains, these genre films intuitively celebrate violence as being consistent with the highest American ideals. Violence almost seems to be the most appropriate expression of American aspirations. The drive for success is by nature violent. "America exalts the *rugged* individualist, the self-made man who wins a place in the sun on his own initiative, regardless of the means that he uses in his struggle to the top. We reward the ruthless businessman, the robber baron, the man with a gun."[73]

Seen in one way, the gangster film or the film noir are only dark parodies of a national myth. A protagonist in these films can be understood as a perverse variation on the American rugged individualist, living a twisted version of the American Dream—he acts out the wishes and values of the successful businessman, but with the high-sounding moral rationalizations stripped away.

Body and Soul:
> ROBERTS
> Everybody dies. . . Ben. . . Shorty. . . Even you.

> CHARLEY
> What's the point?

> ROBERTS
> (casually)
> No point. That's life.

(Roberts [is talking] close to Charley as Charley painstakingly wraps his hand.)

> ROBERTS
> You go in there and just box that kid for fifteen rounds, Charley, like we agreed. Nobody get hurt. Nobody get knocked out. You'll lose by a clean decision. You'll get your money, and we're squared away.
> (Charley doesn't reply)
> You know the way the betting is, Charley. The numbers are in. Everything is addition or subtraction. The rest is conversation.

> CHARLEY
> I still think I could knock that Marlowe on his ear in two rounds.

Roberts takes hold of the long end of the bandage and jerks it with a sudden fierceness.

> ROBERTS
> Maybe you could, Charley. But the smart money is against it, and you're smart.

> CHARLEY
> (resigned)
> It's a deal. . . it's a deal.

                    ROBERTS
            (smiling)
     You gotta be businesslike, Charley, and business-
     men have to keep their agreements. [27-28]

     In the late 1940s, prizefight movies were self-conscious attempts
to comment on the violence that the success drive stimulates. Charley Davis
became a prizefighter because he has been rejected by American society,
and he expresses his resentment in the ring. In releasing his aggressive-
ness, the fighter, like the gangster, is enacting a bizarre parody of the prototypical American success story. The poor boy makes good, portrayed in
montages of shots [69, 112] of the hero's rise to fame cut together to create
the sense of exhilaration associated with "making it" American style. But
for the prizefighter, as for the gangster, success leads finally to corruption
and death.[74]
            Honor is smothered during Charley's ascent, and he is
eventually at the mercy of Roberts to whom he has sold himself. It seems
logical to infer, considering the repeated references to money, that the brutality of the prizefight racket is symbolic of the corruption of the spirit in a
belligerent capitalist society.

                    SHORTY
     You two still getting married?

                    PEG
     Well, I haven't had time to say no.

                    SHORTY
     Then get married right away.

                    PEG
     Why? Have I got a rival. . . .?

                    SHORTY
     Yeah . . . money. You know what Charley is . . .
     what they're making him . . . a money machine . . .
     like gold mines, oil wells, ten percent of the U.S.
     mint. . . . They're cutting him up a million
     ways. . . . [78-79]

     In *Body and Soul*, selling out friends and associates is a way of life.
Davis feels the full weight of perfidy at the end, when Roberts—in a repeti-

tion of his similar betrayal of Ben—decides to violate the agreement for Charley to lose by a decision, and orders Marlowe to knock him out.

Prince and the handler are working furiously over Charley, whose face is well smashed at the mouth, the nose, and over the eyes. As Charley starts to come to, he confronts Quinn.

CHARLEY
(panting)
You sold me out, you rat. Sold out . . . like Ben.[75]
[147]

Death and money, money and death. You kill somebody (one way or another) to get money, then somebody kills you to get yours. Roberts reminds Charley that "everybody dies." By the time that Charley decides not to throw the fight that could let him retire rich, Ben and Shorty have died, at Roberts's hands; so Charlie knows his life will not be "worth much" when he steps out of the ring as the undefeated champ. But he does realize that the years of success and money have made him less his own man, and have brought him dangerously close to Roberts's scrap heap.[76] This, and a transcendent compulsion for revenge, give Charley the courage for this final moment:

ROBERTS
What make you think you can get away with this?

CHARLEY
(smiling)
Whatta you going to do, kill me? Everybody dies.

Peg arrives at the top of the stairs calling Charley's name. She is momentarily stopped by the police.

CHARLEY
Hey, let her through!

Peg rushes down the stairs to Charley.

PEG
(exuding happiness and solicitude)
Are you all right, Charley?. . . Are you all right?
. . . Are you all right?

CHARLEY
(looking up at Roberts)
I never felt better in my life!

Commentators often overlook or ignore the fact that the film's curtain line is not "Everybody dies"—but "I never felt better in my life!" This is a man at peace with himself.

The film's labyrinthine contradictions (of prose-poetry and ghetto tough-talk, of saintly motherhood and a woman's demonic ambition for her son, of money hate and money obsession) find their ironic apogee in the climactic fight, which is photographed and edited so excitingly, so involvingly, that it explains our hero's fascination with "the game," and nearly makes us regret that he has to give it up. Charley may think he finally demolished Roberts with a verbal cut to the jaw ("Everybody dies"), but Charley's last fight helps us realize that he had to put his body on the line before he could pick up the chips of his soul.[77]

POLICING AMERICA'S WRITERS: Abraham Polonsky.

ABRAHAM POLONSKY: The Founding Fathers had the idea that people might be brought up under subpoena or some other way and forced to speak about things that might incriminate them about their political ideas, their conscience, their morality, their feelings, and it was felt at that time—and I feel it very deeply myself—that what the Constitution means, what the Fifth and First Amendments mean, is that this is a kind of country where there is thorough freedom for those things.

CONGRESSMAN HAROLD H. VELDE: Mr. Polonsky, in refusing to answer these questions . . . you leave me with the impression that you are a very dangerous citizen.
—Testimony of Abraham Lincoln Polonsky,
Hearings before the Committee on Un-American Activities,
House of Representatives, 25 April 1951.

POLONSKY: It has been remarked that with a little opportunism the characters I created in *Body and Soul*, *Force of Evil*, and *Tell Them Willie Boy Is Here* could have adapted and survived. And so, with a little opportunism, we all can. That fits into blacklisting. They asked me if I would give the names of people I knew who had been involved in certain radical activities. And if I would just give them those names—they didn't want too many, just a few to establish the fact that I was cooperative—why then I could just go on doing what I was doing. I could have continued to get directing offers, of course. They guaranteed them. I might have made a whole series of Kazan pictures.

But compromise never occurred to me as a possible action. I never thought of doing that—the same way that it doesn't occur to me to hit someone on the head and take his purse.[78]

Thus, the contrast between two writers is eloquently delineated. Two poets of literary betrayal, the sell-out, and the Bitch Goddess—Clifford Odets and Abraham Polonsky—declare themselves before the Committee. Odets preserves his opportunities in Hollywood to produce future screenplays, like *Wild in the Country* (1961) for Elvis Presley; Polonsky is blacklisted for seventeen years.

Mark Kemble's *Names* (1995) is a play about this very contrast, portraying the impact of the blacklist on certain remnants of the Group Theatre. Odets is, of course, a central character in the piece with his sell-out dilemma dramatized. Polonsky, symbolically, is represented by the John Garfield character—who functions as the play's moral center. Garfield's personal moral quandary and his honorable behavior before HUAC are employed expressively—and because of his iconic persona as the "axiom"[79] of several films of rich social texture in the 1940s and early 1950s, he is also able to endow the play with Polonsky's personal ethic and the ethos of *Body and Soul*.

The Garfield character (in *Names*) raises the specter of *Golden Boy* and accuses Odets of lying: "You promised me the lead in *Golden Boy* and you gave it to Luther. You wrote it for me and you kept tellin' me how perfect I was for it. How I inspired you to write the character and then you gave it to Luther." Odets retorts like the gangster Roberts in *Body and Soul*: "It was business. All business." (I.)

Garfield is determined to take a stand against the Committee: "I'm sayin' that I'm gonna fight 'em. And I want to know from all of you, are you with me or not?" Luther Adler: "It's suicide." Odets: "Julie, he's right. I think we should all resist the Committee, I mean, I am going to if I am called, but it's every man for himself. It's a personal decision. If they smell a movement against them, they'll wipe you out." And then, in a final exchange, the ethical contrast is made explicit:

ODETS

What are you going to do? I mean in front of the
Committee?

GARFIELD

I don't know, Cliff. I've done a lot of shitty things
in my life. Hurt a lot of people along the way.
But, I don't think I can name names.

ODETS

I'm going to . . . I may have to cooperate. (II.)

Most tellingly, Kemble uses the anthem of *Body and Soul*—"Everybody dies"—as a motif, interestingly and eloquently through the character
of a bellhop at the Algonquin Hotel, Manny Damski. An admirer of
Garfield, Manny, a young would-be playwright who actually admires
Odets, initiates the existential refrain in Act One :

MANNY

I saw *Body and Soul* three times. I love that film.
You never gave up. You never gave in. Beautiful.
"Whadaya gonna do, kill me? Everybody dies."
What a line. Just beautiful.

At the close of the play, the line takes on a deeper thematic meaning (in light of the Odets-Garfield exchange quoted above), as a significa-
tion of personal—Garfield's, Polonsky's— ethical integrity.
Garfield has signed the bellhop's theater program, and Manny says:
"Be careful out there."

GARFIELD

Sure, sure. "What are they gonna do, kill me?
Everybody dies." Right, Damski?

EXIT JOHN GARFIELD

MANNY reads aloud from his theater program.

MANNY
(to himself)
"Good luck, to Manny Damski. Down but not
out. Julius Garfinkel." Wow . . .[80]

The Final Sell-Out. Abraham Polonsky was blacklisted in Hollywood from 1951 to 1968 (*Madigan*), and when he made *Tell Them Willie Boy Is Here* (1969), it was his first directorial effort in over 20 years. "Anyone looking for a moderation of his views, a gesture of accommodation to his critics or to the larger society, would find no such compromises in *Tell Them Willie Boy Is Here*, his only western and arguably his most vividly political film. He had returned to the director's chair at the age of 58 and was still at the peak of his powers."[81]

And yet he began to experience the ominous presentiment that this would be his last film. "It was just a sense of fate I had about it," said Polonsky.

> I told the studios that I would make only the films that I wanted to make . . . that I will not direct a film that doesn't mean something for me as the particular kind of person I am . . . what I believe about society . . . what I believe about myself . . . and what I believe about film.

> I had written many projects during the years I was blacklisted, and Universal bought a few of them, but they never made the films. I went through 17 or 18 proposals of one kind or another, and suddenly I realized that I was just as blacklisted—even now when they wanted to hire me—as I was when they didn't want to hire me. So I had to assume that there is a kind of aesthetic and social blacklist—*which I create*—which I carry with me . . . like a halo on my head, and, when they see that halo, they say *not him*.[82]

Seduction (one's ability or failure to resist it) has been this essay's connective thread, and the reiteration of this conceit is once again appropriate, because by the late 1980s Abraham Polonsky had decided to disengage himself from the meretriciousness of studio filmmaking. He had recently experienced personal disappointments on several projects: *Childhood's End* (a screenplay of the novel by Arthur C. Clarke, never made); *Avalanche Express* (1979, a script he did mainly at the behest of his old friend, director Mark Robson, who died before the film's completion); *Assassination on Embassy Row* (a very political script about CIA conspiracy in Chile, never made); and *Monsignor* (1982, a screenplay, his final screen credit, that other writers would alter "beyond Polonsky's control and against many of his predilections.")[83] In terms of "seduction," it would take a special set of circumstances to tempt Polonsky back into the dangerous shoals of Hollywood filmmaking, where compromise and betrayal are inherent in the process. Reflective of Polonsky's social values and aesthetic, it would be ideas, not money, that would entice him. Reflective of the Hollywood process, it would end in betrayal.

In 1986, French film director Bertrand Tavernier (who had been a publicist in France for *Tell Them Willie Boy Is Here*, and who had—in a singular tribute—dedicated his film, *The Judge and the Assassin*, 1976, to Polonsky) and producer Irwin Winkler (*Rocky, Raging Bull*) invited Polonsky to write a movie about Hollywood blacklisting. The film was to draw on the experiences of directors like Jack Berry, Joseph Losey, and Jules Dassin. The idea appealed to Polonsky, but he insisted on two conditions for his involvement, *both of which*—and this is important to note—*were agreed to* by Tavernier and Winkler: (1) that the director-protagonist (named David Merrill in the subsequent screenplay) should be a former Communist, "like all but a handful of the witnesses called by the committee in its rowdy and ceaseless search for 'subversion' in the entertainment community," and (2) that his marriage should be a happy one to an independent woman.[84]

"I did not want to do a Hollywood story about a wife who had left her husband because he works too hard," said Mr. Polonsky. In *Guilty by Suspicion*, Merrill and his wife, Ruth, played by Annette Bening, are divorced. "When husbands work too hard, the wives don't leave them, they get lovers. They leave their husbands if they *don't* work too hard. I wanted it to be about Communists because that's the way it actually happened. Besides, they already did the John Henry Faulk story [*Fear on Trial*, 1976]. They didn't need another story about a man who was falsely accused."[85]

So, Polonsky's subsequent blacklist screenplay ("Season of Fear," titled the same as his 1956 novel) concerns David Merrill, a 35-year-old filmmaker, a member of the Communist Party, who made "documentaries that support the New Deal and Roosevelt . . . union pictures, peace pictures, anti-fascist pictures," who supports "the fight against Franco, against Hitler, against Mussolini—even against the Japanese." But most of all— and here one can almost sense Polonsky's excitement with expressing this for the first time in a Hollywood studio picture:

> DAVID
> I'm interested in the theories of social change. I'm
> interested in history. The words haunt my mind
> and the names haunt my imagination: Hegel,
> Kant, Marx, Lenin, Keynes, Socialism, ideas which
> I and a group of friends discuss endlessly with
> passion and enthusiasm. We're interested in social

betterment, what causes the condition that we're in. Is it historical, is it inevitable, is it accidental? I'm not a dope, I'm not a dupe, I'm not a boob. I may be wrong, but I'm not ignorant. And I decide finally that this worldwide depression, this war that is beginning to haunt every horizon in which we live, is a result of finance capitalism and world imperialism. It may not be the only reason, it may not be the real reason, but that's what I believe. And all the facts seem to prove it and it seems to be still true today. Now that's the person I was then. You think I should regret my past? I'm proud of my interest in life and theories about life. It's why I make movies. And now I have to sit down and pretend to this Committee and its witch-hunt in favor of a cold war and nuclear destruction that I'm a boob and a fool and an idiot and I've seen the light and they will save me from my ignorance and stupidity?[86]

That was the approach that was approved by Tavernier and Winkler.

WINKLER: We had several meetings with Polonsky, and went through several drafts with him.

POLONSKY: We saw each other very often, and discussed the picture. He wanted all the details of my life and how they fitted in. And if I may quote Gertrude Stein:

> Little did I know that long before
> the flowers of friendship fade,
> friendship fades . . .[87]

Winkler's sell-out of Polonsky began when Tavernier left the project, and he decided to direct the film himself. But it was a different version of the script that he wanted to direct.

POLONSKY: One day my agent called and said that Winkler had written a screenplay. [See reproduction of Writers Guild of

America's "Notice of Tentative Writing Credits," Figure 1, p. 274.]
Meanwhile, he had been encouraging me to continue with *my* work.
I read it, and I said, I never want to speak to him again.[88]

The film Irwin Winkler eventually wrote and directed is *Guilty by Suspicion* (1991) [working title, "Fear No Evil," Figure 2, p. 275]. Polonsky's central objection to this new Winkler script, which led him to remove his name from the film's credits, concerned the political position of his protagonist. Winkler had changed David Merrill from being a Communist, persecuted for his beliefs, to a liberal, persecuted for his loyalty to friends. [And, sure enough in Winkler's rewrite, Merrill's wife—no longer a scientist as Polonsky had conceived her—now formulaically also became (as Polonsky had feared) his ex-wife, who had left him because he was never around.]

WINKLER: I thought it was more well-rounded if I had an innocent caught up in it. If the principal character were a Communist, the perception would be that everybody involved in these times was Communist.

VICTOR NAVASKY: The Robert De Niro [who played Merrill] character was called before the Un-American Activities Committee, in the film, in 1951; and from 1951 on, almost everybody who was called had a history of involvement with the Communist Party—whereas the protagonist in this movie didn't. And, in that sense, it is not representative.

WINKLER: If we portrayed a Communist as the principal character in the film, somehow all the innocents who were caught up in the blacklist would be unheralded.

POLONSKY: He thought it would be unpopular. He doesn't know how to write about that subject, because he knows nothing about it. He doesn't know why people might possibly be interested in radical philosophy. He doesn't know why they have the courage (or the stupidity) to resist becoming informers. And, so, he did what he thought was safe and what would be more popular.

WINKLER: I don't think that one trip by Ronald Reagan to Red Square can somehow change the attitudes of Americans toward Communism that's been built up over 70 years.

NOTICE OF TENTATIVE WRITING CREDITS - THEATRICAL

Date July 20, 1990

TO: Writers Guild of America, west, Inc., 8955 Beverly Boulevard, West Hollywood, CA 90048, or to Writers Guild of America, East, Inc., 555 West 57th Street, New York, NY 10019

AND

All Participating Writer(s) (or to the current agent if a participant so elects)

NAME(S) OF PARTICIPATING WRITER(S)	ADDRESS(ES)
Irwin Winkler	Irwin Winkler Films 10125 W. Washington Boulevard Culver City, California 90230
Abe Polansky	c/o The Gersh Agency; Attention: Phil Gersh 232 N. Canon Drive Beverly Hills, California 90210

Title of Motion Picture "FEAR NO EVIL"

Executive Producer Steven D. Reuther

Producer Arnon Milchan

Director Irwin Winkler

Other Production Executive(s), and their title(s), if Participating Writer(s) Not applicable

Writing credits on this production are tentatively determined as follows:

ON SCREEN: Written and Directed by Irwin Winkler

ON SCREEN, SOURCE MATERIAL CREDIT, IF ANY: None

ON SCREEN AND/OR IN ADVERTISING, presentation and production credit, IF ANY: An Arnon Milchan Production; An Irwin Winkler Film

SOURCE MATERIAL upon which the motion picture is based, IF ANY: None

The final shooting script is being sent to all participation writers with the notice of tentative writing credits.

The above tentative writing credits will become final unless a protest is communicated to the undersigned not later than 6:00 p.m. on August 3, 1990.

Figure 1. Notice of Tentative Writing Credits.
This official Writers Guild of America form notified Abraham Polonsky that Irwin Winkler had been surrepticiously rewriting his screenplay and is now seeking co-authorship credit.

<u>VIA MESSENGER</u>   July 23, 1990

TO: Irwin Winkler
      Abe Polonsky

<u>RE: "FEAR NO EVIL"</u>

Dear Writers:

The Writers Guild will shortly be conducting an arbitration to determine the writing credits on **FEAR NO EVIL** as a production executive has been proposed for credit.

I am enclosing a copy of the Screen Credits Manual for your use in preparing for the credit arbitration.

You are urged to submit a statement to the Arbitration Committee discussing your writing contribution as it remains in the final script and setting forth what you feel the credits should be. In preparing your statement, please refer especially to pages ten through fourteen of the Credits Manual. Please note that the Screen Credits Manual requires that this statement must be delivered to the Guild within 24 hours after you have received this letter. However, that time limit is dependent upon the submission of the materials by the Company to the Guild. Please contact me at the above number so that we may discuss the appropriate time frame for the delivery of your statement.

I am also enclosing a List of Screen Arbiters. You may delete the names of a reasonable number of arbiters whom you do not wish to read this arbitration. Please return the list (with deletions) to the Guild along with your statement to the Arbitration Committee. As has always been Guild practice, the names of the arbiters selected are confidential.

If you have any questions, please do not hesitate to call.

Thank you for your cooperation.

Figure 2. Arbitration of Screenwriting Credits.

According to Writers Guild contract and procedures, an arbitration of screenwriting credits is mandated whenever a production executive (in this case, Irwin Winkler) claims a writing credit. Since Winkler had violated both his working arrangement with Polonsky and the agreed-upon philosophical essence of the film, Polonsky withdrew his name from the project.

POLONSKY: I think that's a joke. I think if you said that the hero was a member of the Communist party . . . three old ladies would drop dead in Pasadena.[89]

Among the many details in the original screenplay that are retained in the emasculated Winkler version is one that Polonsky drew from personal experience. It is an episode that is a variation of the "sell-out deal" that Elia Kazan and Clifford Odets agreed to (discussed above, p. 261-262). It is a facet of the blacklist phenomenon that had received special condemnation from noted director (and one of the founders of the anti-HUAC Committee for the First Amendment), John Huston: "There are very few who failed to succumb to the general fear. Several . . . who started out bravely had second thoughts and gave 'evidence,' naming names. It was even rumored that they were making deals among themselves: 'You name me, and I'll name you.' This sort of moral rot extended deep into the theater and television, and for me it was sad to see people for whom I had high regard, people of integrity, yielding to this obscene game of blackmail."[90]

In Polonsky's situation, it was David Raksin (the music composer for Polonsky's *Force of Evil*) who asked Polonsky for permission to name him before the committee. And this incident, with Raksin encoded as Bunny, found its way into "Season of Fear":

BUNNY
David, please. I'm stuck. I need your help. I just want permission. I want your permission to use your name.

DAVID
For what?

BUNNY
(exploding)
Why are you making this so hard for me? I'm your old friend. We've been friends since childhood. I have to give them some names, David. It's not enough to eat shit, you know, you have to give them some names. So I'm picking a few, and they want me to give your name.

DAVID
Why me?

                              BUNNY
Because we're friends. That's the whole point of
it, don't you understand? That's the whole point
of this fucking hearing. Screw your friends for the
good ol' U.S.A. That makes you a real patriot for
McCarthy, for HUAC, for Harry Truman.

                              DAVID
                    (lightly)
How did you like the hotel? Pretty crummy, huh?

                              BUNNY
                    (in a frenzy)
Just tell me yes or no.

                              DAVID
                    (quietly, without emphasis; casual)
No.

                              BUNNY
                    (as if struck in the face)
But why? Why not.

He looks around him, surveying the world with a kind of
inspired frightened lunacy, this bewildering world which has
defied him and faced him with disaster. . . . He is suddenly quiet
and though his voice has stopped and the words are gone the
hysteria floats about in the room like a fever. Bunny suddenly
faces David, face-to-face.

                              BUNNY
David, you're dead anyway. You committed
suicide when you got that subpoena, when you
didn't make the deal. You're dead. What difference does it make to you?
                    (and then, in agony)
Ruth, help. Tell 'im.

                              RUTH
Bunny, go. Go before I kill you.[91]

Years later, there is this exchange on "The Hollywood Blacklist" episode of *Mysteries and Scandals*:

DAVID RAKSIN: I will not name anybody who hasn't already been named. And I thought that is a risk I'm willing to take. I'm not going to get anybody into hot water who hasn't already been named.

POLONSKY: And he [Raksin] came to my house one day. He says, "I want to keep on working, Abe. So, will you give me permission to use your name?" I said, "No. Don't be silly." I said, "I can't give you permission to do it. If you have to do it, go do it."

RAKSIN: That's a lie! It's an absolute lie! I would never have asked that son-of-a-bitch anything. Not even his name.

POLONSKY: In my neighborhood, you don't snitch. In fact, you get killed, if you don't watch out. He said he was sorry. He's just embarrassed by the fact that this fact was revealed.[92]

In the end, Polonsky's "sense of fate" about his career was justified. Winkler betrayed Polonsky and then attempted to buy him off, offering him a new contract and a huge bonus to keep his name on the film. For Polonsky, who had authored various ethical dilemmas and moral compromises in his own earlier films, and who had experienced manifold betrayals in his personal life, *Guilty by Suspicion* represented only the most immediate temptation to sell out. Polonsky's comment regarding this latest provocation only serves to confirm and validate a life-long position of ethical beliefs. "You want my comment? I took my name off. That's my comment. It violates my aesthetics, my politics, my morality."[93] Like his seminal hero, Charley Davis in *Body and Soul*, Polonsky had demonstrated courage, discipline, and integrity in the face of moral chaos.

William Butler Yeats writes:

> The intellect of man is forced to choose
> Perfection of the life or of the work.

As well as anyone in our time, Abraham Polonsky came rather close to achieving perfection in both.[94]

Boys—Golden and Otherwise. When Clifford Odets was writing the play *Golden Boy* in 1937, Garfield desperately wanted the lead part. In fact, his talks with Odets about his *own* boxing experiences inspired Odets to write it in the first place. He never got the part in that first stage production, and his disappointment prompted him to not only leave the Group Theatre and sign a contract with Warner Bros., but it influenced his later choice of roles as well. Garfield would get to play the part—but in his *own* boxing movie.

Body and Soul would transform the boxing genre into something different—it made it be about something other than the match itself: a morality play about corruption. It is probably the first urban Hollywood drama to posit a semblance of Jewishness at the center of the film.

Notes

[1]Ernest Hemingway, "The Snows of Kilimanjaro" [1936], *The Short Stories of Ernest Hemingway* (New York: Charles Scribner's Sons, 1966), p. 60.

[2]"Rossen of Films Denies He's Red; Silent on Past," *Los Angeles Times*, 26 June 1951; "$40,000 in Gifts to Reds—Rossen," *Los Angeles Examiner*, 8 May 1953; Norma Abrams and Neal Patterson, "Top Movie Producer Gave 40G to Reds," *New York Daily News*, 8 May 1953; Alan Casty, "The Films of Robert Rossen," *Film Quarterly*, Volume XX, Number 2, Winter 1966-1967, p. 7; Alan Casty, "Robert Rossen," *Cinema*, Volume 4, Number 3, Fall 1968, p. 20.

[3]Richard Hofstadter, *Anti-Intellectualism in American Life* (New York: Random House, 1963), p. 416.

[4]Quoted in Stephen Farber, "Violence and the Bitch Goddess," *Film Noir Reader 2*, edited by Alain Silver & James Ursini (New York: Limelight Editions, 1999), p. 48.

[5]See Jonas Spatz, *Hollywood in Fiction* (The Hague: Mouton & Company, 1969), pp. 81-110, for an excellent review of what he calls the "literature of alienation and seduction."

A brief bibliographical listing of relevant works on this complex theme in both literature and film must begin with the seminal work of Carolyn See, whose extensive studies have influenced all subsequent scholarship: "The Hollywood Novel: An Historical and Critical Study." Ph.D. dissertation, University of California, Los Angeles, 1963; "The Hollywood Novel: The American Dream Cheat." In *Tough Guy Writers of the Thirties*, ed. David Madden, 199-217. Carbondale: Southern Illinois University Press, 1968; "Will Excess Spoil the Hollywood Writer?" *Los Angeles Times West Magazine* (26 March 1967): 34-36.

See also: John Parris Springer, *Hollywood Fictions: The Dream Factory in American Popular Fiction*. Norman: University of Oklahoma Press, 2000; Virgil L. Lokke, "The Literary Image of Hollywood." Ph.D. dissertation, State University of Iowa, 1955; Albert Van Nostrand, *The Denatured Novel*. New York: The Bobbs-Merrill Company, 1962; Michael Millgate, *American Social Fiction*. London: Oliver and Boyd, 1964; Nancy Brooker-Bowers, *The Hollywood Novel and Other Novels About Film, 1912-1982: An Annotated Bibliography*. New York: Garland Publishing, Inc., 1985; Anthony Slide, *The Hollywood Novel: A Critical Guide to Over 1200 Works*. Jefferson, North Carolina: McFarland & Company, 1995; Bruce L. Chipman, *Into America's Dream-Dump: A Postmodern Study of the Hollywood Novel*. Lanham, Maryland: University Press of America, 1999.

[6]Budd Schulberg writes about a process in America involving *seasons of success*: "I suspect that the reason we seem to take special delight in crowning [writers] before they are ready and dethroning them before they are finished, is that we are a nation with a history that is still very short, we are in the main a

pragmatic people better at doing than contemplating, strong on know-how and suspicious of tradition. And so we dig success, instant success, we look for results and are impatient with processes. In Hollywood they like to say you are only as good as your last picture, and this quick count is also used to flag down front-running careers in other arenas of our creative life. Playwrights, novelists, and to a lesser extent even poets are victimized by the psychology of *what-was-your-last-hit?*

"First is the spring season of early success, like Fitzgerald's and Odets's, Saroyan's and Heggen's. The summer season, when men who had put in their apprenticeship, like London and Lewis and Steinbeck, enjoyed the full flowering of their talents and their public's response. The autumn, when talent is still manifestly there, though the public has begun to grow cold. Then the long hard winter of discontent that settled over Melville and Lewis, Farrell and Steinbeck." [Budd Schulberg, *The Four Seasons of Success* (New York: Doubleday & Company, 1972), pp. 26-28.]

See also: Schulberg's "The Four Seasons of Success: Old Scott—The Mask, the Myth, and the Man," *Esquire*, January 1961, pp. 96-101; "The Writer and Hollywood," *Harper's Magazine*, October 1959, pp. 132-137.

[7]Spatz, *Hollywood in Fiction*, pp. 87-88.

[8]Budd Schulberg, *The Disenchanted* (New York, Random House, 1950), p. 180. Italics not in original.

[9]Ben Hecht, quoted in Cecil Smith, "Ben Hecht Returns, Rips Hollywood Apart," *Los Angeles Times*, 26 August 1956.

[10]From the beginning, the suggestion was made that there was something less than respectable about Hollywood employment for (serious) writers. Robert E. Sherwood, in his "Silent Drama" column of film criticism for the old *Life* magazine, 14 April 1921, set the tone: "Eminent authors who were lured out to Culver City (Cal.) by the seductive scent of the Goldwyn gold, have sponsored a great deal of press matter, in which they have frantically attempted to justify their motives in devoting themselves to this new and somewhat more lucrative form of literary endeavor."

The motion picture has been indicted from the earliest days of its history as a corporate, mechanical medium, which designed its product for a mass 14-year-old mentality—and has for many years been denied recognition as an art form, a status which has been granted to its literary, dramatic, and musical counterparts. But the attitude toward and the utilization of writers within the Hollywood studio system (1930s-1950s) requires special attention—to help make the "sell-out" phenomenon comprehensible. The Hollywood studio's peculiar assembly line approach to the "manufacture" of motion pictures produced an artistic environment for the screenwriter which is probably unparalleled in any other form of expression. The established policies seem to be conceptually antithetical to art—the contractual employment of individual writers for weekly increments; the institutional segregation of the authors in "writers' buildings;" the clandestine use of multiple writers on the same script; the ultimate creative decision retained by the producer. As a result of these exigencies of filmmaking, a kind of "slave psychology" enveloped the writers, who were seldom made to feel other than hired minions, paid to conform their visions to the whimsy of their superiors.

As Ben Hecht has written: "However cynical, overpaid or inept you are, it is impossible to create entertainment without feeling the urges that haunt creative work. The artist's ego, even the ego of the Hollywood hack, must always jerk around a bit under restraint." [*A Child of the Century* (New York: Simon and Schuster, 1954), p. 442.] While the writer even today is vulnerable to the judgments of the director, the producer—those who control the money—the irrational essence of the artistic subservience was uniquely intensified during the studio heyday.

That so much witty, vibrant, *artful* work was produced in this period is a tribute to the writers' rich and flexible talents, which managed to assert themselves in spite of the mindless restraints. The writers were understandably cynical about their own positions within the structure and about the artistic value of their work, which was so often truncated and mutilated. But contemporary critics and historians have perceived how felicitously the films of that period bear the stamp of those literary intellects.

[11] Edmund Wilson, *The Boys in the Back Room* (San Francisco: Colt Press, 1941), p. 5.

[12] See John Schultheiss, "The 'Eastern' Writer in Hollywood," in *Cinema Examined: Selections from* Cinema Journal, edited by Richard Dyer MacCann & Jack C. Ellis, (New York: E.P. Dutton, Inc., 1982), pp. 41-75.

[13] George Jean Nathan, "Theater," *Scribner's Magazine*, November 1937, p. 66. See also John Schultheiss, "George Jean Nathan and the Dramatist in Hollywood," *Literature/Film Quarterly*, Winter 1976, Volume 4, Number 1, pp. 13-27.

[14] Wilson, *Boys in the Back Room*, p. 56.

[15] Robert E. Sherwood, "Footnote to a Preface," *Saturday Review*, 6 August 1949, p. 134. See also John Schultheiss, "Robert E. Sherwood," *Film Comment*, September-October 1972, Volume 8, Number 3, pp. 70-73.

[16] Richard Fine, *Hollywood and the Profession of Authorship, 1928-1940* (Ann Arbor MI: UMI Research Press, 1985), p. 3.

[17] Tom Dardis, "The Myth That Won't Go Away," *Journal of Popular Film & Television*, Winter 1984, p.167. See also: Dardis, *Some Time in the Sun: The Hollywood Years of Fitzgerald, Faulkner, Nathanael West, Aldous Huxley and James Agee* (New York: Charles Scribner's Sons, 1976).

[18] The Jewish writer who Updike alludes to is Daniel Fuchs, whose career pattern has received so much scrutiny by anti-Hollywood critics that he has become thought of as the almost classic example of the writer who "sold out." Fuchs wrote three critically celebrated novels in the 1930s—*Summer in Williamsburg* (1934),

Homage to Blenholt (1936), and *Low Company* (1937)—which dealt with Jewish slum life on New York's Lower East Side with such sensitivity and insight that Fuchs was compared to Nelson Algren, James T. Farrell, and Saul Bellow. But the books were commercial failures, and, Fuchs writes, "they became odious to me. I decided to become rich. I was in the middle of a fourth novel but broke it up and swiftly turned it into three or four short stories. I worked away all spring, one story after the other—perhaps a dozen or fifteen in all." He was very successful in placing the stories in the popular magazine market, such as the *Saturday Evening Post*, which would pay the then staggering sum of $600 per story. "Promptly a barrage fell upon me, friends and strangers and wellwishers, wondering what had become of me, why I had sold out, and so on." [Daniel Fuchs, "Author's Preface," *Three Novels* (New York: Basic Books, Inc., 1961), pp. vii-viii.] The moans of remorse increased when he went to Hollywood, where he wrote several good films (*Between Two Worlds*, 1944; *Criss Cross*, 1949; *Panic in the Streets* and *Storm Warning*, both 1950)—but actually only one for Doris Day (*Love Me or Leave Me*, 1955), for which he won an Academy Award for Best Motion Picture Story.

[19]Horst Wessel, a member of the Nazi party in Germany in the 1920s, was a pimp murdered in a street brawl. His major contribution to the Nazi cause was the composition of the words for the first verse of the so-called "Horst Wessel Song," the anthem of the Nazi Party. (The music used was adapted from a North Sea fishermen's song.) [See David Stewart Hull, *Film in the Third Reich* (New York: Simon and Schuster, 1973), p. 29.] It is interesting to speculate about Fowler's motivation, and the degree of self-loathing, that would cause him to employ this reference in a satirical autobiographical lament.

[20]Gene Fowler, "Hollywood Horst Wessel," in *Hello, Hollywood!*, edited by Allen Rivkin and Laura Kerr (New York: Doubleday & Company, 1962), pp. 63-64.
Fowler, in all of his writing, displays a genius for making facts as lively as fiction. In Hollywood he wrote at least 14 scripts, among them *What Price Hollywood?* (1932), *Call of the Wild* (1935), *Billy the Kid* (1941). But he hit his stride writing biographies, particularly accounts of picturesque contemporaries whom he knew personally: *The Great Mouthpiece* (1931), about a New York lawyer of not unblemished renown; *Good Night, Sweet Prince* (1943), a biography of John Barrymore, and probably Fowler's best book; *Beau James* (1949), which brilliantly describes the life and times of Jimmy Walker, once mayor of New York.

[21]George Jean Nathan, *The Entertainment of a Nation* (New York: Alfred A. Knopf, 1942), pp. 84-85.
Nathan could be maddeningly contradictory in his pontificating, however, as in the following he seems to value (a la *Sullivan's Travels*) comedy written solely for the purpose of light entertainment: "Some of the best comedies the modern theatre has disclosed have been written by men of no especial cerebral voltage. They have duly appreciated the fact and have contented themselves with the achievement of merely very brilliant light entertainment." [Nathan, *The Theatre Book of the Year 1942-1943* (New York: Alfred A. Knopf, 1943), p. 125.]

²²Nathan, *Entertainment of a Nation*, p. 86.

²³Quoted in Rick Dubrow, "Studs Lonigan Writer Discusses His Works," *Hollywood Citizen News*, 12 August 1960.

²⁴James T. Farrell, *The League of Frightened Philistines* (New York: The Vanguard Press, 1945), p. 182.

Sidebar on "Selling Out." The nature of creativity is such that it is defeated if anything is substituted for its goal. If an artist in expressing himself succeeds also in giving form to the inarticulate dreams or needs of many people, and is later rewarded with a million dollars, that need not affect him, if his creative drive is strong. But if he works on something he does not believe in or respect, *in order* to make a million, then he and his work deteriorates. It is the change of goals which is important.

• Anthropologist Hortense Powdermaker, who made an intensive study of the artist in Hollywood, substantiates this point:

It is a very different matter for either artist or scientist deliberately to lower his standard in order to make a lot of money. Corruption of both work and man is inevitable, and if it extends over any length of time there is no going back. The artist who thinks he can beat the game, stay in Hollywood and clean up his million, and then return to his own creative works, is usually fooled. There are well-known examples of writers who finally shook the dust of many years of Hollywood from their typewriters, only to turn out mediocre plays and novels which resemble far more the movie scripts on which they had made their million, than their pre-Hollywood work. [Powdermaker, *Hollywood: The Dream Factory* (New York: Grosset & Dunlap, 1959), pp. 291-292.]

• William Bayer presents a perspective not previously encountered:

There is a great deal of miscomprehension about the expression *selling out* and what it means in reference to film. From time to time you will hear someone say that a certain filmmaker has "sold out." When asked for details and a clear definition of the phrase, the speaker will explain that the person in question "took a lot of money and went to Hollywood."

Such a judgment usually reflects less upon the character of the accused than upon that of the accuser. To reproach another person for selling out is a very common habit of those who are filled with envy and looking for a way to rationalize their own position as a "loser."

Back in the 1950s, a girl who went to bed with many different men was called a whore. Actually a whore is someone who sleeps with men for money, whether she likes them or not, which is quite different from actively sleeping around for pleasure. Similarly, a filmmaker who goes to Hollywood and earns a great deal of money does not necessarily prostitute himself. He sells out only when he performs work that he despises in order to obtain something other than artistic satisfaction.

The great myth—that selling out is being famous, making money, and creating films that are successful at the box office—is accepted by young filmmakers as a defense against the hurts and anguish of their own struggles. *Actually, selling out is to betray oneself, and nothing more.*

If a filmmaker wants to make Doris Day pictures, and if he is talented at making Doris Day pictures, then his Doris Day pictures do not signify he is a sellout or a hack. To push the point even further, when a filmmaker whose *metier* is Doris Day pictures fakes an avant-garde film so that he can be screened at the Museum of Modern Art and obtain the approbation of that particular establishment, he is selling out his talent as much as the avant-garde filmmaker who tires of his garret, goes to Hollywood, and tries to direct Doris Day.

An amusing and frequent experience in Hollywood is to spend an evening with a filmmaker who whines and writhes and exhibits self-disgust because, he tells you, he has sold out his talent for worldly goods. Most of the time such people are working at the height of their powers, and their claim that they have sold out is a means to convince themselves that their potential is greater than their work. They are no less pathetic than the filmmaker who tells you that if he were not so independent and incorruptible, he could have amassed a fortune instead of starving for his art.

In the end people do what they want to do, and most of the time they find a proper niche. Probably fewer than one filmmaker in a hundred is so pure that he would not hire himself out if he thought that doing so would lead to a chance to work for himself.

Just as financial success and public recognition are not cachets of quality, so poverty and failure are not proofs of artistic integrity. The filmmaker who is quick to accuse a co-worker of selling out, being a hack, and other heinous crimes, might do well to examine the dimensions of his own talent. He might decide that he is selling *himself* too short. [Bayer, *Breaking Through, Selling Out, Dropping Dead and Other Notes on Filmmaking* (New York: Dell Publishing Company, 1975).]

• Many writers, such as James T. Farrell, saw in Hollywood's utilization of literary talent a clear-cut moral opposition between the vice of non-writing and the virtue of writing. But the careers of most of the best writers who went to Hollywood cogently testify that corruption of literary talent will not *necessarily and inexorably* occur as the result of employment in a mass culture medium.

The temptation to universally ascribe blame to one factor only (e.g., the Hollywood system) must be resisted. The pattern of each individual career must be scrupulously examined.

Edward Shils, in "Mass Society and Its Culture," maintains:

The mere existence of the opportunity will not seduce a man of strongly impelled creative capacities, once he has found his direction. And if he does accept the opportunity, are his creative talents inevitably stunted? Is there no chance at all that they will find expression in the mass medium to which he is drawn? The very fact that here and there in the mass media, on television and in the film, work of superior quality is to be seen, seems to be evident that genuine talent is not inevitably squandered once it leaves the traditional refined media. There is no reason why gifted intellectuals should lose their powers because they write for audiences unable to comprehend their ordinary level of analysis and exposition. [*Daedalus*, Spring 1960, pp. 305-306.]

[25]Irwin Shaw: "Hollywood only ruins those who want to be ruined." [Quoted in William Tuohy, "Author Irwin Shaw's Career Survives Day of the Critic," *Los Angeles Times*, 25 February 1973, p. 14.] William Faulkner: "It's not pictures which are at fault. The writer is not accustomed to money. Money goes to his head and destroys him—not pictures. Pictures are trying to pay for what they get. Frequently they overpay. But does that debase the writer?" [Many writers found ludicrous the charge that writers making as much as two thousand dollars a week were being exploited. (Quoted in Stan Swinton, "Faulkner Hits Writers' Alibis," *Hollywood Citizen News*, 8 March 1953, p. 18.)] Ben Hecht: "For many years Hollywood held this double lure for me—tremendous sums of money, for work that required no more effort than a game of pinochle." [Hecht, *A Child of the Century*, pp. 466, 516.]
See also: Fine, *Hollywood and Profession of Authorship*, pp. 8-9.

[26]Pauline Kael, *The Citizen Kane Book* (Boston: Little, Brown Co., 1971), p.19.

[27]Quoted in Fine, *Hollywood and Profession of Authorship*, p. 9.

[28] John Schultheiss, "A Study of the 'Eastern' Writer in Hollywood in the 1930s," Ph.D dissertation, University of Southern California, 1973.

[29]Michael Blankfort, "Editorial," *Point of View*, August 1964, p. 2.

[30]Quoted in Thomas Flanagan, "The Best He Could Do," *The New York Review of Books*, 21 October 1999, p. 64.

[31]Gore Vidal, "Writers and the World," in *Sex, Death and Money* (New York: Bantam Books, 1968), p. 189. My emphasis.

[32]Hemingway abhorred Hollywood. Many of his novels and short stories were adapted to the screen, but never by him. He had advice for anybody who was considering writing for Hollywood: "First you write it, then you get into a Stutz Bearcat and drive west. When you get to Arizona, you stop the car and throw the script out. No, you wait until they throw the money in, then you throw it out. Then you head north, south or east but for chrissakes don't go west to Hollywood." [Quoted in Sheilah Graham, *The Garden of Allah* (New York: Crown Publishers, 1970), p. 179.]

The films adapted from Hemingway's literary works have nevertheless attracted scholarly attention. For example: *A Moving Picture Feast: The Filmgoer's Hemingway*, edited by Charles M. Oliver (New York: Praeger Publishers, 1989).

[33]Perhaps Odets's most celebrated film script is *Sweet Smell of Success* (1957), co-screenplay credit with Ernest Lehman, directed by Alexander Mackendrick, who said of Odets: "What I really enjoyed about working with Clifford was his craft in the *structuring* of scenes. One of Odets's passions was chamber music. Particularly string quartets. He took great delight in the craft of the composers who knew how to interweave the five 'voices' of the instruments so that each has its own 'line' throughout the work, each distinct from the others but all of them combining to make sure the whole was greater than just the sum of the parts." [Quoted in James Mangold, "Afterword," *Sweet Smell of Success* (London: Faber and Faber, 1998), p. 166.]

[34]The only book-length critical biography of Polonsky is the excellent *A Very Dangerous Citizen: Abraham Lincoln Polonsky and the Hollywood Left* by Paul Buhle and Dave Wagner (Berkeley: University of California Press, 2000).

Other works of thematic relevance: John Schultheiss, "*Force of Evil*: Existential Marx and Freud," *Force of Evil: The Critical Edition*, edited by John Schultheiss and Mark Schaubert (Northridge CA: The Center for Telecommunication Studies, California State University, Northridge, 1996), pp. 151-198; Schultheiss, "A Season of Fear: The Blacklisted Teleplays of Abraham Polonsky," *Literature/Film Quarterly* 24, Number 2 (1996), pp. 148-164; Schultheiss, "A Season of Fear: Abraham Polonsky, *You Are There*, and the Blacklist," *You Are There Teleplays: The Critical Edition*, edited by John Schultheiss and Mark Schaubert (Northridge CA: The Center for Telecommunication Studies, California State University, Northridge, 1997), pp. 11-37; Schultheiss, "*Odds Against Tomorrow*: Film Noir Without Linguistic Irony," *Odds Against Tomorrow: The Critical Edition*, edited by John Schultheiss (Northridge CA: The Center for Telecommunication Studies, California State University, Northridge, 1999), pp. 165-294.

[35]Mark Kemble, *Names*—productions include: Matrix Theater, Los Angeles, Summer 1995; Lee Strasberg Institute, West Hollywood, Winter 2001.

[36]Herbert Mitgang, *Dangerous Dossiers* (New York: Donald I. Fine, Inc., 1988), pp. 61-71.

[37]Testimony of Clifford Odets, 19-20 May 1952, in *Thirty Years of Treason:*

Excerpts from Hearings before the House Committee on Un-American Activities, 1938-1968, Selected and Edited by Eric Bentley (New York: The Viking Press, 1971), pp. 498-531.

[38]Testimony of Abraham Polonsky, 25 April 1951, *Communist Infiltration of Hollywood Motion-Picture Industry—Part 2: Hearings before the Committee on Un-American Activities* (Washington: Government Printing Office, 1951), pp. 395-408.

[39]*Hemingway Short Stories—Sporting Metaphors for Themes of the Sell-Out, Spiritual & Artistic Corruption, and Redemption:*

- In "The Undefeated," Manuel Garcia, like Jack Brennan in "Fifty Grand," endures the punishment of his last (bull)fight to lose on his own terms.

- "The Battler" suggests a dark final chapter for the fighter, Ad Francis, who went too many rounds and now lives in the past with the brutal mercies of his trainer.

- "Today Is Friday" portrays the crucifixion of Jesus Christ (anachronistically) in boxing terms, from the point of view of His Roman soldier killers, who discuss Christ as an "undefeated" boxer. Hemingway claimed to have written "Today Is Friday" and "The Killers" on the same day (16 May 1926). In both there are the hired killers and a waiter of sorts named George in a diner or restaurant; each story opens with ordering food or drinks and is concerned primarily with the varying responses to the manner in which the victims—both "prize" fighters—faced or will face their deaths. Probably the highest tribute that the soldiers could pay Christ for his courage and stoicism on the cross (rendered in a contemporary boxing idiom) is the repeated refrain throughout the story: "He was pretty good in there today."

- "The Killers" may be read as a postscript to "Fifty Grand." The ex-fighter Ole Andreson could have been guilty of double-crossing a syndicate, as was Brennan (ditto Charley Davis in *Body and Soul*), and all three conjure up the ominous likelihood of their being victims of a gangland hit as a consequence. "The Killers," in other words, could be read as a projection of the probable outcomes for Jack Brennan and Charley Davis , if the "Fifty Grand" and *Body and Soul* narratives were to continue past their present closing points. (See section devoted to the debate over the ending of *Body and Soul*, pp. 200-205, in this volume.) [See Paul Smith, *A Reader's Guide to the Short Stories of Ernest Hemingway* (Boston: G.K. Hall & Co., 1989), p. 128.]

- "The Short Happy Life of Francis Macomber" may be profitably seen as a companion to "The Snows of Kilimanjaro" (both African stories)—indeed Hemingway wrote them back to back. In both stories, written during the middle of the Great Depression, Hemingway took the very rich as his subject. There is little mystery about Francis Macomber's character. Born to money and good looks, he is an idle dabbler. He has not had to forge an identity; the inherited Macomber name and wealth have been sufficient. Now in mid-life, he is married to a beautiful woman, Margot. Together they seek adventure on an African safari, Macomber subconsciously eager to realize his manhood or to satisfy his wife's doubts about it. He dies—actually shot by his wife—during an act of bravery, which means, of course, that there will be no long-term testing of his manhood. That makes his death "fortunate." If his bravery is only illusion, he keeps it intact.

• "The Snows of Kilimanjaro" similarly questions the hold that wealth and privilege have upon the American imagination, because even during the Depression human value continued to be measured by materialistic standards. The writer Harry is dying from gangrene, and Hemingway's implication is that the rot that will cause his physical death is a corollary for the spiritual and moral rot that living with the wealthy—and neglecting his talent—have occasioned.

Some critics have found sources for Harry's failings as an artist in Henry James's fiction, such as: (a) "The Lesson of the Master"—A character says to a young admirer: "Don't become in your old age what I have in mine—the depressing, the deplorable illustration of the worship of false gods . . . the idols of the market, money and luxury." (b) "The Real Thing"—Similar to "Snows"'s introspective writer-hero, possessing intelligence, wit, and a high degree of self-knowledge," and the story's central problem "growing out of the interrelatedness of aesthetic and moral issues." [Smith, *A Reader's Guide to the Short Stories of Ernest Hemingway*, p. 353.]

[40] Ernest Hemingway, "My Old Man," in *The Short Stories of Ernest Hemingway*, p. 205.
See Phillip Sipiora, "Ethical Narration in 'My Old Man,'" in *Hemingway's Neglected Short Fiction: New Perspectives*, edited by Susan F. Beegel (Tuscaloosa: The University of Alabama Press, 1989), pp. 43-60.

[41] Frank M. Laurence, *Hemingway and the Movies* (New York: Da Capo Press, 1981), p. 136.
Also see Gene D. Phillips, *Hemingway and Film* (New York: Frederick Ungar Publishing Co., 1980), pp. 98-102.

[42] See James J. Martine, "Hemingway's 'Fifty Grand': The Other Fight(s)," in *The Short Stories of Ernest Hemingway: Critical Essays*. Edited by Jackson J. Benson. (Durham: Duke University Press, 1975), pp. 198-203.

[43] In *Rocky* (1976), a pivotal scene has Rocky emotionally declare how important it is "to go the distance" against Apollo Creed (a split decision validating his effort); in *Raging Bull* (1980), Jake La Motta is defined by his obsession with *not* being knocked out.

[44] Abraham Polonsky, Interview with author, 9 November 1987.

[45]Mitgang, *Dangerous Dossiers*, p. 27.

[46]*Ibid.*, pp. 64-65.

[47]*Ibid.*, pp. 65-67.

[48]*Ibid.*, pp. 70-71.

[49]Fine, *Hollywood and Profession of Authorship*, p. 3. My emphases.

[50]Foster Hirsch, *A Method to Their Madness* (New York: W.W. Norton, 1984), pp. 12-13. This work is an excellent history of the Actors Studio.

[51]Hirsch, *A Method to Their Madness*, pp. 89, 96.
Clifford Odets is the prototype for the eponymous Marxist playwright in the Coen Brothers' *Barton Fink* (1991). The dictionary meaning of "fink" is: 1. a strikebreaker. 2. a labor spy. 3. an informer; stool pigeon. 4. a contemptible or thoroughly unattractive person. "Like his surname, 'Barton is in a lot of respects a shit, but it's not as if we're not interested in the audience having some access to him as a human being. We have a lot of affection for our characters,' say Ethan and Joel Coen. 'Even the ones that are idiots!' . . . Clifford Odets, the hero of the left-wing Group Theater in New York, was also doctoring scripts in Hollywood and being accused by his erstwhile colleagues in the theater of having sold out—in fact, of being a fink. Odets tied himself into psychological knots trying to justify writing for Gary Cooper and Joan Crawford, and, much later, Elvis Presley. 'Great audiences,' he proclaimed in 1937, 'are waiting now to have their own experiences explained and interpreted for them.' Compare this with Barton Fink's language. 'We have an opportunity to forge something real out of everyday experience, create a theater for the masses that's based on a few simple truths . . . The hopes and dreams of the common man.'" [Ronald Bergan, *The Coen Brothers* (New York: Thunder's Mouth Press, 2000), pp. 131, 133.]

[52]"Clifford Odets's bouts with financial and artistic recognition were indicative of the Group Theatre's paradoxical relationship to making it. Odets wanted the kind of acclaim that O'Neill had received in the twenties, but he also craved popular acceptance. He wanted to please both *The New Masses* [Communist Party weekly magazine] and the Broadway crowd, and more often than not wound up finding favor with neither. When he became the thirties' answer to O'Neill, Hollywood tempted him with offers of huge amounts of money. Odets capitulated, thinking all the while that he was betraying his theatre colleagues. 'In the beginning Cliff was beautiful and passionate, but when he went to Hollywood, he ate himself up from within,' says Morris Carnovsky. 'He became disillusioned, and corrupt. He protested, 'I'm not falling for that Hollywood crap, I know what's happening, they're making too much over me.' But he fell for it. He maintained a shrine within himself for members of the Group. He would give us things—records, paintings. He loved us all. But he never got over the feeling that he had sold himself to the

highest bidder, which was the movies.'" [Hirsch, *A Method to Their Madness*, p. 107.]

"It was the classic role of Mr. Inside-Outside. As Mr. Outside, Odets could be the ghostlike conscience of the commercial world: argue for movies that had social content or were time-tested classics. As Mr. Inside, he could enjoy the per-quisites of that same world: attend private parties with friends like Franchot Tone and Eddie Robinson; float in his swimming pool and upon his king-size salary, yet pass them off as 'the contradictions of capitalism.'" [Harold Cantor, *Clifford Odets: Playwright-Poet* (Lanham, Maryland: Scarecrow Press, 2000), p. 40.]

[53]Hirsch, *A Method to Their Madness*, p. 104.

[54] Hirsch, *A Method to Their Madness*, p. 96, 99; Cantor, *Clifford Odets*, p. 38.

[55]Edward Murray, *Clifford Odets: The Thirties and After* (New York: Frederick Ungar Publishing, 1968), pp. 54, 57, 59.

[56] Hirsch, *A Method to Their Madness*, p. 96.

[57]Richard Corliss, *Talking Pictures: Screenwriters in the American Cinema* (Woodstock: The Overlook Press, 1974), p. 131.

[58]John Garfield missed out on the title role in this Group Theatre produc-tion (Belasco Theatre; opened 4 November 1937), and would have to wait until 1952 (American National Theatre and Academy Play Series) to play Joe Bonaparte. In the 1937 production Garfield played Siggie, but "it is impossible to read the play without visualizing him as Joe Bonaparte. It was a bitter disappointment for him, and he left in the middle of the run." [Howard Gelman, *The Films of John Garfield* (Secaucus NJ: The Citadel Press, 1975), p. 197.]

[59]Wendy Smith, *Real Life Drama: The Group Theatre and America, 1931-1940* (New York: Alfred A. Knopf, 1990), pp. 319, 333.
It is ironic, especially in light of the subsequent postwar political turmoil, for John Garfield to be the recipient of Carnovsky's charges of selling out. While Carnovsky would be blacklisted (sold out) as the result of various witnesses' testi-mony to HUAC—such as Lee J. Cobb, in 1953, and Elia Kazan's naming Carnovsky, 10 April 1952—Garfield remained loyal to his friends and refused to inform on others during his appearance before the Committee (23 April 1951). (See Abraham Polonsky's introduction to this volume.)

[60]*Ibid.*, p. 334.

[61]"There was never any possibility that movie careers could fulfill them as actors the way the Group did: the industry required employees, not artists. Good acting happened in Hollywood, but it was mostly at a professional, craftsmanlike level which was antithetical to the Group's way of working. Frances Farmer had

told them how unreceptive film directors were to any leisurely exploration of a part in depth, and Carnovsky had experienced the same haste even in a 'prestige' production like *The Life of Emile Zola*. The pace of filmmaking made a four-week Broadway rehearsal period look positively slow. It took a very special kind of talent to work quickly and still give a good performance and it wasn't necessarily a talent Group actors wished to develop." [Smith, *Real Life Drama*, p. 334.]

[62]Cantor, *Clifford Odets*, p. 38.

[63] Smith, *Real Life Drama*, p. 414.

[64]Lillian Hellman, *Scoundrel Time* (Boston: Little, Brown and Company, 1976), p. 65; Victor S. Navasky, *Naming Names* (New York, Penguin Books, 1981), p. 376.

[65]Elia Kazan, *A Life* (New York: Anchor Books, Doubleday, 1981), pp. 462-463.

[66]Navasky, *Naming Names*, p. 74.

[67]Cantor, *Clifford Odets*, p. 172.

[68]Navasky, *Naming Names*, p. 281.

[69] Smith, *Real Life Drama*, p. 417.
The paradox continued: "Clifford Odets, the Group Theatre playwright who had given the eulogy at the actor J. Edward Bromberg's memorial service (where he blamed HUAC for Bromberg's death), named J. Edward Bromberg." [Navasky, *Naming Names*, p. 75.]

[70]Kazan, *A Life*, p. 463.
"Clifford Odets. I laughed, cried and was inspired by his plays. When he responded to the honey of Hollywood, he frankly answered his critics with, 'The flesh is weak, even though the spirit continues to fight.' Many people supported him and questioned those who dared to cast the first stone. But please explain why this warm, kind man, lover of people, responded to the House Un-American Activities Committee with names of his dearest friends and coworkers in the theatre? Remember the dismal fate of J. Edward Bromberg, a brilliant actor who died a lonely death in England, while seeking work in his field. Have we forgotten the last dreary months of John Garfield? And the many actors and writers whose lives were ruined by the infamous 'Un-American' Committee, with the aid of Mr. Odets? My memories of Clifford Odets emerge with mixed feelings. Can the playwright Odets be the same man who appeared before the Committee? Incredible." [Lillian Gruber, "Mixed Feelings About Odets," *The New York Times*, 8 August 1965.]

A Psychoanalytical Aside on Clifford Odets. In the context of analyzing the subsequent guilt that Odets is presumed (by Kazan and others) to have felt because of his informing, it is tempting to play Freudian critic and uncover a psychoanalytical subtext in his future works. In *The Story on Page One* (1959, a film written and directed by Odets), for example, two lovers (played by Rita Hayworth and Gig Young) are unjustly put on trial for murdering her husband; we as the audience have seen that the death was an accident. [Analysis: Odets is employing a narrative that is suggestive of the "guilty by suspicion" circumstances of the blacklist era's inquisitorial tribunals.] The defense lawyer (played by Anthony Franciosa), who is initially reluctant to take the case, eventually is persuaded that the couple is innocent and decides to help them. The lawyer, in Odets's dialogue, explains: "What impresses me—no ratting out. They're protecting each other, not themselves." [Analysis: the lawyer's specific language regarding *not* selling out another is perhaps implicative of an admirable, idealized action that Odets wished that he himself had been able to accomplish before the committee.]

[71]Larry Ceplair, "Abraham Lincoln Polonsky," *A Political Companion to American Film*, edited by Gary Crowdus (Lakeview Press, 1994), p. 334.

[72]James T. Farrell, *Literature and Morality* (New York: The Vanguard Press, 1947), pp. 73, 77.

Farrell's comments would place him firmly within the so-called "East Coast" category of authorial attitude, according to the distinction Richard Fine makes between conservative and progressive professionals, or what he terms "East Coast and West Coast" factions of writers. East Coast writers wanted to be removed from the crass marketplace and shunned its values of commercial exploitation. They conceived of writing as a calling, a special and privileged vocation, rather than an ordinary career, that necessitates respect for the writer's creative autonomy. West Coast writers, even though they may live in the East, are much more willing to engage the marketplace. They rejected the Victorian idea, so prevalent among East Coast writers, that literature was privileged as a profession. For West Coast writers, authorship is by its very nature a creative and a commercial act. [Richard Fine, *James M. Cain and the American Authors' Authority* (Austin: University of Texas Press, 1992), pp. 242-243.

[73]Farber, "Violence and the Bitch Goddess," p. 46.

[74]*Ibid.*, p. 47.

[75]In that earlier foreshadowing sell-out scene with Ben, in some deleted dialogue from the shooting script, Polonsky again employs language specifically describing the "sell-out." The set up is the same: Roberts violates the agreement that Ben would lose by a "decision."

Charley walks back to his corner and sits down. Ben's handlers rush into the ring and drag him to his corner.

They are working over Ben. Arnold is almost blubbering with violence, pity, *betrayal*. Ben opens his eyes.

ARNOLD

We've been sold out, Ben.

BEN

(mumbling)
Always sold out. . .

ARNOLD

You'll get real hurt, Ben. don't go back in. He'll kill
you.

BEN

I'm the Champ. Let him kill me.

The buzzer SOUNDS. As Ben gets up and they put the rubber in his
mouth, he murmurs again.

BEN

Always sold out. . .

[Dialogue in Polonsky's shooting script, dated December 1946.]

[76]Corliss, *Talking Pictures*, p. 132.

[77]*Ibid.*, p. 133.

[78]Polonsky, "How the Blacklist Worked in Hollywood," *Film Culture*, Fall-
Winter 1970, pp. 42-43.

[79]"The first axiom of *film gris* is John Garfield. Garfield was the first
'method actor' to become a Hollywood star, and he remains the greatest, in my
opinion. . . . Garfield starred in the films that defined and inaugurated the *film gris*
genre, and it was his power as a movie star that allowed them to be made." [See
the references to John Garfield in the essays by Mark Rappaport and Peter Valenti,
in this volume.]
Critic Thom Andersen has intelligently addressed the important question
of whether the most famous victims of the blacklist were talented filmmakers who
were responsible for a distinctive kind of cinema. Abraham Polonsky initiated
with *Body and Soul*—and intensified with *Force of Evil*—a new genre of Hollywood
films, created between the first House Committee on Un-American Activities hearings of October 1947 and the second hearings of May 1951. "Because this genre
grew out of the body of films that have come retrospectively to be called *film noir*
and because it may be distinguished from the earlier *film noir* by its greater psychological and social realism, I will call the genre *film gris*." Andersen associates this
genre with six men who were blacklisted—Polonsky, Robert Rossen, Joseph Losey,
Jules Dassin, John Berry, and Cyril Endfield—and their "artistic fellow travelers."

He identifies 13 films as composing this genre: Polonsky's *Body and Soul* (1947) and *Force of Evil* (1948) [both starring John Garfield], Jules Dassin's *Thieves' Highway* (1949) and *Night and the City* (1950), Nicholas Ray's *They Live by Night* (1949) and *Knock on Any Door* (1949), John Huston's *We Were Strangers* [starring John Garfield] (1949) and *The Asphalt Jungle* (1950), Michael Curtiz's *The Breaking Point* [John Garfield] (1950), Joseph Losey's *The Lawless* (1950) and *The Prowler* (1951), Cyril Endfield's *Try and Get Me* (1951), and John Berry's *He Ran All the Way* [John Garfield] (1951).

Andersen considers *Body and Soul* the first *film gris*. *Force of Evil* is its more ambitious successor, with dialogue "even more stylized than it had been in *Body and Soul*. It becomes a kind of vernacular blank verse, and it is spoken with an uncanny feeling for its rhythms by Garfield, Thomas Gomez, and Beatrice Pearson. Both these films have received eloquent praise, but their thematic originality has not been appreciated."

[Thom Andersen, "Red Hollywood," in *Literature and the Visual Arts in Contemporary Society.* Edited by Suzanne Ferguson and Barbara Groseclose. (Columbus: Ohio State University Press, 1985), pp. 184-187.]

[80]Mark Kemble, *Names*, unpublished manuscript, pp. 19, 77, 107-112.

Philip Brandes (*Los Angeles Times, Calendar Weekend*, 29 November 2001, p. 36) writes: "The play [*Names*] potently evokes a climate of dread as our nation's basic principles and freedoms crumbled before an inquisition with unchecked power."

[81]Buhle and Wagner, *A Very Dangerous Citizen*, p. 204.

[82]Filmed (16mm) interview of Polonsky (with Martin Ritt) by Allan Warren, circa early 1980s, housed in the Abraham Polonsky Collection, Cinema and Television Arts Department, California State University, Northridge.

Polonsky was able to direct one additional film only—*Romance of a Horsethief* (1971).

[83] Buhle and Wagner, *A Very Dangerous Citizen*, pp. 215-223.

[84]Victor Navasky, "Has *Guilty by Suspicion* Missed the Point?" *The New York Times*, 31 March 1991.

[85]*Ibid.*

Navasky provides an abbreviated version of the Polonsky-Winkler dispute in "*Guilty by Suspicion*," *Premiere*, December 1991, p. 134.

For a very lucid overview of how Hollywood has depicted the blacklist, see Jeanne Hall, "The Benefits of Hindsight: Re-Visions of HUAC and the Film and Television Industries in *The Front* and *Guilty by Suspicion*," *Film Quarterly*, Volume 54, Number 2, Winter 2000-01, pp. 15-26.

[86]Polonsky, "Season of Fear" (description on cover: <u>Fourth Version, 25 November 1987</u>), pp. 72-73.

[87]*Late Show* (London, John Claxton Associates Ltd.), broadcast 25 May 1991.

[88]*Ibid.*

[89]*Ibid.*

[90]John Huston, *An Open Book* (1980), quoted in *The Grove Book of Hollywood*, edited by Christopher Silvester (New York: Grove Press, 2000), p. 396.

[91] Polonsky, "Season of Fear," pp. 100-102.
Interestingly, Polonsky delivers Bunny from moral disgrace by having him refuse to testify to the committee in the final moments of the film: "David and Ruth are stunned, with an unexpected jolt of friendship suddenly reborn." ("Season of Fear," p. 122.)

[92]"The Hollywood Blacklist," *Mysteries and Scandals*, E! Entertainment Television, broadcast 24 May 1999.

[93]Polonsky, quoted in Navasky, "Has *Guilty by Suspicion* Missed the Point?"

[94]The Yeats quotation is employed by Roger Kahn to eulogize his friend, Ring Lardner Jr., in "Remembering Ring."

John Schultheiss is Professor of Critical Studies and the Chair of the Department of Cinema and Television Arts, California State University, Northridge.

*Little did I know that long before
the flowers of friendship fade,
friendship fades . . .*

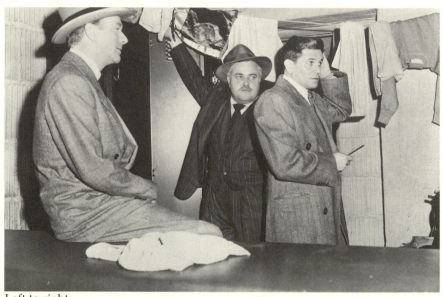

Left to right:
Roberts (Lloyd Gough), Quinn (William Conrad), Charley Davis (John Garfield)

The Forest of the Night for John Garfield.
"The Group trained him, the movies made him, the Blacklist killed him."

—Abraham Polonsky

If the film moves between body and soul, it also moves between success and death, the two poles of life on the streets. "Everybody dies," Roberts comments to Charley. "Everything is addition or subtraction—the rest is conversation." The lessons learned on the East Side and later in Hollywood, particularly at Warner Bros., taught one to be tough, to stick up for your principles, to not let a mug push you around. But shadowy forces lying in wait in the dark—personified by men like Roberts or HUAC—are all too powerful, and good people too often realize too late that a single misstep can doom them.

Body and Soul in the Forest of the Night: Warner Bros. Meets HUAC

by Peter Valenti

By its recurrent rhythmic movements inside—into the depths of the city, the ring, a character's unconscious—*Body and Soul* creates a filmic world unique in its bridging of two substantial cultural forces: the largely populist 1930s-1940s Warner Bros. traditions, and the postwar climate of blacklisting, McCarthyism and human duplicity. It is a film about opposites—set up in terms of structural (conflicts, plots) and thematic (have and have-not, innocence and experience) poles—between two worlds of life and death. *Body and Soul* negotiates between a vertical world of time and a horizontal one of space, with corresponding thematic and visual counterpoints. It occupies a moment in time so well suited to its form and function, so seamlessly connecting numerous cultural and cinematic forces operating in postwar America, that much of its power and meaning might be taken for granted. It signifies the end of John Garfield's Warner Bros. period and the beginning of the period that culminated in his being blacklisted. The film is a document of cultural traditions which solidified the dominant style and content tendencies associated with the Warner Bros. Studio, as well as a reflection of the activist sociopolitical beliefs that underlay the blacklist era. No actor demonstrates more clearly the textured differences between these two periods than does Garfield; the span of time from his last Warners film, *Humoresque* (released in December 1946), through his first independent film, *Body and Soul* (released nearly a year later), shows how profoundly the world changed at this crucial time.

Garfield captures the ethnic uncertainty of social relations in American life, which for Warners operated paradigmatically. As Robert Sklar brilliantly demonstrates in *City Boys*, perceptive observers often found in "Garfield's performance the same social significance once found in Cagney" (90). Nineteen Forty-Seven was the last year of the big-time movie audiences, the last year in which revenues increased. Immediately thereafter, the blacklist accompanied declining box office revenues. The ethnic repertory company that was WB was broken up—now obvious ethnicity was a liability, a potential indication of an individual's foreignness and latent infidelity. These two concerns play over the world of *Body and Soul*, an aptly titled text for such opposing forces at a crucial juncture in the history of American film. The film represents an amazing collaboration of screenplay writer, director, and star—all with New York roots. The viewer feels the film's authentic urban milieu during the trip from northern Jersey into the city: Charley Davis's drive in is like a movement from his unconscious into the larger universe of conflict and doubt, dramatized by his return to his childhood neighborhood and his family, complete with concerned mother and frustrated fiancée. An examination of the Warner Bros. tradition, the verbal, visual, and cultural oppositions of the film itself (against the background of the blacklist period), will reveal the power latent in the complex textual tapestry of *Body and Soul*.

I.

The Warner Bros. "look" was firmly established when Garfield joined the studio in 1938. A 1937 *Fortune* article described the studio as financially the soundest in Hollywood, due in large part to the studio's ability to strike in the public "the nerve that quickens to serious social issues." Crediting "Harry [Warner]'s subtle and race-conscious mind" (110) with establishing a standard of entertainment that moves beyond mere potboiling fiction to reach audiences where they think and how they regard their fellow citizens, regardless of race or ethnicity, the authors of the article go on to suggest that the power of the studio product rests on this unusual social awareness. "Harry has a profound urge to stamp his feelings on the world as well as on his family. He says now that it was the educational possibilities that first attracted him to talking pictures; he is working on an ambitious program of schoolroom films; and . . . he believes that all Warner pictures contain some moral lesson." The authors continue to describe "the genuineness of Harry's messianism" as having "two bases: one is his own lack of schooling; the other is his violent hatred of all forms of human prejudice and persecution." No wonder that the following year saw Harry sign Garfield to a seven-year contract; who better to play a significant role in the Warner Bros. program of socially conscious films, particularly those set in the lower East Side? The authors assure us that "if you see Harry's proselyting hand in a movie, it will be raised against the injustice that he has had to feel and hopes you will not have to" (220). In this sense, the typical WB film is a charm, a talisman against the sort of experience their ethnic protagonists so often had to undergo: by exorcising the patterns of exploitation through film narratives such as those in which Garfield appeared, the world will perhaps see fewer such scenarios enacted in real life. This is the sense in which the WB film could be said to be "educational."

Both Harry and Jack Warner saw their product as educationally effective not only in traditional classroom settings but in shaping general public opinion as well. Taking out an ad in *Variety* in February 1942, Jack says, "We are dedicated to making each precious hour spared for a motion picture count to the fullest in its contribution to American morale" (17). Thus, films like *Casablanca*, *Yankee Doodle Dandy*, and *Air Force* presented images of different nationalities interacting around the globe. *Air Force* in particular featured Garfield as Eastern European in background, and the ethnic melange in this film featured as well several present and former B-western stars—some uncredited—in roles as fighting men. These overlaying paradigms of heroism, particularly when related to ethnic diversity, contributed mightily to morale and the war effort. Sherwood Anderson had wondered about the capacity of the movies to direct public thinking in 1938, when he asked why "simple real life" stories shouldn't be the main focus for film subjects rather than exotic fantasy settings. "Do they want only the escape into the dream?" (93), he asks. Warner Bros. films attempted to answer Anderson's criticism through its narratives.

Though the nature of Warner Bros. productions changed from 1937 to 1947, the studio remained during these years the most willing in Hollywood to address responsibly issues of race, class, and ethnicity. True, Warner Bros. had no monopoly on conscience, and they produced some of the same dreck to be found at the other studios. But no other studio established so effectively (or displayed much interest in establishing) the lower East Side of New York as the birthplace of true American sentiment, as the bedrock of a national personality and character based on fair play for all and a democracy owing nothing to class or racial origins. This paradigm sets Warner Bros. apart from all other studios.

In its Irish ethnicity, the studio supplied a family tree readily exportable for other ethnicities. It did so without patronizing or condescending to its material: screenwriters aimed at characterizations that would satisfy audiences, true, but they were equally concerned with the quality and credibility of their productions. The two prevailing ethnicities in studio productions of the 1930s were Irish and Jewish. Owing at least partially to two of their biggest successes at the beginning of the decade (*Little Caesar* in 1930 and *Public Enemy* in 1931), the studio's establishing of non-WASP protagonists in humble socioeconomic situations contributed an earthy, genuine atmosphere at the beginning of the sound era that sustained the studio for years. Robinson and Garfield were Jewish but played other ethnicities, most notably Italians, in their screen roles. The studio's other great male lead in the early 1930s was Paul Muni, veteran of Yiddish theatre, who became by turns an Italian, a poor white Southerner, a Pole, a Frenchman, a Chinese, and a Mexican. Rudy Behlmer quotes Muni's notes written after viewing the rough cut of *Juarez*: "Mexico and its people are missing in the picture. Juarez would become a greater figure if the audience would have a few visual glimpses and know that Juarez is not simply building up a cause, but that there *is* a cause; a cause which should make every right thinking person feel that he would like to do what Juarez is doing. At present Mexico is hazy and the people foreigners, and as such, it will be very difficult to win sympathy. Actors can only do so much with dialogue. What a vivid flash can do, no actor can do" (85). Muni instinctively comprehends the milieu of the studio and its commitment to making films that succeed because they touch the audience's moral sense. Even in his roles as Pasteur and Zola, Muni emphasized the connections between the screen persona and the lower social classes. Here was a man in whom audiences might place their trust, at least for the duration of the running time; here was a man with whom they could identify. The gradual accretion of various ethnic identities around the Jewish core provided Muni (and the studio) with a formula that would serve them well in such later multi-ethnic propaganda vehicles as *Air Force* and *Between Two Worlds*, two of the films in which Garfield participated as East Side tough guy.

Eliding the difference between his Italian Rocco protagonist in *Little Caesar* and his commitment to Jewish causes, Robinson offered a tougher, more streetwise image than Muni. In a 1938 letter to producer Hal Wallis, Robinson consented to play the familiar role of a gangster in *Brother Orchid*, but in so agreeing he requested special consideration for a role in *Confessions of a Nazi Spy*. Despite his awareness that the story was not strong, he was hopeful that the final treatment would bolster the project. Most telling was his emphasis to Wallis: "*I want to do that for my people.*" Commitment to social and ethnic values played out in so many ways in Warner Bros. films that the cumulative effect was not so much the championing of a single ethnicity, but rather the sense that all ethnic groups were somehow being portrayed. By focusing on a single ethnic group, the studio tapped the well of tribal sentiment that exists in all cultural groups.

Such sentiments demonstrate the social codes common to producers, screenwriters, and actors. In the years preceding WWII, the studio attempted to create support for the antifascist movement with films like *Confessions of a Nazi Spy*, though later HUAC would question such efforts. This is the milieu which Garfield entered when he left Odets and "The Group" for his work with Warner Bros. Typical is producer Sam Bischoff's remark that "his job is no different from running a silk mill, and that he's good at it not because he's a genius but because he's Jewish and shares the racial sense of drama" (*Fortune* 216). Part of Warner Bros.' success is due to their ability to transfer this sense of drama to every racial group they present.

The strong similarity between Jew and Italian was not lost on the Warner Bros. writers. Garfield's last Warners film before he finished his contract and moved on to Enterprise was *Humoresque* (1947), a project born of extra material left over from the studio's biography of George Gershwin, *Rhapsody in Blue* (1945). Clifford Odets had adapted a scenario from Fannie Hurst's original story, but so little of it was used that the property was assigned to screenwriter Barney Glazer for a rewrite. He wrote in an early 1945 memo to producer Jerry Wald:

> "I remind you that what has not yet been decided is the important question of the hero's racial origins. I want to keep him a Jew, as Ferber [*sic.*, Fannie Hurst] and Odets did. You are not sure that is wise. I say we are too sensitive about putting the real Jew on the screen the way they put the Irish Catholic on the screen in *Going My Way* [1944]; that stories like *Abie's Irish Rose* and *Children of the Ghetto* were so enormously successful because they pulled no Jewish punches; that even "Humoresque" owed its popularity largely to the Yiddisha Momma who dominated the story. You answer that we are doing a study of young genius; that for the greater part of it our hero must be portrayed as an out-and-out little son-of-a-bitch; that the same color and sympathy can be had from say an Italian-American family portrait. It is an open question. It ought to be decided before we go much further. Perhaps you may want to consult the opinions of Jack Warner, Charley Einfeld and Steve Trilling. After all it is a matter of policy too.

> "In this outline I am going Italian, but do not blame me too much if the Jewish creeps in. It is more than a choice between serving spaghetti or gefeulte fish; the ingredients I have to cook with *are* Jewish as Ferber [*sic*, Hurst] and Odets contrived them. And musically, Jerry, it could well be a choice between Paganini's 'Perpetual Motion' or the 'Hebrew Melody' of Achron, as Heifitz plays it, or the Kaddish Death Song" (Behlmer 265-266).

Glazer's comments point up the authenticity with which screenwriters attempted to evoke credible ethnic atmospheres, but they also show how one ethnicity might stand in place of others. *Humoresque* presents the family as Italian-American.

The other side of Warner Bros. ethnicity is the Irish. They developed a stable of contract players—Cagney, Pat O'Brien, George Brent, Errol Flynn, Alan Hale—who easily presented a "green" screen persona. These roles operated in a paradigmatic manner, as is evident in Warner's B-unit head producer Brian Foy's letter to Jack Warner, dated 10 March 1939. Foy states his belief that the story of Father Duffy, Chaplain to the WWI 69th Regiment, would make a great film for his unit. Foy had a particular casting request: "I hope that you won't think I'm shooting too high when I ask for Pat O'Brien, because you must understand that I have to invent my own Muni's."

This film did get made, as *The Fighting 69th*, but not as a B-feature; it boasted not only O'Brien but Cagney and George Brent as well. In the cases of Cagney, O'Brien, and Brent, the Irish descent was accurate. In Flynn's case, the studio publicity people took the Tasmanian and gave him a stone cottage in Antrim, northern Ireland, as his birthplace. Flynn's accent of course aided the subterfuge, and in roles such as *Gentleman Jim* he readily became an Irishman. This role is virtually an Irish reprising of *The Adventures of Robin Hood* in its evocation of family and the spirit which binds a group together.

Recognizing the importance of such traits, screenwriter Norman Reilly Raine in a studio memo describes the appeal of Robin Hood: "He has lived [in the popular imagination] because he was a vital, human character who soaked the rich to help the poor; who was a daredevil that stuck his head in a noose for the sheer hell of it; who gathered to himself faithful comrades—Friar Tuck, Little John et al." The convention of the soaking of the rich to help the poor may also be presented in the flaunting of such traditional authority as police or public officials, but the willing complicity of the social group is an absolute necessity. Raine emphatically states that the main appeal of the Robin Hood legend is "the *characterization of Robin in his scenes with his men* so we understand why this great *human* story came down through the ages." Warner Bros. understood perfectly the power of young men, poor and imperfectly educated, to demonstrate assent to the ideals of the hero; this paradigm was imported by the Rossen-Garfield-Polonsky team to the East Side neighborhood so effectively recreated in *Body and Soul*.

Garfield blended East Side, Irish and Jewish effectively. Producer Wallis knew that Cagney's appeal was partially his pugnacious vernacular, as he warned *G-Men* director William Keighley in 1935 "to let the fellow be a mug from the East side." Garfield was that mug from the East Side, but he was also a Jewish mug. Bringing with him to Burbank the glowing reviews he enjoyed in his New York work for Odets in *Awake and Sing!* and the resolve to show what he would have done if he'd been allowed to play *Golden Boy*, Garfield succeeded first in *Four Daughters* and then in *Blackwell's Island*. Returning to New York after his successful early films, he told veteran reviewer Bosley Crowther, "I go up to the Bronx now and see how people live. It makes your hair stand on end. But that's life, and an actor must participate in it if he wants to be a true artist." He added, "If an actor doesn't have a point of view, he doesn't make a dent. And I mean to make a dent" (IX 7:3). Street life translates into an art that obviously touched a nerve with the audiences of the late thirties. At least on the screen, a poor guy with spirit could make a dent.

His next release was *They Made Me a Criminal*, an even more quintessential Warner Bros. vehicle. Playing a boxer with the Dead End Kids to provide an audience for his ring successes, Garfield continued his aloof toughness as a city kid who escaped to the open West. *Newsweek* proclaimed: "The role of Johnnie, a world's champion welterweight with a full set of views, is tailor-made for Garfield. His brilliant characterization in a familiar role will serve as an exciting reminder that another East Side New Yorker is on his way to screen stardom" (24). This East Sider was not exactly Cagney; rather, his darker, swarthier persona extended the repertoire of actors that would appeal to a greater range of audiences and suggested that no matter where this guy ended up, his urban roots would always keep him standing and talking back, no matter who tried to knock him over.

That the studio wanted to align Garfield with Cagney's attributes is evident from Norman Reilly Raine's memo to Wallis on *Each Dawn I Die* (1939). Raine says Garfield will be OK in the Ross role, which Cagney ultimately did play, but adds: "If Cagney plays Ross I think it a definite mistake to dilute his character. What audiences love about the guy is that they get instant blistering, crackling action from the moment his toes are stepped on. He'd start popping and keep popping. He'd be cocky; sure of himself; sure no power could keep him down. He's a realist, a tough newspaperman. Cagney (Ross) is quick to resent indignities and injustice" (4 January 1939). In addition to squaring the Ross role with that of other fighters for justice in the studio's screenplays, Raine's memo indicates Garfield's suitability for the tough reporter roles. Instead of playing a reporter early in 1939 in *Each Dawn I Die*, Garfield played a reporter early in 1939 in *Blackwell's Island*.

In 1944, Warner Bros. released their new model of the 1930 film version of the stage play *Outward Bound*, a fantasy of the borderlands between life and death. Titled *Between Two Worlds* for its remake, it starred Garfield in a role originally played by Leslie Howard. *Variety* announced on 3 May 1939 that Warner Bros. was readying "Garfield's *Outward Bound*" for production (2), though the effort dragged on for five years. The role of the tough reporter clearly paralleled the one he played in *Blackwell's Island*, the film he was just then finishing. This ad suggests other qualities of the studio as well: it was sometimes criticized for its perceived cheapness, though it did attempt to operate efficiently and to cut costs whenever possible. Remakes were one way to cut expenses by eliminating the cost of acquiring new properties; the previous month, Fox won a bidding war over Disney to acquire the rights to Maeterlinck's *The Bluebird*. Disney envisioned an animated follow-up to the success of *Snow White*, but Warners'— shrewdly aware of their own talents and capacities—passed on such high-ticket properties. A property like the remake of a stage play could be developed cheaply: no location shooting, just a few indoor sets and some tank footage of vessels at sea. Despite their desire to present Garfield in effective vehicles, they were also economical vehicles.

Because the studio wanted to save a few bucks, however, does not mean their product was necessarily inferior. The effectiveness of Warner Bros. films stemmed partially from their sensitivity to budget: like the characters they were presenting, a few bucks were always a consideration—often the main consideration. This economy translated into stories that could reach across several audience levels: instead of Paramount or Fox's "white telephone" films suggestive of upscale boudoirs, Warner's would make "black pay phone" films illustrative of life on street corners. This new version of *Outward Bound* would be more like Thomas Mann's *The Magic Mountain*, with individual characters representing different nationalities and character types.

In moving the time of the film from the 1920s to WWII, screenwriter James N. Bilson described his idea of the character of Garfield's movie mother, Mrs. Midget: "This character will symbolize the courage of all the mothers of all American soldiers . . . proud of the divine privilege of giving their sons to protect the heritages of the common people" (UA 12). Aside from the questionable assumption of mothers' willingness to have their sons die in war, Bilson's idea suggests a context for the Garfield character Tom Pryor, who does not realize that Mrs. Midget is his mother. The lack of political power for Warner Bros. characters is perfectly in keeping with the idea that working-class sons are lost in war more quickly and more frequently than other classes; their patriotism, their sense of community, dooms them. Thus the cynical, world-wise smart-aleck newsman Pryor recognizes the score, but at the same time longs to make a social contribution outside individual benefit. This tension was evident in Warner Bros.' shrewd appraisal of Garfield's talent and box office potential.

Robert Rossen as well as Garfield helped establish the Warner Bros. milieu. Teamed together in two films, the pair set a tone which still endures: the gritty urban world of people with a fighting chance, but just barely, engaged in a constant struggle to keep afloat. The in-your-face roles of boxer and reporter typify even the studio's attitude toward abuses of democracy: *They Won't Forget* could well serve as Warner's studio motto.

To a great extent, the blacklist-related problems faced by Garfield, Rossen, and Polonsky came about directly as a result of the unique strengths of their Warner Bros. products: the populist element of their films betrayed a strong social consciousness, affirmation of the value of the individual, and a firm conviction that the existing social order might be changed in order to accommodate demonstrated value of character, even when that character is cloaked in poverty. As Sklar points out, virtually the entire cast of *Body and Soul* shared leftist sentiments (183). This complex of attitudes is borne out by the official pronouncements of the studio on those occasions when Harry or Jack Warner was called upon to respond to criticism.

Body and Soul clearly participates in the Warner Bros. idiom: not just in the speech of the characters—and particularly the streetwise toughness that Garfield displays—but also in characterization, narrative, mood and theme, all of which come from studying New York idioms and the populist-socialist spirit of Odets and The Group. Garfield, Rossen and Polonsky must express their ideas in the form they know best; they shared not only experience working on Hollywood screenplays, but also East Side origins—and, most importantly, that strong sense of social justice very closely allied to lower-middle-class Jewish roots. Polonsky had some experience writing scenarios at Paramount, though his wartime service limited his studio work until *Body and Soul*. Asked to provide a film for Garfield's new endeavor at independent production with Enterprise Productions, Polonsky mined the lower East Side for his characters and ambience. The script received an Oscar nomination because of its confident portrayal of lives pinched by poverty and lack of opportunity, grim lives unrelieved by comfort unless fate were to step in and offer a rare opportunity.

Boxing provided one such opportunity. Having boxed professionally before turning to the theater, Rossen's ring experience exceeded even Garfield's. He discussed the emerging screenplay for *Body and Soul* with Polonsky as the property was being developed, so that the final version resembles Rossen's Warner Bros. work in some important ways. So thoroughly does boxing permeate the ideological project of this film and many Warners vehicles that preceded it, that the language of Odets's response to Garfield's death sums up well the available ethos of a Garfield-boxing property: "His climb from bare poverty to stardom illustrated for him one of the most cherished folkways of our people. His feelings never changed that he had been mandated by the American people to go in and 'keep punching' for them. His success, as he felt it, was the common property of millions, not peculiarly his own. This, I submit, was a basic purity of which not even Garfield himself was conscious" (*New York Times* 7). Rossen understood both the grounds of Garfield's appeal and Garfield's character.

Rossen's first work for Warner Bros. was the screenplay for *They Won't Forget*, which was directed by Mervyn LeRoy. This fictionalization of the Leo Frank case depicted the horror of mob violence, the dark antithesis of the community spirit that underlay the best work of Rossen, Polonsky, and Garfield. Rossen first worked with Garfield in 1939 in *Dust Be My Destiny*, the most frequently televised Garfield film before the advent of cable. His second screenwriting credit with Garfield was *Out of the Fog* in 1941, based on an Irwin Shaw play. In *Dust* Garfield played a poor, hard-luck victim of bureaucratic misunderstanding, while in *Out of the Fog* he plays a tough gangster, thereby comprising the two strands of the Charley Davis character in *Body and Soul*—the poor street kid fighting for a break and the hood who's perfectly willing to bend the law for his own benefit.

In between these two projects, Rossen had his most effective Warners vehicle, *The Roaring Twenties*, which immediately followed *Dust* in 1939 and was a huge box office hit. James Cagney again reprises the urban tough guy, but here, as a returning WWI vet at the start of Prohibition, he demonstrates the economic determinism that forced such figures into crime and racketeering. Rossen exploited the Cagney persona at least partially by establishing so effectively the urban dilemmas of poor people desperate for a better life than the grinding poverty of the slums, so that Cagney's bootlegger Eddie Bartlett arouses audience understanding of his drive for success, though his overweening ambition finally dooms him. *The Roaring Twenties* increased the complexity of the ethnic Warner Bros. lead by showing that an initially sympathetic character might allow pride to drive him too far and estrange him from the larger community; interestingly enough, this formula resembles the one which shot Cagney to fame in *Public Enemy*.

II.

The *Body and Soul* text itself suggests how many of the most important social, intellectual and artistic ideas that made Warner Bros. so successful are carried over by the new Enterprise team. With Polonsky, Rossen, and Garfield collaborating on the initial ideas for the first Enterprise Studios release, creation of an effective, literate script was virtually assured. Securing former Warner Bros. cinematographer James Wong Howe provided his wide expertise for shooting under a variety of circumstances; Howe also had some early boxing experience. The finished film's gritty feel for the ring, then, comes about logically.

Opening with a shot of the "heavy sandbag" hanging over the ring in training camp, casting a shadow like a gallows, the film effectively enters a world in which the bag seems to be a body—that of a victim. Though its producers were of course unaware of the potential suggestiveness this image would hold by 1951, it binds the Warner Bros. traditions with the sad fate of such traditions in the public pilloryings of the HUAC hearings. For Warner Bros. the ring functioned as the site of hope: it became for lower-class kids like Garfield, Rossen, and Howe a place where at least for a few rounds they were equal to whoever else stepped into the ring with them; like the world of the film text, the ring is a place outside time and the constraints of socioeconomic position.

This world of the ring is one center of power in the film; the other is the street corner which faces the Davis candy store. Ring and corner are two instances of what art theoretician E.H. Gombrich calls a "psychologically grounded minimum image"—bits of visual data working together and characterized by an unsophisticated, almost primal response to this extremely basic information which "will make it fit into a psychological lock"—which closes at a "primitive level" (8) of perception. The four sides of the ring, signaled by the horizontal ropes, is one such configuration, a mobilization of space connoting the force to be bound inside the ropes. It is the demarcation of a frame, an exhibition, of the emphasis placed upon the purely physical. This is the site upon which the body asserts itself. We shall see presently how the corner offers another such example.

Howe's camera initiates the rhythms of travel and movement characteristic of the film when he pans from the ring across the tree into the sleeping porch; the first cut is to a close-up of the sleeping man: Garfield as Charley Davis, sweating in his sleep as he jolts himself awake with the cry of "Ben!" This cut has the effect of moving the spectator into Charley's sleeping unconscious, to that primal world that will drive so much of the film. The camera positions the audience in the back seat of the Packard convertible as Garfield heads into Manhattan, revealing little about the situation but establishing a strong, *noirish* sense of the great city at night in long shots. [18]

Such a world echoes the one created in Odets's *Golden Boy*, which was written with Garfield in mind as prizefighter/violinist Joe Bonaparte. Once Bonaparte becomes champ, accidentally killing his African-American opponent in the process, he tries to clear his head with a wild ride out of the city. He promises his girlfriend: "We'll drive through the night. When you mow down the night with headlights, nobody gets you! You're on top of the world then—nobody laughs! That's it—speed! We're off the earth—unconnected! We don't have to think! Lorna darling, we'll burn up the night!" (980). Recalling Howe's basic principle—that the job of the cinematographer is to help the director and writers achieve their ends—illustrates the centrality of the brief drive into the city for the tortured

Charley. The physical motion of the tortured drive into the unconscious world parallels the visual of the filmic world and the verbal of the stage world. Charley returns to his childhood home/world—here, in Freudian terms, the womb—to somehow make things right.

Much shorter focal lengths characterize the cut to the Davis candy store (notice the proprietor is A. Davis—Ma now must run the store by herself to survive). [19] Like the shadows of the bag over the ring, the lines and planes of figures in this scene of Charley driving up are meticulously layered. Close-ups do not obstruct the spectator's view of kids in the background because all is laid out so carefully around Charley. "Hi, Champ!" opens the world of wonder for the neighborhood at its returning son.

Contrasted with this evocation of the street world, very like that of *Angels with Dirty Faces*, is the following sequence in the Davis tenement, where Charley is uncertainly received by his mother Anna (Anne Revere). Arranging the players as carefully as objects in a still life, Rossen and Howe reprise the opening shot of Garfield through a screen, as they shoot first Peg (Lilli Palmer) and then Peg and Charley through one of those strange architectural features in chopped-up and recombined apartments, here an interior window through which we see Peg's anguished response to Charley's kiss. This split screen pits Anna sighing, "Go away, Charley, go away," as Charley and Peg talk soundlessly behind the window. Evoking psychological interiors similar to that in the film's first cut, the camera setup here efficiently provides an understated sense of the inner difficulties of the world of the tenement. [20-22]

Cutting back to the car and Charley's re-entry, the same carefully layered arrangement of human figures, both kids and Charley's contemporaries, create a street world in which Charley is king. The sharp angle of the corner signals a masculine world: like the ring, the corner is a "psychologically grounded minimum image." Unlike the rounded world of the feminine circle, the dramatic angle indicates a world of masculinity. Here male aggression moves from friendly banter to serious threats, as it enacts social dramas and conflicts on the site where human lives intersect and compete.

If the film moves between body and soul, it also moves between success and death, the two poles of life on the streets. "Everybody dies," the promoter Roberts comments to Charley about Ben. "Everything is addition or subtraction—the rest is conversation." As a corrupt authority figure, Roberts wields ultimate power in the boxing world of the film. No publicly sanctioned authority holds any visible sway; people fear and respect only Roberts or his underling Quinn. Ultimately, the only power greater than Roberts's turns out to be that of the social group as demonstrated in Ma and Peg, Shorty and Ben—they provide the direction that leads Charley back to the communion of the street.

Peg comments on success most fully. When Charley says, "I just want to be a success," she counters with, "You mean you want other people to *think* you're a success." [41] This subplot plays out tragically after the welfare worker Miss Tedder leaves Ma Davis's apartment and Peg follows Charley to the rooftop. In declaring her love for him, she allows him to achieve self-expression through boxing—she will support him in whatever he wants.

It is this success that Charley fears is washing away from him before the fight with Marlowe. The dissolve from the flushing drain (over which Charley repeats, "Everything down the drain, all those years, everything down the drain") to the Iroquois Democratic Club banquet [29-31] captures Charley's solitude in the dressing room—in order to contrast it with the tightly packed gathering, the promise of youth alive in the teeming tables of young people, cheering like a fight audience before the main event. The local pol, Jack Shelton, "the man who never said no to a friend," presides over the affair, praising Charley and pushing him to dance with Peg.

Shelton's shove trips Charley's reflexes and he puts up his dukes, going into his boxing stance, opposite Peg. But she reflexively goes into a dance posture, disarming her partner and gliding forward. The first of the film's takes on the title and the first physical contact between hero and heroine, this quick shot prefigures the film's conclusion. Body and soul, boxer and painter, the two sides of the tiger. On the way taking Peg home in a cab, Charley slides over into her, prompting her to ask if he's heard about gravity. "What's gravity?" asks Charley, suggesting that he operates on an inferior intellectual level.

This question parallels the one Charley asks of Peg later when she is attempting to get him out the door and quotes William Blake's poem "The Tyger," which appears in his *Songs of Experience*:

> Tyger, tyger, burning bright
> In the forests of the night
> What immortal hand or eye
> Could frame thy fearful symmetry?

Charley's "What's symmetry?" receives Peg's definition "Well built" immediately before their first kiss. [43] Blake's poem resonates on several levels within the context of the film and its wider cultural universe. The film's title is most evident at this point in the film, just after sculptor Irma has offered to sculpt and Peg has sketched the fighter: Peg uses the lines to refer to Charley's body as object of art, of aesthetic value apart from inner nature—or soul. The Garfield feistiness and the residual toughness that come over from the Warner Bros. tradition of ethnic boxers and strongmen combine to suggest that he's a tiger, hungry and savage, coming out of the night of the great unwashed, the dimly lit streets which are so difficult to leave for good.

Peg senses Charley's inability to see clearly, and the tiger becomes a recurrent motif in the remainder of the film to show Charley's difficulty in comprehending. Just as he asks "What's symmetry?" he also asks what success is, what death is. The limited perception of those who dwell in night protects them from analyzing their situations correctly and looking for answers in some "immortal hand or eye" of some false prophet like Roberts, or in what Charley envisions as the world's estimate of success. Only when Peg helps him to understand his soul in the cold light of day does he begin to see rightly.

Polonsky considered carefully how best to use the poem in the film. As he described the situation to interviewer John Schultheiss:

> Peg is an educated refugee; Charley is a kid of the streets. She possesses a cultural knowledge of such a reference as a William Blake poem. To him it's the first time in his life he's ever heard it. She thinks of the poem because of the natural grace, power, and beauty of this man and the fact that he has no concept about what life will do to a thing like that. But she knows. (10/4:07:54)

Like Blake's speaker, Charley is innocent but at the same time streetwise; he knows some survival skills but not the most crucial ones for his soul. Polonsky worried that such ideas might sound too erudite, and so balanced the serious exchange with the kiss following the symmetry discussion: "That takes the curse off it, makes it amusing for those who know about it, makes it interesting for those who know nothing about it, and takes me out of the scene, which is the greatest thing in the world" (10/4:08:45). The poem and its implications of crucial cultural contexts suit Polonsky's film wonderfully well.

Peg and Charley's mother Anna, the other female with whom Peg will become aligned in the film's characterization, are the forces that will take Charley out of the night and help him to see how his talents can shine. Peg is thus the literal framer of the symmetry, as well as the spiritual one, because she somehow sees what rests in the darkness of Charley's nature. Despite his obsession with success and money, he is the child of his parents and will serve his community despite the influences of people like Roberts and Quinn.

People like Roberts are precisely those against whom Blake rages, because they conspire to keep humanity at bay. For Blake, the world of night was a creation of superstitious and misguided people who failed to see that God exists in other humans—by the light of day. As in Blake's complex divided universe, the film text itself takes on directly the problematic issues of constructing a just and coherent world from the welter of opposing forces which confront the innocent and challenge the process of acquiring knowledge, the decoding of the principles of the universe from sensory data. Thus the shots of the corner refer to the nature(s) of the observer. Blake himself says it best:

> God appears & God is Light
> To those poor Souls who dwell in Night,
> But does a Human Form Display
> To those who dwell in Realms of day.
> —"Auguries of Innocence" (434)

The shots of Charley's corner are nighttime shots, as if to suggest the compromised world in which the characters exist. Contrast with these shots the brightly lit apartment Roberts enables Charley to enjoy. These surroundings are, ironically, the true "forests of the night" because they are the creation of the "fixer," the "businessman," the most powerful authority figure in the film. When Charley realizes this, he leaves Roberts's nocturnal forest for his own neighborhood—which he will illuminate with his soul and Peg's help, as the film's final shot attests.

When Charley returns to his neighborhood after meeting Peg, he comes upon Shorty and the gang in front of the pool hall, the social center of the neighborhood. Shorty's heroic buildup of Charley's exploits ends when Charley approaches and one of the guys takes a look at the drawing, which gives Charley prominent stripes, and says: "Look! Fur!" The tiger image continues even after the end punctuation of this sequence with Quinn's moving by the boys into the poolroom. [45]

The sketch of fighter Charley is useful in other ways. Rolled up, it becomes the club to knock around Quinn's pool balls, after the promoter had suggested that Charley would be fighting only for coffee and doughnut money. This action is what cements Charley's chances because Shorty is then able to deal with Quinn. Charley's belligerence and unwillingness to kowtow to larger powers show Quinn that this fighter is for real.

And when Shorty mistakenly reveals that Charley will be fighting for money, Mrs. Davis rebels at this arrangement. She did not want to raise her children "like wolves" on the lower East Side, where "we live in a jungle so he can only be a wild animal." Charley's unknowing declaration that he does not want to work in a small, run-down candy store selling penny candy and two-cent sodas troubles his father, but only temporarily as the father gives his son his patrimony—ten dollars for equipment, without Mrs. Davis's knowledge, begins Charley's professional career. Unlike the careers or the life in the suburbs that she dreamed for her son, his life will be forever linked to the streets and the neighborhood. Charley is a tiger, but a neighborhood tiger.

This incident parallels a key sequence in another important American film text. In *It's a Wonderful Life*, released less than a year before *Body and Soul*, the main character George Bailey has a talk with his father in which the younger Bailey says he can't live and work like his father, "cooped up in some shabby office." The elder Bailey overlooks the slight and explains that important cultural work goes on in that shabby office and that he sees a talent in his son that should not go unused. This conversation is the last that father and son have in these two films and provides the lessons, however painful, that the son must learn in order to carry on the work of the father, however humble.

Both fathers led circumscribed, strained, and unfulfilled lives in which they found themselves subservient to larger powers beyond the law proper—Davis to the nature of a slum neighborhood rife with bootleggers and gangsters, Bailey to a small town dominated by the corrupt Potter. In their shabby work settings, both men served others and wished for better for their sons. The ultimate benefit of a Warner Bros. aesthetic—or a populist ethic, such as that enunciated in Capra's films—is to demonstrate the pervading sense of group soul, of larger and more positive influence that endures despite temptation to indulge the self. Marxist criticism rightly sees such narratives as perpetuating a restrictive status quo that virtually guarantees the continuation of existing power structures, even though film audiences might see some lessons for the life well-lived. Here is the paradox of the Warner Bros. tradition: though conventional liberal criticism reads such texts as bourgeois, the messages continue to satisfy consumers as legitimate accounts of the movement from privation to some form of satisfaction.

George Bailey absorbs this paternal teaching more quickly than Charley, but they both redeem the lesson of the father by the final frames. The small worlds of drug store, candy store, and building & loan office approximate the workaday world most familiar to the viewers of these films; despite the tendency to sentimentalize such situations (or the Modernist disparagement of them), poor ethnic neighborhoods benefit from their altruistic inhabitants who see beyond the immediate profit to something larger and more encompassing, even when its precise nature cannot be explained. Such inarticulateness partially explains the power the studio held over its audiences.

This feeling is announced commercially in both films. When young George fears that his drunken pharmacist boss—who has just lost his own son—may poison a young boy, he seeks his father's aid after viewing a Sweet Caporal cigar ad: "Ask Dad—He Knows." Charley schmoozes with his cronies in a poolroom in front of another ad for "Dad's Root Beer." The father's presence remains even when he is not onscreen. It is the son's job, however, to redeem the message of the father by working it out in the world and thereby to show the mother that her son is after all the man she hoped he would demonstrate himself to be to that larger world.

This is the stuff of fairy tales and folk legends, probably most apparent in the story of Jack and the Beanstalk. Jack's widowed mother is unhappy because Jack seems to be heading down the wrong track; he's foolishly expended their meager resources. But he ultimately defeats the giant and wins back the valuable prizes that the giant had stolen from his father. While both of these films suggest the ultimate victory of the son, they are realistic in their depiction of the cultural context—Charley still has to reckon with Peters and the boxing commission, and George has the matter of the missing $8,000 and the bank examiner to deal with. The obvious love both fathers hold for their sons demonstrates their assurance that their boys will accomplish what they could not.

The issues of body and soul arise again in the sequence where Peg meets Ma Davis. Easy to miss is the meaning of the "For Rent—Apply Next Door" sign on the abandoned candy store. [53] The Davis family now has no income. In a carefully arranged series of interior shots, Charley's extended family—his mother, Peg, and Shorty—are grouped first around the table in order to show Peg's shrewd deference to Ma and to establish a relationship between the two ladies. [60] Ma gets up from the table to show Peg Charley's basketball medal, only to be interrupted by Miss Tedder's knock at the front door. In this sequence, Charley's sense of self and self-worth are most directly challenged. "We don't want any help—tell them we're dead!" screams Charley—and perhaps they are. With no source of income and no education, Charley has no life. So when he commands Shorty to get him a fight, Ma yells at her son, "Better to get a gun and shoot yourself!" Charley keys the dispute by telling her that he needs money to buy a gun. Death assumes many forms in this film world. [63-66]

Howe's careful lining of figures and expressions in the wake of Charley's expulsion of Miss Tedder shows how the principals in the film relate to one another, and then the rhythm of flight and pursuit begins anew as Peg follows Charley to the rooftop. Here Charley has a rooftop soliloquy musing on death and the city (worthy of comparison with the one Elia Kazan wrote for Francie Nolan in *A Tree Grows in Brooklyn*)— seeing boxing as his only way to escape his wretched life: "Tiger, tiger, I got claws, but not for you, Peg, not for you." He realizes that he still has lessons to learn, but he knows when he can avoid hurting those he loves—or thinks he does.

The punctuation of this sequence emphasizes the verticality presented in the earlier interior shots. The camera pulls back from a frontal shot to a reverse shot, presenting the street corner below. [67] And here is a point overlooked since the film's release—though critics have always praised the newsreel look of the low-angle roller-skate shots of the final fight sequence and Howe's effective use of low-angle shots generally, they have missed the basic psychological impact of the high-angle shots which look down at the street corner from the Davis apartment. Critical response has been slow to recognize the power of such high-angle shots over the subconscious. Peg's presence with Charlie and her declaration of support indicate a position superior in terms both of relationship and social power, as they embrace above the masculine "V" of the street corner, certainly one of the most crucial sites in American cultural history. The kiss shows the couple above the world of the street and corner, and yet still very much a part of it. Here the viewer sees perhaps most fully the nature of the film's soul, the feminine presence of the anima that tempers the masculine body. Peg helps Charley to see how he can transcend the corner's limitations by giving in to his capacity for human connection. This, too, fueled Warners' street corner stories, and the same sympathetic vision later led to charges of fellow traveling being leveled against the creators of such texts.

As if to dispel this delicate image and mood, Rossen offers a dramatic change: a whirlwind montage of posters, fights, trains and phone calls creates a taking-off for Charley, a jumping into space, into an abyss from the security of the corner—site of his first triumphs and his securing of Peg's love. [68-69]

He displays this same lack of sophistication when he claims that as champ he can give orders to Roberts, and then immediately cuts himself while shaving. The blood suggests the power Roberts still has over him. [72-73] Similarly, when he sets himself up in his grand apartment, he crows from behind the fancy bar, "Just like the candy store!" [77] Only he has mistaken the lesson of the father and must travel further in his descent before he can recognize that trajectory. Howe again helps the viewer to appreciate this, as he sets up a banquet scene in deep focus, recalling Kane's victorious celebrations in Welles's film, that is very different from the packed shots of the Iroquois Democratic Club.

Howe returns to this layered style again, though, when the conversation moves to the singer Alice and the spectator sees Quinn's reactions to Roberts's comments about her. [115-116]

Narrative structure reflects the Warner Bros. milieu as well. The East Side is going for Charley in a big way: when Charley has put the sixty grand on Marlowe and returns home, the grocery boy tells him that he has his five bucks on Charley and the whole Jewish neighborhood is behind him. As he says, "Like you was the Irish sweepstakes!" [131] This ethnic identification again brings the two groups together, as the Cagney/Garfield fighter paradigm recurs. Finally, the melodramatic plot turn involving a flawed character seeing the right and reforming—Cagney, for example, in *Angels with Dirty Faces*—recurs not once but twice here. Quinn forgets that Charley has alienated the grasping affections of his former girlfriend Alice and overlooks his own bets when he decides to help Charley win the fight. Charley, of course, provides the crucial turnaround when he understands that, as the pawn of Roberts, he will never know exactly where he stands and he determines to knock out Marlowe.

The final fight sequence, justifiably famous for its effective cinematography created by Howe's using roller skates to empower a mobile camera, displays other strengths as well. Earlier fight films and sequences, even those from Warner Bros., displayed a studio sheen. The scene of the intimacy of the arena was not effectively realized. But here in *Body and Soul*, Howe has created a new look. The darkness is truly dark in the far reaches of the arena, and the cigar and cigarette smoke hangs in that darkness in a way that had not been captured before. That Howe was willing to overstep boundaries and try new techniques is borne out by recalling his three-month suspension from using Technicolor equipment, after he shot the cave scenes for *The Adventures of Tom Sawyer* using only a quarter of the light the color consultants prescribed. What he produced for *Body and Soul* is a new look in boxing, one that captures Gillette's Friday Night at the Fights—the look of a new era.

III.

Sadly, the film looked forward to a new era in other ways. Though it was highly successful with both critics and the ticket-buying public, the seeds of future trouble are apparent. Polonsky, Rossen, and Garfield shared the lower East Side sense of wrongs to be righted; their intellectual interests led them naturally to others who shared their critical views of society. To varying degrees they embraced the Communist party as a means of righting the wrongs they viewed in the world; to their credit, they increased such efforts as their growing stature enabled them to raise their voices more effectively.

Speaking out on behalf of equalitarian ideals that even remotely related to the party, however, meant trouble for the three principals. The sort of trouble associated with political activism in 1940s film has been capably studied before. Jonathan Rosenbaum points out that "a fear of the social movements of the Thirties was an important ingredient in American life in the Forties and Fifties" (42). Thom Andersen points out, however, that "Surprisingly, none of the histories of the blacklist have addressed" two questions: "Were the films of the blacklist victims *politically* distinctive? Were the films of the blacklist victims *artistically* distinctive?" (Part II). Since Andersen coins the term "film *gris*" to characterize the dismal greyness of a subgenre introduced by *Body and Soul*, he obviously does believe that this body of film represents significantly distinctive political interests and artistic qualities.

The blending of political and artistic concerns finds a perfect counterpoint in Blake's poem. If, as Andersen argues, *Body and Soul* is the first example and Garfield the patron saint of *gris*, then "The Tyger" is its anthem. The poem's speaker is mired in the world of experience—he knows that there is much that is wrong, even evil, in the universe, but he has come to accept such negativity as a given. He imagines a dark and fearsome God at the center of this universe who is omnipotent and who operates from a wilderness unfathomable to the speaker. This spirit of energy cannot help but manifest itself, because in its unquenchable power it necessarily overpowers all who observe it, and in turn causes the narrator to fear it.

Such is the situation of the citizen of the society that allowed—in many cases, even encouraged—first the hearings and then the blacklist. Citizen and Blake's narrator dwell in realms of night because they alike have mistaken the manifestations of hatred and repression in the world for the God of that world. They reason that since these qualities are the most powerful, they in turn must be the ultimate power, or God. In this way, a Warner Bros. refugee like Ronald Reagan can think that as a "friendly witness" he is serving a legitimate god, when he takes a page from the book of the narrator in the night and imagines a fearful symmetry in the thinking patterns of many of his former coworkers and colleagues. Blake never knew of the blacklist, but he knew intimately the human and social factors that produced such an age of Reagan and Roberts.

The example of Blake also serves as a corrective to Rosenbaum's parting assertion of "an ongoing tradition of political avoidance and omission whereby blacklist victims become worthy of our attention only to the extent that they become stripped of their political beliefs" (57). The example of *Body and Soul* and Garfield show how, in the starkest terms possible, people think they are performing the will of a higher power when they operate on principles apparent in the world they observe, when they see the body and not the soul. *The Songs of Experience* are songs of woe sung in a land of plenty, songs sung at least partially to rebuke a power structure that worships forms of strength, even negative ones, and prosecutes the weakness it perceives in human sympathy, in feeling for the plights of others.

A final Blakean instance is the character of Alice. Like Quinn, she comes directly from the wet nocturnal streets of film *noir*. In her art of singing, she parallels Peg's painting; but in her sense of the world, she becomes one of Blake's little girls lost or singing bird heroines, either herself caged up or caging others in a vain attempt to control them. Charley's vision of success, a dream born of the night on his corner, provides Alice the money she wants, but it cannot provide the true love that Peg requires. As Peg points out to Charley, his idea of success is based on what other people think. He must allow his true successes to arise from his own ability, as she allows Charley his freedom to find his way. Even Quinn realizes that his efforts to keep Alice in a cage have failed; he moves out of the world of Blakean night when he overlooks Charley's having taken his girl and encourages Charley to win the final fight.

We should thus construe Rosenbaum's comment in a slightly different manner—the politics appear correctly; the problem is that we're still trying to see the world from the vantage point of the forests of the night. The useful work done by Andersen, Rosenbaum and other commentators on the effects of the blacklist increases in resonance when considered against the qualities which all filmmakers absorbed consciously or unconsciously from the Warners traditions.

In 1947 the Hollywood Ten were indicted by the House Committee on Un-American Activities (HUAC). In May of that year, Jack L. Warner was called to testify in private before the committee. Unbelievable as it is today, the Committee was raking Warner over the coals for what it perceived as pro-Communist sympathies in the 1942 film *Mission to Moscow*. Never mind that the Russian initiative against the Nazis in 1942 required all the support the U.S. could muster; in 1947, the WWII effort was evidently forgotten in the zeal of waging the new Cold War. But Warner defended his studio's work, and by extension the movie industry as a whole, in both the May meeting and a second round of testimony in October, when he stated: "That picture was made when our country was fighting for its existence, with Russia as one of our allies. It was made to fulfill the same wartime purpose for which we made such other pictures as *Air Force*, *This Is the Army*, *Objective, Burma!*, *Destination Tokyo*, *Action in the North Atlantic*, and a great many more.

"If making *Mission to Moscow* in 1942 was a subversive activity, then the American Liberty ships which carried food and guns to Russian allies and the American naval vessels which convoyed them were likewise engaged in subversive activities. This picture was made only to help a desperate war effort and not for posterity . . ." (Behlmer 288-89). In linking his product with the food and guns necessary to wage war, Warner points out how vital a role Warner Bros. played in shaping national consciousness. If the general perception in 1947 was not so, then neither Jack Warner nor the three collaborators on *Body and Soul* would have been so crucial to HUAC. Affiliations with the Communist party for Polonsky, Rossen, and Garfield were of interest to the HUAC investigators largely in terms of their influence on the films with which they were associated.

Rossen was one of nineteen scheduled to be investigated as "unfriendly" when the Committee broke off hearings in late 1947. He was blacklisted in 1950. After providing some information to the Committee in 1953, he was able to resume working in Hollywood the following year. Garfield frequently reiterated his belief that actors should speak their convictions, although he did not actually have to appear before the Committee until 1951. Following his testimony, he was unable to find film or theater work until he played in a late-spring 1952 revival of *Golden Boy*. Polonsky was named as a Communist to the Committee in 1951, invoked the Fifth Amendment, and was blacklisted until 1968, when he wrote *Madigan*.

Polonsky's exile was the longest of the three. He was perhaps more frank about his Communist party acquaintances and experiences than any other subpoenaed witness, calling the party "the best club to belong to in Hollywood, because all the smart guys were in it" (Goldstein 1997). Certainly it was the organization for someone with a social conscience. Though Polonsky did not work for Warner Bros., his work certainly breathes the spirit of that company's operational philosophy. When he scripted Blake's lines for Lilli Palmer, he was invoking a fearless fighter against all sorts of tyranny. Nothing put Blake into a greater rage than the abuse of power, whether through such private institutions as slavery or the use of chimney sweeps, or through public institutions of organized religion and a standing army. One of Blake's constant themes was the recognition of energy in life and the need to purify it, to enable energy to take forms that would lead to a more just world in which poetry and not tyranny held sway. Blakean subtexts fit perfectly a film project that reprises a hallowed tradition at the same time it declares war on the forces of tyranny. Like Blake's chimney sweeps, Garfield, Polonsky, and Rossen knew there had to be a better world beyond the tough life of the streets.

IV.

The lessons the three learned as savvy kids on the East Side and later in Hollywood, particularly at Warner Bros., taught them to be tough, to stick up for your principles, to not let a mug push you around. But in the McCarthy era, such values were a liability. The shadowy forces lying in wait in the dark—forces sometimes personified by men like Roberts— were all too real and all too powerful in the early 1950s. The final decades of the century brought fuller understanding of the venality of the committee's motives and wider appreciation of the men and women strong enough to oppose them—but such understanding came too late. Like the ending Rossen proposed for *Body and Soul* in which Roberts's gunsels kill Charley after the fight and dump him in an alley, the good guys too often realize too late that a slight misstep can doom them. The very qualities that made *Body and Soul* a great film in the traditions established by Warner Bros. doomed its creators.

Works Cited

[Warner Bros. correspondence related to specific films is housed according to film titles. The most complete archive is housed at the University of Southern California School of Cinema-Television; a parallel set, nearly as complete, is housed at the United Artists Collection of the Wisconsin Center for Film and Theater Research. A third set—comprised mainly of Warner Bros. legal files from its New York office— is housed at the William J. Seymour Theater Collection of Princeton. *The Warner Bros. Archive of Historical Papers*, a multi-volume index, lists materials at all three sites. All citations of correspondence in this essay refer to these files.]

Andersen, Thom. "Red Hollywood" in *Literature and the Visual Arts in Contemporary Society*. Eds. Suzanne Ferguson and Barbara Groseclose. Columbus: Ohio State UP, 1985. Pp. 186+.

Anderson, Sherwood. "Listen, Hollywood!" *Photoplay*, March 1938, 28-29, 93.

Anonymous. "They Made Me a Criminal." *Newsweek*, 30 Jan. 1939, p. 24.

Behlmer, Rudy. *Inside Warner Bros. (1935-1951)*. New York: Simon & Schuster, 1985.

Between Two Worlds. United Artists Collection, Wisconsin Center for Film and Theater Research. Scripts Files. Box 27, Folder 7.

Blake, William. *The Complete Poetry & Prose of William Blake*. Ed. David V. Erdman. Rev. ed. New York: Doubleday, 1988.

Crowther, Bosley. "A Man Who Means to Make a Dent." *New York Times*, 18 December 1938 IX, 7:3.

Editors of Fortune. "Warner Brothers." *Fortune* 16:6 (December 1937), 110-13, 206+.

Goldstein, Patrick. "Hollywood Blacklist: Cornered Rats and Personal Betrayals." *Los Angeles Times*, 20 October 1997 1.

Gombrich, E. H. "Meditations on a Hobby Horse." *Meditations on a Hobby Horse and Other Essays on the Theory of Art*. London: Phaidon Publishers, 1963.

Odets, Clifford. *Golden Boy*. *A Treasury of the Theatre: From Henrik Ibsen to Eugene Ionesco*. Ed. John Gassner. Third ed. New York: Simon and Schuster, 1961. 952-82.

_____. "Letter." *New York Times*, 25 May 1952 II, 3:7.

Polonsky, Abraham. Filmed Interview with Prof. John Schultheiss
     on *Body and Soul*. 13 May 1987. Passage from documentary currently in
     production.

Rosenbaum, Jonathan. "Guilty by Omission." *Film Comment* 27:5 (September-Oc-
     tober 1991) 42-46, 50+.

Sklar, Robert. *City Boys: Cagney, Bogart, Garfield*. Princeton: Princeton UP, 1992.

Variety. 10 February 1942, p. 17.

⚜

Peter Valenti is Professor and Chair, Department of English, Fayetteville
State University, Fayetteville, NC, and is presently Distinguished Visiting
Professor of English at the United States Air Force Academy. He has written on numerous film-related subjects including Errol Flynn, Frank Capra,
and John Huston. He is completing *Angel Spoken Here*, a study of the
discourses of sentiment in popular film and literature.

Guys in the neighborhood: Shorty (Joseph Pevney, third from left); Charley Davis (John Garfield, second from right holding sketch)

A Tiger in the Neighborhood. Peg has sketched Charley's "well built" body as an object of art, of aesthetic value apart from inner nature—or soul. His feistiness and toughness suggest that he is a tiger, hungry and savage, roaming in dimly lit streets which are so difficult to leave for good. Peg's drawing has given Charley prominent stripes, and one of the guys says, "Hey, look . . . fur!" It is a wonderfully ambiguous image: Charley is streetwise, but at the same time innocent. He knows survival skills, but not the most crucial ones for his soul. Charley is a tiger, but a neighborhood tiger. (See pp. 311-314.)

The Candy Store
That Dare Not Speak Its Name

by Mark Rappaport

Although boxing movies or, rather, movies about boxers were a sub-genre before *Body and Soul* was made, *Body and Soul* transformed the genre into something different—a morality play about corruption. The success of the film, in the true spirit of Hollywood, spawned a rash of imitators hoping to duplicate its success, all of which added aspects of parable to the form. Hard on the heels of *Body and Soul* came *Champion* (1949, morality play in which corrupt boxer succumbs to the corruption) and *The Set Up* (1949, morality play in which washed up boxer goes up against corruption to regain self-respect). Subsequent visits to the ring produced *Somebody Up There Likes Me* (1956, cautionary tale about bad boy who becomes a good boy through boxing), *Rocky* (1976, fable about a lunk who beats the odds)—all the way through *Raging Bull* (1980, cautionary tale about angry lunk who can find nothing, not even himself, in the ring).

Along the way, *Body and Soul* changed the direction of the sports film insofar as it made it be about something other than just the game itself. What is *The Hustler* (1961) if not a morality tale that takes place on a pool table instead of the ring—morality tale of guy with too much pride who wins the game *and* his soul, but is deprived of the possibility of playing again?

The variations on the theme have been and will be endless, but the basic premise remains the same—the ring or the pool table, the diamond, the bull ring, or the race track become the crucible in which the hero tests his mettle and finds out what he's really made of. Perhaps it was that post-World War II films had to validate their existence by finding a meaning in a shopworn format, or that the tired formula, of necessity, had to be recharged by the horrors that everyone who was alive at the time became privy to. It was no longer an innocent world. One could not have lived through World War II, even at a distance, and imagine the world was still the same place as it was prior to the war. If sports films became invested with a new and darker meaning and became metaphors for how the world works, the same was true of other genre films like westerns, "women's" films, gangster films. Suddenly genres which, a few years earlier, reveled in their innocence became battlegrounds where conflicts of good and evil, innocence and corruption, individuals versus communities, have-nots against haves were waged. And *Body and Soul* was there. As was Polonsky's *Force of Evil* the following year.

Body and Soul changed the face of sports movies in other ways as well. Even though films like *Somebody Up There Likes Me* and especially *Raging Bull* grounded themselves in the communities and specifically the ethnic environment from which the boxers emerged, prior to *Body and Soul*, ethnicity was used as another instance of local color, to add a bit of flourish to an otherwise undernourished background. If Cagney is a boxer, the background can easily be filled in with drunken pals and barroom scenes peppered with lilting brogues—and *voilà*—we got Irish. Ethnicity in Hollywood movies was as casual and inessential to the films themselves as the authenticity of a foreign setting—we are shown an establishing shot of the Eiffel Tower and, poof, we know that the rest of the movie despite the variety of American accents of the actors takes place in Paris. *Body and Soul* is probably the first urban Hollywood drama to posit a semblance of Jewishness at the center of the film.

Although one could be of Irish or German or Italian descent in Hollywood movies, one could never be Jewish. Was it too close to the bone for the studio heads who were all, with the exception of Darryl Zanuck, Jewish themselves? Was it the fear of "calling attention" to themselves as minorities (in terms of the general population), even though they are in the majority in Hollywood? Was it the shame of providing, for audiences who might prove hostile to any kind of portrayal of Jews, convenient templates of negative stereotyping? Or was it perhaps an acting out of some distorted form of a lost, unwritten commandment—Thou Shalt Not Make Images of Thine Own People? Or maybe it was the notion that it was too self-serving and at the same time too close to home to depict Jews. Or was it, if we don't mention it, maybe they'll forget? None of these complicated questions can be answered by a simple true or false or a yes or a no. Obviously, Don't Make Waves was one of the unwritten, implicit commandments among the large Jewish community within the Hollywood community.[1]

Despite the fact that the studio heads were Jewish and many top directors and writers were as well, the first and only mention to my knowledge, of Jews in concentration camps was in *Once Upon A Honeymoon*

(1942)—by Leo McCarey, the Irish Catholic director of *Going My Way* and *The Bells of St. Mary's*. One solemn scene occurs in this otherwise tasteless yukfest about the Nazi takeover of Europe. Ginger Rogers has given her passport to her Jewish maid to help the maid escape the Nazis (a scene accompanied by a "Yiddish"-sounding mournful melody on the soundtrack), and she is stuck with the maid's passport that identifies Ginger as a Jew. Because they are mistaken for Jews, she and Cary Grant are subsequently incarcerated for a very brief spell in a concentration camp (and it wasn't the showplace camp Theresienstadt, either), where a whole bunch of Orthodox Jews are colorfully and mournfully *davening* in the background. It appropriately takes place at night, an opportunity for a lot of chiaroscuro and fog effects and maybe you can even make out some smokestacks in the distance. So here's proof positive that they *did* know, even then! Or at least they knew *something*! Still earlier, in *The Man I Married* (1940) a.k.a. *I Married A Nazi*, made by Fox, Zanuck's studio, Joan Bennett learns that her husband, Francis Lederer, the eponymous villain, is involved in concentration camps, which are, parenthetically, in that version, Jew-free zones.

Jewishness was a subject not much talked about in films, although sometimes it hung around insidiously and tenaciously in the background. For example, whenever the Lower East Side is mentioned in films it *probably* means "Jewish" although it's hard to prove. The Lower East Side became the signifier for a racially diverse, culturally mixed, not-so-glorious melting pot where Germans, Italians, Irish, and Jews all lived cheek to jowl not-so-harmoniously together in a romanticized studio-bound idea of realistic tenement life (cf. *Street Scene*, 1931; *Dead End*, 1937). The Lower East Side becomes something like the polyglot roll call in war movies, which always included someone named Schwartz and someone from Brooklyn—sometimes embodied by one actor. But most of all, Lower East Side meant Jews. And if the hero were John Garfield from the Lower East Side it almost definitely meant Jewish. Garfield, although not the first Jewish movie star (think Paul Muni, Edward G. Robinson, Danny Kaye, Melvyn Douglas, Leslie Howard, and on the distaff side, Sylvia Sidney), was the first one to allow himself to be identified as such. When seen as the army veteran Dave Goldman, Gregory Peck's best friend in *Gentleman's Agreement*, there is almost a nakedly clandestine thrill of Julius Jacob Garfinkle being allowed to play a Jew without the disguises, masks or shorthand that had become familiar, if not always immediately recognizable, to moviegoers.

But the shorthand still applied. If Chinese laundries always signified "Chinese," and Italian restaurants always meant "Italians," similarly "candy store" (certainly in New York) means "Jewish." There aren't many candy stores in film literature—but the ones that are there are Jewish. This is not to be confused with the drug store or soda shop or soda fountain, all of which could be found in dozens of Hollywood films of the 30s, 40s and 50s. But you can bet you couldn't get an egg cream or a cherry lime rickey or a copy of the *Jewish Daily Forward* at any of *those* emporiums. Similarly, I'd like to bet that you *could* ask for any of those items at the Davis candy store run by Garfield's parents (Art Smith and Anne Revere) in *Body and Soul*.

Precedents and Antecedents

Although I was certain that I wasn't making this up, that the candy store *is* a signifier for Jewishness, I wanted to be on firmer ground and checked with a variety of friends and acquaintances who have seen more films than I have, and/or have more prodigious memories than I do, and/or have more of an interest in the representation of *Yiddishkeit* than I do. I also checked with friends who are experts in theater literature and one who has a broad knowledge of Yiddish theater. *Everyone* said, "That sounds right," and were sure that they could come up with several example. None did. But I found a few on my own. As Lily Tomlin says, "I got evidence."

In Clifford Odets's play, *Golden Boy* (1937), the father's pal from the neighborhood is a Jewish candy store owner named Carp (parenthetically, the major ingredient in gefilte fish), which is certainly something he does a lot of. He is a cranky (but lovable) guy who has a lot of opinions about the world and begins every sentence with, "As Schopenhauer says…" In the original Group Theater production, he was played by Lee J. Cobb.[2] In the film version *Golden Boy* (1939, directed by Rouben Mamoulian), Cobb, only 28 at the time, plays the father of William Holden, the Golden Boy of the title, in a blubbering, *Saturday Night Live* impersonation of an Italian immigrant. The candy store-owning friend (William H. Strauss), who has no relation whatever to the plot, and is retained perhaps to suggest diversity in the neighborhood, or perhaps as a reminder that the play might just as easily have been about Jews as about Italians, is still a cranky (but lovable) philosopher-type although the references to Schopenhauer are minimized.

More Jewish candy store owners? Try *Somebody Up There Likes Me* (1956, directed by Robert Wise). Even though Joseph Buloff, a luminary of the Yiddish Theater, is a self-described "two-cent soda *schlepper*," he is as handy at dispensing philosophy as he is at making egg creams. He is the one that Rocky Graziano (Paul Newman) goes to when he needs advice on how to straighten out his life. And then at the furthest end of the time frame when the idea of "candy store" was well on its way to becoming an anachronism and a nostalgia-worthy memory, there's *West Side Story* (1961, also directed by Robert Wise). Tony (Richard Beymer) works in Doc's candy store, which is a hangout for the Jets and where the Jets and the Sharks conduct their war council. Doc, too, is a lovable old Jewish man who is quick to give anyone who will listen the benefit of his hard-earned wisdom. He is played by character actor Ned Glass who has a special place in my heart as the man who tries to palm off his ratty cat men costumes on Kirk Douglas and Barry Sullivan in *The Bad and the Beautiful* (1952) for a low-budget horror movie they are making. "Lotsa character in the tail," he says, casually fondling a moth-eaten piece of *schmatte*. There are, doubtless, many more scenes of Jewish-owned candy stores hovering at the peripheries of forgotten and almost-forgotten movies (the Bowery Boys movies have been suggested to me), but my purpose is not to excavate them all. A few examples will to suffice to suggest that, as a phenomenon, it *does* exist.

Naming Names

In *Body and Soul*, Polonsky spares us the candy-store-owner-as-philosopher trope. They're only candy store owners, not philosopher kings. But we're also wooed away from the notion that they're Jewish. First the family name Davis. Not Jewish. The owners? Art Smith, Anne Revere. Not Jewish or, rather, not particularly Jewish. Where are the tell-tale accents? So, wherein does this Jewishness reside? The mere fact of the candy store itself. In the 30s and 40s, candy stores were as quantifiably Jewish as Korean green grocers are "Korean" today. Or as newsstands are Pakistani-owned today. That the names and the actors do not suggest any ethnic affiliation may be an attempt to neutralize the situation and make it more palatable (within the frame of the film, less stereotypical) for a larger audience. Or, to cast it in a more positive light, it was an attempt to deflect the Jewishness of the situation by de-emphasizing it or ignoring it completely.

Art Smith—perhaps best remembered today for his roles as Louis Jourdan's mute butler in Max Ophuls's *Letter From An Unknown Woman* (1947), as the shrink who advises Robert Ryan not to marry Barbara Bel Geddes in Ophuls's *Caught* (1949), and as Humphrey Bogart's agent in Nicholas Ray's *In A Lonely Place* (1950)—was in the Group Theater, and, like many other cast and crew members on *Body and Soul*, was a victim of the blacklist. He had the dubious distinction of being denounced by his former Group Theater colleague, many-time Oscar winner Elia Kazan. Smith's last appearance in films was a small role, ironically enough in another movie directed by Robert Rossen, *The Hustler* (1961). This was *after* Rossen had given names to the House Committee on Un-American Activities and Smith was finally allowed to work in films again.

Anne Revere was a large-boned woman whose face and demeanor suggested she would brook no nonsense. That her name rhymes with "severe" is probably an accident, but her New England bearing and demeanor are not. In the 1940s and early 1950s, before she was blacklisted, she specialized in strong mother roles on the screen and was, in fact, the Mother of All Mothers. Her brood included, besides Garfield, Jennifer Jones in *The Song of Bernadette*, Elizabeth Taylor in *National Velvet*, Gregory Peck in *Gentleman's Agreement*, and Montgomery Clift in *A Place in the Sun*—a stunning looking bunch of stellar dark-haired children.

None of these actors conveys any ethnic coloring other than good American stock. We are not offered caricatures of ethnicity, like J. Carrol Naish who plays Garfield's father in *Humoresque* (1946, directed by Jean Negulesco). Without any ethnic specificity, is he Italian? Jewish? Greek? What *is* he? The family name is "Boray." But don't think French. It's too hoity-toity. Naish owns a grocery store, but "Boray" betrays no recognizable ethnic traces, while at the same time suggests an unaggressive but not unpleasant ethnicity. To say that Naish is *generic* ethnic, without filling in any details, provides enough information to the audience without, in Hollywood terms, overstating the case. That his nondescript accent suggests an indeterminate foreignness is all that is required. (On second thought, maybe Naish *was* supposed to be Italian—in a warm-up for his radio and television series in the early 1950s, *Life with Luigi*.)

Secondary characters could be played by actors who by the very nature of their foreign accents or looks were signifiers of "foreignness," and were presumably accepted by the audience as members of any nationality. Akim Tamiroff, J. Carrol Naish, Vladimir Sokoloff, Anthony Quinn, Nestor Paiva, who never stopped working, quickly come to mind as actors who suggested all-purpose foreignness, and who would obligingly "pass" for any and every nationality that Hollywood required. Were those more innocent times? Or more isolationist times—when a Spaniard could play an Italian and a Frenchman could play a Spaniard and any actor could apply a thick fake accent and no one would take offence? Consider, for example, that scruffy pick-up band of Spanish Republican fighters in *For Whom the Bell Tolls* (1943)—Katina Paxinou, Akim Tamiroff, Vladimir Sokoloff, Mikhail Rasumny, not to mention Ingrid Bergman. Ethnicity was another form of local color that need not impinge itself on the foreground, which was usually occupied by the romantic entanglements of the stars. Having *somewhat* ethnic characters was a method of suggesting a background, but a background undifferentiated by nuance or troubled by facts.

Without putting too fine a point on it, the candy store, despite the conflicting signals it may send (Anne Revere/not Jewish, Davis/not Jewish, candy store/Jewish), is fully in keeping with the Hollywood tradition of scrambling up the coding, partly not to offend those who are all too willing to be offended, partly to hedge the filmmakers' bets by not putting all the cards on the table, and partly by having it every which way at the same time. Plausible deniability rules if one is asked whether or not a situation represents ethnic authenticity.[3]

Then there is the problematic case of Charley's girlfriend "Peg," Lilli Palmer. Now, we all know that Peg is an Irish name, but since Lilli Palmer (née Lilli Peiser) is playing the part, how to explain her untraceable trace of an accent? [39] The movie flirts with the convention that Irish and Jews are destined to fall in love with each other, as they do in other movies and plays that situate themselves on the Lower East Side (*Street Scene*, *Abie's Irish Rose*). But the reality is a little more dangerous. When Garfield asks her where she learned to talk so funny, she says she went to school in London, Berlin, and Paris. But in reality, Berlin is the answer. Palmer, a Jewish actress, fled Germany in 1933. To have two Jews in starring roles fall in love on screen was unheard of—not that there were enough Jewish women to go around in any case[4] The audience is instead invited to read through the Peg/Irish invention and reposition Lilli Palmer as a Jewish character. Or, to put it another way, the audience is encouraged to go along with the fiction that Peg is Irish, while knowing that Palmer isn't. Peg, Irish or not, is the nice Jewish girl who always sticks by her guy and even has his mother's approval—as opposed to the slinky *shiksa* seductress embodied by Hazel Brooks, goldigger and nightclub chantoosie, who is all for Charley being as corrupt as he possibly can. This dichotomy is repeated in *Force of Evil* as well, *sans* ethnic baggage. Polonsky posits the mother and the whore as two extremes as to what a woman could or should be—the improbably innocent Doris (Beatrice Pearson) pitted against the impossibly jaded Edna (Marie Windsor), who keeps throwing herself at Garfield's head. Polonsky more than makes amends for these stereotypically drawn good girls versus slutty dames in *I Can Get It For You Wholesale* (1951), in which he creates an amazingly complex woman character who transcends genre typecasting.

Candy Store as Metaphor

In the flashback that comprises the bulk of *Body and Soul*, we see Charley at the beginning of his career enter the candy store as his father and mother are closing up. Charley wants money to buy boxing equipment, but his mother refuses to give it to him. He says he doesn't want to wind up in a candy store like his father. His mother lashes out at him for the remark but his father lets it slide. After his mother leaves the store, his father gives him the money he needs. His father understands that boxing can be a way out of the cycle of working class poverty, as it always has for generations of what are now euphemistically called inner city kids. There was a wave of Irish fighters, followed by scores of Jewish boxers, followed by children of Italian immigrants, just as today young blacks and Hispanics see the game as a way out of the ghetto. But Charley is a Jew, and that's not something you can mention in a movie. Shortly after Charley receives the money, the candy store, unfortunately located next door to a bootlegging joint, is bombed and Charley's father is killed.

Although Charley is in no way responsible for his father's death, he chooses to become involved with the same kind of racketeers who caused his death. And although he never acknowledges his connections to the subsequent deaths in the film, he is nevertheless responsible for them. Once he hooks up with Roberts (Lloyd Gough), a big-time fight racketeer, the die is cast. Although we've seen the last of the candy store when Mr. Davis is killed, the candy store gets mentioned several more times during the film—most saliently whenever somebody dies.

When Charley becomes a success, he has a palatial uptown apartment, complete with a hidden, secret panel bar. When the bar swings into view, Charley, delighted, gets behind the counter and offers everyone drinks. "Bourbon, scotch. Like milk, like cream. What'll you have, folks? Just like the candy store. Want a two cents soda, Peg?" [77] You can take the boy out of the Lower East Side but you can't take the Lower East Side out of the boy. Is it nostalgia for his lost youth or an awareness of how far, as a once-impoverished Jew, he's come from his origins? And how, as a Jew, he doesn't really fit into the world he's fought so hard to make for himself?

When his pal and boyhood friend Shorty, played by Joseph Pevney,[5] who has become his unofficial manager, is beat up by Roberts's henchman and dies, Peg tells Charley that he must give up the boxing racket. "What can I do?" he asks Peg? "Go back to the candy store?"[6] [110] The death of Shorty is Charley's first major betrayal, because he didn't adequately protect Shorty from Roberts's fury and greed. But Charley's response is a realization that there's no going back to the innocence of the past. Or to the old neighborhood. Like Macbeth, he's set himself on a bloody course and there's no way back. So, he must continue on.

Similarly, Charley is seriously implicated in the death of Ben (Canada Lee), a former champ who has a blood clot and whom Charley fought. Charley is unaware of Ben's fragile state, but nevertheless fatally exacerbates his condition when he knocks him out. Charley accepts the responsibility of taking care of Ben by taking him on as his trainer. But he lets Ben down, too, when he allows Roberts to fire Ben. The excitement and humiliation so dangerous to Ben's high blood pressure kill him when Charley refuses to go to bat for him.

Charley, in fact, is very closely related to Joe Morse, the character Garfield plays in *Force of Evil*, because Joe Morse is responsible for the fix he put his brother in and his brother's inevitable death. Joe pretends to himself and to his brother that he is helping his brother, but he is really his chief gravedigger. In the book *Tucker's People* by Ira Wolfert, which *Force of Evil* is based on, Joe betrays Leo many, many times before Leo finally dies from Joe's treacheries. Their greediness and headlong flight from the poverty of the slums they grew up in permit neither Charley in *Body and Soul* nor Joe in *Force of Evil* to admit or even acknowledge their roles as emissaries of death and destruction. They are so corrupt themselves that they choose to blame the corrupt organizations they willingly joined. At the end of both films both heroes/anti-heroes decide to buck the system. Garfield, in both cases, enjoyed all the riches and he's going to call a stop to it when *he's* had enough. But since he/they profited so handsomely by partaking of the system's ill-gotten gains during the course of the two films, one has to wonder how long the final reel conversion will last after "The End" appears on the screen. This is a serious flaw that both movies have to contend with, but it also provides an interesting tension by positing a totally corruptible hero/anti-hero who can (but chooses not to) recognize the element of choice in his decisions. As Joe, who is more articulate than Charley Davis, says in *Force of Evil*, "I didn't have enough strength to resist corruption but I was strong enough to fight for a piece of it." The trail of death that they both leave behind them wakes them up. But very late in the game. And it's almost a given that Charley/Joe/Garfield will ultimately be no more successful in turning their backs on the criminals than the other characters, who had committed many more minor infractions against the rackets and paid with their lives.

When Roberts first tells Charley he wants him to take a dive, Charley assures Roberts that he can lick his opponent. Roberts tells him he's become soft. All that high living has taken a toll on him. Why even bother fighting it? Why not just go down for the count? He suggests to Charley that he could open up a club. "You punch the cash register instead of getting punched." [116] This is yet another reminder of Charley's humble origins, when he punched the cash register for his father. Even if his first instinct is to avoid a return to what can't be returned to, the instinct is to go back to revisit it.

The first thing he does after Ben's death is run for the security of the candy store. He's already agreed to throw the fight but he wants reassurance from his mother, who still lives on the Lower East Side above the candy store, that it's O.K. While he is visiting his mother, groceries are delivered. The grocery man (Shimen Ruskin), who speaks with a trace of an accent but not that of a recent refugee, tells Charley he's betting on him for the big fight, which Charley has already agreed to throw. "People shouldn't bet," Anne Revere advises him. "No, no, Mrs. Davis, it isn't the money. It's a way of showing. Over in Europe the Nazis are killing people like us—just because of their religion. But here Charley Davis is champeen.

So you win and you retire champeen. And we are proud. Period."[7] [132] People like us? Who does he mean? Grocery delivery boys? The movie was made in 1947. The war was already over. There are no textual indicators within the film itself that situate the film during the war.[8] This bolt out of the blue and the reference to "people like us" can only mean one thing. Every return to the candy store is a return to his Jewish roots, even though the "J" word isn't, couldn't, and wouldn't be mentioned.

Ben's death, followed by Shimen's pride in Charley as a representative of his people, and especially Peg's repudiation of Charley for what he's become, turn Charley around and tell him what he's come to hear. His transforming visit to the apartment above the candy store gets him back to his traditional Jewish/liberal roots, fighting for what you believe in and fighting corruption, even if you're part of it. His mother said to him earlier in the film, when he first started out and said he wanted to fight, "Fight for something. Not for money." [51] It took him three deaths later, two of which he caused, to understand what that meant.

Boys—Golden and Otherwise

When Clifford Odets was writing the play *Golden Boy* in 1937, Garfield desperately wanted the lead part. In fact, his talks with Odets about his *own* boxing experiences inspired Odets to write it in the first place. That and a Fannie Hurst short story, "Humoresque." Odets, even though he was not in a position to do so, promised Garfield the part and Garfield knew it would have made him a star. Harold Clurman, the director, felt that Garfield, then 24, did not have the acting ability to play the role of Joe Bonaparte, who is 21, and the role was given to Luther Adler, who was 34 at the time. Garfield was offered instead the role of Siggie, Joe Bonaparte's Jewish brother-in-law, which he grudgingly played, and then went off to Hollywood to become a star in his first movie, *Four Daughters* (1938, directed by Michael Curtiz). To say that Garfield was obsessed by *Golden Boy* may be going a bit far but he clearly felt that it would have provided him with an opportunity that few other roles would. The resentment at not having gotten the part rankled him so much and, clearly, for such a long time that at his 1951 HUAC hearing he admitted, "Well, I had turned down Hollywood for five years. Then I was promised the lead in a play. It is a very personal story but I don't mind telling you. I had a falling out with some of the directors in the Group on the basis of the part I was supposed to get and didn't get, so I was a little angry and signed a contract. Warner Bros. signed me at the time." His disappointment in not playing the Golden Boy of the title influenced his choice of roles once he fulfilled his Warner Bros. contract as well.

When Garfield and Bob Roberts formed Enterprise Pictures, an independent company, in 1946, specifically to create for Garfield the roles he wasn't getting from Warners, the first project was going to be a boxing story based on the life of Barney Ross. Barney Ross was a Jewish prizefighting champ who went into the marines during World War II, was a hero during the war, and became addicted to morphine as a result of his bout with malaria. When Polonsky started writing the script of *Body and Soul*, the Barney Ross idea got tossed out. But, like Barney Ross, Charley Davis's father owned a candy store *and* was accidentally killed in a gangland skirmish! Once again, as Lily Tomlin might say, I got evidence! So even though Garfield does not get to play Joe Bonaparte on stage or on screen—the movie *Golden Boy* was made by Columbia, and since Garfield was a Warner contract player and not yet a major star, that automatically put him out of the running—he gets to play it anyway. But in his *own* boxing movie.

The big conflict that Joe Bonaparte has in *Golden Boy* is that he must decide whether to become a professional boxer or fulfill his father's dream for him and become a concert violinist. The fiddle or the ring. Quick easy money versus hard art. The year before *Body and Soul* was made, Garfield made *Humoresque* for Warner Brothers. Here the *Golden Boy* conflict between boxing and fiddling evolves further. In *Humoresque*, Garfield plays a guy from the Lower East Side who *does* become a successful concert violinist. His father, like Joe Bonaparte's in *Golden Boy*, owns a grocery—and the script, rich in zingers, was written by none other than *Clifford Odets*. In a way, *Humoresque* is about the road not taken in *Golden Boy*. And, in a way, it makes the conflict clearer. Playing the fiddle was not genetically encoded in Italians the way it was in Jewish immigrant children in an earlier era. Garfield, in a sense, rips away the Italian trappings in *Golden Boy* and reveals them for the Jewish background that they probably should have been but for a variety of reasons couldn't have been. Nor was Garfield unaware of the connection between *Golden Boy* and *Humoresque*. He said, "You find out what would have happened to Joe Bonaparte if he had bumped into Helen Wright (Joan Crawford in *Humoresque*) instead of Lorna Moon (the female protagonist in *Golden Boy*)." *Body and Soul*, in conjunction with *Humoresque*, gives Garfield the opportunity he never had, to play *Golden Boy* when he was the right age. And perhaps it worked out for the best.

Although *Golden Boy* created quite a stir when it was first produced, today it reads as very clanky and tired, and, I suspect, is all but unactable. The 1939 movie, with William Holden, Barbara Stanwyck and Lee J. Cobb, feels like a musty antique, whereas *Body and Soul* has dialogue and situations that are as sizzling as they ever were. The same is true of *Humoresque*, a movie that is compellingly watchable. It's a fascinating examination, among other things, of a sado-masochistic relationship between Garfield and Crawford—"You might be sorry the word love was ever invented, Paul," she promises, and makes good on it. It is also another one of those culture-mongering Hollywood movies that tells us a great deal about the respect and honor Hollywood awarded or at least the lip-service they paid to high culture, complete with warnings about artists having to choose between the demands of art and the dubious comforts of love. For Garfield, *Body and Soul* + *Humoresque* = the lost chance of *Golden Boy*. Almost.

But, he still hadn't exorcised *Golden Boy*. In 1950, he performed a ten-minute scene from the play, with the then unknown Kim Stanley playing Lorna Moon, on a variety show, "Cavalcade of Stars." He was 37 and Kim Stanley, who plays a somewhat older or certainly worldlier, wiser woman, was 25. If I seem insistent on mentioning everyone's age, it's only because in the play and the scene they did, it's mentioned many times that Joe Bonaparte is 21. At 37, Garfield was already too old to suggest the freshness and innocence of a 21 year old. Certainly, too old to be playing a young boxer who has the world before him. And it's not just that the camera is less forgiving than the stage. Everyone who can add and had seen him in the movies *knows* Garfield is on the wrong side of twenty one. But Garfield is not through with "Golden Boy" yet.

In late 1951, he plans to do a revival of *Golden Boy* on Broadway. His movie career was at a standstill because—despite a somewhat cooperative session with HUAC in which he repudiated communism—he didn't give any names, and hadn't therefore cleared himself in the eyes of the studio heads. Kazan, by now a legendary theater director (*Death of a Salesman*, *Streetcar Named Desire*) as well as an Oscar-winning film director, was supposed to direct the play, but had to bow out to prepare for his first HUAC hearing in January 1952. Odets decides to direct the play himself. For Garfield it becomes an opportunity to re-visit the past, re-insert himself in it, and finally get it right. It's a nostalgic effort to erase the past 15 years—both the successes *and* the failures—and return to a more innocent time before the war, before the hearings and the blacklist—when all the people in the Group Theater were in it for idealistic reasons. In a way, doing the play, in the midst of McCarthyism, was in itself a political statement, a reminder of an earlier time when political commitment meant fighting *for* something, to use Anne Revere's line. Even Lee J. Cobb and Art Smith were on board again, Cobb playing Garfield's father this time and Smith playing his manager—promotions from the last time they played it on stage. And once again, the choice of who would play Lorna Moon was Odets's—based on amatory and personal reasons. This time, he chose his wife, Bette Grayson, as he had chosen the movie star Frances Farmer, with whom he was having an affair, in 1937.

It *was* a homecoming—and a vindication, certainly for Garfield. He got some of the best reviews of his career. It was to be the last part he played before he died. He had his 39th birthday on March 4. The play opened for a four-week limited engagement on March 12, 1952, but was so successful the run was extended for another three weeks. On April 10, Kazan testified a second time, this time naming names, including those of Odets, Art Smith and Tony Kraber, a former Group Theater actor who was also in the current production. Canada Lee, who had played Ben in *Body and Soul* and who was also a victim of the blacklist, died on May 9 at the age of 45.

Garfield was convinced that he wouldn't be able to work again unless he could somehow clear his name. It was asserted that he debated whether to take his problem into a more public arena. There was speculation that he wrote an article for *Look* called "I Was A Sucker For a Left Hook," the title itself once again conflating the boxing metaphor with left-leaning liberalism. The article was never published, nor were any copies of the manuscript ever found.[9] On May 19 and 20, Odets testified as a friendly witness for HUAC. Like Kazan, he was asked about Garfield's activities as a communist. And like Kazan, he said that Garfield had never been a communist. Without having been told about it, however, Garfield had already been cleared by both by HUAC and the FBI. On March 21, Garfield died of a heart attack. But by this time, *Golden Boy*, the part that had always eluded and haunted him and that bracketed his film career and even helped shape it, became his at last.

❧ ❧ ❧

If Garfield was the first Jew in the movie ring, he certainly wasn't the last. In fact, Jewish actors in Hollywood, after the war, strangely enough *always* ended up in the ring: Kirk Douglas in *Champion* (directed by Mark Robson), Paul Newman in *Somebody Up There Likes Me*, Jeff Chandler in *Iron Man* (1951, directed by Joseph Pevney), Tony Curtis in *Flesh and Fury* (1952, also directed by Joseph Pevney), and even Danny Kaye in *The Kid from Booklyn* (1946, directed by Norman Z. McLeod). It's almost like a ritual testing ground or rite of passage. If you were Jewish, in order to be able to play the sensitive guys, you first had to prove that you could take a good pummeling as well as give your opponent a good shellacking—not unlike Jewish guys going into the marines to prove to themselves and especially others that they were tough enough to take it.

As for the Barney Ross story, it was made into a movie in 1957 after the success of Preminger's *The Man with the Golden Arm* (1955), trying to capitalize on the drug addiction aspect which had been taboo in films before *Golden Arm*. Incidentally, or not so incidentally, at one point Garfield optioned Nelson Algren's novel, *The Man with The Golden Arm* as a possible project for himself and Enterprise. In the movie, *Monkey on My Back* (1957, directed by André de Toth), the emphasis is on Barney Ross (Cameron Mitchell) the junkie, kicking his habit, rather than on the boxer. His Jewishness is never alluded to, although he does have a mother with an accent who offers him and his future wife chicken for dinner. No candy store is ever mentioned.

The Candy Store of the Future

The candy store is, for better or worse, no longer with us. Even though the candy store has long since disappeared from the socio-economic landscape, edged out at first by somewhat upscale fast food chains like Chock Full O'Nuts and ultimately by the disintegration of immigrant neighborhoods as the children grew up and fled to the suburbs or to fancier addresses, the problems of representation of Jews on the screen is as tricky and thorny as it ever was. The word "Jew" it seems, is as big a taboo for the big screen as those pesky four-letter words are for the newspaper of record, *The New York Times*.

Even though the word "Jew" never rears its ugly head, when Spike Lee depicts people who *might* be Jews in *Mo' Better Blues*, cries of anti-Semitism are sounded. When Danny De Vito holds an army of penguins in thrall in *Batman Returns*, everyone seems to notice that he *seems* to be too Jewish for comfort: that prosthetic nose that is much too hooked, and what is that *mittel-Europeische* coat with the fur collar (could it be beaver?) supposed to mean?[10] The same people who seem to be so upset at discovering what they see as anti-Semitic slurs in movies by *goyim* and, even worse yet, *schwarze* filmmakers like Spike Lee, are not moved to complain about ugly caricatures of Jews in *Barton Fink* and *The Big Lebowski* by the Coen Brothers. If the Jews do it, it's O.K. On the other hand, the Coens are equal opportunity offenders—everyone who is *not* fortunate enough to be a Coen brother is in for a healthy dollop of their unfocused scorn. But the casual and repeated appearances of Jews-for-a-laff scattershot contempt have, to my knowledge, not raised any cries of protest by watchdog critics who claim to be so sensitive to this sort of thing.

Same goes for Woody Allen, who has found a gold mine in his Jewishness and has never stopped digging. All he has to do is say my date with her was . . . like . . . like a . . . a weekend in Auschwitz and it's a given that he'll bring the house down. Comparing an encounter with a former girlfriend or an unpleasant acquaintance to a visit by the Gestapo is a guaranteed laugh-getter. The mere mention of Nazis as a source of sure-fire humor—especially when evoked by Jews who trade on their Jewishness and get away with self-degrading jokes that others would be called on the carpet for—is a distressing signpost of how far we've come from the original revelation of the horrors of Nazism.[11] That the trivialization of Nazi atrocities can become the punch line of almost any joke is a disturbing reminder of the fact that—before, the word "Jew" couldn't be uttered unless it was a "problem" picture about the "Jewish problem" (*Gentleman's Agreement, Crossfire, Judgment at Nuremburg*) now, Jewishness, or what are perceived as attributes of Jewishness, is immediately recognizable and has its own built in laugh track. Certainly the entire career of Woody Allen is built on that premise, and more recently we have, on the small screen, *Seinfeld* and *The Nanny*. To question whether or not Fran Drescher as "The Nanny" is good for the Jews begs the issue. Can Drescher be good for *anyone*? Jewishness as *shtick* has become part of the American cultural landscape in a way that Polonsky and the makers of *Body and Soul* could never have predicted or recognized. Although it's totally permissible for comics to flaunt their Jewishness today, paradoxically, being Jewish has much less meaning than it did then. Now it's merely a comfortable comedic tool, one in a large arsenal, that by its very presence predictably primes the audience's responses.

To look at it another way: 50 years from now, if anyone bothers to unearth episodes of what they may yet call the "lost" episodes of *The Nanny* and *Seinfeld* (or, worst case scenario, readily viewed in endless syndication on many of the 1,000 cable channels available) or research copies of Woody Allen's movies, they will see depictions of Jewishness that will seem remarkably quaint and exotic. By that time, all connections to immigrant life, first generation Jewish-Americans, Jews without money, Jewish neighborhoods, and even the connection to Borscht Belt humor (Milton Berle, Sid Ceasar, Mel Brooks, Jerry Lewis, etc.) which is still so strong and influential today, will have completely disappeared and Jewishness will only be a fact of birth—not a cluster of cultural or social or behavioral affinities or shared memories, or experiences, or history. The "Jewishness" of current day representation will look as quaint 50 years from now, as *Body and Soul* does 50 years after its making, in its inability to say the one word that needs saying but can't be said. But we know that Jews, who today are seen as so much fun and so funny, were not such a laughing matter then. That Hollywood did not want to and thought it *couldn't* deal with the "Jewish question" in almost any manifestation was and remains a singular example of self-imposed political repression and willful self-denial. It required a great deal of skill and finessing in those days to find a way around this intractable obstacle—how to say it and, yet, not say it at all. One had to deal with coded signs and symbols, unable to reveal themselves, nonetheless revealing themselves fully, but in a very proscribed way. Now, when it no longer refers to anything, it's hip and chic to be Jewish and eminently flauntable. People do watch shows like *Seinfeld* and *The Nanny* and Woody Allen's movies—well, why not throw in Mel Brooks and Albert Brooks's movies as well? Fifty years from now, will anyone have an inkling what the mannerisms and arcane references refer to? Will there be evidence and traces of a *truly* lost tribe? Hard to say. Do stay tuned. But by then, even though everyone will probably still know what bagels and lox means, they will need footnotes at the bottom of the screen explaining, as if it were Shakespeare, what and how much a candy store meant in the middle of the 20th century in America.

Notes

[1][*Editor's Note*: To help make this complicated dynamic more comprehensible, see Neal Gabler's *An Empire of Their Own: How the Jews Invented Hollywood* (New York: Crown Publishers, 1988), which is a detailed social history of the political, religious, and economic milieu of Hollywood—and an examination of the psychology of the movie moguls themselves. *Hollywoodism: Jews, Movies and the American Dream* (1998) is a documentary, written and directed by Simcha Jacobovic, based on Gabler's book.]

[2] Also in the original production with Cobb were Garfield (billed as Julius), Art Smith, Elia Kazan, Martin Ritt, Morris Carnovsky, Howard Da Silva, and Michael Gordon, who directed *I Can Get It for You Wholesale* (1951) from a script by Polonsky, as well as *Pillow Talk* (1959). All of these actors and/or directors were later in varying degrees affected by the blacklist. The title role was played by Luther Adler and Lorna Moon was played by Frances Farmer, who was herself a political casualty of a different nature. Karl Malden was also in the play.

[3] While doing homework for this article, I watched *Kid Galahad* (1937, directed by Michael Curtiz)) in which Edward J. Robinson plays an Italian fight promoter, Donati. His mother, born in the Old World and who speaks very heavily accented English, is played not by an Italian woman but by an actress named Soledad Jiminez. Her thick accent is, in fact, *Spanish*. When the two of them talk Italian to each other, as if to suggest they always spoke Italian at home, it's an elaborate charade—but for whose benefit? To convince the audience of the verisimilitude of the "Italian-ness" of it all? Or to suggest that all foreign accents, Spanish or Italian—what difference does it make?—are the same? Or probably something less sinister than that. Hollywood's nonchalant relationship to foreignness, despite the high percentage of immigrant directors, reflects a casualness that should not be explored too deeply. Anything that can and does suggest foreignness or other-ness will work as effectively as another combination of elements. On a more authentic level of artifact, when you actually have the real thing like Marcel Dalio, who plays Frenchie in how many American movies, his presence suggests more than Frenchness. He *is* France! A refugee from Nazi-occupied France, his profile adorned Nazi posters alerting people to what a typical Jew looked like. Born Israel Moshe Blauschild, he was in all likelihood, however, no Frenchman's idea of the Idea of a Frenchman.

[4] When I saw *Young Man With a Horn* (directed by Michael Curtiz) for the first time, sometime in the mid 1980s I tried to imagine what it must have been like in 1950 when the movie was first released, seeing two major stars like Kirk Douglas and Lauren Bacall, neither of whom had made any bones about their Jewish origins, kissing each other on the screen. Did it mean as much to Jews in a post-Final Solution world as it meant to black people in pre-civil rights America seeing two beauties like Dorothy Dandridge and Harry Belafonte kissing in *Carmen Jones* (1953)?

⁵ Pevney subsequently became a contract director for Universal, where he directed without any great distinction several movies every year during the 1950s, including a slew of Rock Hudson, Jeff Chandler, and Tony Curtis vehicles.

⁶[*Editor's Note*: In Polonsky's shooting script (FINAL—Revised 1-13-47), there is a scene between Charley and Alice, *deleted* during production, that includes one more symbolic refrain about the candy store. Charley is having second thoughts about his agreement with Roberts to throw the fight. He now thinks that, "I can knock that Marlowe on his back in two rounds." Alice: "And end up in the candy store with your old lady . . ." Charley (wheeling furiously): "Shut up!" Alice (driving it home): "Or in the gutter with a bullet in your back."]

⁷[*Editor's Note*: See Annotation #19 to the *Body and Soul* screenplay for notes regarding the variations of this dialogue.]

⁸[*Editor's Note*: The only precise indication of a year occurs in Polonsky's shooting script with the reference to the 1938 license plate (p. 18), but it is not viewable in the actual shot (diegesis).]

⁹[*Editor's Note*: John Garfield testified before the House Committee on Un-American Activities on 23 April 1951. His approach was to deny all allegations and avoid naming names. This did not satisfy the committee. The one statement by Garfield that they tried to contradict concerned his never having known a Communist. An attempt was made by the FBI to secure witnesses who would acknowledge Garfield's having known Communists and thus make his statement perjurious. In the year after his testimony all such attempts failed—but in the meantime he was unemployable.

The lack of work was debilitating to him, and in the months before his death there were various assertions and speculations by a number of anti-Communist newspaper columnists (the "I Was a Sucker for a Left Hook" allusion was one of them) that Garfield was on the verge of a full confession. "The right made an immediate effort to claim him, as it were, as a deathbed convert. [But] all these revelations were delivered secondhand, because the actor was no longer able to speak in his own 'warm voice.'" See Robert Sklar, *City Boys: Cagney, Bogart, Garfield*. (Princeton NJ: Princeton University Press, 1992), p. 224.

"In retrospect, it is apparent that those who publicized this undocumented confession had a vested interest in anti-Communist disclosures. Certainly they were not concerned with exposing the pressure tactics that were used to obtain confessions. Many of these people were in the business of 'exposing Reds.' It is still a fact that Garfield's name does not appear on any document disavowing his past, and he made no public confession or second appearance before the HUAC." See Howard Gelman, *The Films of John Garfield* (Secaucus NJ: The Citadel Press, 1975), p. 213.]

[10] No one, however, noticed that the scene in which he implores his fellow penguins to follow him if necessary to the death is an homage to the trial scene in Lang's *M* (1931).

[11][*Editor's Note*: Behold the amazing success of Mel Brooks's *The Producers*, the Broadway version of the 1968 movie. On the day after it opened, the show sold 33,598 tickets, taking in a total of $3,029,197 (it recouped its $11 million investment—almost 12 times the cost of the movie—in 36 weeks); these are the biggest numbers ever in the history of Broadway. (See John Lahr, "Gold Rush," *The New Yorker*, 7 May 2001, pp. 84-86.)]

For a hilarious mud wrestling match between a Woody Allen-type *kvetch* from New York and an Elie Weisel-type Holocaust survivor, both of them visiting a concentration camp-as-theme-park site, check out Francine Prose's alternately very funny and very upsetting novella, *Guided Tours of Hell*. Neither Woody Allen nor Elie Weisel, who uses his horror stories to score with babes, comes out smelling like a rose.

Mark Rappaport is a writer, director, and critic whose credits include *The Silver Screen: Color Me Lavender* (1998), *From the Journals of Jean Seberg* (1995), *Rock Hudson's Home Movies* (1992).

Left to right:
Peg (Lilli Palmer), Charley (John Garfield), Ma Davis (Anne Revere)

A Long Way from the Candy Store. When Charley becomes a success, he has a palatial uptown apartment, complete with a hidden panel bar [frame right]. When the bar swings into view, Charley, delighted, offers everybody drinks. "What'll you have, folks? Just like the candy store. Want a two-cent soda, Peg?" You can take the boy out of the Lower East Side but you can't take the Lower East Side out of the boy. Is it nostalgia for his lost youth or an awareness of how far, as a once-impoverished Jew, he's come from his origins? And how, as a Jew, he doesn't really fit into the world he's fought so hard to make for himself?

Canada Lee. "In the history of the American film industry [through the 1940s], there are few pictures, possibly half a dozen, which present Negro personality as a normal part of the action. Ben [Canada Lee] in *Body and Soul* is responsible for the decision that brings the film to a climax." (John Howard Lawson, 1949.) "Canada Lee gets at his character's insides slowly but steadily. It's a classic example of a black performer taking a supporting part and beefing it up with his talent and also his mad conviction and desire to make a statement, to create. This is also a prime example of the gradual change in the depiction of Negro characters in Hollywood films of the post-World War II era. No longer simply comic characters, the black figures are treated more sensitively, used occasionally as statements on the effects of a tight, restrictive capitalistic system." (Donald Bogle, *Blacks in American Films and Television*, 1988.)

Shadowboxing

by Kevin Lewis

"All my life I've been on the verge of becoming something."
—Canada Lee

This statement dates from interviews soon after Canada Lee's spectacular Broadway debut in his breakout performance as Bigger Thomas in *Native Son* in 1941. It is a modest self-evaluation of his various setbacks as a jockey, boxer, musician, and actor before he achieved fame on Broadway.

When Lee died in 1952, the *New York World Telegram and Sun* quoted his words in his obituary.[1] A note of failure, of dreams unfulfilled, is implied, and the statement was used to damn Lee as either a misguided idealist or a failure. Lee, who had the natural naiveté of the athlete rather than the actor, was open-handed in his relations with the world. He was not clever in dealing with the media or even columnists who were friends from his youth. His words became his epitaph in the few articles about him in succeeding years, and one senses that he was writing his own eulogy. He wasn't.

Canada Lee is virtually forgotten today, even by historians of African American culture. The last major biographical entry written about him that is available in libraries was a profile written for *Current Biography* in 1944. Recent encyclopedias of African American history ignore him. Yet, in his time, he was perhaps second only to Paul Robeson as a black theatrical star, and essentially the only black actor to appear in major roles in significant film productions. Though he is not shown to best advantage in films, even in classics such as *Lifeboat* (1944), *Body and Soul* (1947), *Lost Boundaries* (1949), and *Cry, the Beloved Country* (1951), these movies have given him whatever visibility he retains. He was the only black actor of his time to play in several prominent productions of Shakespeare.

To say that his performance in *Native Son* was a breakout performance is an understatement. It was a breakout performance for African Americans in the arts. The frustration expressed in Lee's own assessment was a metaphor for African Americans in the United States. There were phantom strides by blacks in the pre-Civil Rights era of the 1960s. The political work and the artistic accomplishments of Lee damned him, and only served to make other black people in the United States frustrated, fearful, and isolated when they saw what happened to him. In many ways, in every aspect of his life, he was shadowboxing against political, artistic, and social forces beyond his control.

It was Lee's political career that perplexed both black and white elements in America. Lee walked the fine line between liberal Democratic thought and left-wing ideology. As Frances Lee Pearson (Lee's widow) expresses it: "Canada was known to work actively against discrimination and the segregated armed forces. Any organization that asked him to speak on those topics he was happy to accept. He would never think to question their affiliation." Lee always fought for economic and artistic opportunities for African Americans, which made him a sacrificial lamb in Jim Crow America. It could be argued that he sacrificed his thespian career for political action. His career choices were motivated by what he wanted to do rather than what was commercially feasible. Like the Harlem Renaissance, which was always on the verge of becoming something, Lee never really had a topper to *Native Son*.

Born in 1907 in New York (as Leonard Lionel Canegata), Lee had more economic advantages than many other African Americans—even in Manhattan. His father, James Cornelius Lionel Canegata, was a Pullman porter, a coveted position among Negroes (as they were referred to at the time), but he left behind a more prosperous life in St. Croix, The Virgin Islands. David Canegata, Lee's uncle, was a physician who was at one time head of the Privy Council on St. Croix; his grandfather and his great-grandfather were ship owners; his grandfather owned the largest mercantile store on the island. But Lee's father married a woman his family wouldn't accept, so he ran away to New York and became a Pullman porter. Lionel/Canada learned about the underprivileged in an extraordinary way—his mother, Lydia Whaley Canegata, organized an orphanage for Negro children.

When he was a child, Lionel experienced the first Spring of the Harlem Renaissance—that constellation of writers, sculptors, painters, musicians, and poets which revealed to the world that African American culture was vibrant and no longer dormant. He studied painting with Bessye Bearden (mother of Romare Bearden), piano with Thomas "Fats" Waller, and violin with J. Rosamund Johnson (brother of the poet James Weldon Johnson). But, Lionel, who possessed the kinetic energy of a Rodin sculpture, rejected his background, and ran away from home at the age of 14 to become a jockey in Saratoga, New York.

He became a boxer next, a usual route out of the black ghetto for underprivileged boys, but hardly a necessity for Lionel. The Salem-Crescent Athletic Club in Harlem spawned many a black fighter, and Lee was promising. After winning the Amateur Metropolitan championship, the Junior Nationals, and the Inter-City Finals, he turned professional. As a welterweight, he was a New York State title-holder, and notched up 175 fights, only being floored three times, and never knocked out against such fighters as Tommy Freeman, Lou Brouillard, and Vince Dundee. A fight announcer, Joe Humphries, changed his name because he couldn't pronounce Lee (his nickname) Canegata, and reversed it in any case. So he became Canada Lee.

An examination of the scrapbook kept by Lee reveals much about how ethnic groups were isolated in melting pot America. The Negro fighter Canada Lee fought boxers identified first by their nationality, whether Spanish or Italian. Jews were identified by their religion; thus Canada Lee fought the *Hebrew* boxer Yale Okun. Years later, the Charley Davis character in *Body and Soul* was thought to be based on Barney Ross, the boxer who was always identified as being Jewish. So it was fitting that the movie which refers back to Lee's career as a boxer shows him fighting a boxer who was Jewish.[2]

An eye injury in 1930, caused by a punch from William Garafolo during the welterweight title fight, curtailed his boxing career. A detached retina ended it completely, except for work as a sparring partner to Joe Louis.

His second career, as band leader of the Cotton Pickers, and as proprietor of a Harlem nightclub, the Jitterbug, was eventually KO'd by the economic circumstances of the Depression. He had to support his wife Juanita and his boy, Carl Vincent Canegata, who was born when Canada was just 21 in 1928, during a time when over half of Harlem was unemployed. Ironically, he found his destiny when he went to the unemployment bureau of the YMCA. The WPA Federal Theatre Project was auditioning actors for a Harlem Unit, and he got a part in the Federal Theatre production of *Brother Moses* (1934). (Carl Vincent Canegata became the actor Carl Lee. He died in 1986.)

Hallie Flanagan organized the WPA Federal Theatre Project through President Franklin Delano Roosevelt's economic relief programs. Actors, directors, writers, and technical personnel were given a weekly wage to put on original shows and revivals of classics. Though the Federal Theatre has been mythologized in later decades as a great left-wing organization which was closed down in 1939 because of alleged seditious propaganda, it conformed to social ideas of the time, one of which was segregation.

Canada Lee became an actor because of the auditions at the YMCA for the Federal Theatre, but he acted with his Harlem neighbors in what was always referred to as the Harlem Unit. As his widow Frances Lee Pearson wryly states, "Orson Welles and John Houseman were the whites."[3] The Federal Theatre couldn't have picked better theater people to direct African Americans, because Welles and Houseman reveled in innovative theater production. During his time with the Federal Theatre, Lee became noticed for his Banquo in *Macbeth* (1936) and his Christophe in *Haiti* (1938), in which he replaced Rex Ingram. Later on, apparently the Federal Theatre had integrated casts because *Haiti* used white and black actors. He also replaced Ingram in *Stevedore*. A quartet of Eugene O'Neill one-acts about the sea (Lee appeared as Yank in *A Moon for the Caribees* and *Bound East for Cardiff*) was less successful, because O'Neill's characters were identifiable as Swedes and Irish, and didn't translate well as black characters.

Lee made his formal Broadway appearance in *Mamba's Daughters* with Ethel Waters in 1939. In 1940, he played the lead in the Negro Playwright Company production, *Big White Fog*. Two years later, Orson Welles remembered Lee when he was casting *Native Son*, written by ex-Federal Theatre playwright and Pulitzer Prize winner Paul Green and Richard Wright, from the latter's novel. He created a sensation in the role, though at nearly 35 years of age, he was at least 15 years older than the character he played.

Bigger Thomas revealed the black man's fear of white reprisals if he were discovered with a white woman. Thomas is a chauffeur to a white family. When the daughter he is driving from a party is so drunk that Thomas has to take her to her room, he accidentally kills her when he tries to silence her loud comments. Instead of the black stud raping the white woman (the stereotypical white fear of black males), Wright showed a black man so fearful that he kills through panic. The true circumstance wouldn't be believed because he is black. In the moving trial scene, he explains his compulsions, his anger, and his fear of white society. In real life, Canada Lee kept his anger in check, because as an ex-professional fighter his hands were considered by the law to be lethal weapons. All his life, he realized how tenuous his rights as a man were because he was black, so he took no chances. Frances Lee Pearson recalls an incident in an after-hours bar when she was with Canada. He was prodded to come on-stage and jam with the jazz band. Finally, he agreed, but he played only a minute before rejoining Frances. She asked him why he played for so short a time, and he told her that he could not afford to defend her in public if a man made a play for her. He could be arrested. [4]

In another, later era, Canada Lee would have been a natural celebrity. He played characters with dark sides on stage, but presented a positive, pleasant, sexy aura offstage. *Pic* magazine, a clone right down to its layout of *Life* magazine in the 1940s, shows a smiling Canada Lee getting into his limousine and working out in his hotel room. Ironically, the photo session was in the Hotel Theresa, site of many significant African American events, and where Canada Lee was later to bury his career in a 1949 press conference with Paul Robeson and Howard Fast. Though Lee never lived in the Hotel Theresa (actually living in a penthouse on Edgecombe Avenue in the Sugar Hill section of Harlem), the article stated that he lived there because Lee wanted to protect his privacy. Lee instinctively knew what the press wanted, giving the reporter great quotes. "Honest, I haven't gone through any of the things Dick Wright talks about in the play. Nobody's ever treated me badly because I'm colored. But, of course, I know Wright was talking about Negroes in general, not just me. Me! I've been lucky."[5]

Native Son had the distinction of opening twice on Broadway— once in March 1941 and again in October 1942. Alexander Clark, who played the prosecuting attorney in the second production and on the subway circuit, recalled in a letter to Frances Pearson how delightful Lee was as an actor and as a colleague. Clark, who was a distinguished Shakespearean actor in supporting roles, asked Lee to perform scenes from *Othello* at the 1942 Lambs Gambol. Clark also played Iago to Lee's Othello in two engagements at the New School in 1944 and 1947, the later of which was directed by Erwin Piscator.

"He had a great sense of humor," wrote Clark. During one performance on the subway circuit tour, Clark had to point an accusatory finger at Lee during the trial scene. But Lee had sidled away into a corner out of the lights where Clark couldn't find him. "I must say I sensed his presence because I could hear him giggling, knowing that if I had a hard time finding any actor in that predicament, finding a black one was almost impossible. Saying that, we had a hell of a good laugh afterwards.

"He phoned me at one time and put on a British accent with a phony name, and when I pressed for more information, he said he was from Canada. But even then I didn't get it. He finally had to say, 'It's me.' He was a charming gent, with great integrity. I really mean it when I cannot recall anyone in all my years who had such innate, true, unphony charm. It was completely natural. I think if he had had to do a TV commercial, he would have thrown up rather than put on the smarm which seems to be the basis of our commercial advertising."[6]

William Herz was company manager of *Native Son*. Herz recalls that Orson Welles rehearsed *Native Son* with Canada Lee at its inception at Lee's restaurant in Harlem called The Chicken Coop. After its first Broadway run, the play toured throughout the North—but not the South (except for Baltimore)—in 1941. Herz also remembered that Lee stated, "I want to go on the road, but I want to stay in white hotels." He succeeded to a great extent, but there were occasional problems. Lee minimized the dilemma by staying with black friends he knew in various cities from his years as a boxer. In Pittsburgh and in Detroit, he stayed in hotels. But, As Herz points out, "All of the problems we had on the road, he never paid any attention to them." Discrimination "didn't seem to phase him." According to Frances Lee Pearson, the discrimination bothered him a great deal but he was determined that the cast would not realize that he was angry.

As Herz says, "We played at the Cass Theatre in Detroit, and I thought the manager was going to have a hemorrhage because there were so many blacks coming to the show. So we played only one week at the Cass, and then the owner of the Shubert Lafayette Theatre said, 'Why don't you come here, and you can have an open-end engagement.' We played five or six weeks and sold out." Even with some price reductions, "It was very successful there. It was an interesting tour."

All 750 second-balcony seats at the Ford Theatre in Baltimore, the only area where blacks could be seated, were sold out. William Herz:

> The opening night in Baltimore was one of the most frightening things that I've ever experienced. There must have been about 200 people in the orchestra, a few people in the balcony, and 750 in the second balcony. I thought we were going to have a race riot, especially during the trial scene. So I got on the phone to New York, and I said, 'This man who's the manager is an idiot. When we played St. Louis [the theater manager] was a very smart man, and he saw that he was going to have a lot of Negroes, so instead of just keeping the second balcony, he opened the regular balcony. Then he made divisions in the orchestra to take care of the orchestra prices and the balcony prices. So that way, the balcony and the second balcony were sold out and we had a good representation in the orchestra. We didn't have any problems. But in Baltimore, it was horrible. The second night in Baltimore, the New York booking office called the idiot and told him to invite the soldiers from Camp Meade.

> The soldiers from Camp Meade came in busfulls, and there was a white sergeant and a lot of blacks. And the manager didn't want to let the black soldiers in the orchestra. So the white sergeant took the manager, grabbed his necktie, he nearly choked him, and said, "They're going to fight with us, they're going to sit with us." And it's the first time any black sat in the orchestra in the Ford

Theatre in Baltimore. But that experience was so horrible, and we knew that there was segregation in Washington, and I said we weren't going to play any place where there was segregation. It was ridiculous. So we went back on what in those days was the subway circuit that Jules Leventhal used.

Socially and temperamentally, Lee was always a boxer, and emphasized that fact in interviews. He associated with fighters, and Herz recalls, "The theatre people that he knew were very few and far between."[7]

In a 1941 interview with Stanley Frank, Lee defined what boxing meant to him, long after the eye injury that sidelined his career. "Boxing is beautiful. Boxing is rhythm, grace and finesse. To me, it is the highest expression of skill and science. Boxing is more than busting a guy on the chin. I had more than 200 professional fights and I had a good punch. I could knock them dead. But I got greater satisfaction slipping punches and moving gracefully out of danger. You know, there is something peculiarly exciting in the knowledge that danger can strike you at any instant. I got a terrific bang by sustaining that suspense while making every move a picture."

Stanley Frank referred to Lee as a "welterweight with class." Lee was not a brute in the ring, and relished the dramatics involved rather than the killer instinct. "Maybe I could have been a champion if the artistic nature of boxing had not appealed to me so much. I liked to see a fellow drop when I hit him with a good right hand, but I took more pride in my skill rather than my strength. I liked to make the other boy miss me by a fraction of an inch. I wasn't hit often."[8]

Because he was independent and an athlete who brooked no opposition, Lee more than tested the limits of Jim Crow America. "When he was staying at a hotel," says Herz, " I could sort of keep tabs on him, but when he lived in private homes, or with friends, or in Negro hotels, then it was a little bit difficult, but he had a great kind of animal magnetism for white ladies. From time to time he was fighting them off. White ladies would end up in his room at the hotel," he recalled. When hotel managers complained to Herz, he told them to speak to the women themselves. "If they go up to his room, they go up voluntarily. He does not drag them up."[9]

Despite being thought of as rivals, Lee and Paul Robeson were close friends. Lee was more committed to performing in Shakespeare than Robeson was, though Robeson is a more famous Othello because of the legendary Broadway production he starred in with Uta Hagen and José Ferrer. Both appeared in films called *Body and Soul*, though they have completely different plots. And, of course, they shared political activism. In retrospect, Lee's career in both theater and film was more distinguished than Robeson's. Lee made three film classics—*Lifeboat*, *Body and Soul* and *Cry, The Beloved Country*—and one minor classic, *Lost Boundaries*. All of these movies examined in significant ways the different images and aspects of black culture. Robeson made two classics—*Body and Soul* (1925) and *Show Boat* (1936)—and many flawed British films, of which the best was *The Proud Valley (1940)*. Some of these British films are among the most racist—*Sanders of the Rivers* (1935) and *King Solomon's Mines (1937)*—and others, *Song of Freedom* (1936) and *Big Fella* (1937), are badly acted and scripted. Robeson's film career was over by World War II, when Lee's was just beginning.

Lee's fame on Broadway was the reason he was signed for *Lifeboat* (1944), written by John Steinbeck, directed by Alfred Hitchcock. But the film industry did not know how to use African American performers, except in two-dimensional or stereotypical ways. *Lifeboat* was a difficult experience for Lee on an artistic and a personal level. His role of the stalwart stoker was changed to a more traditional movie stereotype, and he became a passive, isolated character, only good for reciting prayers and stealing a compass from the Nazi. In an interview for *Opportunity: The Journal of Negro Life*, Lee wrote about how demoralizing the *Lifeboat* experience was. "My *Body and Soul* experience was in contrast to the time I worked in *Lifeboat*. Though I had been assured the role of the Negro sailor would do much to advance the cause of colored people, production wasn't very far along when I noticed that the script called for the Negro to be in a corner by himself, while the Nazi mingled freely—and, in fact—dominantly among the group. I didn't like it, but couldn't do anything about it. There was even a prominent actor in the cast who repeatedly spoke of 'niggers' and how he wished they were all still slaves. These were his personal views, mind you, not speeches from the script. Of course, he was unpopular with the other actors, who wondered why I didn't 'sock the big ham.'" [10] The unnamed actor was Walter Slezak, who would be a busy character actor in films until his death over three decades later. Significantly, his father, Wagnerian tenor-turned-film-actor Leo Slezak, became a state artist in the Third Reich.

However, Henry Hull, another actor in *Lifeboat*, whose fame rested on creating the ultimate white trash character Jeeter Lester in the Broadway production of *Tobacco Road* (1933), was in his way just as nasty to Lee. His pet name for Lee was Dichty, a Southern term for a black man with pretensions. Years after Lee's death, Hull expressed his disdain for the boxing actor to his daughter Joan.[11]

His ally on the movie was Tallulah Bankhead, a pal from their Broadway days and many social engagements. Ironically, for many years she was blamed for insulting Lee because of a humorous story (never printed but oft repeated in theatrical circles). Supposedly, she (because she was from Alabama) started prompting Lee to speak in a Southern black dialect, at which point Canada turned to Alfred Hitchcock, the director, and said, "Would you kindly tell Miss Bankhead that I've been a black man longer than she has." Other racial terms were substituted as the story made the rounds. Frances Lee Pearson denies the truth of that story because Canada told her everything that went on each day on the set. He seethed with fury every night in mentioning the Slezak/Hull remarks, but he never mentioned Bankhead except fondly. Bankhead, Frances recalled, often used to call Canada in the wee hours to talk.[12]

Lee admitted that he was "boiling all the time" because of these insults, but he was determined to leave Hollywood with the industry saying, "He's a fine actor and a gentleman." Lee tempered his criticism with the statement, "Fortunately, people like that actor are few and far between in Hollywood. Most folks I met out there are liberal and progressive minded."[13]

[One of the liberal people Lee met in Los Angeles while making *Lifeboat* was Frances Pollack (maiden name of Frances Lee Pearson), who was Executive Secretary of the Federation for Civic Betterment and active in the Democratic Party in Los Angeles, with whom he spent a significant portion of his last decade. Though they planned on marrying (Lee was divorced from Juanita)—a daring act for a white woman and a black man in an America where interracial marriage was illegal in 36 states—they separated in 1945. They met again in 1948 at a Henry Wallace for President rally and finally married in 1950.]

Hollywood was never a fit for Lee, and one looks in vain for any connection between the real Canada Lee and the characters he portrayed on film. The support system was never in the film industry for black actors. For a black actress, there was the hope of becoming an Ethel Waters or a Lena Horne rather than a Hattie McDaniel, but a black actor could only aspire to be another Eddie "Rochester" Anderson or Leigh Whipper. Robeson, as has been said, was finished in Hollywood by the 1940s. Sidney Poitier reveals how unsavory Whipper could be toward other black actors. Whipper claimed to be the first black actor to join Actors Equity Association, and he may very well have been since he was born in 1876, and was the founder of the Negro Actors Union. Poitier considers Whipper to have been a Judas goat in league with producers and studios unwilling to deal with black actors. One day, Whipper accosted Poitier on 125th Street in Harlem, chastised him about his left-wing friends, opened his coat to reveal a gun in his trouser waistband, and said, "that he would use it on me and all my friends if we fucked with him."[14] Ironically, Whipper's most famous movie role was portraying Haile Selassie, the Ethiopian ruler who fought Mussolini's fascist army, in *Mission to Moscow* (1943).

Lee did not make another movie until *Body and Soul*, over three years later. His Broadway career throughout the 1940s was dotted with such failed shows as *Across the Board on Tomorrow Morning* (1942) and *South Pacific* (1943—the drama, not the musical). There was no follow-up to *Native Son* because plays and musicals with black themes and characters were not generally produced on Broadway during the war years, with the exceptions of *Carmen Jones* (1943), *Deep Are The Roots* (1945), *Strange Fruit* (1945), and the revival in 1942 of *Porgy and Bess*. His only triumphs were in such classic plays as *The Tempest* by William Shakespeare in 1944 and the Jacobean tragedy *The Duchess of Malfi* by John Webster in 1946. In the former he was praised for portraying Caliban in all of his twisted anger.

In *The Duchess of Malfi* he created a cause célèbre for playing the villainous 17th century nobleman in whiteface. If it was acceptable for a white actor to portray Othello in blackface, it should have been equally satisfactory for a black man to play a Caucasian character. His characterization divided many in the theater and in the press. Right-wingers regarded it as a stunt and a symbolic hate letter to white America. Ironically, left-wing critics and theater people praised it because it deconstructed an incomprehensible and clunky melodrama. Howard Fast in *Being Red* [Laurel, 1990] writes about its effect on Communist Party theory of theater production. Fast said that Communist theorists regarded it as a new articulation of bourgeois theory and the suspension of disbelief, which Fast states was important in Communist Party dogma. Fast's play, *The Hammer*, was then cast with 18-year-old James Earl Jones as the son of white Jewish parents.[15] The experiment was a fiasco, and a disgusted Fast left the Party soon after, citing the Communists' tenuous grip on reality.

Anna Lucasta (1944) was a hit, but did nothing for Lee because he had agreed to play a small part for a limited time only because the producers needed a name actor to sell the show. Lee starred in and co-produced *On Whitman Avenue* (1946) with Mark Marvin. Though it ran for only a few nights, it was a well-remembered show by African American audiences, and its theme about a black family trying to live in a white neighborhood anticipates *A Raisin in the Sun* (1959) by a decade. His last show *Set My People Free* (1948), about the slave revolt led by Denmark Vesey in South Carolina in 1822, was also political and controversial and did not last long on Broadway.

Throughout the 1940s, Lee was active in radio, narrating and hosting such black-oriented shows as *New World A-Coming*, produced by WMCA in cooperation with the Citywide Citizen's Committee on Harlem, and *The Canada Lee Show* on WNEW.

He had great hopes for *Body and Soul* because it was about a sport he still loved. Though *On Whitman Avenue* didn't concern boxing, Lee allowed Irving Rudd of the boxing magazine, *The Ring*, to discuss the sport with him in conjunction with *Whitman* publicity. Lee announced that he wanted to become a boxing manager. "There's nothing basically wrong with the game if supervision is stringent and things are run competently. I hope to build a stable of good, earnest kids who want to learn, and hope to have them competing against the best in their class." He emphasized the worthiness of the sport. "The fight game never had a color line. A good Negro, if he had the ability, could go on to win the championship in any class in which he competed. I don't have to enumerate. Louis, Armstrong, Gans, Wolcott, and even going all the way to Molyneaux are good enough examples. Therefore, it surprises me that a sport which is so progressive and liberal-minded has over a period of so many years failed to provide for simple, essential care of its health, finances, and general welfare of its own." Lee proposed that each fighter donate a percentage of his purse to a fund which would provide medical insurance and nursing homes. Education and job training could be provided for fighters who leave the game. Later in the article, he echoes the Abraham Polonsky script for his forthcoming film. Fighters "come from poor families and fighting is a quick way to earn money and keep body and soul and family together. The average boxer possesses little education, possibly no more than two years of high school." He usually winds up broke and jobless.[16]

Body and Soul was not the first time he played a boxer or a trainer. Several years earlier, in his first film *Keep Punching* (1939), produced by the Sports Melodrama Company at the Film Art Studios, he played the trainer to a real boxing champion, Henry Armstrong. By 1938, Armstrong (1912-1988) had become the first boxer in history to hold three world titles in three weight classes simultaneously: Featherweight Champion, Welterweight Champion, and Lightweight Champion. The first was earned in 1937 and the latter two in 1938. Interestingly, Armstrong, whose nickname was "Perpetual Motion," won the welterweight title against Barney Ross, the Jewish boxer who may have been the inspiration for Charlie Davis in *Body and Soul*.

Keep Punching was directed by John Clein, who was primarily a producer of British film dramas, and the script was written by Marcy Klauber, whose largely undistinguished career includes *Tevye*, the 1939 Yiddish film derived from the same Sholem Aleichem stories which became *Fiddler on the Roof*.

Both *Keep Punching* and *Body and Soul* share similar incidents, themes, and plot points. Both Henry and Charley, in their respective films, are seduced by the bad girls in a nightclub setting. (The Democratic party club in poor neighborhoods is a primary social location.) They also reflect the different periods in which they are set. *Keep Punching*, though set in the 1930s complete with jitterbug contests, reflects the aspirations and promise of the Harlem Renaissance of the 1920s, rather than its ashes in the 1930s. Its theme song, "Lift Every Voice and Sing" (written by James Weldon Johnson and J. Rosamund Johnson, who was in the movie), was written years earlier and became the anthem for the National Association for the Advancement of Colored People (NAACP). *Body and Soul*, though set in roughly the same Depression era as *Keep Punching*, is really about the individual repression and white-collar crime which dominated post-WWII America. Though on the surface it is a boxing movie, replete with the cliches of the genre, it is about corporate crime and payoffs. Polonsky himself said it was about capitalism rather than about boxing. Only a few years after *Body and Soul*, General Electric was convicted for price-fixing, and the network television quiz show scandals showed America that producers manipulated the contests and gave payoffs if contestants threw the game.

In *Keep Punching*, Henry Jackson (Henry Armstrong) is an honor student who wants to be a boxer because, as he tells his fiancée, he wants to do what he does best. His mother (Hilde Offley) agrees with him and opposes his father (Walter Robinson) who wants him to become a lawyer. "There are plenty of lawyers around here and they're all broke," says the mother. Later, when Henry is a successful fighter, his parents come to New York on the evening of his championship fight. "Ain't no dignity in fighting, there ain't no dignity in it," the father says, continuing his opposition. "There's plenty of dignity when he sends those checks home after every fight," replies the mother. (Notably, this is a complete reversal of the parents in *Body and Soul*. Anna Davis says her son should shoot himself rather than fight. "You need *money* to buy a gun," is the Charley Davis retort.) Henry goes to New York, where he is trained by the worldly-wise Speedy (Canada Lee). Speedy tries unsuccessfully to stop him from living the high life in nightclubs. However, he falls in with an ex-schoolmate (Willie Bryant), now a gambler and bookie, and his moll (Mae J. Johnson) who seduces Henry. The bookie has bet heavily against Henry and, to make sure he doesn't win, has his moll slip Henry a mickey. Henry's friend (Hamtree Harrington) sees the spiked drink and takes it himself. The moll, not knowing that Henry didn't take the drink, repents her ways at a mission, led by a preacher (J. Rosamund Johnson) who tells her, "Your arms' too short to box with God." Henry wins but decides to leave boxing to get an education. (In real life, Armstrong became a Baptist minister in 1951.)

In *Body and Soul*, Charley Davis, disgusted by the Lower East Side poverty and the death of his candy-store owner father in a speakeasy rubout, becomes a fighter over the objections of his mother. She runs a very kosher Jewish home and thinks money for fighting is akin to criminal activity. When he makes a lot of money, she hates the game more. Ben Chaplin, a black boxer, is the champion controlled by the same fight promoter, Roberts (Lloyd Gough) as Davis. Chaplin has a blood clot in the brain and is finished as a boxer. However, he owes Roberts $40,000 and has no way to repay it except to throw the bout against Davis. Chaplin agrees, but tells Roberts, "People don't count with you, do they Mr. Roberts." When Davis almost kills him because he is not in on the fix, he takes the broken Chaplin on as a trainer and a friendship develops. Ben becomes Charley's doppelganger, his conscience—and his death in fruitlessly defying Roberts is the catalyst for Davis not throwing the fight as Chaplin did. [*Editor's Note*: See "Fifty Grand," Note #11.] That and a visit from his Jewish grocer who tells him that people are betting on him because he is the great Jewish challenge to the extermination of Jews that Adolf Hitler is performing in Europe.

Lee is so remarkable in this film that the viewer doesn't realize he is only in the movie physically for just four short scenes. Because of the flashback structure of the film, Ben is talked about more than seen.

Ben Chaplin is first introduced in the film on the dreaming lips of Garfield. Chaplin is already dead at this point, but in flashback Davis recalls the first time he knew Chaplin's name, via a headline proclaiming that Chaplin has a shot at the welterweight championship title.

In September 1947, after *Body and Soul* opened in New York, Lee gave an interview in Sardi's Restaurant, the watering hole for thespians, in which he also expressed anger about people who resented a black man portraying anything other than a buffoon. What impressed Canada Lee most about the script was the fact that, "There's a good, man-to-man relationship between us. It's remarkable—in the whole picture you never heard the word 'Negro.' There is no differentiation made. I am just accepted as a character in a story. That must be the first time the movies have handled an American Negro like any other human being." Clenching his fist, he said, "The stupidity of it. All of a sudden you feel the viciousness of these people who won't accept a picture because it may affect these ideas about superiority and inferiority. You feel the futility, you wonder, you really wonder how a man can be a Negro and a good American at the same time. It calls for a lot of guts. I started to say intestinal fortitude, but the hell with intestinal fortitude. It takes guts." Lee told the interviewer that director Robert Rossen didn't expect the movie to be released in the South—not because Lee was involved with a white woman, but because Garfield and

Lee were presented as equal boxing colleagues. Lee had nothing but praise for Garfield, both as actor and producer. Garfield was so sensitive to Lee that at one point he slipped and called him "boy" rather than Ben. Garfield insisted on re-shooting the scene, despite Robert Rossen's insistence that it wouldn't be noticed. Lee stated that Rossen first approached him about the project in 1943 when Lee was acting in *Lifeboat*. "A year went by, and another went by and another went by and here it was 1947. And then I got called. Bob was going to make the picture and he had remembered me all that time."[17]

Lee's conclusion was prescient: "We need more pictures like *Body and Soul* and I don't think the people out there can be pressured not to make them, either by Washington probes or by local witch-hunts."[18]

Garfield and Lee shared many characteristics, though they were not close friends. Both were brought up in Manhattan in lower middle-class neighborhoods. Lee became involved in theatre through the WPA Federal Theatre. Garfield because of his performances with the Group Theatre, was signed by Warner Bros. They died within weeks of each other, both harried into their graves by HUAC.

Garfield and Lee believed so strongly in the film that they wrote tandem essays, entitled "Our Part in Body and Soul," for *Opportunity: The Journal of Negro Life* in the January 1948 issue. In "Fists, Fights and Brains," Garfield wrote that as a Lower East Side boy, which was "a sort of jungle" because of poverty, he had two choices if he wanted to survive—"to fight or run." He learned how to fight. But he was impressed one day by how a runt in his class defeated him in a debate and made him look like a fool. He joined the debating society and became interested in acting. His success as a Hollywood star enabled him to produce the independent film *Body and Soul*, and more importantly, to realize the "right of an artist to exercise a choice in the selection of story and roles and to have a voice in all phases of production."[19]

Lee wrote in the previously quoted *"Body and Soul* Has Heart, Too" that he plays "a fighter who happens to be a Negro. Not a Negro fighter." Significantly, " nowhere in the film is the word 'Negro' used. As a human being I liked that." Garfield calls him Ben and he calls Garfield Charley. "There isn't a single 'Yessuh, boss.' My role happens to be a meaty one and a significant one. That I liked as an actor. Though shown as a has-been champion welterweight who has taken many a beating and sustained a head injury, the character I play has integrity and pride and intelligence." Though Lee says that Ben doesn't take bribes in the essay, the character does seem to be prepared to allow Charley to win by "a decision." He is also powerless in advising Charlie not to throw the final fight. Ben is a victim throughout the movie and is powerless against Roberts. "My big scene carries terrific impact. It's a death scene, in which Ben's head injury is aggravated. In a fury of frustration, I engage in a fight with an imaginary opponent in a training camp ring, until I sink to the canvas dying."[20]

Throughout his life, Lee was always a tireless activist, perhaps because he was a lifelong friend of Walter White and Adam Clayton Powell, Jr., who with Powell and other black district leaders organized the Greater New York Coordinating Committee in February 1938. This event was launched in the Abyssinian Baptist Church in Harlem, of which Powell's father was minister. Lee participated in picket marches against stores and businesses in Harlem which did not hire blacks. Jews owned most of the stores, because it was mostly Jews who populated Harlem before they moved to the Bronx in the 1920s. In fact, Harlem at that time housed the third largest settlement of Jews in the world. Lee did not picket on anti-Semitic grounds but on economic principles only. Over half of Harlem was unemployed during the Depression.[21]

Throughout the war years and until his death, Lee delivered many speeches about the interdependency of African Americans and Jews in ending job and economic discrimination. He viewed the American South as the nemesis of democracy. He campaigned indefatigably throughout 1944 for the re-election of Franklin Delano Roosevelt, determined that Republican presidential candidate Thomas Dewey would not make inroads into the black vote. He admired Roosevelt especially for creating the Fair Employment Practice Commission (F.E.P.C.). Dewey not only "killed a bill which would make it illegal in New York State to refuse to hire a man or woman because of his race, creed or color," but opposed F.E.P.C. "How can he condemn an Administration which has given the Negro a chance to own a home, a farm, a business, by such agencies as the Farm Credit and Home Owner's Loan Corporation?" How can he fail to appreciate the fact that one-third of all the housing financed by the Government in the past ten years is tenanted by Negroes? Nearly one-half million Negroes live in Federal Housing projects financed by the Roosevelt Administration." In his speech, Lee pointed out that Dewey wanted to have Social Security administered by the individual states, rather than on a federal basis. "How do you suppose the Negro would make out in Jim Crow states if the Federal government stepped aside? You know, and I know."[22] This was a longtime concern of Lee's. In 1942, he narrated a documentary, *Henry Browne, Farmer* for the Department of Agriculture that showed how African American farmers contributed to the war economy. Lee also credited Roosevelt with creating the Federal Theatre, which gave him his start (ignoring the fact that it was segregated).

One of the most incendiary speeches for FDR's campaign that he delivered was in Philadelphia in 1944, in which he linked Southern politicians with Hitler during the Second World War. "As I see it, there are today two choices open to us. It is the choice of democracy versus fascism. I don't have any doubt about which choice you people here have made in your minds. But we do know our enemies—the enemies of democracy—who have chosen the fascist solution to the way out. We know the Rankins and the Bilbos—those fascists in our midst who would lynch all Negroes and thus end the so-called 'Negro problem.' Just as Hitler has found an answer to the so-called 'Jewish problem' in the slaughter houses."[23] Representative John Rankin and Senator Theodore Bilbo of Mississippi were both supporters of the Ku Klux Klan and launched a filibuster against the Federal Employment Practices Commission, which was defeated year after year. They also served on HUAC with Martin Dies in 1938.

Robert Washow in the essay "The Legacy of the 1930's," written in 1947 and published in *The Immediate Experience* (Altheneum, 1970), presents the dilemma of American progressive thinkers and intellectuals in a conservative era. "For most American intellectuals, the Communist movement of the 1930's was a crucial experience. In Europe, where the movement was at once more serious and more popular, it was still only one current in intellectual life; the Communists could never completely set the tone of thinking, in Europe, and Communist intellectuals themselves were able to draw a part of their nourishment from outside the movement. But in this country there was a time when virtually all intellectual vitality was derived in one way or another from the Communist party. If you were not somewhere within the party's wide orbit, then you were likely to be in the opposition, which meant that much of your thought and energy had to be devoted to maintaining yourself in opposition.

"In either case, it was the Communist party that ultimately determined what you were to think about and in what terms." (p. 33)

(After the war, when right-wingers tried to link Jews with left-wing sympathies, especially during the Rosenberg spy trial, Lee spoke many times before such groups as the Conference of Christians and Jews.)

"The riddle of the day to me is the existence in America of the anti-semitic Negro and the anti-Negro Jew," he said to the Jewish War Veterans in New Rochelle, New York in 1949. Anti-semitism among Negroes was self-defeating, he stated, because the "economic and political weakness of the Negro people" meant that Jews were not affected by this enmity. "Negro anti-semitism it is assumed—even in a pro-fascist America —can have little repercussions on the Jewish people. The vote controlled by Negroes is negligible in most communities and constitutes no immediate political threat. The economic strength of the Negro is weak from mal-remuneration for work performed."

Rather, the anti-Negro Jew was a more crucial problem because that character could be exploited by fascists in politics. In the Weimar Republic era, wealthy Jews "aided the growth of fascism" because of their fear of Communism, and made the Nazis powerful. This action of course doomed them in Germany. "Jews who persist, who are possessed with the naiveté to imagine that an American fascism would be less vicious than the German species, and loan their money, press and energies to fostering American fascism, are deluding no one but themselves. The suicide note of distinction already is tagged with your name."

Defending civil rights for all, Lee quoted Thomas Paine, "who said that civil rights, like blood, cannot be taken from any of the parts without being taken from the whole mass and circulation, and every part will feel the loss."

Turning the knife, Lee said, "Many people believe they have no anti-Negro feeling in their makeup. They hire Negro servants and boot blacks and janitors. But has it ever occurred to them to hire a Negro secretary, clerk or technician?" After stating that "neither Jew nor Negro can survive in a fascist America," he pointed out that discrimination and lack of opportunities cause racial conflicts, not race itself.[24]

At the very end of the war, in June 1945, he campaigned to save the Fair Employment Practice Commission (F.E.P.C.), which was threatened with extinction by the end of that month. Again, he named Rankin and Bilbo, as well as Reverend Gerald L. K. Smith and Father Coughlin as culprits in fighting the commission.[25]

Frances Lee Pearson surmises that Lee's problems with the FBI began, however, with his espousal of desegregation of the Armed Forces in 1942. Ignored by the FBI, however, was Lee's sterling record of selling a massive number of war bonds.[26]

Despite the premise of a contemporary play, *Becoming Something* by Mona Z. Smith, Canada Lee and Ed Sullivan were not close friends, just acquaintances. In the 1920s, Sullivan wrote columns espousing African American athletes in competition with Caucasian and/or white athletes, but his commitment was superficial. In fact, Sullivan was irresponsible as a journalist by printing innuendo that Lee was a Communist because he spoke to groups that were openly socialist. When Lee asked Sullivan to retract his charge that Lee was a Communist, Sullivan didn't reply.[27] Instead, Sullivan delivered his own eulogy to Lee and Garfield after their deaths in May 1952. "*Body and Soul*, as a case history, is of tremendous importance to Americans fighting Communism because it illustrates the manner in which Commies and pinks, in the field of communications and ideas, gave employment to one another." Sullivan intimates that Garfield lied to HUAC in April 1951 by denying that he knew Communists when he was a close friend of playwright Clifford Odets, who admitted prior membership in the Communist Party.

Sullivan, without explaining any left-wing ideology in *Body and Soul*—other than the HUAC probes of actors Lee, Garfield, and Anne Revere, the director Robert Rossen and the screenwriter Abraham Polonsky—states that the film itself "should open the eyes of those confused liberals who have assailed the House committee as witch-hunters. It should open the eyes of those who have fought every attempt to clear up the Commie's attempted infiltration of the TV industry. *Body and Soul* is the pattern that the Commies and their sympathizers in TV networks, agencies and theatrical unions would like to fasten on the newest medium. From the director on down, the Commies insert their members, freeze out those who are on the American side of the fence." After a thumbnail analysis of the Communist takeover of the communications industry through its crafts unions, Sullivan concluded his diatribe with the statement: "The deaths of Garfield and Canada Lee should dramatize to all youngsters that the Commies take over, body and soul. Both of them, Garfield and Lee, were warm-hearted kids, easy prey for the bait that Commies dangle before confused liberals."[28] [See Figure 3.]

The irony of his guilt-by-association is that most of the actors in the film were apparently kosher to HUAC. Lilli Palmer, then married to Rex Harrison, continued to have an enviable dual career as a theatrical and a film star. Joseph Pevney, who played Shorty, became a busy Universal Studios director; William Conrad, the star of radio's *The Fat Man*, became a television star in the series *Cannon*. Hazel Brooks never became a star, and Lloyd Gough always worked. The cinematographer James Wong Howe remained one of the masters in his field, eventually winning an Oscar for *Hud* (1963), directed by the formerly blacklisted Martin Ritt.

If *Body and Soul* expresses left-wing thinking, it can be found in the character of the fight promoter Roberts. As Polonsky has stated, the film is not per se a boxing melodrama. It is about business and how it manipulates the entrepreneur and his/her employees. Charlie and Ben are expected to do as they are told. Though they were trained to be champions, they must be ready to be bribed, take a fall, and deceive the public. Roberts is portrayed as a kingmaker, the one who decides who will get a fight. The fallacy of this is that if Roberts fixed a majority of fights, the word would get around that betting on a Roberts fighter is foolish. Merit and skill are not factors. However, if one looks at the film as a metaphor of business, it works. The public is deceived about the merits of a product if the manufacturer wants the new product to succeed. The older product is discredited by the company that created it in order to introduce this year's model. When Peg Born refuses to marry Charley because it would be the same as marrying Roberts, she is correct. Charley and Ben belong to Roberts body and soul. When Ben ineffectually but bravely tells Roberts that he can't tell him how to live, Roberts replies that he *can* tell him how to die. Roberts is right. Ben does die on Robert's farm, just as Uncle Tom died on Simon Legree's plantation.

The last play Canada Lee did was *Othello* in 1948, which was produced in New England theaters for a summer run before a Broadway production was considered. Despite hypertension, Lee worked zealously to realize a Broadway production that would rival the one which starred Paul Robeson three years earlier. Unfortunately, it was not to be.

Because he considered the theme of black people passing as white an important and timely subject, Lee accepted a supporting role in *Lost Boundaries* (1949), produced by the docudrama creator Louis de Rochemont. As the sympathetic Harlem cop who counsels the confused runaway teenage boy who learns his family is black rather than white, Lee was praised.

Then it all turned around. In June 1949, two FBI agents knocked on the door of his 58 W. 57th Street office apartment. Frances Pollack [Pierson] was in the next room and heard an angry Lee screaming at the FBI agents that they wanted him to divide his people. He would not denounce his old friend, Paul Robeson. They left, but they won the battle.[29] This was an especially perilous time for Lee because he was already defending himself against charges that he was a Communist (as his name was written in a notebook, suggesting that he was at a social gathering for Communists). The notebook, belonging to a State Department worker named Judith Koplon, was confiscated by the FBI after she was arrested for passing government documents to a Soviet agent.

Instead of being intimidated by his association with the now-targeted Robeson, Lee held a press conference with the actor/singer at the Hotel Theresa on 9 July 1949 to protest racial bias in broadcasting. *The New York Times* reported that, "Mr. Lee, who has repeatedly denied that he was a Communist, joined with Paul Robeson, the singer, William L. Patterson of the Civil Rights Congress, and Howard Fast, the author, in violent attacks on American radio owners for alleged efforts to distort and conceal Negro problems and what he termed their refusal to hire qualified Negro workers. They spoke at a conference sponsored by the Committee for the Negro in Arts held in the Theresa Hotel [*sic*], Seventh Avenue and 125th Street. "

In a recent interview for this essay, Fast recalled those days. "Whenever we needed him to speak, he would speak," Fast said. "And he spoke because if he believed in a cause, he didn't ask about the political affilia-tion of the hosting group." Was Lee a Communist? "I don't think Canada was a Communist," he said.[30]

In many ways, this may have been the most disastrous day for Lee. He was there to state, as reported by the *New York Times*, "that failure to enact civil rights legislation, renewed terrorism by the Ku Klux Klan and other acts of violence toward Negroes were all part of a movement to maintain an 'iron curtain' between Negroes and white persons in the United States." Robeson went overboard, and this probably did more to harm both men than anything else they had said earlier. Unfortunately, for Lee, he left before Robeson spoke, so he didn't know the content of Robeson's speech. But because it was covered by the *New York Times* with no mention that Lee gave his speech on bias and left, he was tarred with Robeson. "Mr. Lee's enunciations were reiterated by Mr. Robson, who predicted the death of American democracy if Negroes and 'progressive' artists in this country did not unite with the twelve indicted leaders of the Communist Party to overthrow the 'guys who run this country for bucks and foster Cold War hysteria.' The famous baritone, recently returned from a trip through Eu-rope, told the 300 Negro workers in radio, television and the theater that they were deprived of all rights, whereas inhabitants of the Soviet Union and the 'people's democracies in Eastern Europe' are in no danger of los-ing any of their civil rights.' He accused the State Department of deliber-ately falsifying attempts of Negro artists to depict the struggle of his race for freedom, but said that a solid Communist-Progressive front, backed by all Negroes, could stop 'those who railroad the Atlantic Pact through con-gress while they can't do anything on civil rights.'" Lee delivered a similar speech as the keynote speaker on 6 September at a conference held by the Committee for the Negro in the Arts in New York.

It got far worse for Robeson. On 27 August 1949, he appeared for the Civil Rights Congress at a gathering in Peekskill, New York. It soon turned into a riot instigated by right wing elements and war veterans an-gered by what they regarded as a Communist gathering. Robeson was blamed for the whole affair.

On 13 October, an item appeared in Walter Winchell's column stat-ing that, "Canada Lee, the Negro star, will address a Vets' rally near Peekskill, Nov. 6th. He will wallop P. Robeson's 'line.'"[31] It was a plant, and Lee sent a letter to Winchell demanding a retraction. Instead, Winchell sent the letter to J. Edgar Hoover. Then Lee did the unthinkable. When he received no reply from Winchell and no retraction, Lee wrote the editor of the *New York Mirror* telling his side of the story. One sentence in particular would have made the venomous Winchell laugh. "Relying upon his own integrity for truthfulness, I have been waiting for him to publish a correction on the item." The rest of the letter, which the editor also sent to the FBI, is painful to read because such sincerity and faith in the system fell on deaf ears. "As everyone must know by now, I am for complete democracy, and for the Negro in terms of his participation in this democracy! His right to act, sing, speak or play ball without fear of mob violence any place in these United States. This is a great nation, and at no time in its history had there been any doubt of the Negroes' [sic] love, loyalty, and contribution to this nation's safety and culture.

"I am against all isms, including that kind of Americanism which permits Jim Crow, Klanism, prejudice, lynching —and all other indignities and lack of opportunities that keep the Negro from being a first-class Citizen [sic] in this America for which so many have fought and died.

"Learning that the false item had spread beyond Winchell (other radio commentators and columnists), I realized that it was necessary to notify all the press before it got completely out of hand. I hope this completely clarifies my position in this matter." [32] Lee was a victim of FBI disinformation, long before the public knew the practice.

The damage was done. Though Lee did not address the veteran's group, did not denounce Robeson, the consensus even among some African Americans was that he did. Frances Pearson always had to contend with that rumor. Paul Robeson Jr. had heard the rumor, and when he was asked to refute it for this essay, gave a statement. According to his son, Robeson didn't believe that Canada Lee had denounced him. Moreover, Robeson did not harbor ill feelings toward black artists, like Josh White, who did denounce him, because he realized the desperate circumstances in which they found themselves. "For my father," says Robeson, Jr., "the enemy was HUAC. I'm not aware of any reliable evidence that Canada Lee informed on or denounced my father. So I think it's unfair to accuse him. Dad had only good feelings for Canada Lee, and had great respect for him as an actor."[33] Victor Navasky in *Naming Names* [Penguin, 1981] repeats the false story, told by Stefan Kanfer in *A Journal of the Plague Years* [Atheneum, 1973], that Lee caved in to pressure. The documentary *Scandalize My Name* (2000) insinuates that Lee gave in and then died from shame. In any case, Lee was blacklisted and worked very little in America from 1949 until his death.

Ironically, the one project which may have cemented Lee's stardom in American movies was denied him because of racism. Ironic because *The Set Up*, based on the narrative poem written by Joseph Moncure March in 1928, was about an African American boxer named Pansy. Because Pansy refused to throw a fight, he was hunted down and killed on the subway tracks by vengeful gamblers. When the movie was produced by RKO in 1949, it starred Robert Ryan as the fading boxer, now named Bill

"Stoker" Thompson. Robert Wise, who a decade later was to direct Harry Belafonte's finest movie, *Odds Against Tomorrow* (1959), which also starred Ryan, stated to the author (on 23 August 2002) that Canada Lee was never considered for *The Set Up*. The American film industry, said Wise, didn't have any black stars at that time, and RKO had Robert Ryan, who had been an intercollegiate heavyweight champion boxer at Dartmouth, under contract. So it seemed only natural that RKO do the film with him instead of a black actor.

Lee lost the chance to immortalize his Bigger Thomas on film when Richard Wright made the misguided decision to cast himself as Thomas in a strange version of *Native Sons* made in Argentina in 1950. There was no way that the 40-year-old Lee could have portrayed the youthful Thomas, but pudgy 43-year-old Wright in a leather bomber jacket was laughable.

When *Body and Soul* was remade in 1981, the lead boxer was changed from white to black (Leon Isaac Kennedy). When it was again remade in 1998, with Ray "Boom Boom" Mancini as Charley Davis, the lead boxer was white. The 1998 adaptation was really a loose remake, and the Ben Chaplin character was missing, as he was from the Kennedy version.

Lee's final American project was appropriately enough about a conflicted fighter, much like Charley Davis in *Body and Soul*, entitled *The Final Bell* (1950). Frances Lee Pearson, who married Canada that year, regards the television show as a fluke and a mystery as to why CBS allowed the casting of Lee.[34]

Fate was kind to Lee, however. The British film industry, which had given Paul Robeson a film career, gave Lee one last great role—Stephen Kumalo in *Cry, the Beloved Country* (1951), the film version of the Alan Paton novel about the murder of a white planter's son by the black son of a rural minister. Lee desperately wanted the part, though he was already suffering from the hypertension that would kill him. In some respects, it is intriguing that the man who played Bigger Thomas on stage should now play the father to a South African version of Bigger Thomas in this film.

Lee befriended a young Sidney Poitier, who played a priest, Reverend Msimangu, in the film. Poitier regarded him as a spiritual father. (By coincidence, an incident linked Poitier with Lee, Garfield, and Joe Louis. Just before he made *Cry, the Beloved Country*, Poitier made his film debut in *No Way Out* (1950) at 20th Century Fox. On his way back to New York, his seatmate on the plane was John Garfield. It was a turbulent flight, and Garfield showed Poitier a trick taught him by Joe Louis to calm his nerves. Louis told Garfield to lie back with a handkerchief over his face and think of nothing.) Years later, when Poitier was hired to play in *The Blackboard Jungle* (1955), the MGM legal department demanded that he sign a loyalty pledge—because of his association with dangerous men such as Paul Robeson and Canada Lee. Poitier walked out, prepared to give up the job rather than sign. "It drove me wild that these men could see red but couldn't see black. That was galling enough. But what also appalled me was that I was accused of being sympathetic toward, respectful of, even admiring of Paul Robeson and Canada Lee—men I did respect tremendously. How could I not admire men of such courage and integrity?" He didn't have to sign, and credits the director Richard Brooks with standing up for him. The situation was repeated a few months later at NBC when Poitier was cast in *A Man Is Ten Feet Tall*. Again, the long-deceased Canada Lee was called a dangerous man and Poitier walked out, to be backed up by David Susskind.[35]

The success of the *Cry, the Beloved Country* in the United Kingdom didn't make Lee's phone ring in America. He was ignored in his country, and he was unemployed at a time when his illness, hypertension, was draining his coffers. The Italian producer Dino Pasanissi, however, signed Lee for a film starring him as Othello, to be shot in Technicolor. Lee went to Rome for pre-production work on the film but kept a promise to Zoltan Korda to appear at the New York premiere of *Cry, the Beloved Country* in early 1952. He had to return to the United States to renew his expiring passport in any case. If he had stayed in Rome, and renewed his passport at the American Embassy, perhaps the tragedy would have been deferred. He had been hospitalized in London for hypertension during the production of *Cry, the Beloved Country*, and he was still ill.[36]

Despite his blacklisted state, he was able to promote *Cry, the Beloved Country* on The Tex McCrary-Jinx Falkenburg Show on radio in January 1952. At the time, they were perhaps the most admired and glamorous commentators on radio (and later television). How was Lee able to appear on commercial radio? I asked Tex MCrary that question. The McCrarys were ardent Democrats, knew Canada for many years, and were seemingly not afraid of the consequences. "We had many on who were liberal," he said.[37]

Lee turned in his passport for renewal, but months passed and no passport was forthcoming. He could not return to Italy and no work was offered in New York. During his waiting period, he spoke constantly about discrimination, reconciliation between African Americans and Jews, and right-wing America. Lee's commitment to Adam Clayton Powell Jr. remained steadfast. Just a month before he died, Lee spoke at the Abyssinian Baptist Church about apartheid in South Africa, based on his eyewitness accounts while filming *Cry, the Beloved Country*. Just two weeks before he died he marched in White Plains, New York to protest the shooting of two black people by the police.

His frustration turned into anger. The hypertension, which always threatened his health, turned into deadly uremia. Frances was told there was no hope, and she watched over him as he died in agony at their 235 W. 4th Street apartment in New York on 9 May 1952. He was 45 years old.[38]

(The remake of *Cry the Beloved Country* in 1995 starred James Earl Jones as Kumalo. Fifteen years after Canada Lee's aborted attempt to present his Othello on Broadway, Jones became a star in the Joseph Papp production of that work. It is interesting to speculate that Jones had the career which would have been Lee's, if the times were favorable in the 1940s. He was the only African American actor after Lee to become celebrated as a Shakespearean actor, and he won his first Antoinette Perry "Tony" Award for playing the black boxer Jack Johnson in *The Great White Hope* in 1969. A year later he was nominated for a Best Actor Oscar for the film version of the play. Two decades later, he won another Tony Award for portraying the father in *Fences* by August Wilson. Lee would have been ideally suited for the plays of Wilson.)

Three days after Canada Lee's death, Frances Pearson met with Adam Clayton Powell, Jr., Walter White, and Oscar Hammerstein II to ensure that Lee's life and legacy would not be appropriated by the Communist Party of America. White, always sensitive about Communism because of charges over the years that the NAACP was a Communist front organization, wrote extensively about exploitation by Communists of blacks in Harlem. Powell was also accused over the decades of Communist-leaning leadership, particularly during the Harlem boycott of stores. According to Frances Pearson, they believed that Canada Lee, especially because of his sudden death, would be proclaimed a black hero of Communism. With Frances, they set up the Canada Lee Foundation, whose purpose was to raise money for scholarships.[39]

(In 1956, Frances married Henry Pearson, a volunteer with the Canada Lee Foundation.)

Hammerstein spoke at the memorial for Lee at the Abyssinian Baptist Church (where an estimated 6000 to 8000 people flooded the area), and expressed the essence of Lee's ambitions and dreams. "The life of Canada Lee will itself have many lives in our combined and varied memories. His death is a single incident in that life," Hammerstein said. Celebrating his accomplishments, Hammerstein emphasized that the primary reason for Lee's lasting impact is the wholeness of his life:

> There are all kinds of artists in the theater and out of it. Some keep their art in one compartment and their lives in another. In the case of Canada Lee there was a close and deep relationship between the actor and the man. He approached the part on the stage as he

approached every problem in life—with a basic, uncompromising honesty. He had no use for cheap theatricalism, nor did he build his career with cool, calculating steps. He chose parts and plays for what they had to say to the public, not merely for what they might do for him. So, he became a versatile actor, always interesting to watch and listen to, not merely for the mastery of any superficial technique, but because he threw his heart and soul into every part he played. And you could feel his heart beating beneath every character he depicted. The last time I had a chance to talk to him he had just returned from Africa after finishing *Cry, the Beloved Country*. He was most unhappy at what he had seen there—misery, injustice, poverty, cruelty. He was consumed with pity and bursting with anger. His capacity for feeling the heartbreak of others is what made him a good actor and an important man. He was no mildly interested spectator of the world's affairs. He lived them. He threw himself into every scene where he was needed. He spent himself on the rest of us, wore himself out, perhaps. He gave all of himself to us. Let us never forget to be grateful for the gift.[40]

This essay is dedicated to Frances Lee Pearson, the keeper of the flame, without whose cooperation it would not have been possible.

Notes

1. *New York World Telegram and Sun*, May 10, 1952, p. 22

2. Scrapbook in Schomburg Center, New York Public Library, Box 6.

3. Author telephone interview with Frances Lee Pearson [FLP], telephone July 9, 2002.

4. Author telephone interview with FLP, telephone, June 29, 2002.

5. *Pic*, August 5, 1941, pp 28-29.

6. Letter from Alexander Clark to FLP, October 1978.

7. Author interview with William Herz, New York, April 26, 2001.

8. Stanley Frank, "Canada Lee's Love for the Ring Is No Act," *New York Post*, May 16, 1941.

9. Author interview with WH, April 26, 2001.

10. Canada Lee, "*Body and Soul* Has Heart, Too," *Opportunity: The Journal of Negro Life*, Jan-March 1948, V. 26, #1, p. 21.

11. Author interview with Joan Hull Turner, March 21, 2001.

12. Author interview with FLP, Atlanta, July 26, 2001.

13. Lee, "*Body and Soul* Has Heart, Too," p. 21.

14. Sidney Poitier, *The Measure of a Man: A Spiritual Autobiography*. (NY: Harper, 2000), pp. 86-87.

15. Howard Fast, *Being Red*. (Boston: Houghton Mifflin, 1990) p. 272.

16. Irving Rudd, "Canada Lee, Former Boxer, Eyes Return," *The Ring*, June 5, 1946, pp. 7 & 34.

17. Seymour Peck, "Lee Put Heart and Soul Into *Body and Soul*," *PM*, September 4, 1947, n.p.

18. Lee, "*Body and Soul* Has Heart Too,"p. 21.

19. John Garfield, "Fists, Brains and Breaks," *Opportunity: The Journal of Negro Life*, Jan-March, 1948, V. 26, #1, p. 20.

20. Lee, *"Body and Soul* Has Heart Too,"p. 21.

21. Charles V. Hamilton, *Adam Clayton Powell, Jr.,* (New York: Collier Books, 1991), p. 97.

22. Speech written and delivered by Canada Lee before the Industrial Union of Maritime and Shipbuilding Workers, Baltimore, Maryland, October 29, 1944, (Frances Lee Pearson collection.)

23. Speech written and delivered by Canada Lee in Philadelphia and other places in 1944: "Harmony Among the Races, Among All People, Black and White, Jews and Gentiles, Capital and Labor." (Frances Lee Pearson collection.)

24. Speech written and delivered by Canada Lee titled "Differences" before Jewish War Veterans and possibly B'Nai Brith in New Rochelle, c. 1949.

25. Speech written and delivered by Canada Lee titled "Save the F.E.P.C.," at Town Hall, New York on June 19, 1945; public rally. (Frances Lee Pearson collection.)

26. Author interview with FLP, June 23, 2002.

27. Author interview with FLP, May 26, 2002.

28. Ed Sullivan, syndicated column appearing under various headlines, "Little Old New York and "Today in New York;" entitled "Body and Soul," May 21, 1952, from Burrelle's Clipping Service. (Frances Lee Pearson collection.)

29. Author's interview with FLP, Atlanta, July 26, 2001.

30. Author telephone interview with Howard Fast, April 21, 2001 and March 28, 2002.

31. Walter Winchell, "Walter Winchell in New York: Ham & Eggs, Broadway Style," *NY Daily Mirror*, Oct. 13, 1949. (Schomburg Center, Canada Lee Papers, New York Public Library.) The term "wallop" is a boxing term, meaning to knock an opponent senseless. The "line" is a clever double reference to both a huckster's scam and the Communist party line.

32. Letter retrieved from the FBI files on Canada Lee under the Freedom of Information Act; sent to Frances Lee Pearson by Howard Blue. (Frances Lee Pearson collection.)

33. Author interview with Paul Robeson, Jr. July 14, 2001; letter from Paul Robeson, Jr., on July 15, 2001, with approved text.

34. Author interview with FLP, June 22, 2002.

35. Poitier, *The Measure of a Man*, pp. 87-92.

36. Author interview with FLP, July 26, 2001.

37. Author interview with Tex McCrary, March 20, 2001.

38. Author's interview with FLP, Atlanta, Ga., July 26, 2001

39. Author interview with FLP, July 26, 2002.
Frances Lee Pearson supplied a letter which Lee wrote in 1949 to a newspaper editor which clarified his political position. Stating that he was not a Communist, he wrote in part: "I believe this constant screech of 'Communism' is only a smoke screen designed to hide very unpleasant facts. These facts are that Negroes, among other minority groups, do not have full civil rights; that housing is very, very inadequate; that serious unemployment threatens us; that the peace of the world is indeed very shaky. In passing, I might also inquire, where is the FBI in the frame-up of the Trenton Six, in the case of Rosa Ingram, in the case of Willie McGee, in the case of Caleb Hill, Jr., in the case of the seven men in Martinsville, Virginia, and in a host of other lynch justice cases—VICIOUSLY UN-AMERICAN!!! I say, and very sincerely, let us better examine those who do most of the screeching. It is they who have an axe to grind. It is they who are un-American!" Deliberate smear motives were at work. "It is the intent to frighten people into silence and submission by implying a connection with, or association in, a 'so-called' subversive organization labeled so by the offices of the Attorney General rather than through the due process of democratic law."

40. "Canada Lee Memorial Album," privately issued recording, 1952.

Kevin Lewis, who covers New York news for *DGA Magazine* (Directors Guild of America), has published in *Films in Review, Irish Voice,* and *Collector Editions*, among other publications. He was the curator of several exhibitions at the New York Public Library at Lincoln Center and the 82D Airborne Division Museum. His most notable exhibition *Something for the Boys: Trouping in America's Wars*, first shown at the New York Public Library at Lincoln Center, was brought to Deauville, France for the American Film Festival by the Academy of Motion Picture Arts and Sciences in 1994. He has lectured on film in guest appearances at the American Museum of the Moving Image, The Brooklyn Museum, and the United States Military Academy at West Point. He served as special projects coordinator in the 1980s for the American Theatre Wing and the Shubert Archive.

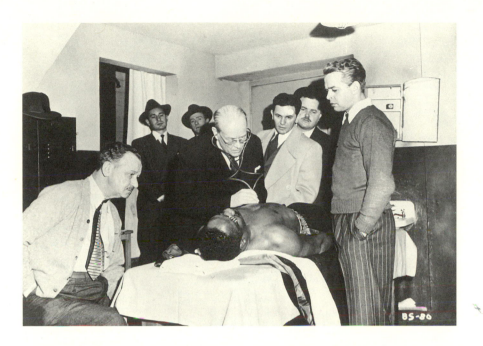

The Black Christ. *Body and Soul* was the first Hollywood film to place at its center the relationship between an African American and a Jew, according to Michael Rogin. The film created one of the first "substantial, ungrotesque" African American film roles—but it "fails to free the African American actor from inheriting the sacrificial role."

Once Charley is champ, his agreement to throw his title defense and bet against himself is an "investment." There is thus interracial solidarity between black man and Jew: not only is Charley following Ben in selling out; he has also risen on Ben's back, as the graphic shots of the Jewish fighter knocking down the African American make all too literal. "*Body and Soul* insists that the black face represents the sacrificed immigrant Jewish community. In finishing off Ben and elevating Charley, the film tells the truth about the contrasting prospects in the United States for African Americans and Jews. When the white fighter became Jewish, he inherited the culture's wish for a victory of white over black. *Body and Soul* wanted to repudiate that wish, but it could not film black victory. Although the word *Negro* is never uttered in *Body and Soul*, Canada Lee plays the black Christ. Eventually, the Jewish boxer follows the African American as mob-sponsored champion paid to throw away his crown. Charley was warned that he would end up like Ben, but he does not. Ben dies for Charley's sins." [Michael Rogin, *Blackface, White Noise: Jewish Immigrants in the Hollywood Melting Pot* (University of California Press, 1998.)]

MAY 2 6 1952

UNIONTOWN, PA.
HERALD
Circ. D. 10,713

Little Old
NEW YORK

By ED SULLIVAN

Body and Soul

The grim and curious coincidence of the deaths of John Garfield and Canada Lee within a few days spotlights the fact that both appeared in "Body and Soul," made by United Artists in 1947.

"Body and Soul," as a case history, is of tremendous importance to Americans fighting Communism because it illustrates the manner in which Commies and pinks, in the field of communications and ideas, gave employment to each other.

The picture was directed by Robert Rossen, written by Abe Polonsky, included in its cast Garfield, Canada Lee and Ann Revere. All of them later were probed by the House Committee on Un-American Activities. Rossen, Polonsky and Miss Revere defied the committee on the grounds of the Fifth Amendment, and were shelved by moving picture companies.

Garfield, just before his death, had tried to make atonement. He appeared voluntarily before the FBI, after being so advised by the Anti-Defamation Committee, and was testifying fully to his knowledge of Commie tactics and strategy, acquired from his association, but not his membership in the party.

"Body and Soul" actually caused his death. When the picture was being made, Garfield, as the fighter, did a rope-skipping scene. The girl playing opposite him in the scene repeatedly fluffed her lines. The scene had to be re-shot, over and over. When he went home that night, Garfield complained of illness. The doctor found that the rope skipping had torn a muscle of this heart.

Figure 3. Ed Sullivan's Syndicated Column, Originally Published 21 May 1952.

376

Up to just before his death, when he decided to come clean, Garfield had twisted and turned in a vain attempt to escape responsibility for his stupidity. After his appearance before the House committee in April 1951, this column challenged Garfield's sincerity. At that time, he told the committee that he wouldn't know a Communist if he saw one. Pointing out that he was a close friend of Clifford Odets, who later admitted having held a party card, I said that Garfield's testimony was worthless.

"Body and Soul" should open the eyes of those confused liberals who have assailed the House committee as witch-hunters. It should open the eyes of those who have fought every attempt to clear up the Commies' attempted infiltration of the TV industry. "Body and Soul" is the pattern that the Commies and their sympathizers in TV networks, agencies and theatrical unions would like to fasten on the newest medium. From the director on down, the Commies insert their members, freeze out those who are on the American side of the fence.

Edward Dmytryk, who rose from a $6-a-week studio messenger to a $2,500-a-week director, told the House committee in 1951 that as a result of the Alger Hiss revelations, he had determined to talk freely. In 1947, he had refused to answer questions. Dmytryk, who did a magnificent American job, explained that Communism in Hollywood had three targets:

(1) To profit from large dues or assessments taken from high salaried persons; (2) to gain prestige for the party through its own actions and the work of "front" organizations collecting large sums from stupid liberals; (3) The eventual control of the picture industry through its guilds and craft unions.

This is the same pattern that the Commies seek to work out on the Broadway stage and in TV.

The deaths of Garfield and Canada Lee should dramatize to all youngsters that the Commies take over, body and soul. The frustration that Garfield voiced in film roles followed him right to his death, not even permitting him to live long enough to know the country's appreciation for his voluntary testimony before the FBI. Canada Lee, equally talented, died in distress. Both of them, Garfield and Lee, were warm-hearted kids, easy prey for the bait that Commies dangle before confused liberals. Each of them, in the lyrics of Oscar Hammerstein, in "The King and I," was trapped because he "thought with his heart—his heart was not always wise."

Editor's Commentary on Ed Sullivan's **"Body and Soul"** *Column.* Ed Sullivan's piece on *Body and Soul* (21 May 1952), prompted by the deaths, a few days apart, of John Garfield and Canada Lee, is a perfect example of the "Cold War opportunism" that was such a symptom of that politically pathologic era. Sullivan—very much in his fervent anti-Communist mode (see page 174) in criticizing Lee, Garfield, and *Body and Soul*—was *reversing* a demeanor toward John Garfield that he had exhibited in "safer" times.

On 19 December 1948, Sullivan had John Garfield as a guest on his nationally televised *Toast of the Town* show to promote—and note this—Garfield's latest movie, (mispronounced by Sullivan as) "*Forces* [*sic*] *of Evil*." This is a film, remember, that would inflame the red-baiters as a product of the highly-suspect Enterprise Studios, a perceived citadel of Communist conspiracy (see pages 157-158). But here Sullivan is giving this film and Garfield a major plug on national television.

> ED SULLIVAN: A great movie star . . . started out on the New York stage . . . so New York has always gotten a terrific rap out of his success . . . he is in New York now for the opening of a new picture, *Forces* [*sic*] *of Evil* . . . it's a terrific . . . I saw it out on the coast . . . terrific story of the numbers racket. It is opening in New York on Christmas day. Ladies and gentlemen . . . *John Garfield.*

> Garfield comes on stage and is warmly greeted by Sullivan.

> SULLIVAN: [warmly holding Garfield's hand throughout this exchange] John-O! How are you? How are you, John? How are you, boy?

> GARFIELD: How are you, Eddie? [Looks and points at the television cameras.] These kind of cameras kind of make me nervous. I've never seen anything like this before, and they're absolutely fascinating!

> SULLIVAN: [ironically] *You're* upset by cameras!

They laugh and the audience laughs at their friendly, good-natured jesting. The inference to be drawn from this dynamic is that these are two affectionate colleagues who respect each other.

Sullivan now refers to a discussion that he, Garfield, and the postmaster of New York (Al Goldman) had before the show dealing with letters that children send to Santa Claus at Christmas time. He asks Garfield to read one. Garfield charmingly does so, and the segment concludes with the announcement that the child's requests for toys are being granted—including, in Dickensian fashion, the providing of a job to the child's out-of-work father.

The audience applauds in appreciation of the touching solicitude shown to this humble family at Christmas time.

Sullivan and Garfield embrace graciously, and their body movements (especially Garfield's) evolve into a kind of mock-boxing choreography, in which Garfield feigns punching Sullivan. This causes Sullivan to joke: "No *Body and Soul* with me, boy! No *Body and Soul* with me, huh!" And Garfield replies: "We'll leave that to the movie."

SULLIVAN: John, it was grand to have had you here—and now, let's have a real sock hand for a very fine youngster, John Garfield! Thank you, boy!

[Audience applauds enthusiastically.]

I told you that his picture, *Forces* [sic.] *of Evil*, is about the numbers racket—opening throughout the country—and John just whispered to me up here . . . he said the winning number tomorrow is "606."

[Audience laughs.]

(Ed Sullivan Broadcast, 19 December 1948; Andrew Solt Productions, time code: 11:39:49:00—11:44:09:10.]

Now, the point of this extended quotation is to dramatize the essence of Ed Sullivan's attitude and treatment of John Garfield (and *Force of Evil*)—on network television—in December of 1948. This entertainment encounter took place in advance of the 1951 U.S. Supreme Court decision which validated HUAC's inquisitions of Hollywood. After this later date, all reactionaries and political opportunists began to seek a safe refuge. This group included Ed Sullivan.

Thus, the attitude toward John Garfield needed to change. What was applauded in the past (*Body and Soul, Force of Evil*) now needs to be revised or deconstructed in light of contemporary political reality. Garfield, who was portrayed by Sullivan as a great star and friend on that 19 December 1948 CBS broadcast, is scornfully derided by Sullivan on 21 May 1952.

Had Garfield substantially changed as a human being from late 1948 to 1952? What had changed about *Body and Soul* or *Force of Evil* or Enterprise Studios since 1948 that would bring about such a shift in viewpoint from that warm acceptance on the *Toast of Town* broadcast to this condescending *Little Old New York* column? Answer: the political climate in the United States had changed. Certain Hollywood entities had now been identified as "unfriendly" or "uncooperative." It now became socially or politically dangerous to have certain friendships, associates, or affiliations. Accordingly, it becomes politically expedient to adopt an anti-Communist posture.

The affectionate allusion to "No *Body and Soul* with me," and the praise for a "terrific story of the numbers racket" (*Force of Evil*), now are superceded by an ideological position more conforming to Cold War politics. Attitudes and values change, but, as Abraham Polonsky used to say, if they change only when they put a gun to your head, the change is too late to preserve moral and intellectual integrity.

—John Schultheiss

"No *Body and Soul* with me," says Ed Sullivan (right) to John Garfield.

That Affable Familiar Ghost . . .
(a *Body and Soul* memoir)

by Joseph Janeti

The first time I saw Abe Polonsky was in Room 201 of the Lucas Building in the Cinema/Television complex at the University of Southern California (USC). I had been a product and presenter of East Coast and Midwest education, and was attending my first faculty meeting in the West. I didn't know what to make of the kinds of topics being offered up for consideration or the ways they were being discussed. Fearful of being engaged for an opinion in such unfamiliar territory, I kept my eyes cast down, sweeping the room every now and then to identify the speaker of the moment. At length, I noted an elderly bespectacled fellow who looked like he could have played Robert De Niro's father in a movie. He was seated off to my left, at the far end of the table; he was doing the same kind of scanning that I was, but his eyes twinkled and had a hint of mischief in them. When the meeting ended, I got up from my seat and headed over to say hello to this kindred spirit, but before I had moved very far, I saw that he was circling my way, and more quickly. He came up and extended his hand: "I'm Abe Polonsky."

At the time, I knew nothing of Abraham Lincoln Polonsky. It wasn't until he invited me to dinner sometime soon thereafter that I began to get a picture of him and his career, though years later I would recall that I *had* known something of Polonsky, something I would remember from my childhood—a TV screening of *Force of Evil*, the same film, by chance, which had influenced the career of Martin Scorsese. I recalled sitting on the floor of the downstairs rec room in our house in Elmsford, New York, when the words, "Written and Directed by Abraham Polonsky," came on the screen. I had wondered at the look of those words. "Such a big name!" I had mused, "He must a be an important man, and with such big thoughts!"

That initial dinner date with Polonsky was at Anna Maria's on Wilshire Boulevard in Santa Monica. It was the first of innumerable such evenings over the next 15 years, right up in fact to his last venturing out, some 48 or so hours before he died. But going back to that first dinner,

Polonsky was expansive. He began what would be an unswervingly regular game between us: always opening a topic of conversation or answering an important question by quoting from some obscure piece of literature—in this case, a Shakespeare sonnet, the one, in fact, from which our title is taken. Also over that dinner, Polonsky filled me in on his professional doings, and ran off a list of his novels and screenplays. I duly memorized the titles and vowed to myself to get them all out of the library and/or video rental store as soon as I could.

I began my viewing of the films with *Body and Soul*, the initial title he had clicked off and, of course, the subject of this memoir. Aside from *Golden Earrings* (extensively re-written by others), *Body and Soul* was Polonsky's first produced work as a screenwriter, and (as I hope to demonstrate in these pages) telling the story of *Body and Soul* provides a mechanism for recounting various of his most important personal themes. Eerily, conversation regarding the film marked not only the very beginning of my communication with Polonsky, but the very ending of that communication as well.

There are many places to begin the story of *Body and Soul* and how it wove through Polonsky's life, but perhaps some perspective may be gained by beginning our tale with the commencement of World War II. Most Americans at the time were swept up in a combination of predictable patriotism and outrage at the events going on across the seas. It was not uncommon for young men to attempt to join the fray, and Polonsky was no exception. Poor eyesight, however, kept him from being accepted into any branch of the armed forces. A visit by his brother, however, added an unexpected nuance to the discussion: "Abe, they're starting something called the Office of Strategic Services (OSS). They're looking for smart people; your eyesight won't be a problem. Why don't you contact them?" Polonsky did just that, and he was inducted into the fledgling service which was to be the direct predecessor of the Central Intelligence Agency (CIA). But how does this fit into the *Body and Soul* saga? As it turns out, Polonsky's entering the OSS dove-tailed precisely in time with another of his major life events.

Polonsky had been interested in writing since he was a boy, but his father had prevailed upon him to go to law school ("as a back-up" to a literary career). Dutifully, Polonsky graduated from Columbia Law, was admitted to the New York Bar, and proceeded to work for a firm that had radio celebrity Gertrude Berg as a principal client. Without going into that story, suffice it to say that Gertrude Berg gave Polonsky his first work as a writer, though he still wasn't doing anything in the way of film.

About that time, in 1942, Polonsky completed what was to be his first published solo-effort novel, *The Enemy Sea* (initially serialized in a magazine called *America*), a WW II adventure story set off the Gulf Coast that he would later refer to as "a pot-boiler." The story was highly visual, filled with entertaining characters and dialogue, and spoke to current government preoccupation with Nazi infiltration of American life. The novel enjoyed a modest success and led to a flurry of interest from the screen trade.

Polonsky's acceptance of an offer from Paramount came at virtually the same time as his induction into the OSS. Unsure of what was to be done in such a bifurcating situation, Polonsky reported the combination of events to senior OSS officer, "Wild Bill" Donovan. Rather than being disturbed in any way, Donovan responded with glee: "Perfect! You go ahead and accept the offer. It will be a perfect cover: you will say that you are in Europe to put together war documentaries for Paramount!"

As it turned out, the OSS's gain was Paramount's loss. A federal bill at the time required all employers to rehire at full pay any individual who had to take leave of his or her job to serve in the military. This, of course, made for a lot of red tape and for the freezing of long-term hiring plans by many employers. Paramount was no exception. So when, after signing his multi-year contract with the studio, Polonsky reported that he had been inducted to serve overseas, the Melrose mavens were furious. Nevertheless, at war's end, together with his wife Sylvia and their daughter Susan, Polonsky returned to Hollywood.

At first, things were slow on The Coast, and—telescoping a great deal—we might sum up the time in Polonsky's own words. In the last year of his life, when he was given the Lifetime Achievement Award by the Los Angeles Film Critics Association, Polonsky was asked how he felt about his long career in the screen trade. He responded, "To paraphrase the words of Swann near the end of the first volume of Proust: `To think—I spent the best years of my life making love to a woman that wasn't my style!'" Polonsky's interlocutor didn't know quite what to say; meanwhile, the audience howled. But the comment does arc over one important aspect of Polonsky's life—how he felt about Hollywood as a career choice. It began with that stint at Paramount: he was writing, but he was not getting any of the stories he really wanted to tell approved for production. But soon, "random events" (as he was fond of characterizing life's transforming factors) would turn the tide of the monotony.

Polonsky had befriended writer Arnold Manoff early on, and their relationship criss-crossed over various important domains in both their lives. As it turned out, Manoff was on contract at Enterprise (now Raleigh) Studios, situated just a block from Paramount's main gate. Manoff was over at Polonsky's office one afternoon, just generally kibbitzing. He looked at his wristwatch and said, "I've got to get over to a meeting at Enterprise; why don't you walk me back?"

As the two fellows set out on the short stroll down Melrose Avenue, Manoff mused, "Abe, I've got a problem. Garfield wants to do a boxing picture, but I just can't seem to come up with anything he likes." Polonsky vamped, "Why don't you do a story about . . ." And he proceeded to just make up some situation off the top of his head as the two men continued along. By the time they reached the Enterprise gate, Manoff said, "You know, I'm going to be meeting with Garfield right now; why don't you come in and say hello?"

In fact, Polonsky had been introduced to John Garfield at a recent social event. Besides some personal warmth between the two, they shared similar views on various political issues. They had gotten along quite well at that earlier meeting, so when they met up again at Enterprise, they greeted each other enthusiastically. "Abe's got a story for your boxing picture," announced an unabashed Manoff. "Let's hear it!" enthused Garfield. And audaciously, Polonsky complied, further weaving his piece of five-minute extemporary. The best part of the story is that Garfield loved it: "Wait right here; I'm going to call the brass!" And, on Garfield's request, the Enterprise decision-making team was willing to assemble to hear about Polonsky's "boxing picture."

And so, a short while later, Polonsky went through the story for the third time. He was becoming an expert, after all—with two full prior tries at his tale, he had spent perhaps a full twenty minutes with the material! He wove his character, Charley, through the drama's various feints and weaves, until he got to the story's last few minutes. We will come back to this point later, but for now we need to relate merely that at this climactic moment of the drama, Polonsky got up from his chair and moved toward the door. "Wait a minute, Polonsky," said the studio chief, "You haven't finished the story!" To which Polonsky replied, "Yeah, but I don't work for you. I work for Paramount!"

Polonsky left Enterprise and walked back down the block-and-a-half to Paramount's main gate. As he passed through the entrance, the guard at the kiosk hailed him, "Mr. Polonsky, the boss wants to see you." Polonsky headed up to the studio chief's office.

When he got upstairs, Polonsky was ushered into a seat: "Abe, you're going to work for Enterprise; we just loaned you out." Polonsky sat there, listening. The executive continued gleefully, "And we're getting $2,000 a week for you!" (almost $17,000 per week in 2002 dollars). "What do you mean, *you're* getting? You mean *I'm* getting . . ." Polonsky liked to recount. "No, Abe, that's not how it works. You're on contract; you get your regular salary. We get the extra money." Polonsky took a different view of things and, such was the magical fortune which surrounded his life, it was he who walked away with the majority of the windfall.

Making a film in the 1940's was still a relatively straightforward affair: a script was executed soon after there was agreement on a project, and shooting commenced quickly thereafter. Consequently, *Body and Soul* was released in 1947, and here we will return to the cliff-hanger with which Polonsky had left the Enterprise brass.

When *Body and Soul's* editing was completed, Polonsky received a phone call one evening from Arthur Loew, one of the Enterprise principals. "Abe, a few of us are going down to Long Beach to do a test screening of the picture; do you want to come along?" They picked up Polonsky, and the carload of movie people headed off to that sleepy seaside town. John Garfield was among the biggest box office attractions of the day, so inasmuch as there would be a sizeable built-in audience, the production team chose for the test screening a theatre which was then playing one of Garfield's films. The scheduled feature was to be the last show of the evening, but before it began, the lights in the theatre were turned up and the audience members were advised that if they would like to see a screening of John Garfield's new picture, they need only stay in their seats once the slated film was over. Of course, a shout went up from the house. The scheduled feature commenced, and after it was over, *Body and Soul* rolled for the first time before a theatre audience.

For a dramatic artist, on the stage or on the page, the capacity to handle decision is the telling challenge. When *Body and Soul* got to the moment of decision—Charley's moment of decision, the moment referred to earlier where Polonsky had left the Enterprise executives hanging—audience members sprang from their seats as one, screaming at the action on the screen. Loew turned around to Polonsky who was sitting just behind him: "I guess we've got a hit on our hands."

And what a hit it was! Not only was the film one of the most financially rewarding of the year, making millions for Enterprise (its most successful film ever), but it also garnered a host of critical raves, three Academy Award nominations (one for best screenplay), and an Oscar for best editing. It also insured Polonsky's career as an important Hollywood screenwriter.

What was it about *Body and Soul* that was so compelling, and why do I say it encompassed some of the most important themes of Polonsky's life? Although it is not uncommon for writers to use aspects of their lives in their work, Polonsky used such elements liberally and quite directly throughout his literary material. *Body and Soul* is the story of Charley Davis, a poor boy from the Lower East Side of New York. Polonsky had spent his formative years in a different section of New York—the Bronx—in an area bordering the Bronx Zoo. He eventually would write lyrically of this magical time, in Part I of *Zenia's Way* (1980), his final novel. However, he was intimately familiar with the Lower East Side since his father had a pharmacy in that neighborhood. Polonsky had spent a fair amount of time there while growing up; therefore, the pharmacy and the surrounding neighborhood figure prominently in many aspects of his history, from his earliest sexual experiences to his scrappy sense of always wanting "to be where the fight was." The pharmacy stood near the corner of Second Avenue and Second Street, just a few blocks from the neighborhood Martin Scorsese was later to portray as "Mean Streets."

An almost-personal anecdote may contribute to conveying something of the flavor of the neighborhood. My brother, an artist, lived for a while just off that very same Second Avenue/Second Street intersection, in a front apartment of a building directly next door, as circumstance would have it, to the New York Chapter of the Hell's Angels. The mid-section of the block was lined with expensive motor cycles, and as in all neighborhoods ruled by thugs, no one would dare touch anything on the street; it was one of the safest blocks in New York. A noisy row late one night brought my brother to the front window. From there he witnessed a score of Angels spilling through the doorway of their building, out onto the sidewalk. At the head of the mob was a particularly angry individual who shoved a woman to the ground, then kicked her until she rolled off the curb and into the street. A second fellow just behind him finally grabbed his cohort's arm, and in a thick New York accent, jawed, "Hey Sal, she didn't mean nothin' by what she said!" To which the first, turning back toward the building and away from the woman lying in the gutter, responded, "I know; that's why I didn't punch her." This was the neighborhood in which *Body and Soul's* Charley Davis grew up.

In the film, Polonsky's father's pharmacy is only slightly morphed into Charley's father's candy store. In fact, David (Charley's father) so closely resembles Polonsky himself that we may easily imagine the fellow being cast along the lines of Polonsky's image of his own father. Additionally, the candy store would, in almost all respects, resemble a Lower East Side pharmacy of the time. In trying to characterize the atmosphere of rough justice that ruled the neighborhood, Polonsky frequently told one particular story. Embedded in the tale, on the one hand, is some old-fashioned mean-street decorum, but it also contains some stand-up-decisively-against-wrong-doing honor, a street version of the kind of honor Polonsky respected, the kind of honor that would eventually result in his subpoena to appear before the House Committee on Un-American Activities, an action which began when he was visited in France while writing his novel,

Season of Fear.   A New York buddy had arrived and warned, "Abe, what-ever you do, don't go back to the States just now." "Oh, yeah, and why is that?" "For sure they'll call you in to testify in front of the House Commit-tee." Polonsky turned to his wife: "Sylvia, start packing." As he would later say, "No one was going to tell me what I could or couldn't say in my own country!" And back to the States they went. Polonsky did appear before that Committee, but that's another story. As to the kind of hard line street equity we are here trying to characterize as being an influence on *Body and Soul*, Polonsky often told the following anecdote about life on the Lower East Side.

During Prohibition, the only alcohol that moved legally through the United States was that used in pharmacies for certain medical prescrip-tions. In those earlier, less complicated days, and especially as noted above, in those neighborhoods ruled by gangsters, certain things could be counted on as being safe and off-limits to criminals—among them residents of the neighborhood and their property. So it was that a pallet containing a large shipment of alcohol was delivered late one night and allowed to be left on the sidewalk, to be brought into the pharmacy the next morning when it opened for business. Someone misread the rule of the jungle, however, and absconded with the entire pallet.

The following morning, when Polonsky-the-elder came to open the store, there was no alcohol in sight. He wrung his hands a bit about it, but went on with his work. Later in the day he received a visit from one of the neighborhood Dons. When asked about the shipment, Mr. Polonsky acknowledged that it was missing. "Don't you worry, Mr. Polonsky, you'll get it back."

The next day, when Mr. Polonsky arrived to open the store, the missing pallet was indeed sitting right on the sidewalk where it should have been the morning before. The astonished pharmacist stocked it away. Later in the day he was again visited by the Don: "You found your prop-erty OK, Mr. Polonsky?" "Yes, sir, I did." "Was it all there?" "Yes, it was." "OK, well, the guy who took it, he wants to come in and apologize." "Oh, that's OK. As long as everything is back . . ." "No, you don't understand, he wants to come in." "Well, OK, I'll be here all day." "No, he won't be able to come in for a coupl'a months." The pharmacist was puzzled. "He's in the hospital right now, and he can't talk so good, so maybe in a coupl'a months . . ."

Charley's mother (Anna) is quite sensitive to the effect that such a rough-and-tumble place will have on her son. When Charley comes into the candy store after his amateur win, she speaks out in anger about his boxing career. **[49-51]** She feels things can come to no good in this place. And, in fact, with beautiful story-telling economy, Polonsky dramatizes this truth immediately. Once his wife has left to go up and make dinner, Charley's father, David, hands him ten dollars for boxing equipment. Charley takes off like a gleeful kid. When David turns back to close out the cash register, a bomb is hurled out of a speeding car, blowing in the candy store window and burying him in the rubble. Charley's prescient mother is made a widow in less than three minutes of screen time. The premise of money destroying a person's life and/or character was never far from Polonsky's consciousness. We will return to this later.

Another of Polonsky's life themes that is limned in early in the film is altogether different: the joy and magic possible in love between two individuals. Polonsky's life was truly blessed by his early and enduring marriage to his wife, Sylvia. In fact, that relationship was the single most important element in Polonsky's life, a fact expressed repeatedly in numberless variations over all the years I knew him. In his version of the initiation of his and Sylvia's courtship, a 17-year-old Polonsky was sitting in his room reading one day, when a firm knock came at the door leading from his sister's bedroom. "What is it?" The door opened and in walked 14-year-old Sylvia Marrow. "I just wanted to tell you that I'm going to marry you," she said. "Oh, is that right? Did you ask your mother!" The affection and playfulness in the relationship is what is important here—it is how Polonsky saw love.

When, in *Body and Soul*, Charley first meets Peg, she is a local beauty and a kind of door prize for the winner of an amateur boxing competition. Charley, of course, is the winning competitor, and the presentation of Peg to him as his dance partner for the evening brings out every awkward boyish thing in the young man. The two most charming expressions of this come in the sequence directly following their meeting. For Peg the evening is, after all, merely a way to earn a little extra money to help support her career as an artist. In spite of this, some early sparks are evident between the two. The boyish quality in Charley shows up immediately, when he is called to the floor to share that first dance with Peg. With his buddies catcalling from the sidelines, Charley blushes and trips over himself as he sets out to do a turn with the comely young woman.

It is after the cab ride home, in Charley's saying good-night to Peg at her door, where the playful quality we are tracking in the relationship is most noticeable. Hoping for a good-might kiss, Charley jams his foot in the door to keep Peg from closing it. She stomps down on the foot, and when he withdraws it in pain, Peg slams the door shut. Charley changes his tack: he gestures over his shoulder to indicate his buddy (Shorty) and the cab driver, who are eagerly watching to see whether Charley will "score."

INSIDE THE DOOR

From within, Peg draws the curtain of the glass door back and peeps out at Charley, who leans closer to the glass and pantomimes. He holds up his hands in prayer, then indicates the cab and the two watchers over his shoulder. Peg starts to smile. Charley pronounces soundlessly "Five Minutes," holding up five fingers for additional clarity. Again he points over his shoulder. Peg hesitates, and then slowly opens the door. She is in full command now and somewhat intrigued by this muscular naivete.

As described on innumerable occasions, this bantering and sparring playfulness with a person of sensitivity and intelligence and equality characterized the relationship Polonsky shared with Sylvia. For example, at his Los Angeles Film Critics Association Lifetime Achievement Award presentation, when he told the story of the Paramount executive ordering him over to Enterprise, Polonsky noted, "He should have known better: he should have known that I didn't take orders from anyone —except my wife!"

One of the things Polonsky loved most about Sylvia was her practicality. "She knew how to do all these kinds of things," he would note, when faced with one of those daily tasks of life which he might find confusing, like replacing a light switch. Robert Johnson, in his extraordinarily beautiful book on relationships, *We*, notes the rarity of modern Westerners' ability to identify and/or appreciate an "Iseult of the Fair Hands," a partner of practical virtue, willing to roll up her or his sleeves to work to make a loving life with another actually possible. This was not a burden for Polonsky: he loved Sylvia in a practical way, specific and earthbound. He touches on those feelings most clearly in his novel *Season of Fear* (Cameron Associates, 1956):

Restlessly he turned his head and saw his wife's living face, her mouth a little open as she breathed in her sleep. This dry wind would irritate her delicate sinuses. He thought of it as a husband should.

Her face did not fade and melt in the luminous darkness flooding from the sky. Her face was sharply etched, in relief. Like her body, her face did not have any of the usual beauties to which this generation of hungry consumers had been trained. She was of a different race, his own, a different time, an era special in his consciousness. His wife was special, delicate and strong, as if built of a new kind of flesh and bone that did not need a heavy mass of body, of sensuality, to sustain its life.

She had, so to speak, arrived in development as the modern bridge had, no longer encumbered with a useless weight of decoration, concrete and bricks that supported nothing but the memory of what men were used to. She was all grace and strength as some of the springing bridges he had built, all practical and wonderful as the idea of health brought as water from the mountains and the far rivers, the wild water brought into the very house to run coolly on the hand from the tap. She was then natural and yet more than the perfect shapes of natural things, human. . . .

[He was aware of] . . . the supreme confidence of the woman who lay asleep beside him, this marvelous person, the old, old love he had for her, this girl whom he had known in the fields and dirt roads of Goshen, this girl, this woman who contained more of his life than what he could force himself to recall, this person with whom he had discovered life, affection, friendship, marriage, passion, children, maturity. Everything. Whatever had been written or said about love seemed inadequate to him for between him and his wife all barriers had fallen and only death could now intervene.

What is love?

What is love that melts bodies, a double turning of separate persons into each other until matter immaterializes and becomes emotion, thought, memory, a new kind of fact, weightless, bodiless, spaceless, whose direction is always intention and whose motion is only by meaning? It is not desire, which is only a falling as a weight drops . . . In love the body moves and then it happens, the miracle of matter becoming mental energy. It is related because it exists, and it is relevant because it is real, but it is a mystery since it has no physical quantity, only meaning. (pp. 61-63.)

Polonsky loved the way Sylvia could rule him in everyday matters and lead their lives forward in sensible ways. In the further adventures of Charley and Peg, we see that although an out-of-towner and newcomer to New York, it is Peg, not Charley, who has managed to set up a cozy little home for herself. Moreover, she is an artist. She holds crayons in her hands and makes things, practical things that can go out into the world, things such as one of the artifacts of this first date—a portrait of Charley [p. 323]. And so, the getting-to-know-you that takes place between the two is set against a backdrop of practicality and aesthetics, two of the qualities Polonsky most voiced in telling of his relationship with Sylvia.

As in his own real marriage, in *Body and Soul* Polonsky gives the lady of the house the last word. When it is Charley's time to leave, it is Peg who lets him know that the time has come. Further, he is putty in her hands, not only in being the more moon-eyed of the two at this early point in their relationship, but clearly in the way which Polonsky allows Peg to dominate—though dominate in the playful, cuffing way Polonsky reserved for love as he understood it.

CHARLEY
(trying)
Could I see you again, sometime.

PEG
What for?

CHARLEY
(earnestly)
Well, just to see you, anything. . . .

PEG
(with a slight smile)
Try some time. [41-42]

[See additional analysis of the "Tiger! Tiger! Burning bright" scene in Peter Valenti's "Forest of the Night," pp. 311-312.]

Recounted in endless variation, it was precisely this kind of playful, affectionate enjoyment of two people for one another, which Polonsky so treasured in his own life, in the home he had made with Sylvia. But love has a difficult time of it in *Body and Soul*—in almost every case it is damaged and/or destroyed by the quest for money.

Money is a principal character in *Body and Soul*. Polonsky cared tremendously about the movement of money in the world. Whether it was the optimistic valuation of Marxism, calling for a world without private ownership, the creeping concentration of capital via the globalization of the world's economy, or the greed of a private individual appropriating the financial right or well-being of another, the topic was never without discussion at a dinner with Polonsky. He pondered, too, the money he himself earned.

And it is money that provides the greatest press on Charley. Earlier, in the candy store episode, Charley had lashed out at the idea of working for a living in a repetitive, earth-bound way. There is an obvious crudeness to his speech in front of his parents who, themselves, have worked so hard to do the best they could for him. In a sense, Charley is there parroting one of the vilest streaks in a world where money rules—get as much as you can, as fast as you can, any way that you can. His mother, of course, rebukes him, but the most famous scene regarding money in *Body and Soul* is coming up.

Charley has done rather well in the amateur boxing world, and his manager-friend Shorty has managed to make a connection for him with Quinn, a shady conduit to big fights and big money. Teetering in the balance as to whether or not to go ahead with such a life, Charley has a healthy influence pulling at him—his relationship with Peg. He brings Peg home to meet his mother. Interestingly, Polonsky uses two bits from his own past in constructing Peg's history—her father is a pharmacist, and she is from Highland Falls, the same upstate New York town where Polonsky's family lived for a brief time after they moved from the Bronx. But what is important for present purposes is the tug of agendas at work in the scene. Shorty is waiting for an OK from Charley to allow Quinn to set up boxing matches for him; Charley is interested in his mother and Peg meeting, for by now, he and Peg have clearly fallen in love. The provocation that actually ignites the scene is the unexpected arrival of a social worker who wants to interview Charley's mother about her application for welfare assistance. Charley is outraged when he realizes what the woman is there for. He lashes out in fury and throws her out of the apartment. His mother turns on him.

ANNA
(desperately)
I did it to buy myself fancy clothes? Fool! It's for
you . . . to get an education, to make something of
yourself.

CHARLEY
(wheeling to Shorty)
Shorty! Shorty! Get me that fight from Quinn. I
want money!
(hysterically)
You understand? Money! Money! Money!

ANNA
(with same hysteria as Charley's)
No! I forbid! I forbid! Better buy a gun and shoot
yourself.

CHARLEY
(yelling)
You need *money* to buy a gun!

Polonsky truly felt disturbed by what people would do for money: the manipulation of truth, the twisting of intention, the destruction of continuing or potential relationships. He spoke of it frequently, sometimes in disturbing and altogether surprising ways. The word itself appears in *Body and Soul* 48 times.

But money is not the end of our tale. More than anything, *Body and Soul* is a story about honor. The basic question of the drama is whether or not Charley will throw a fight. At first the question seems one of only minor import—a single humiliation will turn him into a wealthy man for life. By the point in the film where Charley must actually make the decision as to whether or not he will throw the fight, however, the situation has grown into a monster casting an evil shadow over numerous lives. It involves the mob as well as an uncountable number of everyday people, all of whom have bet according to their various views of the meaning or outcome of the match. As noted above, there was no more important quality to Polonsky than honor, or as he chose to root it in the individual—*character*. Character was Polonsky's most constant topic of conversation, and he always spoke this word with a very pronounced "C."

Perhaps because he had seen how words and intention could be twisted to undermine the basic rights of individuals, Polonsky had a great affinity for people who spoke straightforwardly and could be taken at their word. In a certain way, this penchant lies at the root of his problem with the House Committee on Un-American Activities: he hated their distortion of motive and meaning. Polonsky believed that one should be allowed to speak one's mind and live one's private life, however these might be expressed, and that no individual should stand in the way of another's enjoyment of such rights. In the largest sense, protection of this enjoyment is the basic premise of the First Amendment, which has been so regularly threatened in American history. Quiet, front-line opposition to such threats is provided by the kind of person Polonsky most respected—an innately noble, plain-speaking individual with unselfconscious native dignity and an unshakeable code of honor. Polonsky joyfully celebrated such individuals. His sister-in-law Ruth was such a one, and he enjoyed her intelligent company until the very end of his days. So too was his housekeeper Maria; her bantering with him was one of the greatest pleasures of the last year of his life. Charley, potentially, is such an individual, but in his case his sense of honor is shaky. Will he throw the match and thereby violate his most fundamental nature, his core and native self?

It is an old axiom of dramatic writing that it is by a minor character that a story's most incisive views are spoken and its most provocative questions asked—often in an almost off-hand way. In spite of his appearing in *Body and Soul* (in what at first glance might be dismissed as an ancillary scene), the clearest carrier of the code of honor we have been discussing is Shimin the grocer. In dramatic terms, he appears at the moment before the fall. Things are practically euphoric among Charley, Peg, and his mother; Charley's career has never looked better—a championship fight is about to take place and everyone is excited about it; and most important to the well-being of all, the match will be Charley's last. However, looming darkly in the background is Charley's secret question: will he or will he not throw the fight? Just now, it's looking as though he will. The family is together in Mrs. Davis's apartment. Shimin the grocer arrives and, in humble terms, tells how the neighborhood is standing behind Charley, betting on his winning the match. [131-132]. [See additional discussion of this scene in Mark Rappaport's "Candy Story" essay, pp. 333-334.]

Not only does Shimin stand for the community, he also, in psychological terms, stands for what Carl Jung would call Charley's "shadow," his unaccepted, unrealized self. For ultimately, Charley will be forced to make a decision: whether to incorporate his shadow (the simple, hardworking, honest world of his mother and Shimin), or to avoid it—and thereby live only that segment of his psyche currently at the fore (the corrupt, manipulative, money-driven world of Roberts and Quinn). That Shimin has touched this acute psychodynamic nexus is evident in Charley's explosive outburst as the scene continues after Shimin's exit.

> The women are emotionally stirred, laughing happily. Anna is even proud. But Charley has turned away, his face clouded. In that same moment the women notice it and exchange a look.

CHARLEY
What's the matter with people? Why do they have to bet? It's a racket. They know it's a racket.

ANNA
People gamble.

CHARLEY

They're suckers. Tell 'em not to bet on me, Ma.

ANNA

I'm too old to walk up and down New York telling
people not to bet . . .
        (smiling)
. . . especially when they win.

CHARLEY

They can lose. You don't always win. Suckers like
Shimin shouldn't bet.

ANNA

Suckers like Shimin! You didn't hear what he said,
did you, Charley? It isn't the five dollars that's
important, it's . . . [the principle.]

And it is the strength and clarity of these principles, these simple
gifts of quiet dignity and unadorned faith, which illuminate Charley's
mother, Shimin, and the community from which they spring. And although
he knows that they could cost him his money and even probably his life, it
is these same principles which will propel Charley to choose to face the
odds against tomorrow, and complete his personal development, a winner
at last. And so we need to spend a bit more time on this seemingly expend-
able apparition, this Greek Chorus on Second Avenue. But in order to understand this situation from Polonsky's perspective, it would be helpful to
recount his favorite piece of personal lore, a story he repeated over the
years I knew him more times than any other.

Although Polonsky maintained a scrappy persona with a superficial crusty cynicism and sometimes caustic speech, he was actually rather
a romantic, with a gentle, kindly soul. He consequently loved a certain
sort of person, a humble individual without airs, a plain and natural being
whose faith and loyalty and sense of right could be relied upon, even to the
edge of doom. Such dependability was a question of character, as Polonsky
would have put it, and, as noted earlier, character was Polonsky's greatest
preoccupation. An incident which illustrates this predilection took place
at the New York City premiere of *Tell Them Willie Boy Is Here* (1969).

But before we begin this story we need to share some Italian-American pigeon-English and some bits of New York custom. As to the first,
inasmuch as many Italian immigrants could not speak English, they would
sometimes resort to hand gestures and child-like renditions of words to

express ideas; thus "good-bye" might be "bye-bye," with a child-like cupping of fingers into the palms of the hands. Additionally, most of those early Italian-American immigrant families were Roman Catholic, and for the ones living in New York, the most customary manner of dealing with their dead was by burial in one of the large cemeteries in the vicinity of Brooklyn. Finally, there generally was (and is) an alcove in Roman Catholic Churches where donations could be exchanged for the right to light a candle and offer a prayer for a deeply desired wish or a longingly missed loved one. With that, we can return to our *Willie Boy* premiere.

Although *Willie Boy* had already opened in Paris, the American debut was slated for New York City's Museum of Modern Art. The gala evening began with festivity and good will in the air. After the feature concluded, the audience members exited the theatre. Many stopped to share a few words with Polonsky who stood in the vestibule just outside. All the while Polonsky was chatting with these critics, friends and movie buffs, he kept noticing a lone figure pacing back and forth at the far end of the vestibule. The fellow was dressed in a dark suit, a tie, a white shirt . . . and the whole time, he just kept pacing.

The line of fans slowly dwindled, and eventually Polonsky said good-night to the last well-wisher. He looked up, and yet again noted the lone figure, still in his solitary pacing. Polonsky moved across the lobby, and extending his hand, said, "Hello, I'm Abe Polonsky." The fellow looked up and responded, "I know you, Mr. Polonsky." Between the gentleman's accent and mannerisms, Polonsky sensed right off that this was a good fellow "from the neighborhood" as Polonsky put it, the Lower East Side, his Lower East Side, the Lower East Side of his father's pharmacy and his own exploring youth, the lower East Side portrayed in *Body and Soul*.

So, sensing instinctively the gentleman's origin, Polonsky ventured, "You're from the neighborhood!" The fellow loosened just a bit, and with a touch of shyness, answered "Yeah, that's right." "How is everybody?" asked Polonsky, "How is Sal?" The gentleman brightened: "Oh, Sal, he's'a business do good!" and extending all the fingers of his outstretched hand: "He's'a got five trucks!" "And what about Johnny?" asked Polonsky, now amused. "Oh, not so good," the man shook his head sadly, "Bye-bye Brookaleenah . . ."

But still Polonsky could not figure why the fellow was there. He cast around more broadly: "Did you see the picture." "Yeah, I see the pi'tch. But I no like'a go see the pi'tch; I no come'a see the pi'tch; I come'a see you." The man shifted around from one foot to the other; Polonsky waited. "The pi'tch . . . You make'a good money?" "A whole fleet of trucks!" roared Polonsky with a laugh. "`At's'a good," the gentleman mumbled, then looked down at the floor. Polonsky waited. There was another awkward moment. At last the gentleman reached into the inner pocket of his jacket; he pulled out an envelope and extended it across the divide.

Polonsky took the envelope and pryed it open. With curiosity, he pulled out seventy-four dollars. "What's this?" Polonsky hazarded. The man shuffled around a bit, then took an awkward breath: "My mother, in the Depression, she's'a sick; she no can pay for the medizeen'a. Your father, he's'a give'a: `Signora, you pay me when'a you can.' When she's'a die, she calls me come; she's'a tell me, `You find'a Mr. Polonsky; you geev'a him.' She's'a give me the envelope. When my mother, she's'a die, I go find'a you father; they's'a tell me he's'a die too. I no can'a find'a you; they's'a tell me you go to Hollywood, make'a the pi'tch. So, I watch'a the newspaper all'a time for you' name. When I read about the pi'tch and you be here, I come give'a you the money."

Polonsky stood there speechless for a moment. He put the money back in the envelope. Then referencing Little Italy's *Our Lady of Mount Carmel*, he asked, "You still go to the Church?" The fellow loosened yet more visibly. "Oh, yeah, I go." "They still have the Poor Box there?" queried Polonsky, referring to the simple wooden box affixed to the back wall of the Church where the faithful could leave donations for the parish poor. "Oh, yeah, they have." "OK," said Polonsky, handing the envelope back to the gentleman, "Then, how about if you go to the Church and you put this into the Poor Box; then maybe you can light a candle—for your mother and for my father." The man's eyes misted over as he accepted the beau geste; he said a humble farewell and moved off into the night. Polonsky stood there thinking of the old lady, sick back in the days of the Depression and of her life-long mindfulness of his father's generosity, of the 40 years which had passed between then and this evening in 1969, of the long patient vigil of this gentle man, and the quiet, graceful completion of his appointed round. Character.

When Charley rants after the Grocer's exit, the words on the surface are of disgust that anyone would be such a fool as to bet on a boxing match, but really the true object of the tirade is Charley himself. In fact, this place in the screenplay stands out as the beginning of Charley's own transformation, the one which will lead him to his dramatic decision at the movie's end, and the only choice he truly could have made in order to fulfill the drama's premise and his own destined individuation. But things are never so simple with Polonsky, and triumph will be mixed up with the idea of death.

The single most famous coda of *Body and Soul* is the variously repeated: "Everybody dies," and it would be impossible to consider the intellectual history of the movie without considering death and dying. The first time "everybody dies" appears in the film is in the scene where we first learn of the cold-blooded manipulation of human affairs that is possible when motives are ruled by money. Roberts, the gangster behind organized boxing, mixes up money, amorality, and death, in a speech chilling in its lack of feeling. At the time of the speech, Roberts notices that Charley is distant and withdrawn. We will come to know that Charley is thinking of his buddies Ben and Shorty, good people who were sold out and are now dead, of his family and relationships and love, of money, morality, community and history. And although the throwing-the-fight scheme has been on the boards for a while now, Roberts realizes for the first time that Charley may be having second thoughts about going ahead with the charade. The scene ends with one of Polonsky's own all-time favorite lines of his writing.

> ROBERTS
> You know the way the betting is, Charley. The
> numbers are in. Everything is addition and
> subtraction. The rest is conversation.

When we next hear the coda, we are in a flashback. We now learn how cancerous the situation is. Ben, the title-holder Charley has just beaten in the ring, lies comatose on a gurney. Although Charley has won the fight, there is no joy in the locker room. The men hover about the supine Ben. And again Roberts mutters, "Everybody dies."

The final time the line appears, it is Charley's, and this time, ironically, spoken *to* Roberts. Polonsky has managed to keep us in suspense right up to the final moments of the film, the point, noted above, where he had left the brass at Enterprise hanging, the point where the preview audience members had risen to their feet as one, screaming at the screen. Anyone who has ever watched *Body and Soul* cannot have escaped spine-tingling chills at the moment when Charley finally decides what he is going to do: he stands up for principal and right action and the various good people in his life and suddenly begins to fight, and fights unambiguously to win! In his most decisive action in the film, Charley is engaged, focused, unstoppable. In dramatic terms, in the terms spoken of above, this has been as expert a protraction of the process of "decision" as we can ever hope for from an artist. [See "Fifty Grand," Note #11.] As to the match itself, there is a quick knock-out. The various crooks in the audience are furious; Charley's fans and loved-ones are ecstatic.

Of course, there will be hell to pay for this. It is unlikely that Charley will live very long; in fact, the director shot a variant ending of the film, where Charley was executed right after he exchanged words with Roberts and exited the building. [See Screenplay Annotation #23.] But as *Body and Soul* was finally presented (the way it was originally written), there is a moment of triumph. Charley has come out of the arena and is in the corridor next to Roberts.

> ROBERTS
>
> What makes you think you can get away with this?

> CHARLEY
> (smiling)
> Whatta you going to do, kill me? Everybody dies.

As noted above, the ideas of death and triumph are often woven together in Polonsky. Certainly, none of the innumerable dinners I shared with him was ever without talk of the two. In his last years, Polonsky used to tell a very touching story, as poetic as it was heroic. In her final minutes, his beloved Sylvia called her husband to her to say good-bye. Polonsky looked on quietly at his partner of over sixty years. So many things flooded through his mind. At last, he ventured: "Will I ever see you again?" "Of course," spoke Sylvia, decisive to the end. "How will I find you?" Polonsky queried softly. "I'll be stardust . . ." The two were silent for a minute. "But you'll be so far ahead of me." mused Polonsky. "Have I ever had trouble finding you before?" bantered Sylvia. "There are just two things I want to tell you before I go," she continued. "Keep on teaching, and don't try to balance the checkbook." From that moment on, in his consciousness, Polonsky held the promise of only one future engagement.

When I think of this continuous blending in his thinking of the notions of death and triumph, I think of the existentialists with whom Polonsky was so frequently associated. Interestingly, I think not of the first generation of these thinkers, the ones for whom death spelled a final damnation to an eternal annihilation, but rather of the movement's second generation, those writers often referred to as "Christian existentialists." For them, if indeed physical death was to be the inevitable final scene of a life drama, could not an individual take some comfort in that knowledge? Did not that leave the individual free to extemporize fancifully in every one of life's preceding scenes? Certainly it is a philosophic presupposition under which all of the contradictions variously ascribed to Polonsky make complete sense. As he once put it himself: "If you're still alive, spring comes every year. This time, use it."

And so it is that Charley, in accepting death, is thereby free to choose life, the "right action"—as the Greeks would have termed it— which holds forth the promise of greatest meaning for him, the choice honoring community and the values which he can respect without compromise. In this way, in spite of being reminded of the inevitable consequence of his action ("What makes you think you can get away with this?"), Charley can articulate his final position forcefully, a fully-individuated, animated, decisive human being. And for this statement, we return to the screenplay.

Peg arrives at the top of the stairs calling Charley's name. She is momentarily stopped by the police.

CHARLEY
Hey, let her through!

Peg rushes down the stairs to Charley.

PEG
(exuding happiness and solicitude)
Are you all right, Charley? . . . Are you all right?
. . . Are you all right?

CHARLEY
(looking up at Roberts)
I never felt better in my life!

Charley has met his challenge squarely; his transformation is complete. As Polonsky once put it, "That is the very notion of a truthful life, to be shaken up, to be disturbed, to be awakened." And Polonsky's life, I think, carried this same kind of message: leaning philosophically toward a universe of numbers and vast distances where human beings cannot dream of making an impact, Polonsky, nevertheless, created situations, characters, and indeed life events, where an individual had the choice to either throw away the opportunity to rise to the occasion, or stand up and meet it, against all odds. Charley was a hero of this latter stripe. So, I believe, was Polonsky. As Nikos Kazantzakis's Zorba the Greek puts it, "Life is trouble; only death is not. To be alive is to undo your belt and look for trouble."

We come now to the last section of our *Body and Soul* story. Death, as noted, was never far from Polonsky's consciousness. He once wrote of "the facing of death, the ultimate nothing, and the liberation that comes from its recognition." During that last dinner together, the topic had its usual turn on center stage, more ceremoniously, as it turned out, than was customary. However, in addition to the eerie talk of death, there was one other topic on the table that evening which is part of our story.

About a week before that final venturing out, Polonsky and I had decided to join our classes at USC for a day, and screen *Body and Soul* for the assembled group. This had come about, in part, because he had suggested that I read the actual screenplay for *Body and Soul*, something I had never done. In fact, I had never read any of Polonsky's screenplays. Nevertheless, after going through the first five or six pages of the manuscript, I realized why he was considered such an important scenarist. Where most writers struggle for a phrase, an image, a cinematic turn wherein they can say something important in some unique, original way, Polonsky hit this stride repeatedly, even in the script's first few pages. I picked up the phone to call him and make some comment on the writing.

I dialed Polonsky's number, and after a ring or two, his voice crackled his signature question/exclamation, "Hello?!" "So, that's why they pay you all that money!" I said. "I can't talk to you right now," he said, "there are some people here." "OK, call me when you can." I hung up. When Polonsky returned the call, without even saying hello, his first words were, "So, you were going to tell me about what a great writer you think I am!" I chuckled; we talked. We arranged for the joint-class screening of *Body and Soul*.

Now it was Saturday night, a week later, and we were at that last supper. It was at Hamburger Hamlet, on Beverly Drive. We sat against the wall, in a booth, on the left-hand side of the rear dining room. Polonsky ordered "regular-cut" fries, a hamburger (the "classic"), and a glass of white wine; for dessert he ordered "real tea," and an apple cobbler with vanilla ice cream. He couldn't help playing with an infant at the next table. With great pride he announced to the parents that he was almost 89 and had a great-granddaughter with red hair! We talked about a number of things, but germane here was our discussion *of Body and Soul* and the arrangements for its screening which was to be held the following Thursday.

The next afternoon, Sunday, Polonsky's son, Hank, brought over tongue sandwiches (Polonsky's signature deli choice) to share with his father. That night, Polonsky's daughter, Susan, on a professional visit to the Northwest, phoned from her hotel to talk for a while. On Monday, there were three phone calls between Polonsky and me, oddly spiritual, but not the topic here.

The following morning, Tuesday, I was to talk with Polonsky about the topic of the phone calls, and more pressingly, the screening of *Body and Soul*. I would have stopped by his Beverly Hills home on the way to USC, but, as fate would have it, a lengthy phone call with another very promi-nent blacklistee, Pete Seeger (about a topic raised recently in conversation with Polonsky just before he had gotten out of my car) collapsed the brief time I would have been able to spend with Polonsky that morning. Pressed to make a one-o'clock class, I decided to head off to USC and ring him up from there to go over the business at hand.

As soon as I reached the Adjunct's Office in the Writing Division, I picked up the phone and dialed. His housekeeper, Maria, answered and blurted, "Oh, Mr. Joe, you better come quick! Mr. Polonsky . . . he dead."

I drove over to Polonsky's home on McCarty Drive. There I was greeted by the doorman, who shrugged his arms helplessly while shaking his head back and forth. Upstairs I found Hank and his wife, Iris. Maria sat silent in the kitchen. When I went into the room where Polonsky lay, two things stood out: he was only an extended arm's reach away from the spot where Sylvia had breathed her last, and he had a peaceful, rather ironic expression on his face. My mind raced through the poetry and gestures and conversation, the tales and the teasing, the politics and family and friends, the work, the War, the blacklist, death and triumph—and love. The mouth I had watched pour forth endless streams of words was un-characteristically still. But as I looked at him, I stood corrected. That affable familiar ghost rightly haunted me with intelligence: "I never felt better in my life!"

Joseph Janeti is a teacher and a writer living in Los Angeles.

DEDICATION

The editor and publisher of the *Film as Literature* series dedicate this book—what, sadly, is likely to be the final volume in this sequence of critical editions of the screenplays and teleplays of Abraham Polonsky—to Mr. Polonsky himself. Access to these valuable media texts began with his kindness and generosity in not only donating their publication rights, but with his gracious and inspiring relationship with the Cinema and Television Arts Department at California State University, Northridge—endowing scholarships; mentoring faculty; teaching (never accepting financial remuneration) an extended number of classes on film history, aesthetics, philosophy, and blacklist studies—always imbuing every moment of his physical and spiritual presence with a bracing existential wisdom, a small extract of which we invoke to honor his body and soul:

> Unlike the eye, which is like science, the ear is like religion and knows everything by rumor. And now, the rumors began upon the edge of sleep—the men crying out their hates and fears of the civilization that had borne them:
> Whatever stupidity contradictory intention can execute, will be executed; whatever sentimentalities can confuse existence, will be felt; whatever brutality and willfulness, whatever selfishness and silliness, can be imposed on existence, will be imposed. In peace or war it was the same. The contradictions of external reality created the internal conditions of human life.
> And there is no instant solution. There is no general answer. There is no secret formula. The formula, as always, is simply passion, indignation, and necessity.
> —Abraham Polonsky

Bibliography

Andersen, Thom. "Red Hollywood." In *Literature and the Visual Arts in Contemporary Society*, ed. Suzanne Ferguson and Barbara Groseclose, 141-196. Columbus: Ohio State University Press, 1985.

Anderson, Sherwood. "Listen, Hollywood!" *Photoplay* (March 1938): 28-29, 93.

Anonymous. *Communist Infiltration of Hollywood Motion-Picture Industry—Part 2: Hearings before the Committee on Un-American Activities*. Washington: Government Printing Office, 1951.

_____. "Rossen of Films Denies He's Red; Silent on Past." *Los Angeles Times* (26 June 1951).

_____. "$40,000 in Gifts to Reds—Rossen." *Los Angeles Examiner* (8 May 1953).

_____. "They Made Me a Criminal." *Newsweek* (30 Jan. 1939): 24.

_____. *Variety*. (10 February 1942): 17.

Abrams, Norma and Neal Patterson. "Top Movie Producer Gave 40G to Reds," *New York Daily News* (8 May 1953).

Arnold, Edwin T. and Eugene L. Miller. *The Films and Career of Robert Aldrich*. Knoxville: The University of Tennessee Press, 1986.

Bayer, William. *Breaking Through, Selling Out, Dropping Dead and Other Notes on Filmmaking*. New York: Dell Publishing Company, 1975.

Belcher, Stephen. *New Movies* Vol. 22, No. 6 (November 1947): 9-10.

Bentley, Eric, ed. *Thirty Years of Treason: Excerpts from Hearings before the House Committee on Un-American Activities, 1938-1968*. New York: The Viking Press, 1971.

Bergan, Ronald. *The Coen Brothers*. New York: Thunder's Mouth Press, 2000.

Between Two Worlds. United Artists Collection, Wisconsin Center for Film and Theater Research. Scripts Files. Box 27, Folder 7.

Blake, William. *The Complete Poetry & Prose of William Blake*, ed. David V. Erdman. Revised Edition. New York: Doubleday, 1988.

Blankfort, Michael. "Editorial." *Point of View* (August 1964): 2.

Bogle, Donald. *Blacks in American Films and Television*. New York: Garland Publishing, 1988.

Bowles, Jerry. *A Thousand Sundays: The Story of The Ed Sullivan Show*. New York: G.P. Putnam's Sons, 1980.

Bowles, Scott. "Body and Soul." *CinemaTexas Program Notes* Vol. 20, No. 1 (18 February 1981).

Brandes, Philip. *Los Angeles Times, Calendar Weekend*. (29 November 2001): 36.

Brenner, Teddy (as told to Barney Nagler). *Only the Ring Was Square*. Englewood Cliffs NJ: Prentice-Hall, 1981.

Brooker-Bowers, Nancy. *The Hollywood Novel and Other Novels About Film, 1912-1982: An Annotated Bibliography*. New York: Garland Publishing, Inc., 1985.

Buhle, Paul and Dave Wagner. *A Very Dangerous Citizen: Abraham Lincoln Polonsky and the Hollywood Left*. Berkeley: University of California Press, 2000.

Bywater, Tim and Thomas Sobchack. *Introduction to Film Criticism*. New York: Longman, 1989.

Cantor, Harold. *Clifford Odets: Playwright-Poet*. Lanham, Maryland: Scarecrow Press, 2000.

Casty, Alan. "The Films of Robert Rossen." *Film Quarterly*, Volume XX, Number 2 (Winter 1966-1967): 3-12.

_____. "Robert Rossen." *Cinema*, Volume 4, Number 3 (Fall 1968).

Ceplair, Larry. "Abraham Lincoln Polonsky." In *A Political Companion to American Film*, ed. Gary Crowdus, 333-336. Lakeview Press, 1994.

Ceplair, Larry and Steven Englund. *The Inquisition in Hollywood: Politics in the Film Community, 1930-1960*. Berkeley: University of California Press, 1983.

Chapin, Henry B. ed. *Sports in Literature*. New York: David McKay Company, 1976.

Chipman, Bruce L. *Into America's Dream-Dump: A Postmodern Study of the Hollywood Novel*. Lanham, Maryland: University Press of America, 1999.

Christopher, Nicholas. *Somewhere in the Night: Film Noir and the American City*. New York: The Free Press, 1997.

Corliss, Richard. *Talking Pictures: Screenwriters in the American Cinema*. Woodstock: The Overlook Press, 1974.

Crowther, Bosley. "A Man Who Means to Make a Dent." *New York Times* (18 December 1938) IX, 7:3.

Dardis, Tom. "The Myth That Won't Go Away." *Journal of Popular Film & Television* (Winter 1984): 167.

_____. *Some Time in the Sun: The Hollywood Years of Fitzgerald, Faulkner, Nathanael West, Aldous Huxley and James Agee*. New York: Charles Scribner's Sons, 1976.

Dubrow, Rick. "Studs Lonigan Writer Discusses His Works." *Hollywood Citizen News* (12 August 1960).

Early, Gerald. *The Culture of Bruising: Essays on Prizefighting, Literature, and Modern American Culture*. New York: The Ecco Press, 1994.

Eyles, Allen. "Films of Enterprise: A Studio History." *Focus on Film* 35 (April, 1980): 13-27.

Farber, Stephen. "Violence and the Bitch Goddess." In *Film Noir Reader 2*, edited by Alain Silver & James Ursini, 45-55. New York: Limelight Editions, 1999.

Farrell, James T. *The League of Frightened Philistines*. New York: The Vanguard Press, 1945.

_____. *Literature and Morality*. New York: The Vanguard Press, 1947.

Fast, Howard. *Being Red*. Boston: Houghton Mifflin, 1990.

Fine, Richard. *Hollywood and the Profession of Authorship, 1928-1940*. Ann Arbor MI: UMI Research Press, 1985.

_____. *James M. Cain and the American Authors' Authority*. Austin: University of Texas Press, 1992.

Flanagan, Thomas. "The Best He Could Do." *The New York Review of Books* (21 October 1999): 64-67, 70-72.

_____. "Master of the Misbegotten." *The New York Review of Books* (5 October 2000): 14.

Editors of *Fortune*. "Warner Brothers." *Fortune* 16:6 (December 1937): 110-113, 206+.

Fowler, Gene. "Hollywood Horst Wessel." In *Hello, Hollywood!*, ed. Allen Rivkin and Laura Kerr, 63-64. New York: Doubleday & Company, 1962.

Frank, Stanley. "Canada Lee's Love for the Ring Is No Act." *New York Post* (16 May 1941).

Friedman, Lester D. *Hollywood's Image of the Jew*. New York: Frederick Ungar Publishing Co., 1982.

Fuchs, Daniel. *Three Novels*. New York: Basic Books, Inc., 1961.

Garfield, John. "Fists, Brains and Breaks." *Opportunity: The Journal of Negro Life* (January-Marc, 1948).

_____. *Negro Digest* (November 1947).

Gelman, Howard. *The Films of John Garfield*. Secaucus NJ: The Citadel Press, 1975.

Giles, Ronald K. "The Reflexive Vision of Sport in Recent Drama and Film." In *The Achievement of American Sport Literature: A Critical Appraisal*, ed. Wiley Lee Umphlett, 100-106. Rutherford: Fairleigh Dickinson University Press, 1991.

Goldstein, Patrick. "Hollywood Blacklist: Cornered Rats and Personal Betrayals." *Los Angeles Times* (20 October 1997): 1.

Gombrich, E. H. "Meditations on a Hobby Horse." *Meditations on a Hobby Horse and Other Essays on the Theory of Art*. London: Phaidon Publishers, 1963.

Graham, Sheilah. *The Garden of Allah*. New York: Crown Publishers, 1970.

Gruber, Lillian. "Mixed Feelings About Odets." *The New York Times* (8 August 1965).

Hall, Jeanne. "The Benefits of Hindsight: Re-Visions of HUAC and the Film and Television Industries in *The Front* and *Guilty by Suspicion*." *Film Quarterly*, Volume 54, Number 2 (Winter 2000-01): 15-26.

Hamilton, Charles V. *Adam Clayton Powell, Jr.* New York: Collier Books, 1991.

Hamilton, Ian. *Writers in Hollywood*. New York: Carroll & Graf Publishers, 1990.

Hecht, Ben. *A Child of the Century*. New York: Simon and Schuster, 1954.

Hellman, Lillian. *Scoundrel Time*. Boston: Little, Brown and Company, 1976.

Hemingway, Ernest. *The Short Stories of Ernest Hemingway*. New York: Charles Scribner's Sons, 1966.

Herman, Daniel J. "Sport, Art, and Aesthetics: A Decade of Controversy (1978-88)." In *Achievement of American Sport Literature: A Critical Appraisal*, ed. Wiley Lee Umphlett, 158-164. Rutherford: Fairleigh Dickinson University Press, 1991.

Hirsch, Foster. *A Method to Their Madness*. New York: W.W. Norton, 1984.

Hoffman, Irving. "Tales of Hoffman." *The Hollywood Reporter* (1 May 1951): 3.

Hofstadter, Richard. *Anti-Intellectualism in American Life*. New York: Random House, 1963.

Huston, John. *An Open Book* (1980). In *The Grove Book of Hollywood*, ed. Christopher Silvester, 396. New York: Grove Press, 2000.

James, Nick. "Raging Bulls: Sexuality and the Boxing Movie." In *Boxer: An Anthology of Writings on Boxing and Visual Culture*. London: First MIT Press edition, 1996.

Kael, Pauline. *The Citizen Kane Book*. Boston: Little, Brown Co., 1971.

Kazan, Elia. *A Life*. New York: Anchor Books, Doubleday, 1981.

Kemble, Mark. *Names* (1995). Productions include: Matrix Theater, Los Angeles, Summer 1995; Lee Strasberg Institute, West Hollywood, Winter 2001.

King, Susan. "Going Glove to Glove with Some Greats." *Los Angeles Times Calendar* (27 December 2001): 22-26.

Lahr, John. "Gold Rush." *The New Yorker* (7 May 2001): 84-86.

Laurence, Frank M. *Hemingway and the Movies*. New York: Da Capo Press, 1981.

LaValley, Albert. "The Emerging Screenwriter," *Quarterly Review of Film Studies*, Volume 1, Number 1 (February 1976): 22-27.

Lawson, John Howard. *Theory and Technique of Screenwriting*. New York: G.P. Putnam's Sons, 1949.

Lee, Canada. "*Body and Soul* Has Heart, Too." *Opportunity: The Journal of Negro Life* (January-March 1948): 21.

Lokke, Virgil L. "The Literary Image of Hollywood." Ph.D. dissertation, State University of Iowa, 1955.

Mangold, James. "Afterword," *Sweet Smell of Success*. London: Faber and Faber, 1998.

Martine, James J. "Hemingway's 'Fifty Grand': The Other Fight(s)." In *The Short Stories of Ernest Hemingway: Critical Essays*, ed. by Jackson J. Benson, 198-203. Durham: Duke University Press, 1975.

Millgate, Michael. *American Social Fiction*. London: Oliver and Boyd, 1964.

Mithani, Sam. "Giving Voice to Ben Chaplin: Afro-American Representation in Abraham Polonsky's *Body and Soul*," Unpublished manuscript, July 1999.

Murray, Edward. *Clifford Odets: The Thirties and After*. New York: Frederick Ungar Publishing, 1968.

George Jean Nathan, *The Entertainment of a Nation* (New York: Alfred A. Knopf, 1942), pp. 84-85.

_____. "Theater." *Scribner's Magazine* (November 1937).

_____. *The Theatre Book of the Year 1942-1943*. New York: Alfred A. Knopf, 1943.

Navasky, Victor. "*Guilty by Suspicion*." *Premiere* (December 1991): 134.

_____. "Has *Guilty by Suspicion* Missed the Point?" *The New York Times*, (31 March 1991).

_____. *Naming Names*. New York: Penguin Books, 1981.

Neve, Brian. *Film and Politics in America: A Social Tradition*. London: Routledge, 1992.

Oates, Joyce Carol. *On Boxing*. Garden City: Doubleday, 1987.

Odets, Clifford. *Golden Boy*. *A Treasury of the Theatre: From Henrik Ibsen to Eugene Ionesco*, ed. John Gassner. Third ed. New York: Simon and Schuster, 1961.

_____. "Letter." *New York Times* (25 May 1952) II, 3:7.

Oliver, Charles M., ed. *A Moving Picture Feast: The Filmgoer's Hemingway*. New York: Praeger Publishers, 1989.

Palmer, Lilli. *Change Lobsters and Dance*. New York: Warner Books, 1975.

Parrish, Robert. *Growing Up in Hollywood*. New York: Harcourt Brace Jovanovich, 1976.

Peary, Danny. *Cult Movies*. New York: Dell Publishing, 1981.

Peary, Gerald. "Odets of Hollywood." *Sight and Sound* Volume 56, Issue 1 (1986): 59-63.

Peck, Seymour. "Lee Put Heart and Soul Into *Body and Soul*." *PM* (4 September 1947).

Phillips, Gene D. *Hemingway and Film*. New York: Frederick Ungar Publishing Co., 1980.

Piper, Keith. "Four Corners, A Contest of Opposites." In *Boxer: An Anthology of Writings on Boxing and Visual Culture*, 76-77. London: First MIT Press edition, 1996.

Poitier, Sidney. *The Measure of a Man: A Spiritual Autobiography*. New York: Harper Collins, 2000.

Polonsky, Abraham. "How the Blacklist Worked in Hollywood." *Film Culture*, (Fall-Winter 1970): 42-43.

_____. Filmed Interview with John Schultheiss on *Body and Soul* (13 May 1987).

_____. *Season of Fear*. New York: Cameron Associates, 1956.

Powdermaker, Hortense. *Hollywood: The Dream Factory*. New York: Grosset & Dunlap, 1959.

Rainsberger, Todd. *James Wong Howe: Cinematographer*. New York: A.S. Barnes & Company, 1981.

Reed, Rex. "Anne Revere Looks Ahead!" *Los Angeles Times* (2 May 1975).

Rogin, Michael. *Black Face, White Noise: Jewish Immigrants in the Hollywood Melting Pot*. Berkeley: University of California Press, 1998.

Rosenbaum, Jonathan. "Guilty by Omission." *Film Comment* 27:5 (September-October 1991): 42-46, 50.

Schulberg, Budd. *The Disenchanted*. New York: Random House, 1950.

_____. *The Four Seasons of Success*. New York: Doubleday & Company, 1972.

_____. "The Four Seasons of Success: Old Scott—The Mask, the Myth, and the Man." *Esquire* (January 1961): 96-101.

Rudd, Irving. "Canada Lee, Former boxer, Eyes Return." *The Ring* (5 June 1946).

Schulberg, Budd. "The Writer and Hollywood." *Harper's Magazine* (October 1959): 132-137.

Schultheiss, John. "The 'Eastern' Writer in Hollywood." In *Cinema Examined: Selections from* Cinema Journal, ed. Richard Dyer MacCann & Jack C. Ellis, 41-75. New York: E.P. Dutton, Inc., 1982.

_____. "*Force of Evil*: Existential Marx and Freud." *Force of Evil: The Critical Edition*, ed. John Schultheiss and Mark Schaubert, 151-198. Northridge CA: The Center for Telecommunication Studies, California State University, Northridge, 1996.

_____. "George Jean Nathan and the Dramatist in Hollywood." *Literature/Film Quarterly* Volume 4, Number 1 (Winter 1976): 13-27.

Schultheiss, John. "*Odds Against Tomorrow:* Film Noir Without Linguistic Irony." *Odds Against Tomorrow: The Critical Edition*, ed. John Schultheiss, 165-294. Northridge CA: The Center for Telecommunication Studies, California State University, Northridge, 1999.

_____. "Robert E. Sherwood." *Film Comment* Volume 8, Number 3 (September-October 1972): 70-73.

_____. "A Season of Fear: Abraham Polonsky, *You Are There*, and the Blacklist." *You Are There Teleplays: The Critical Edition*, ed. John Schultheiss and Mark Schaubert, 11-37. Northridge CA: The Center for Telecommunication Studies, California State University, Northridge, 1997.

_____. "A Season of Fear: The Blacklisted Teleplays of Abraham Polonsky." *Literature/Film Quarterly* 24, Number 2 (1996): 148-164.

_____. "A Study of the 'Eastern' Writer in Hollywood in the 1930s." Ph.D dissertation, University of Southern California, 1973.

See, Carolyn. "The Hollywood Novel: An Historical and Critical Study." Ph.D. dissertation, University of California, Los Angeles, 1963.

_____. "The Hollywood Novel: The American Dream Cheat." In *Tough Guy Writers of the Thirties*, ed. David Madden, 199-217. Carbondale: Southern Illinois University Press, 1968.

_____. "Will Excess Spoil the Hollywood Writer?" *Los Angeles Times West Magazine* (26 March 1967): 34-36.

Sherwood, Robert E. "Footnote to a Preface." *Saturday Review,* (6 August 1949): 134.

Shils, Edward. "Mass Society and Its Culture." D*aedalus* (Spring 1960): 305-306.

Silver, Alain and James Ursini. *What Ever Happend to Robert Aldrich? His Life and His Films.* New York: Limelight Editions, 1995.

Sipiora, Phillip. "Ethical Narration in 'My Old Man.'" In *Hemingway's Neglected Short Fiction: New Perspectives*, ed. Susan F. Beegel, 43-60. Tuscaloosa: The University of Alabama Press, 1989.

Sklar, Robert. *City Boys: Cagney, Bogart, Garfield.* Princeton: Princeton UP, 1992.

Slide, Anthony. *The Hollywood Novel: A Critical Guide to Over 1200 Works.* Jefferson, North Carolina: McFarland & Company, 1995.

Smith, Cecil. "Ben Hecht Returns, Rips Hollywood Apart." *Los Angeles Times* (26 August 1956).

Smith, Paul. *A Reader's Guide to the Short Stories of Ernest Hemingway.* Boston: G.K. Hall & Co., 1989.

Smith, Wendy. *Real Life Drama: The Group Theatre and America, 1931-1940.* New York: Alfred A. Knopf, 1990.

Spatz. Jonas. *Hollywood in Fiction.* The Hague: Mouton & Company, 1969.

Springer, John Parris. *Hollywood Fictions: The Dream Factory in American Popular Fiction.* Norman: University of Oklahoma Press, 2000.

Sugden, John. *Boxing and Society: An International Analysis.* Manchester UK: Manchester University Press, 1996.

Sullivan, Ed. "Little Old New York." *New York Daily News* (21 May 1952).

Tackach, James. "Whose Fix Is It, Anyway?: A Closer Look at Hemingway's 'Fifty Grand.'" *The Hemingway Review*, Vol. 19, No. 2 (Spring 2000): 113-117.

Talbot, David and Barbara Zheutlin. *Creative Differences: Profiles of Hollywood Dissidents.* Boston: South End Press, 1978.

Taylor, Clarke. "Blacklist—Horror Role for Anne Revere." *Los Angeles Times Calendar* (20 June 1976): 39.

Thoreen, David. "Poor Ernest's Almanac: The Petty Economies of 'Fifty Grand's' Jack Brennan." *The Hemingway Review*, Vol. 13, No. 2 (Spring 1994): 24-36.

Van Nostrand, Albert. *The Denatured Novel.* New York: The Bobbs-Merrill Company, 1962.

Vidal, Gore. *Sex, Death and Money.* New York: Bantam Books, 1968.

Wilson, Edmund. *The Boys in the Back Room.* San Francisco: Colt Press, 1941.

Winchell, Walter. "Walter Winchell in New York: Ham & Eggs, Broadway Style." *NY Daily Mirror* (13 October 1949).

Wolfenstein, Martha and Nathan Leites. *Movies: A Psychological Study.* New York: Atheneum, 1970.